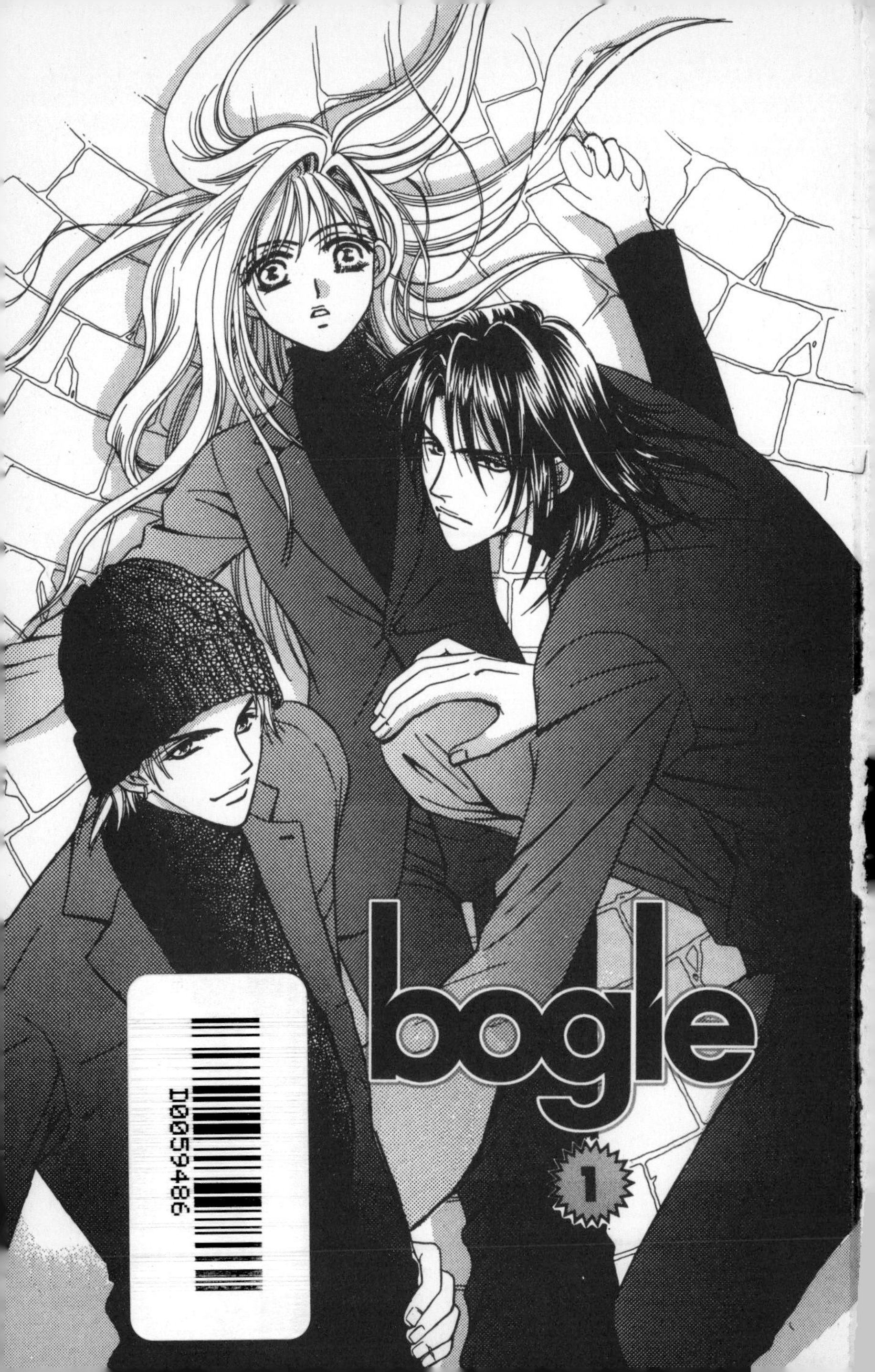
bogle
1

Translation – Christine Schilling
Adaptation – Brynne Chandler
Editorial Assistant – Mallory Reaves
Retouch and Lettering – Erika Terriquez
Production Assistant – Suzy Wells
Production Manager – James Dashiell
Editor – Brynne Chandler

A Go! Comi manga

Published by Go! Media Entertainment, LLC

Bogle Volume 1
© SHINO TAIRA & YUKO ICHIJU 2002
Originally published in Japan in 2002 by Akita Publishing, Co., Ltd., Tokyo.
English translation rights arranged with Akita Publishing Co., Ltd.
through TOHAN COPORATION, Tokyo.

Visit us online at www.gocomi.com
e-mail: info@gocomi.com

ISBN 978-1-933617-96-1

First printed in July 2008

1 2 3 4 5 6 7 8 9

Manufactured in the United States of America

BY
SHINO TAIRA & YUKO ICHIJU

VOLUME 1

go!comi

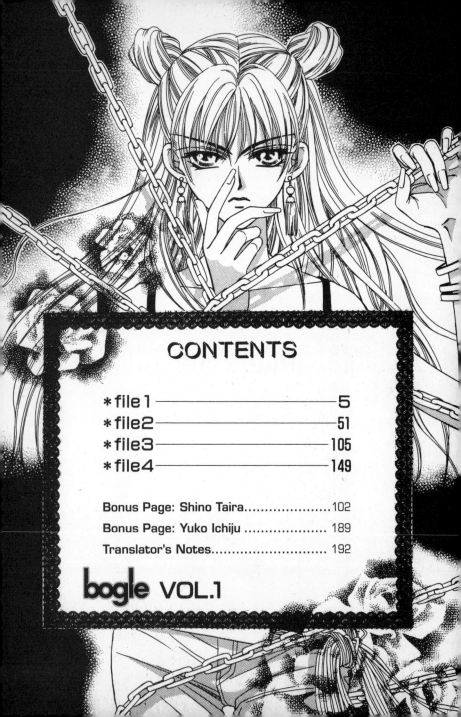

CONTENTS

bogle VOL.1

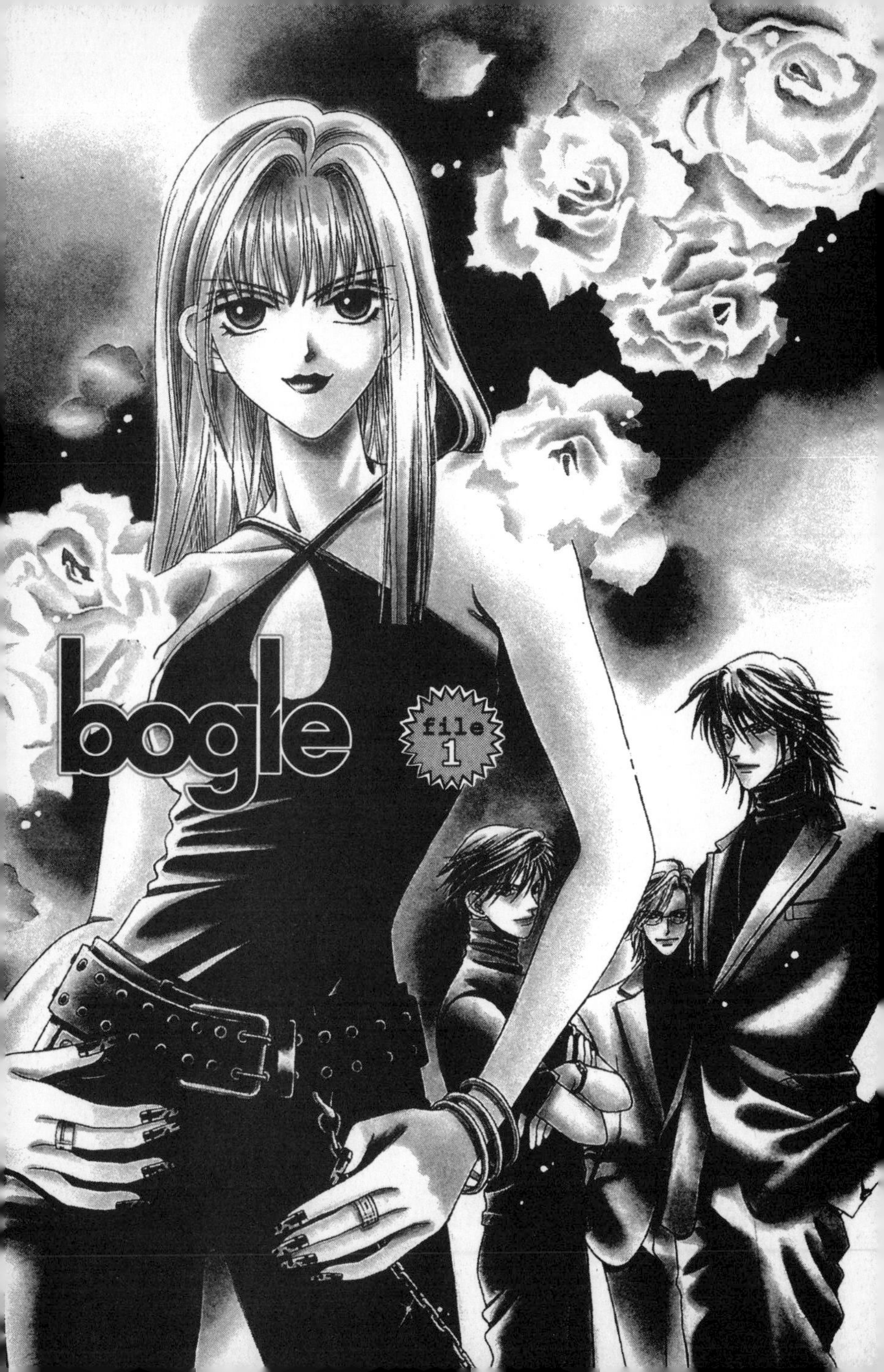
bogle
file 1

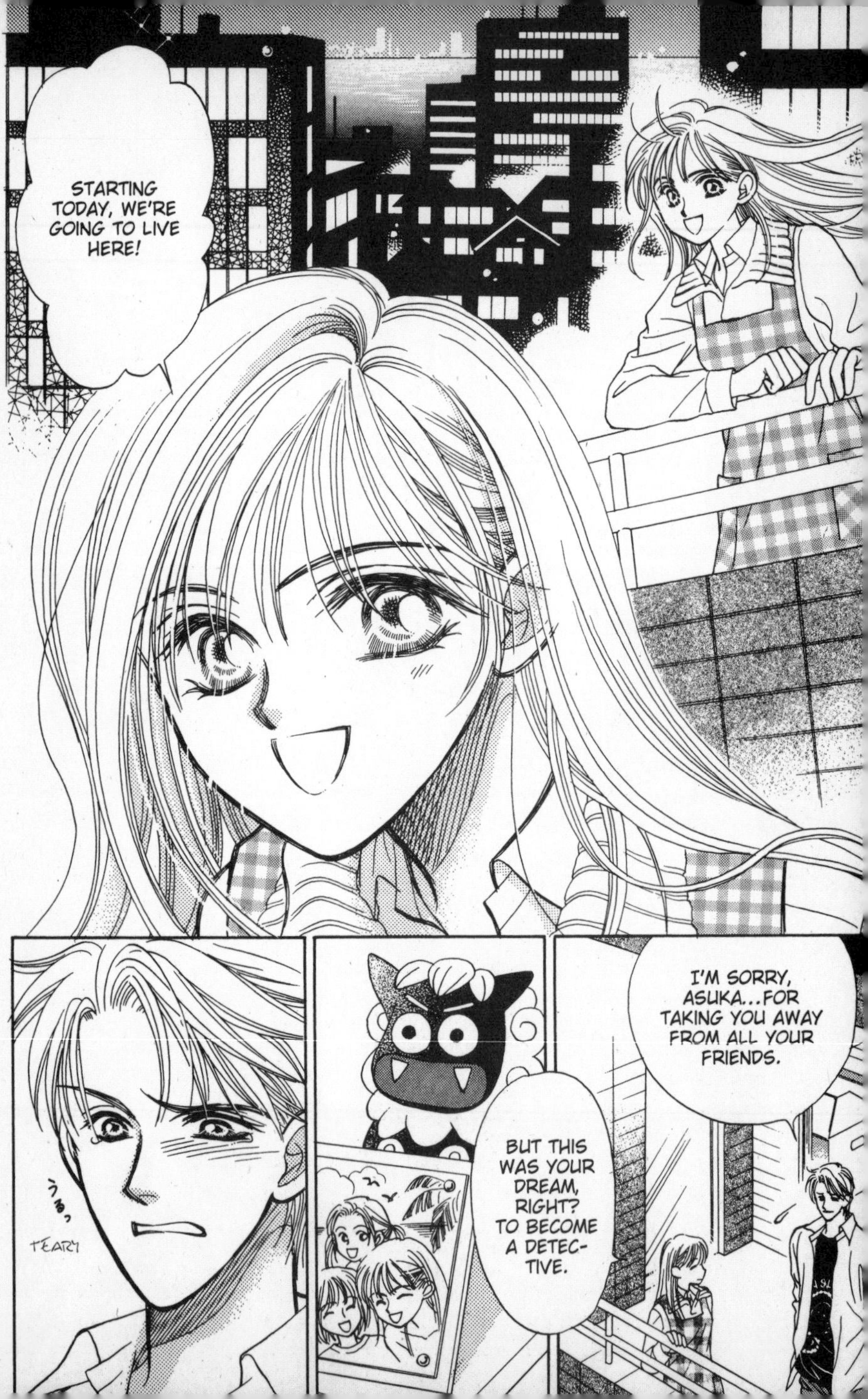
STARTING TODAY, WE'RE GOING TO LIVE HERE!
I'M SORRY, ASUKA...FOR TAKING YOU AWAY FROM ALL YOUR FRIENDS.
BUT THIS WAS YOUR DREAM, RIGHT? TO BECOME A DETEC-TIVE.
うるっ
TEARY

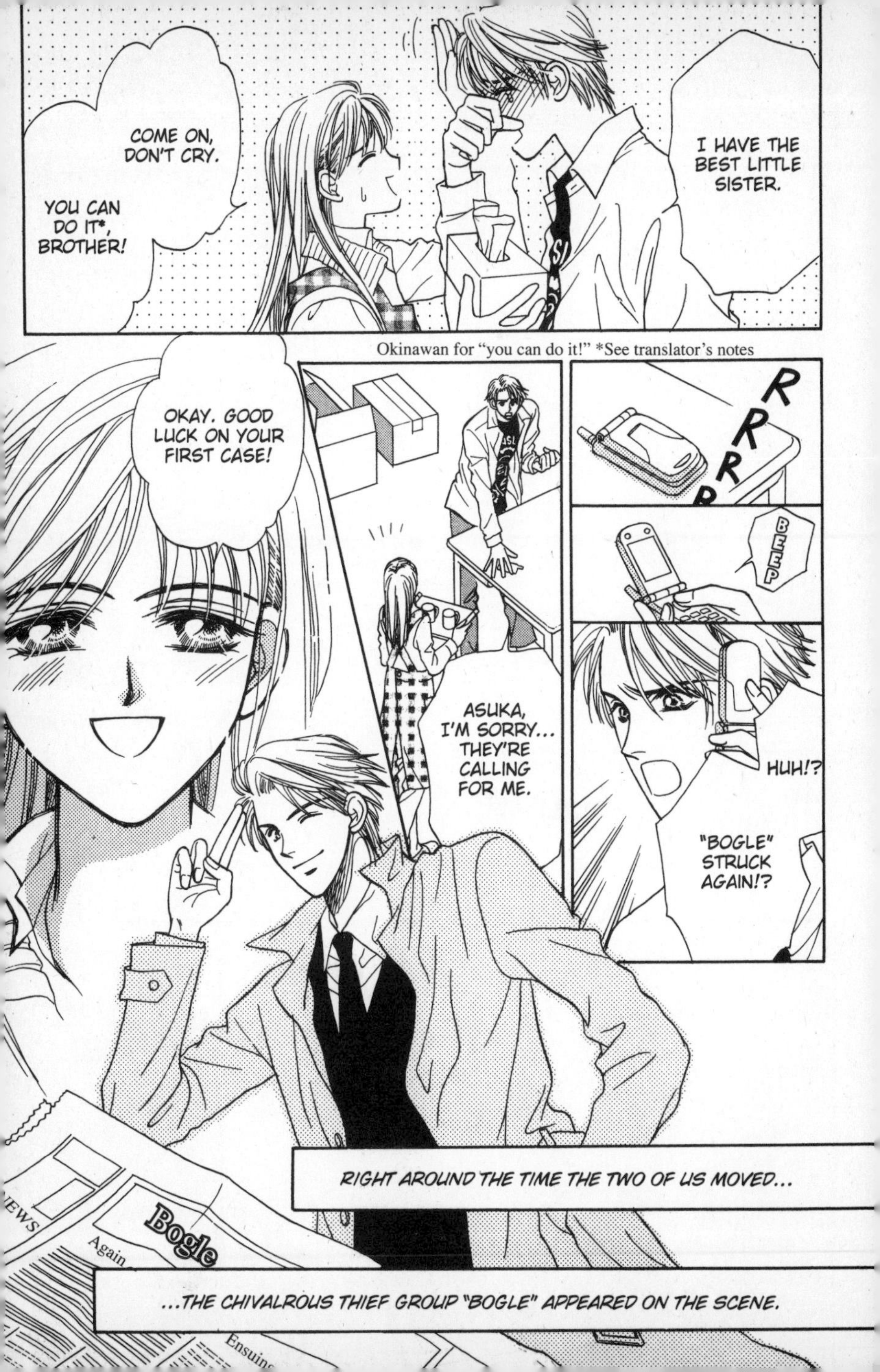
I HAVE THE BEST LITTLE SISTER.
COME ON, DON'T CRY.
YOU CAN DO IT*, BROTHER!
Okinawan for "you can do it!" *See translator's notes
RRRR
BEEP
HUH!?
"BOGLE" STRUCK AGAIN!?
ASUKA, I'M SORRY... THEY'RE CALLING FOR ME.
OKAY. GOOD LUCK ON YOUR FIRST CASE!
RIGHT AROUND THE TIME THE TWO OF US MOVED...
...THE CHIVALROUS THIEF GROUP "BOGLE" APPEARED ON THE SCENE.
NEWS
Bogle
Again

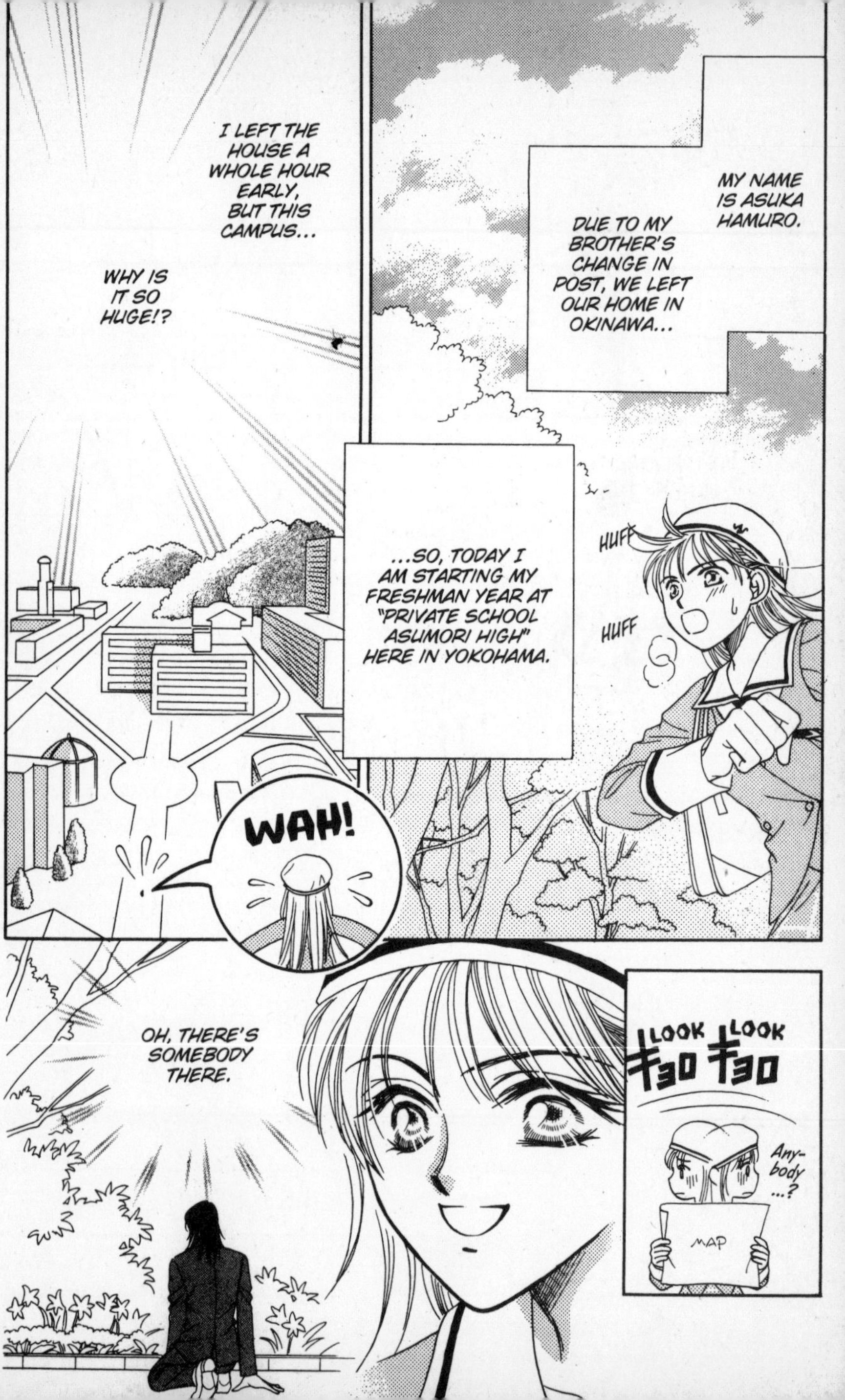

MY NAME IS ASUKA HAMURO.
DUE TO MY BROTHER'S CHANGE IN POST, WE LEFT OUR HOME IN OKINAWA...
...SO, TODAY I AM STARTING MY FRESHMAN YEAR AT "PRIVATE SCHOOL ASUMORI HIGH" HERE IN YOKOHAMA.
HUFF
HUFF
I LEFT THE HOUSE A WHOLE HOUR EARLY, BUT THIS CAMPUS...
WHY IS IT SO HUGE!?
WAH!
LOOK LOOK
キョロ キョロ
Any-body ...?
MAP
OH, THERE'S SOMEBODY THERE.

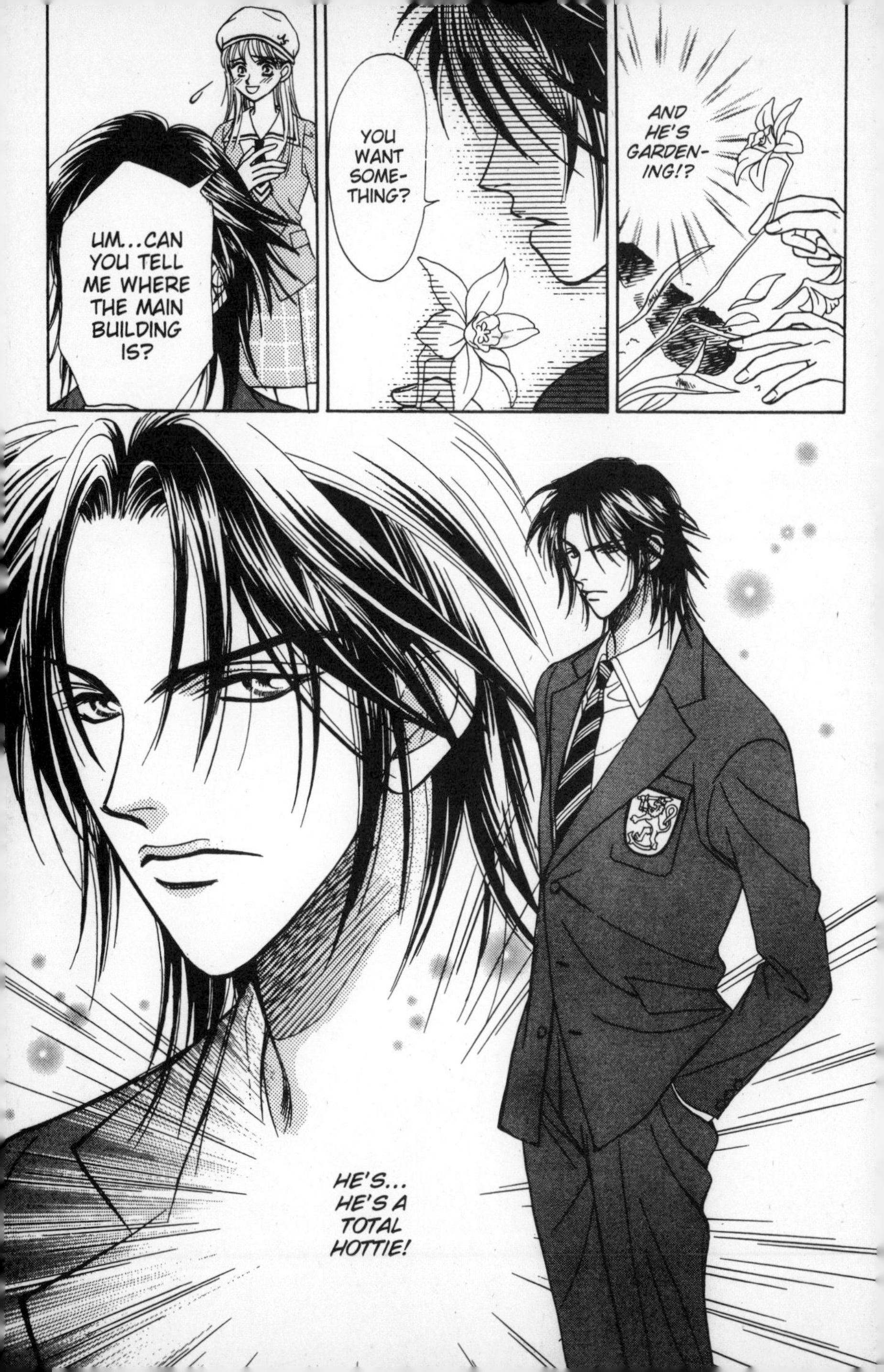
AND HE'S GARDEN-ING!?
YOU WANT SOME-THING?
UM...CAN YOU TELL ME WHERE THE MAIN BUILDING IS?
HE'S... HE'S A TOTAL HOTTIE!

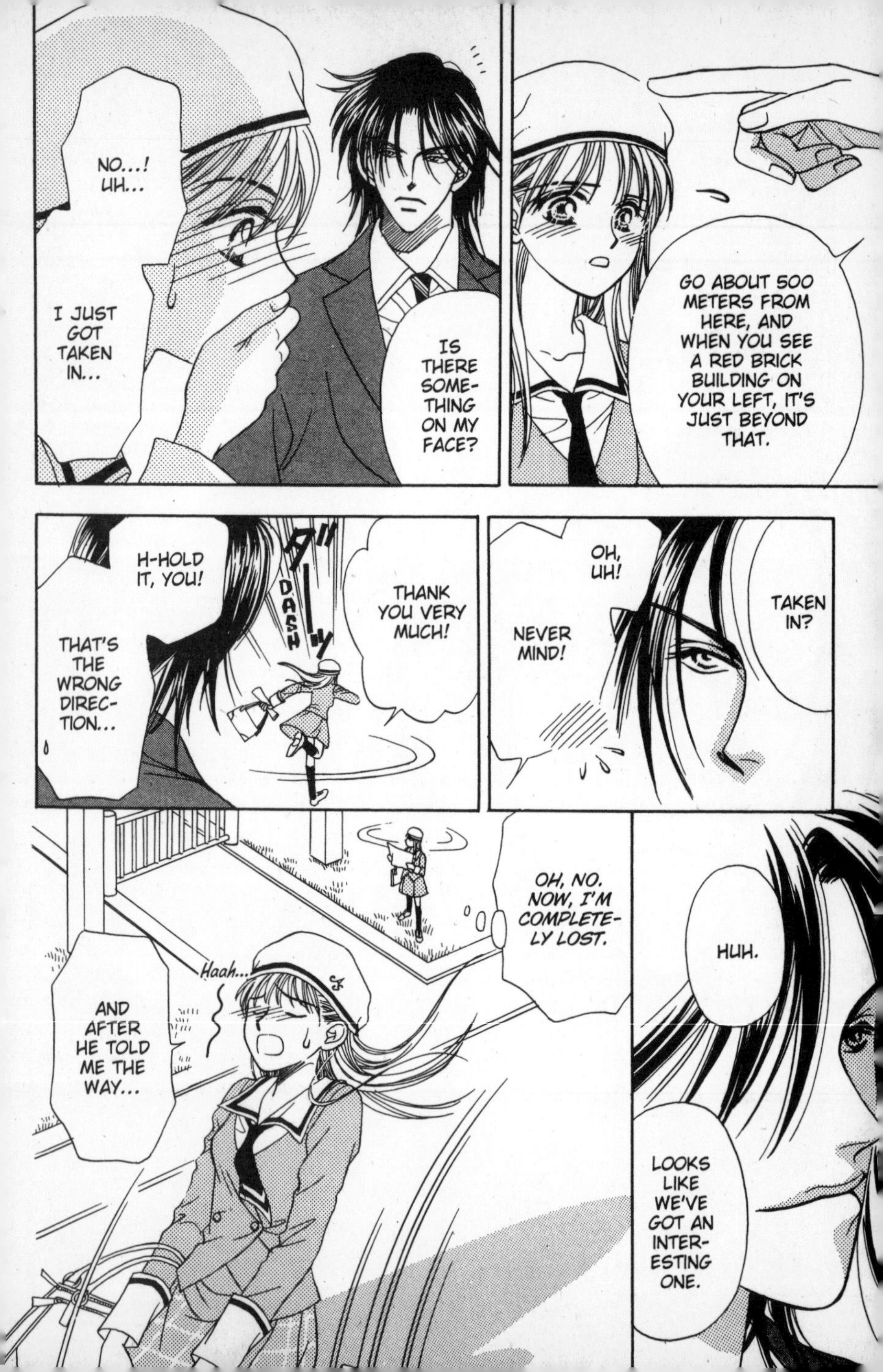
GO ABOUT 500 METERS FROM HERE, AND WHEN YOU SEE A RED BRICK BUILDING ON YOUR LEFT, IT'S JUST BEYOND THAT.
IS THERE SOMETHING ON MY FACE?
NO...! UH...
I JUST GOT TAKEN IN...
TAKEN IN?
OH, UH!
NEVER MIND!
THANK YOU VERY MUCH!
DASH
H-HOLD IT, YOU!
THAT'S THE WRONG DIRECTION...
HUH.
LOOKS LIKE WE'VE GOT AN INTERESTING ONE.
OH, NO. NOW, I'M COMPLETELY LOST.
Haah...
AND AFTER HE TOLD ME THE WAY...

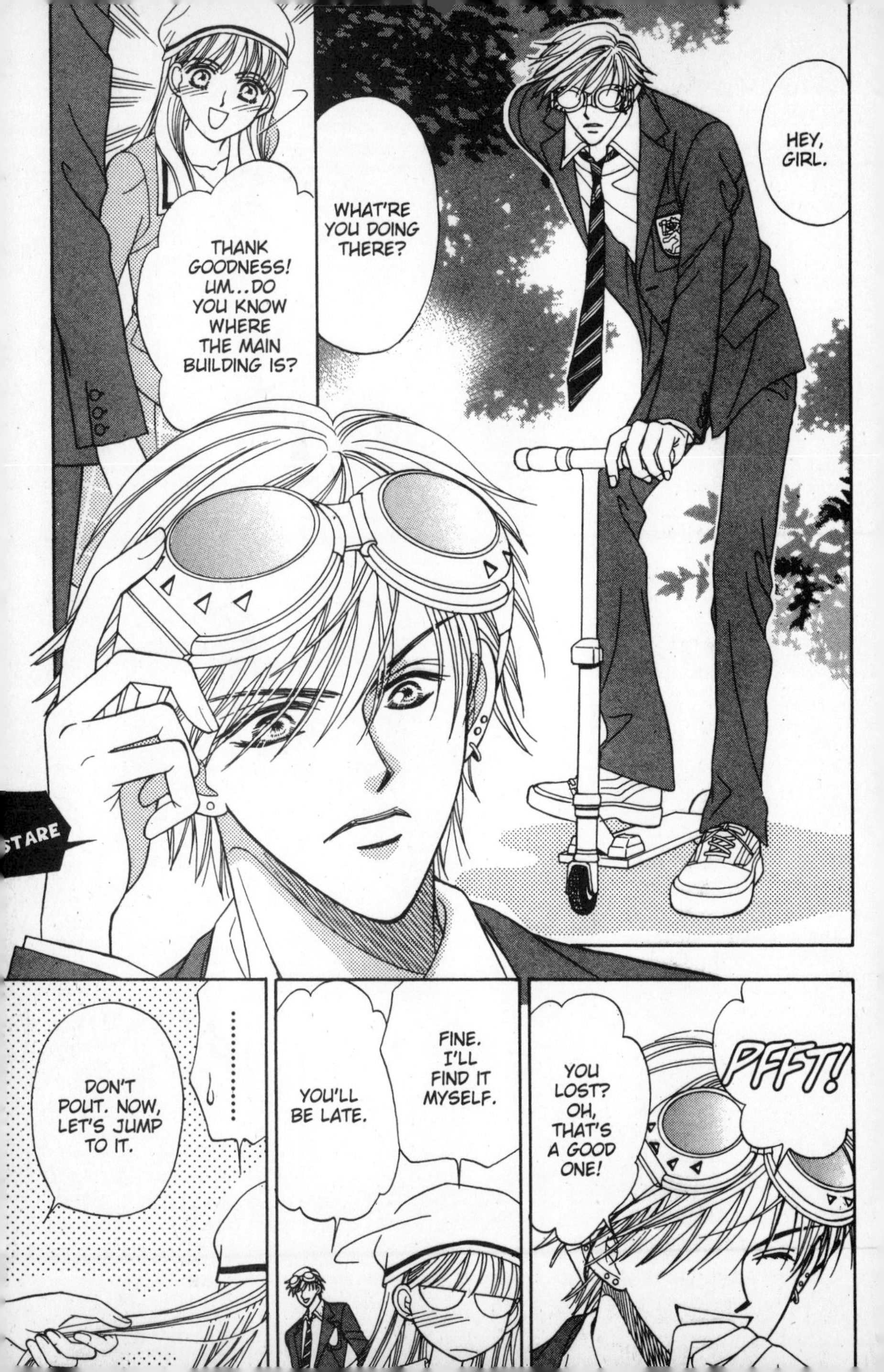
HEY, GIRL.
WHAT'RE YOU DOING THERE?
THANK GOODNESS! UM...DO YOU KNOW WHERE THE MAIN BUILDING IS?
STARE
PFFT!
YOU LOST? OH, THAT'S A GOOD ONE!
FINE. I'LL FIND IT MYSELF.
YOU'LL BE LATE.
....
DON'T POUT. NOW, LET'S JUMP TO IT.

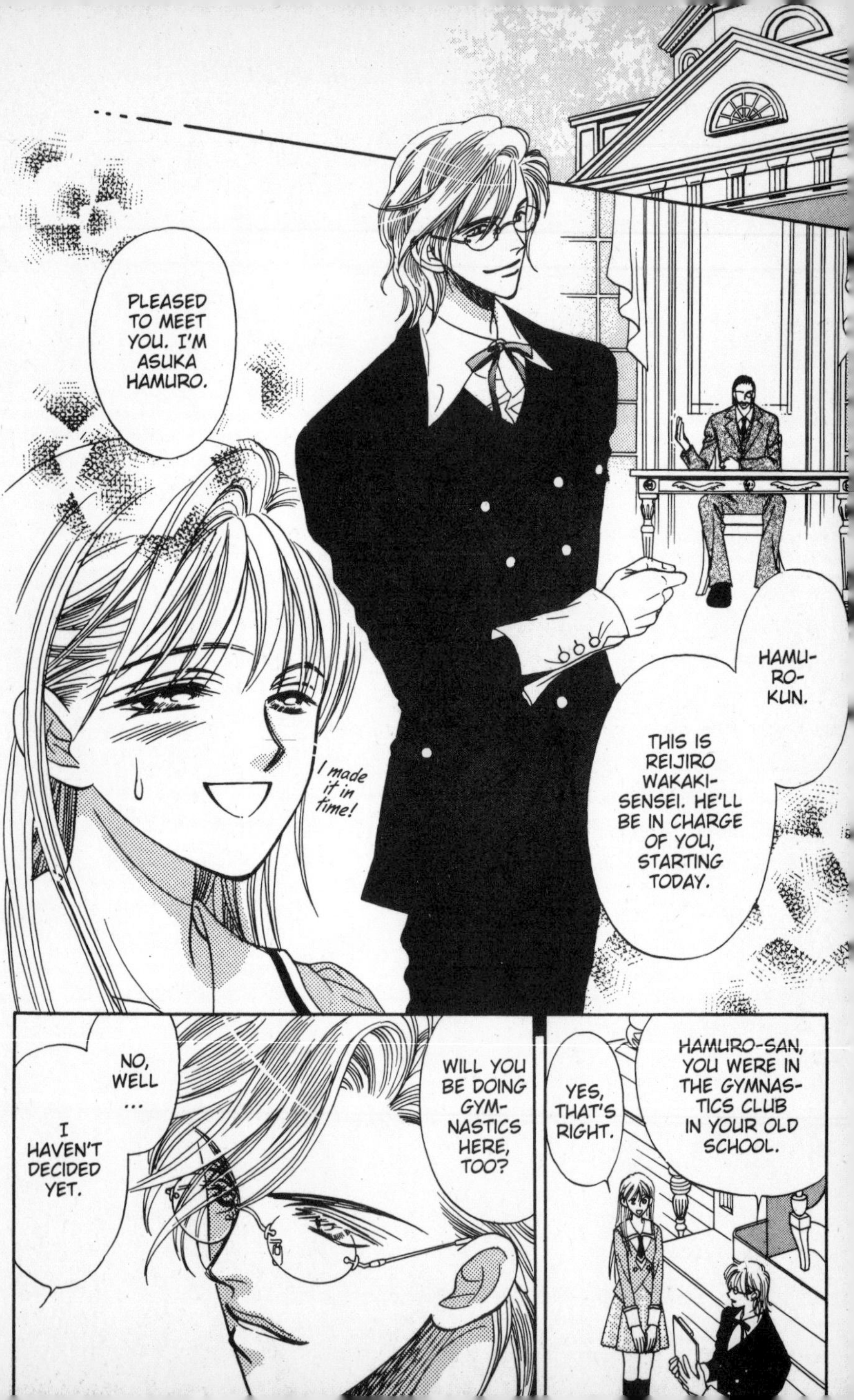

HAMU-RO-KUN.
THIS IS REIJIRO WAKAKI-SENSEI. HE'LL BE IN CHARGE OF YOU, STARTING TODAY.
I made it in time!
PLEASED TO MEET YOU. I'M ASUKA HAMURO.
HAMURO-SAN, YOU WERE IN THE GYMNAS-TICS CLUB IN YOUR OLD SCHOOL.
YES, THAT'S RIGHT.
WILL YOU BE DOING GYM-NASTICS HERE, TOO?
NO, WELL ...
I HAVEN'T DECIDED YET.

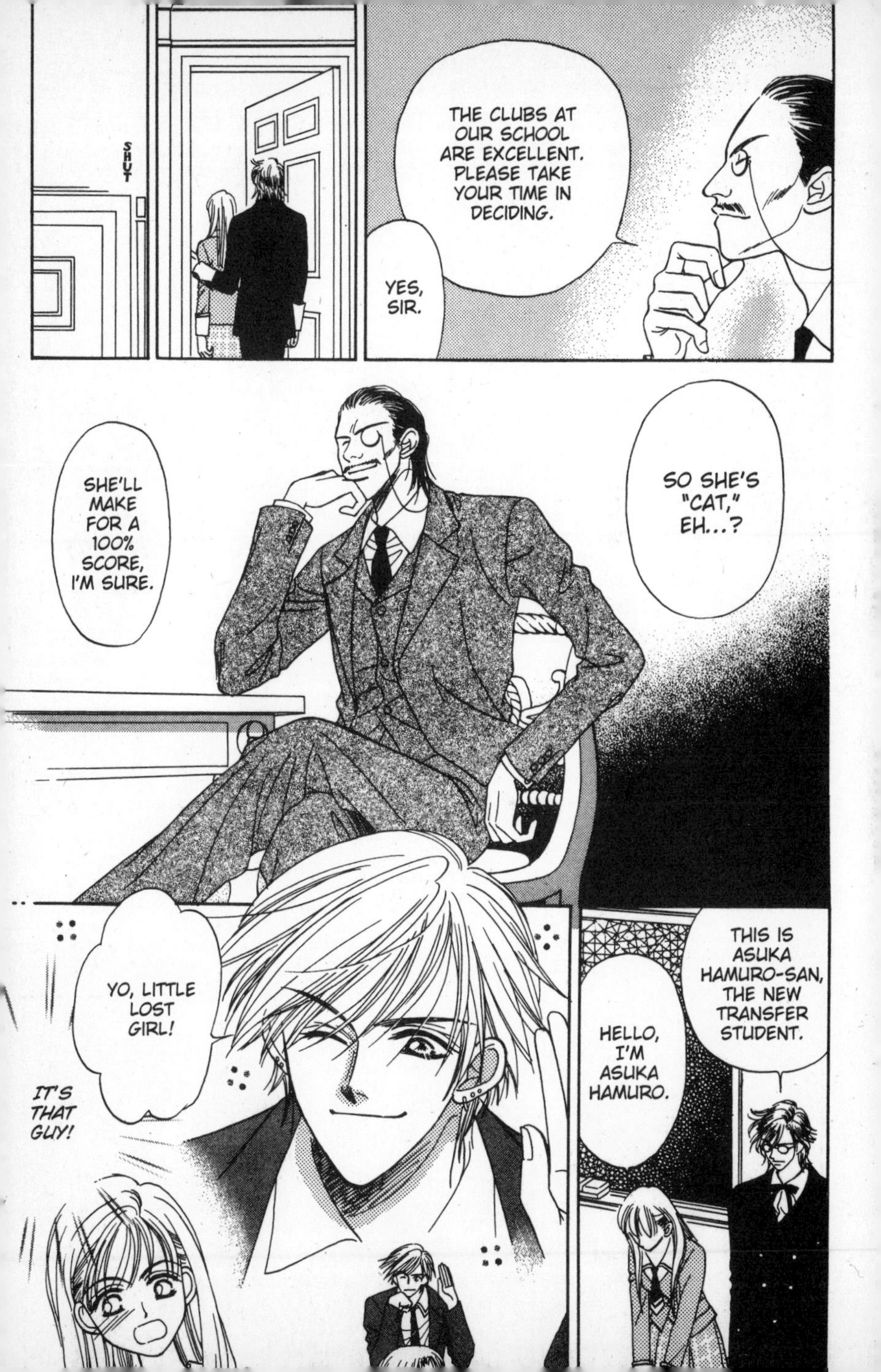
THE CLUBS AT OUR SCHOOL ARE EXCELLENT. PLEASE TAKE YOUR TIME IN DECIDING.
YES, SIR.
SHUT
SO SHE'S "CAT," EH...?
SHE'LL MAKE FOR A 100% SCORE, I'M SURE.
THIS IS ASUKA HAMURO-SAN, THE NEW TRANSFER STUDENT.
HELLO, I'M ASUKA HAMURO.
YO, LITTLE LOST GIRL!
IT'S THAT GUY!

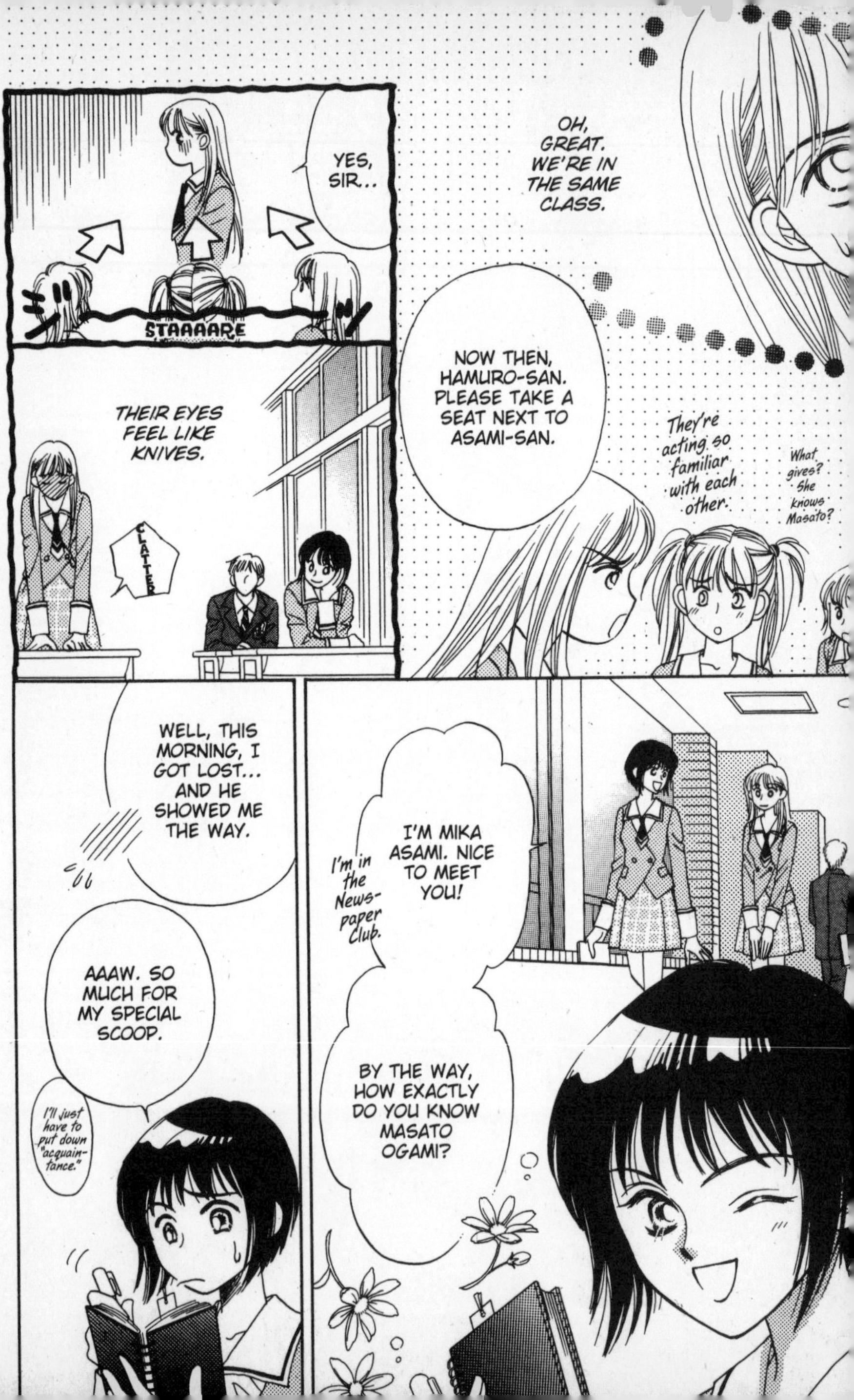
OH, GREAT. WE'RE IN THE SAME CLASS.
YES, SIR...
STAAAARE
NOW THEN, HAMURO-SAN. PLEASE TAKE A SEAT NEXT TO ASAMI-SAN.
They're acting so familiar with each other.
What gives? She knows Masato?
THEIR EYES FEEL LIKE KNIVES.
CLATTER
I'M MIKA ASAMI. NICE TO MEET YOU!
I'm in the News-paper Club.
BY THE WAY, HOW EXACTLY DO YOU KNOW MASATO OGAMI?
WELL, THIS MORNING, I GOT LOST... AND HE SHOWED ME THE WAY.
AAAW. SO MUCH FOR MY SPECIAL SCOOP.
I'll just have to put down "acquaintance."

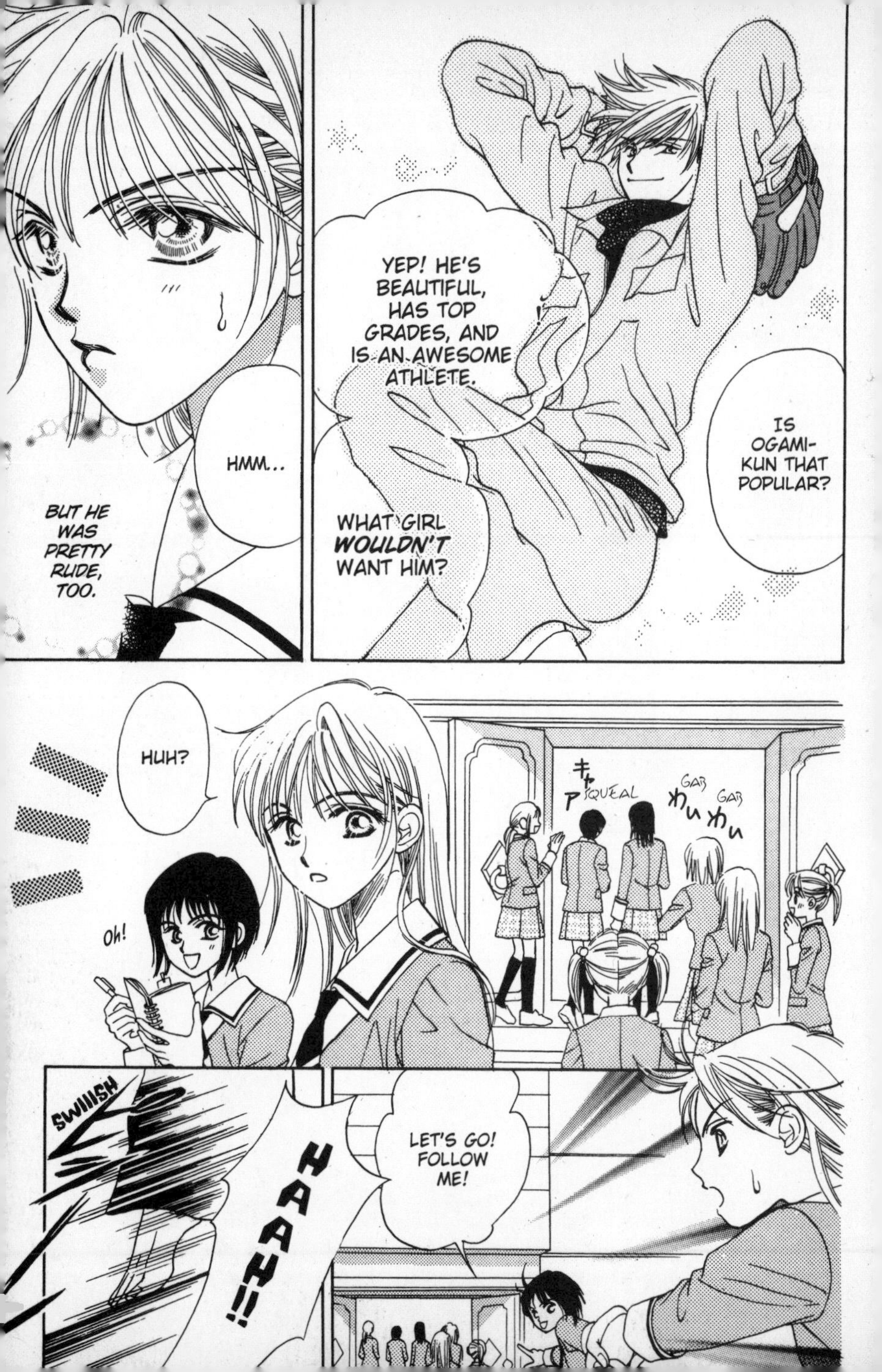
IS OGAMI-KUN THAT POPULAR?
YEP! HE'S BEAUTIFUL, HAS TOP GRADES, AND IS AN AWESOME ATHLETE.
WHAT GIRL WOULDN'T WANT HIM?
HMM...
BUT HE WAS PRETTY RUDE, TOO.
キャ SQUEAL
わいわい GAB GAB
HUH?
Oh!
LET'S GO! FOLLOW ME!
HAAAH!!
SWIIISH

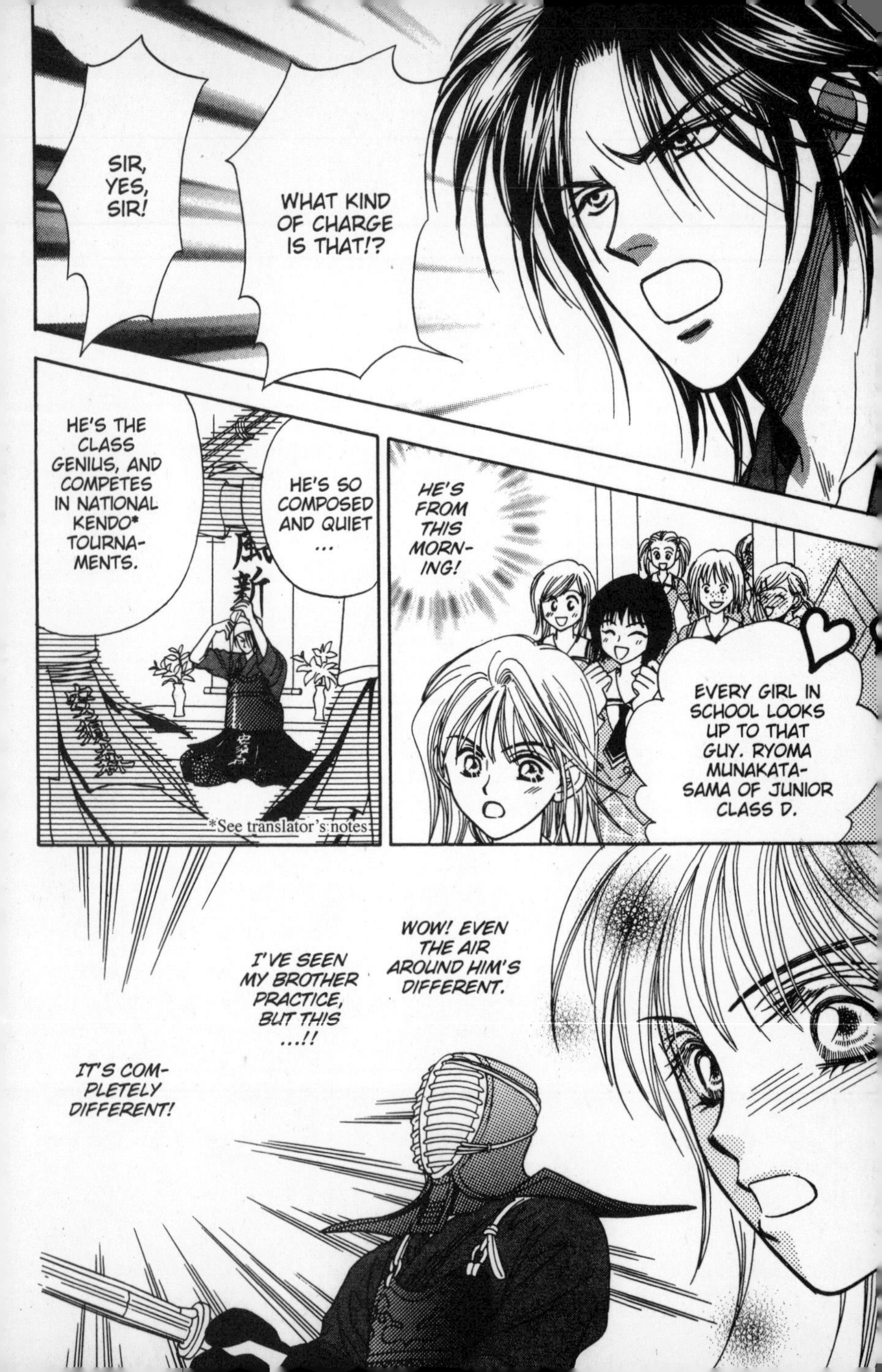
WHAT KIND OF CHARGE IS THAT!?
SIR, YES, SIR!
EVERY GIRL IN SCHOOL LOOKS UP TO THAT GUY. RYOMA MUNAKATA-SAMA OF JUNIOR CLASS D.
HE'S FROM THIS MORNING!
HE'S SO COMPOSED AND QUIET ...
HE'S THE CLASS GENIUS, AND COMPETES IN NATIONAL KENDO* TOURNAMENTS.
*See translator's notes
WOW! EVEN THE AIR AROUND HIM'S DIFFERENT.
I'VE SEEN MY BROTHER PRACTICE, BUT THIS ...!!
IT'S COMPLETELY DIFFERENT!

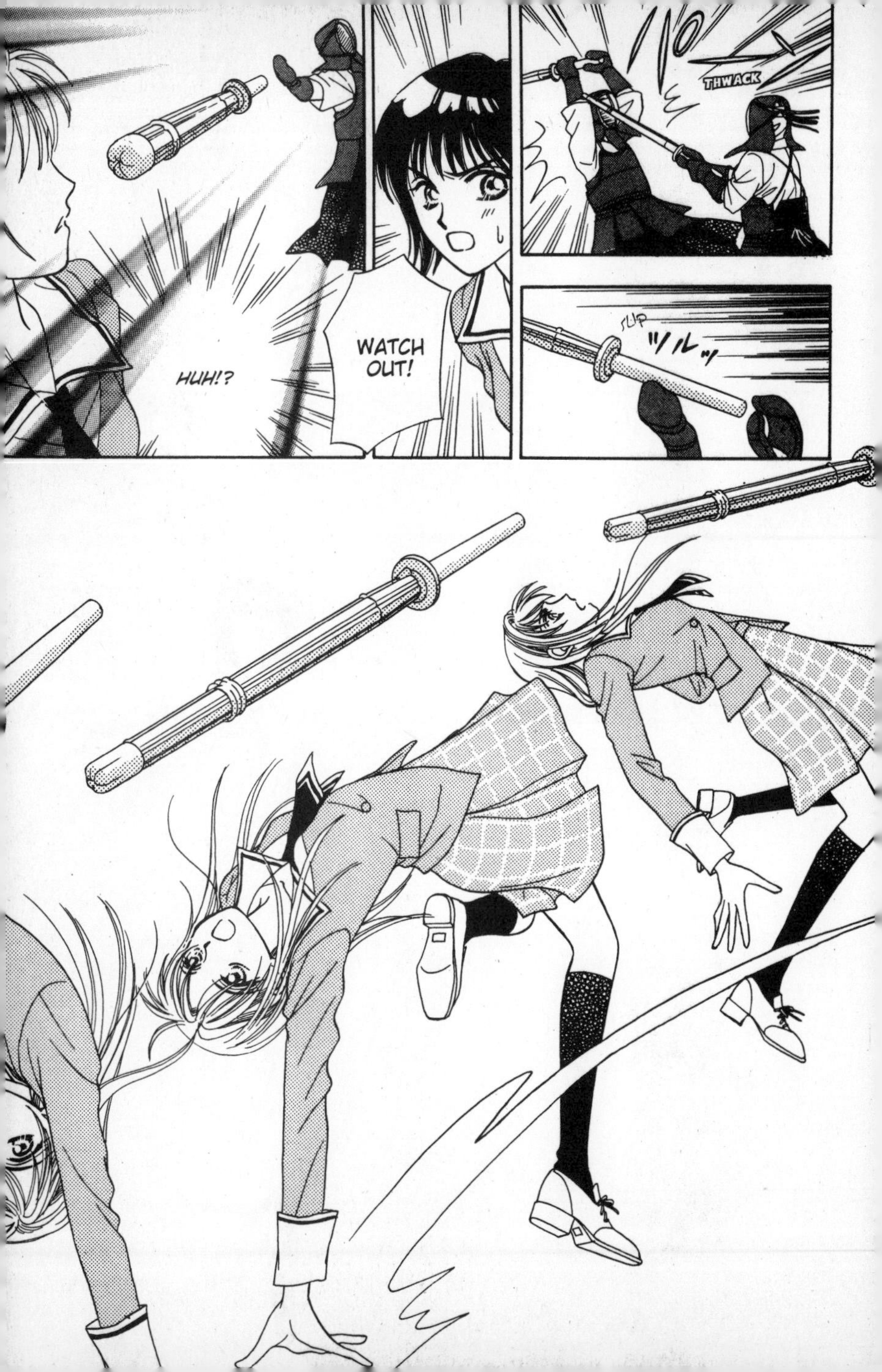
THWACK
SLIP
ツルッ
WATCH OUT!
HUH!?

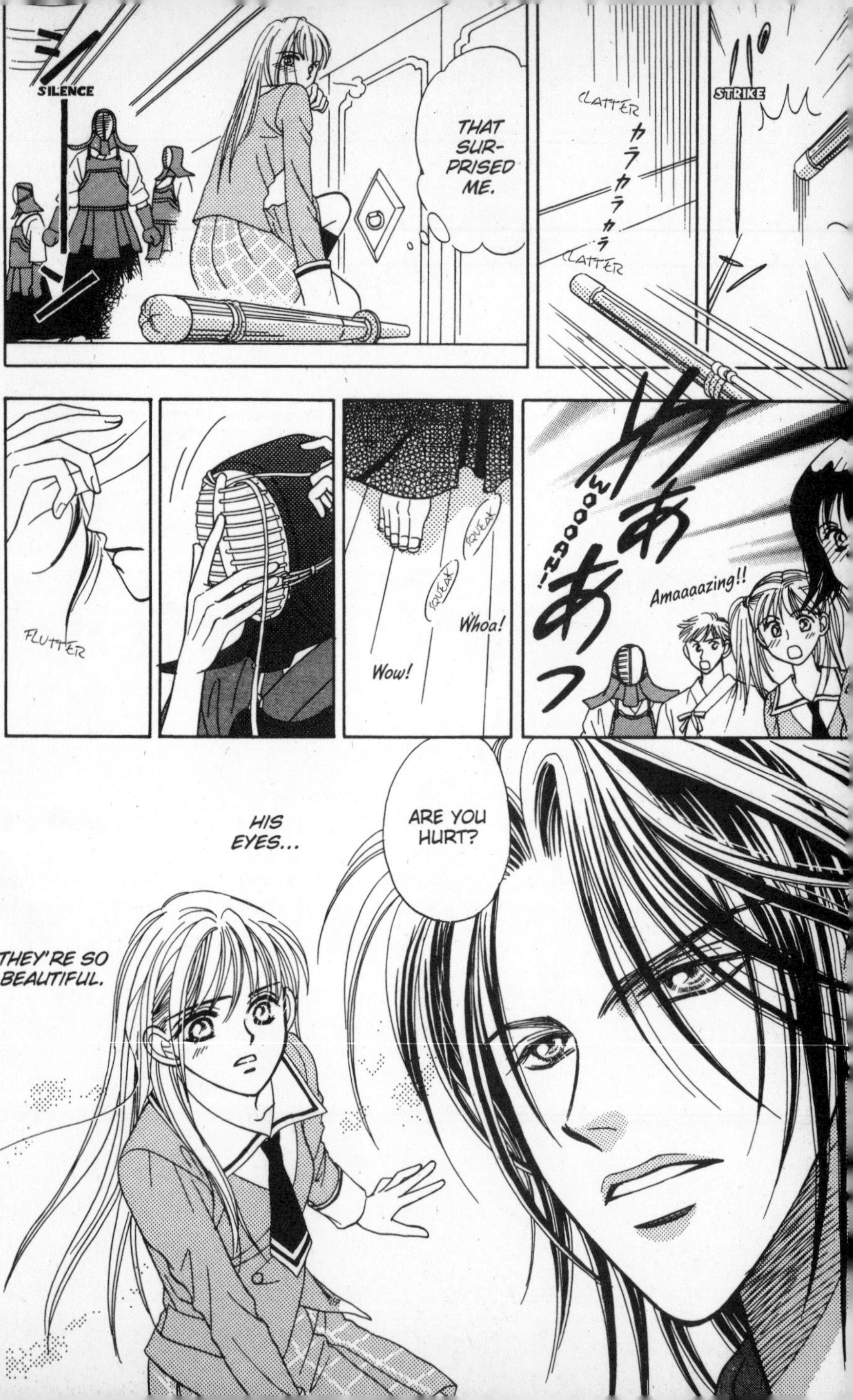
STRIKE
パ
CLATTER
カラカラカラ
CLATTER
THAT SURPRISED ME.
SILENCE
シン
WOOOOOOW!!
わあああっ
Amaaaazing!!
Whoa!
SQUEAK
SQUEAK
Wow!
FLUTTER
ARE YOU HURT?
HIS EYES...
THEY'RE SO BEAUTIFUL.

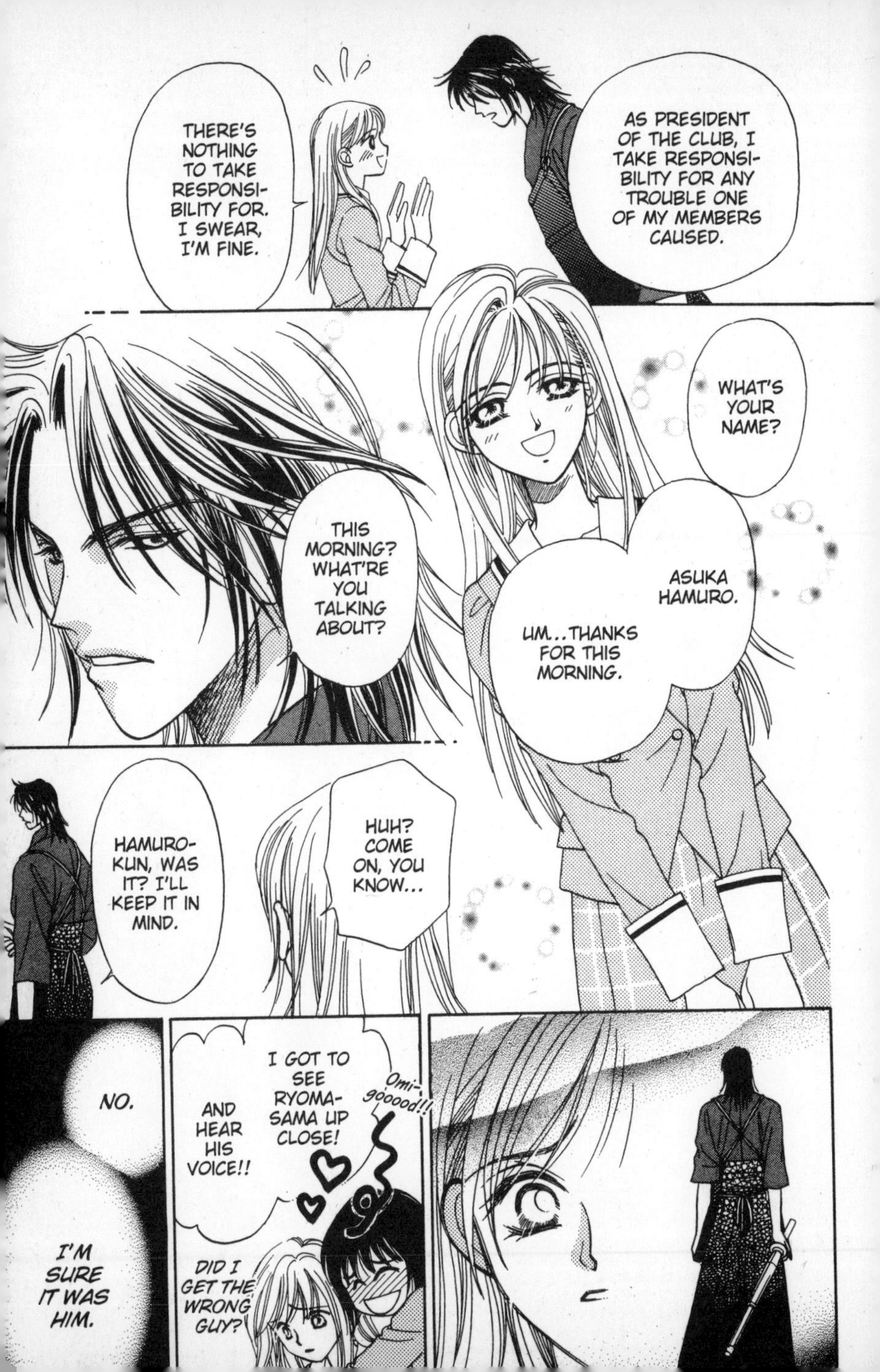
AS PRESIDENT OF THE CLUB, I TAKE RESPONSIBILITY FOR ANY TROUBLE ONE OF MY MEMBERS CAUSED.
THERE'S NOTHING TO TAKE RESPONSIBILITY FOR. I SWEAR, I'M FINE.
WHAT'S YOUR NAME?
ASUKA HAMURO.
UM...THANKS FOR THIS MORNING.
THIS MORNING? WHAT'RE YOU TALKING ABOUT?
HUH? COME ON, YOU KNOW...
HAMURO-KUN, WAS IT? I'LL KEEP IT IN MIND.
I GOT TO SEE RYOMA-SAMA UP CLOSE!
Omi-gooood!!
AND HEAR HIS VOICE!!
DID I GET THE WRONG GUY?
NO.
I'M SURE IT WAS HIM.

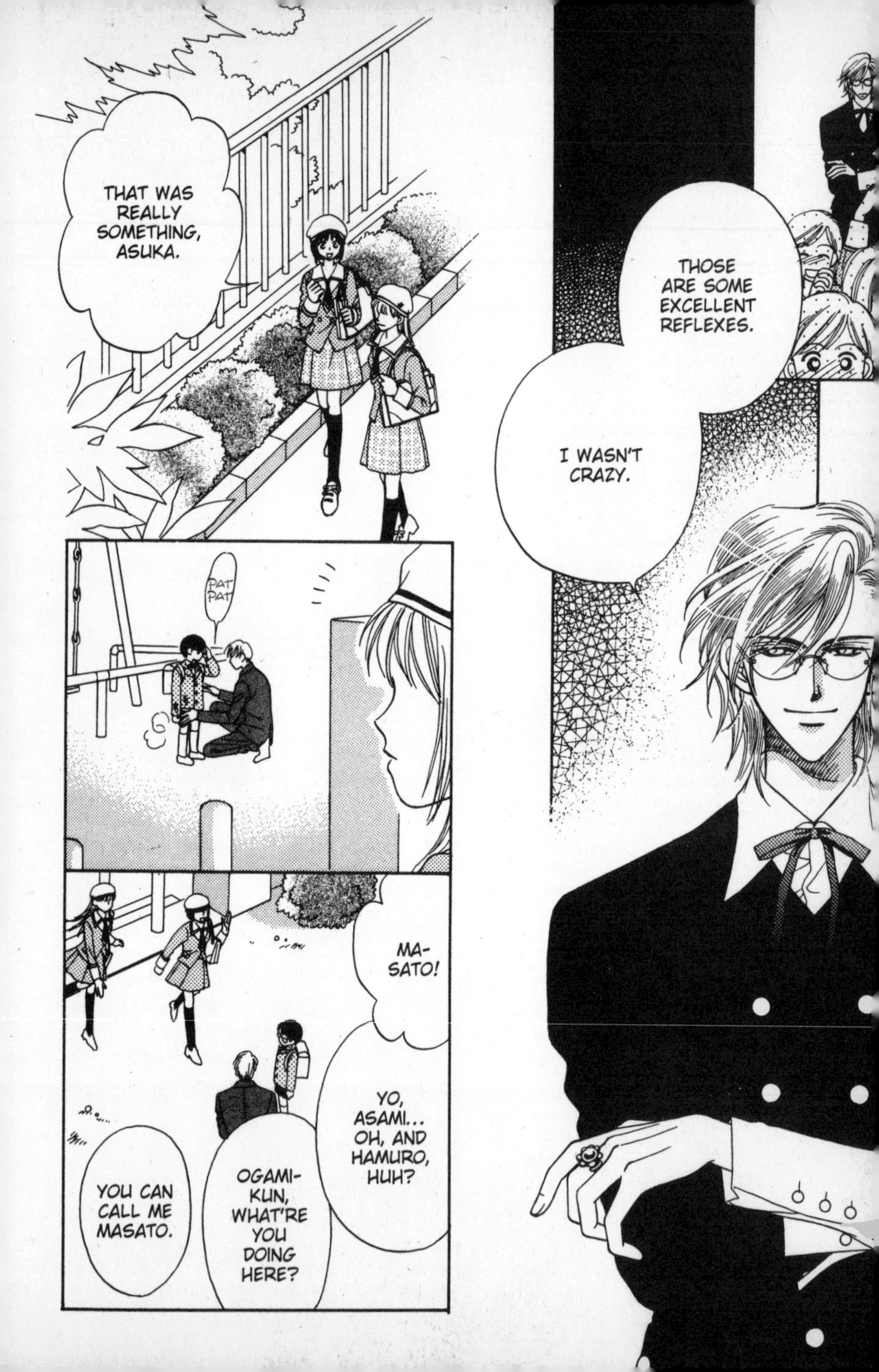
THOSE ARE SOME EXCELLENT REFLEXES.
I WASN'T CRAZY.
THAT WAS REALLY SOMETHING, ASUKA.
PAT PAT
MA-SATO!
YO, ASAMI... OH, AND HAMURO, HUH?
OGAMI-KUN, WHAT'RE YOU DOING HERE?
YOU CAN CALL ME MASATO.

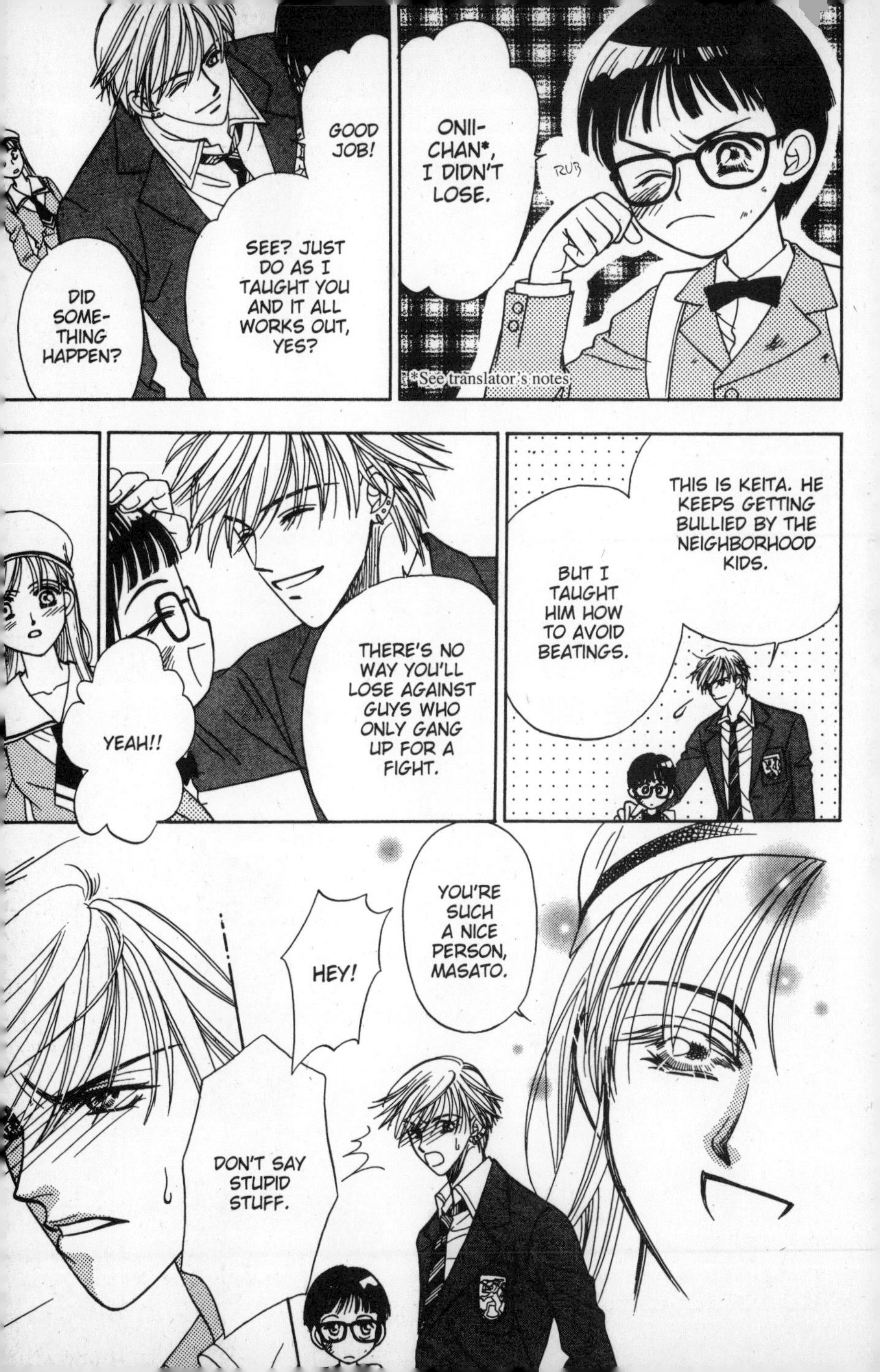
ONII-CHAN*, I DIDN'T LOSE.
RUB
GOOD JOB!
SEE? JUST DO AS I TAUGHT YOU AND IT ALL WORKS OUT, YES?
DID SOME-THING HAPPEN?
*See translator's notes
THIS IS KEITA. HE KEEPS GETTING BULLIED BY THE NEIGHBORHOOD KIDS.
BUT I TAUGHT HIM HOW TO AVOID BEATINGS.
THERE'S NO WAY YOU'LL LOSE AGAINST GUYS WHO ONLY GANG UP FOR A FIGHT.
YEAH!!
YOU'RE SUCH A NICE PERSON, MASATO.
HEY!
DON'T SAY STUPID STUFF.

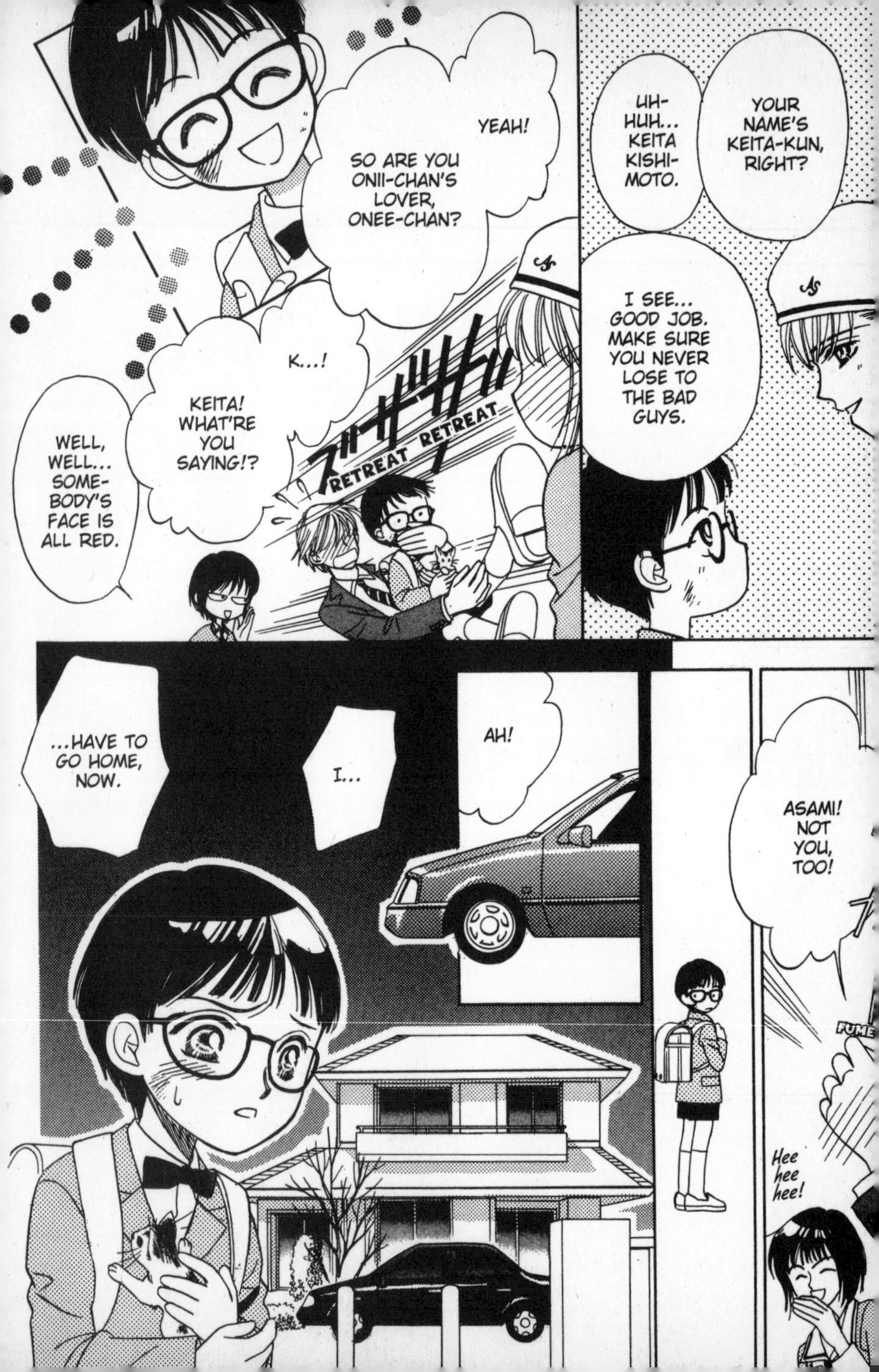

YOUR NAME'S KEITA-KUN, RIGHT?
UH-HUH... KEITA KISHIMOTO.
I SEE... GOOD JOB. MAKE SURE YOU NEVER LOSE TO THE BAD GUYS.
YEAH!
SO ARE YOU ONII-CHAN'S LOVER, ONEE-CHAN?
K...!
KEITA! WHAT'RE YOU SAYING!?
RETREAT RETREAT
WELL, WELL... SOMEBODY'S FACE IS ALL RED.
FUME
ASAMI! NOT YOU, TOO!
Hee hee hee!
AH!
I...
...HAVE TO GO HOME, NOW.

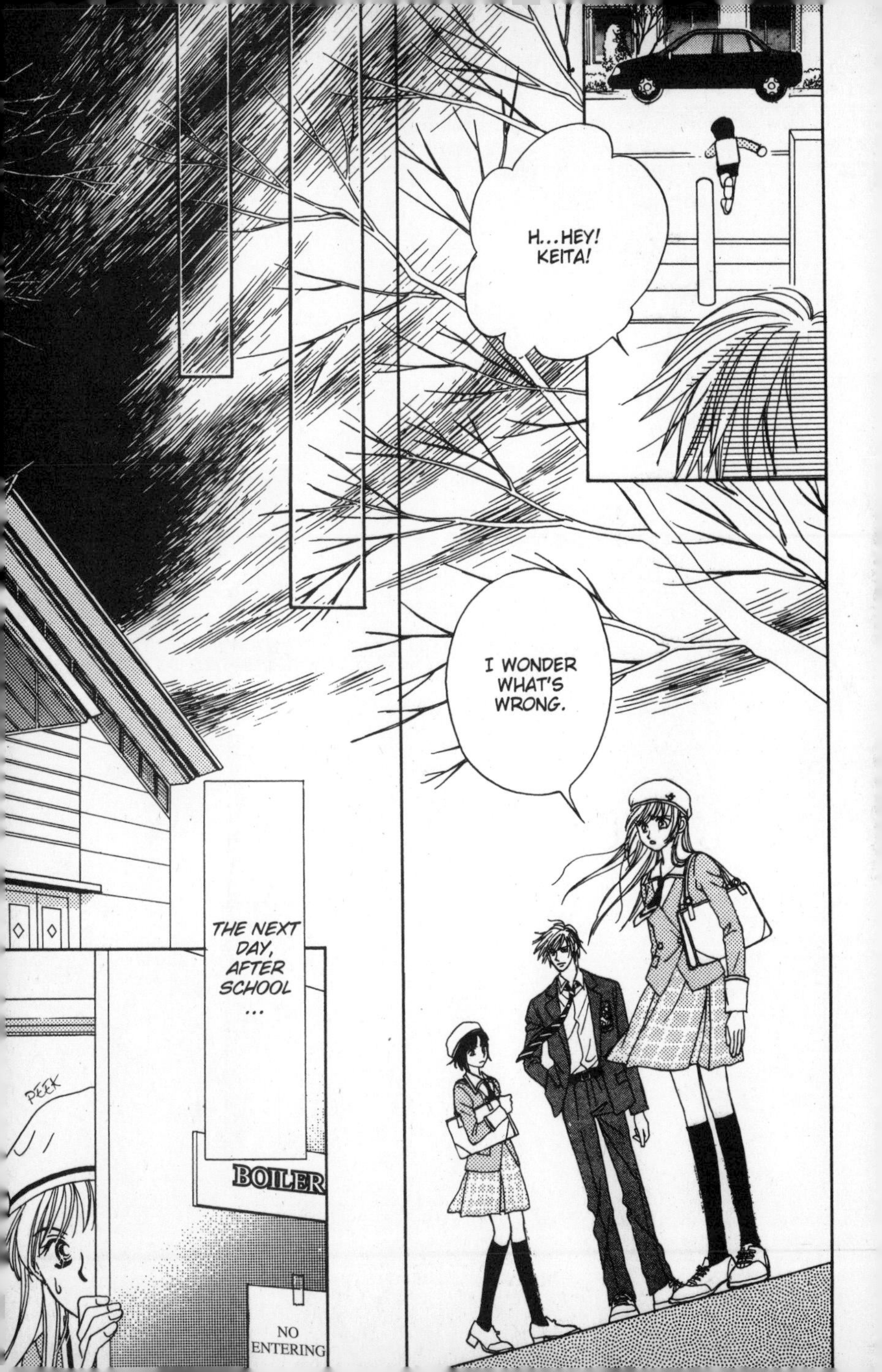

H...HEY! KEITA!
I WONDER WHAT'S WRONG.
THE NEXT DAY, AFTER SCHOOL ...
BOILER
NO ENTERING
PEEK

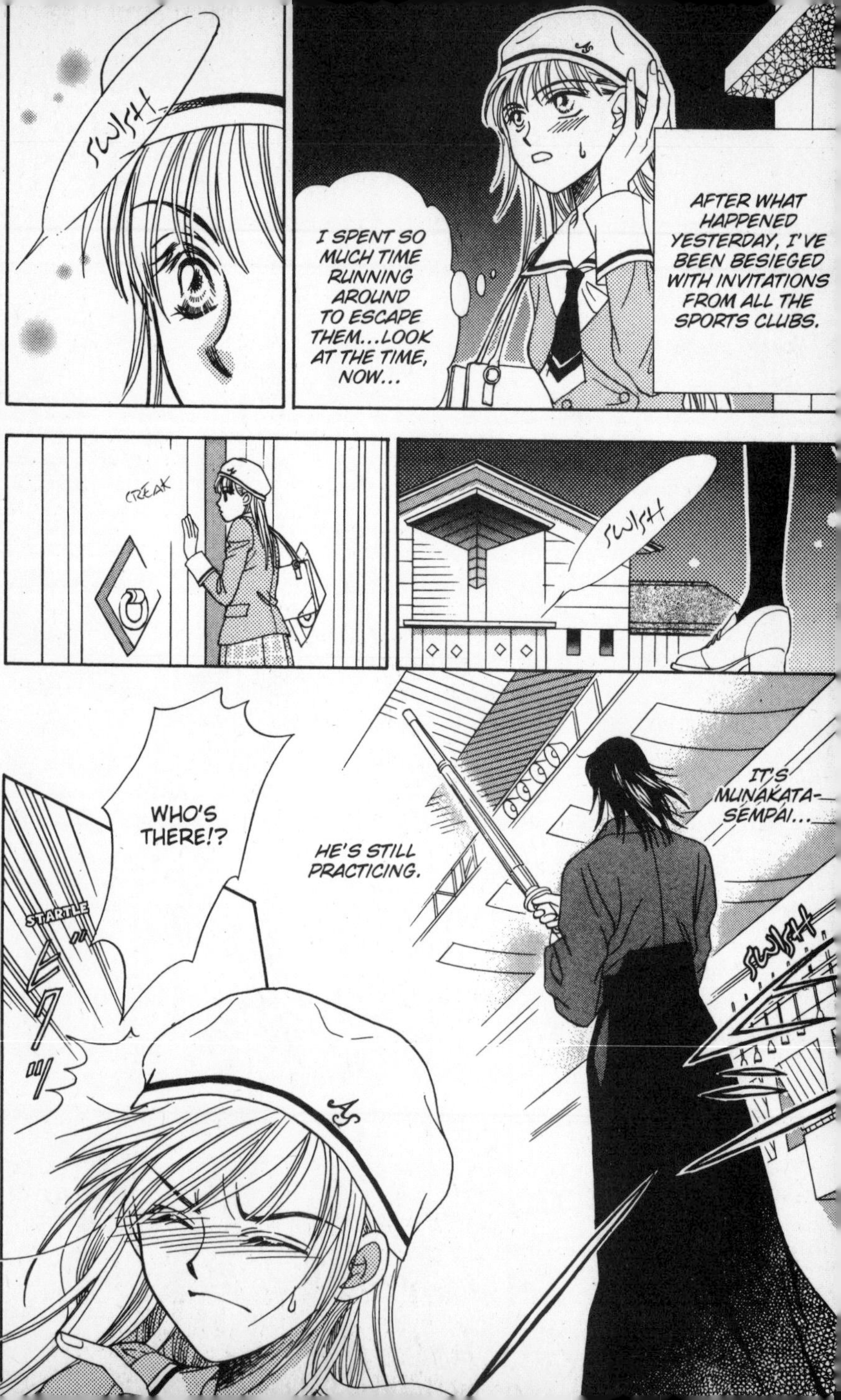
AFTER WHAT HAPPENED YESTERDAY, I'VE BEEN BESIEGED WITH INVITATIONS FROM ALL THE SPORTS CLUBS.
I SPENT SO MUCH TIME RUNNING AROUND TO ESCAPE THEM...LOOK AT THE TIME, NOW...
SWISH
SWISH
CREAK
SWISH
IT'S MUNAKATA-SEMPAI...
HE'S STILL PRACTICING.
WHO'S THERE!?
STARTLE

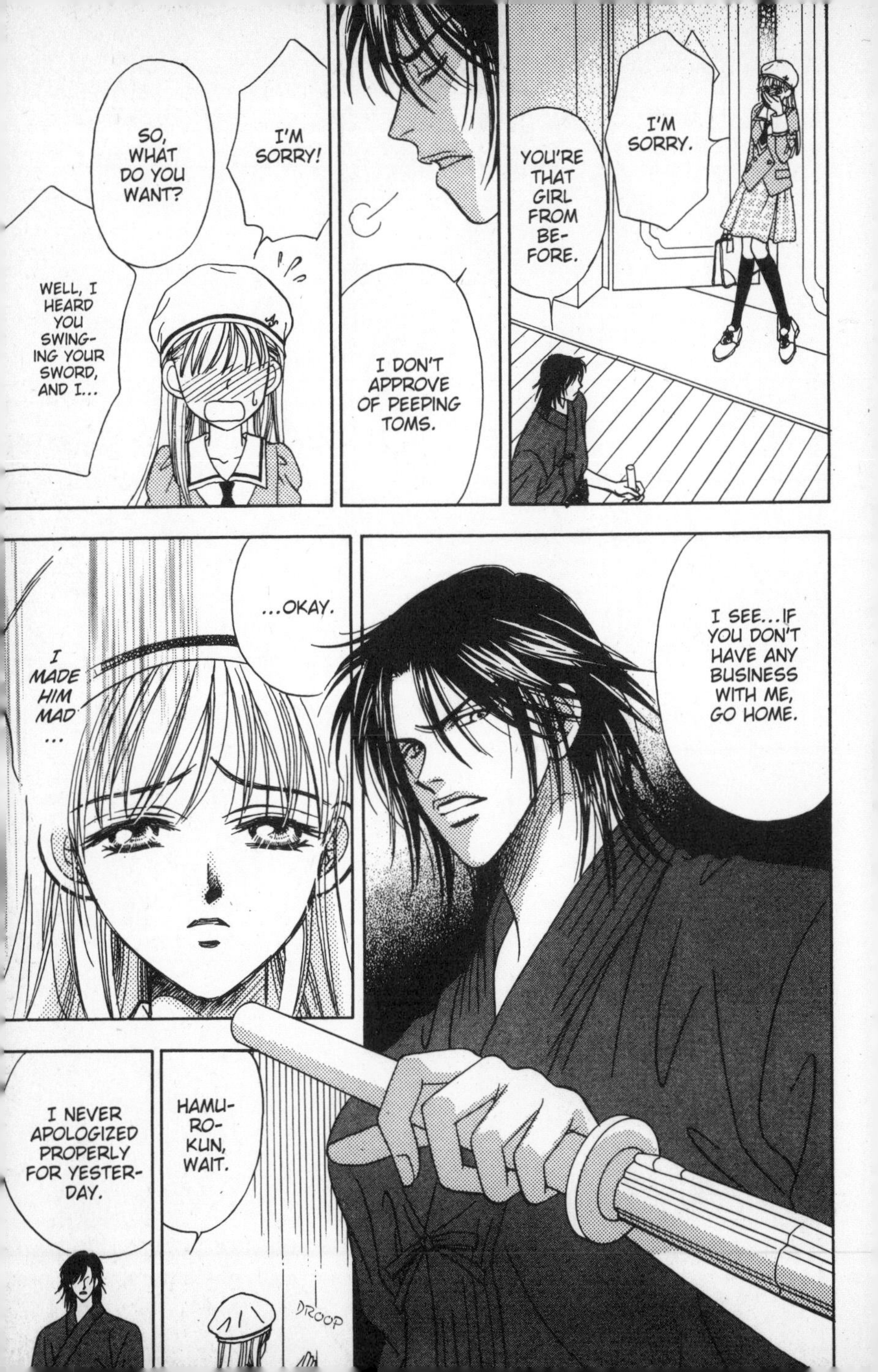
I'M SORRY.
YOU'RE THAT GIRL FROM BEFORE.
I DON'T APPROVE OF PEEPING TOMS.
I'M SORRY!
SO, WHAT DO YOU WANT?
WELL, I HEARD YOU SWINGING YOUR SWORD, AND I...
I SEE...IF YOU DON'T HAVE ANY BUSINESS WITH ME, GO HOME.
...OKAY.
I MADE HIM MAD...
HAMURO-KUN, WAIT.
I NEVER APOLOGIZED PROPERLY FOR YESTERDAY.
DROOP

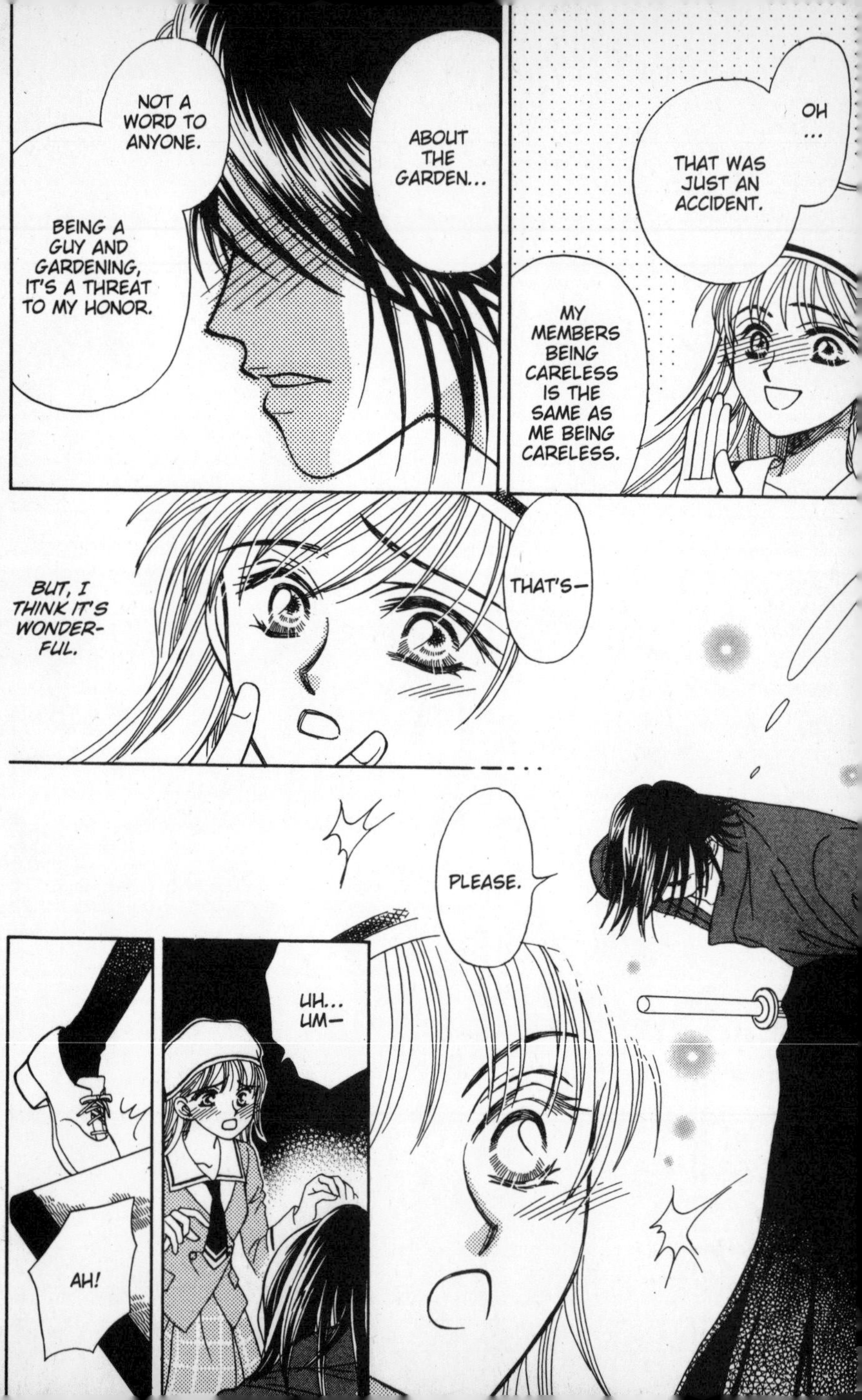
OH ...
THAT WAS JUST AN ACCIDENT.
MY MEMBERS BEING CARELESS IS THE SAME AS ME BEING CARELESS.
ABOUT THE GARDEN...
NOT A WORD TO ANYONE.
BEING A GUY AND GARDENING, IT'S A THREAT TO MY HONOR.
THAT'S—
BUT, I THINK IT'S WONDER-FUL.
PLEASE.
UH... UM—
AH!

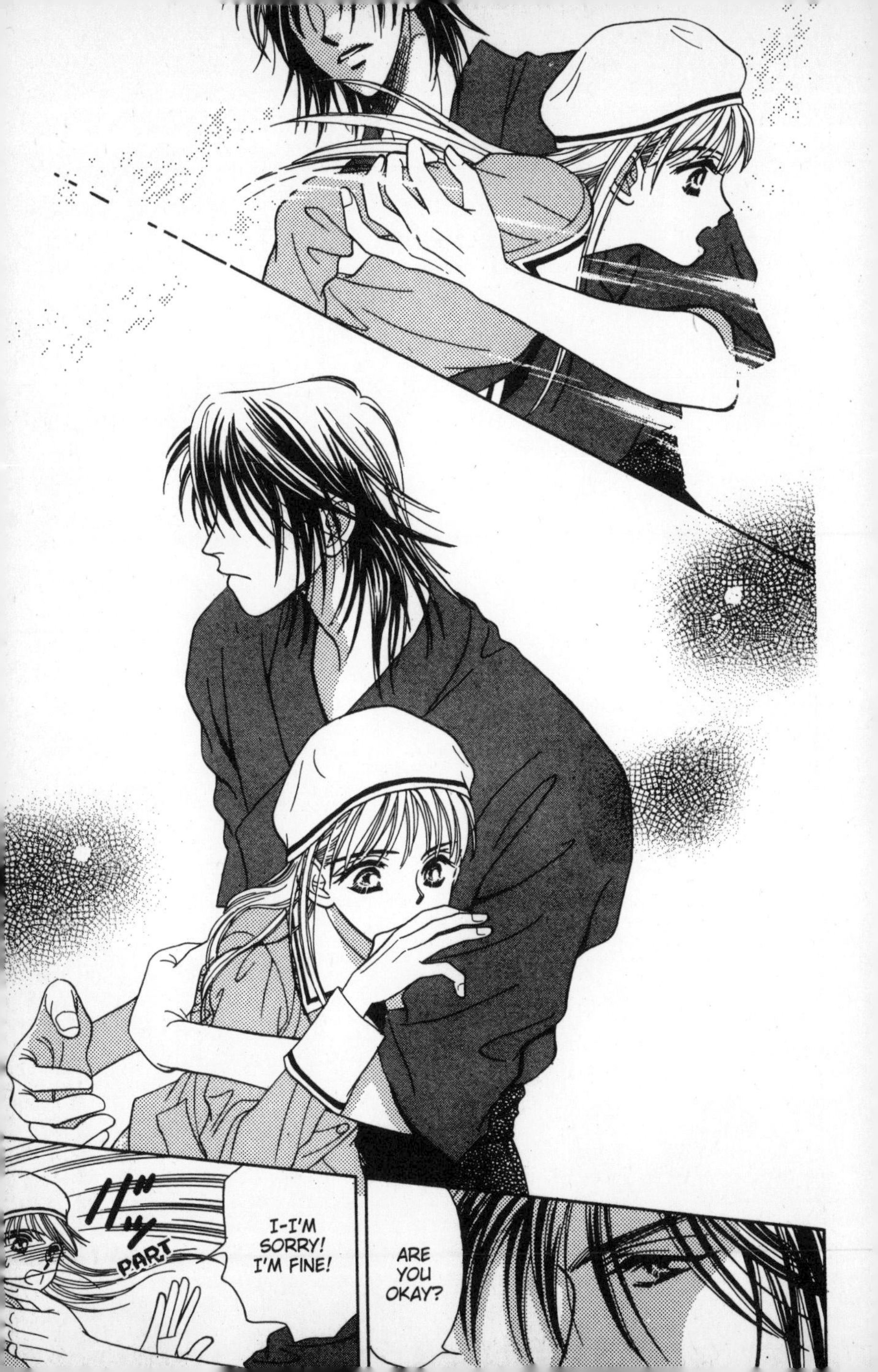

ARE YOU OKAY?
I-I'M SORRY! I'M FINE!
PART

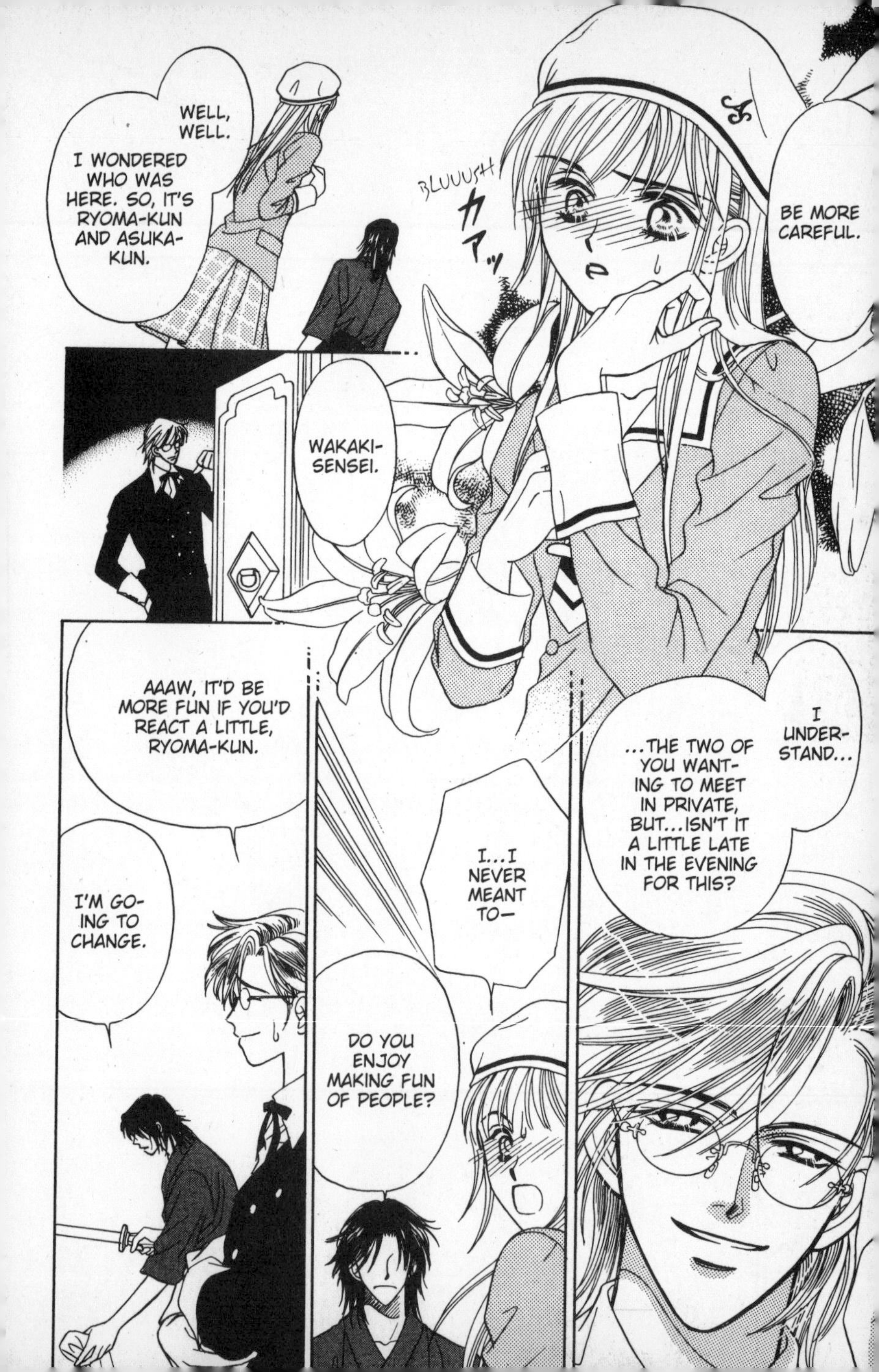
BE MORE CAREFUL.
BLUUUSH
カァッ
WELL, WELL.
I WONDERED WHO WAS HERE. SO, IT'S RYOMA-KUN AND ASUKA-KUN.
WAKAKI-SENSEI.
I UNDERSTAND...
...THE TWO OF YOU WANTING TO MEET IN PRIVATE, BUT...ISN'T IT A LITTLE LATE IN THE EVENING FOR THIS?
I...I NEVER MEANT TO—
DO YOU ENJOY MAKING FUN OF PEOPLE?
AAAW, IT'D BE MORE FUN IF YOU'D REACT A LITTLE, RYOMA-KUN.
I'M GOING TO CHANGE.

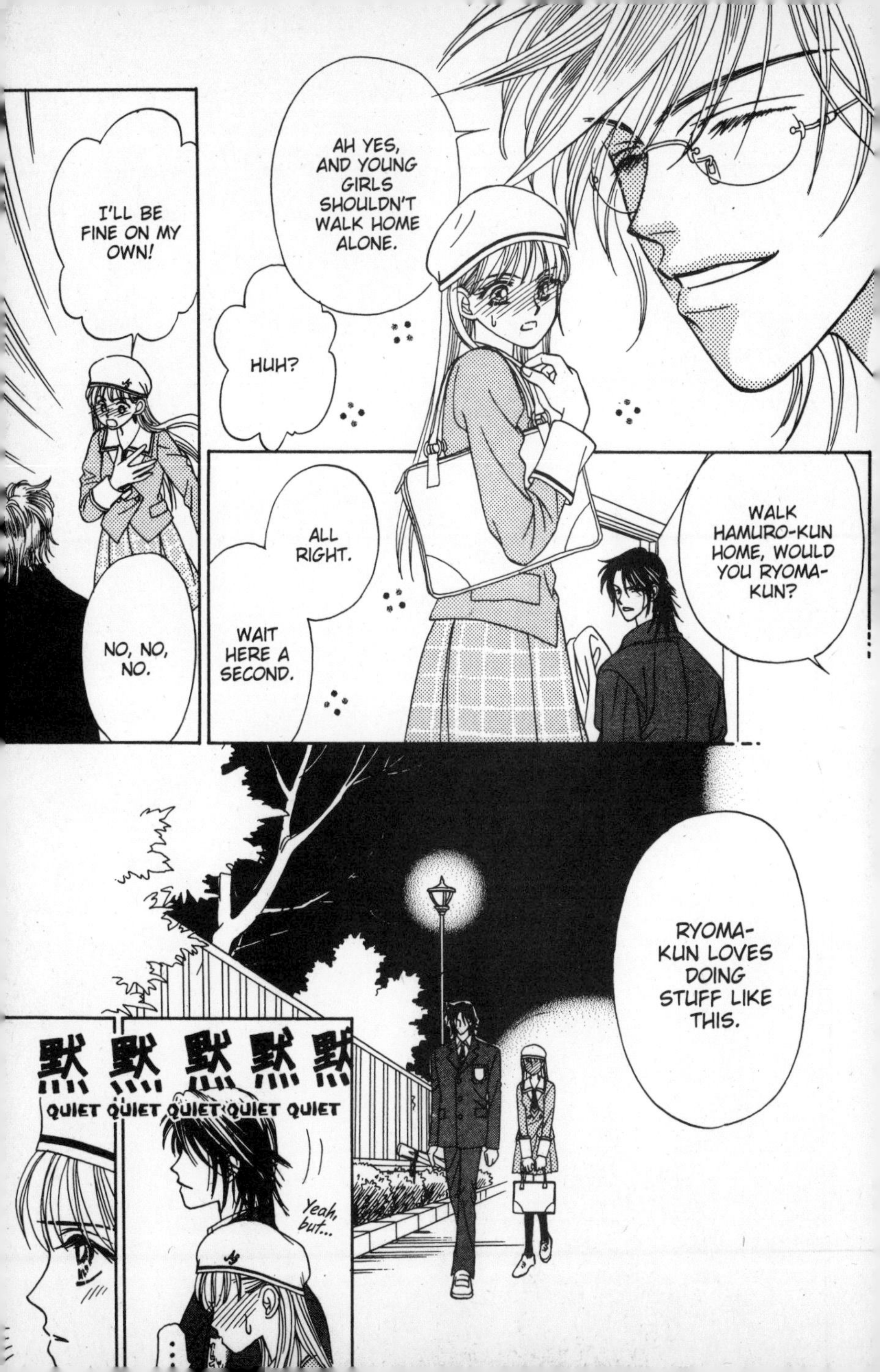
AH YES, AND YOUNG GIRLS SHOULDN'T WALK HOME ALONE.
HUH?
I'LL BE FINE ON MY OWN!
WALK HAMURO-KUN HOME, WOULD YOU RYOMA-KUN?
ALL RIGHT.
WAIT HERE A SECOND.
NO, NO, NO.
RYOMA-KUN LOVES DOING STUFF LIKE THIS.
默默默默默
QUIET QUIET QUIET QUIET QUIET
Yeah, but...

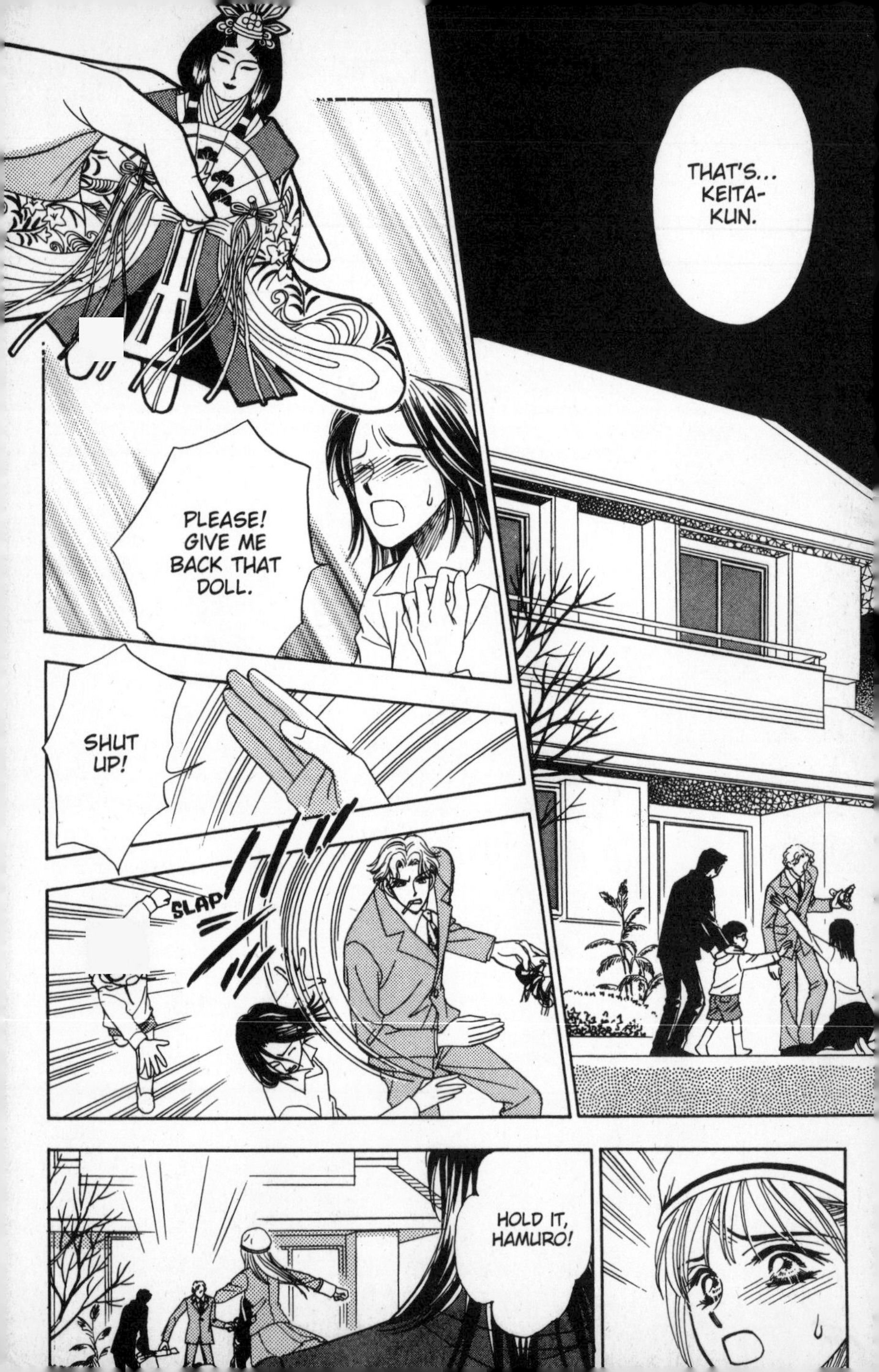
THAT'S... KEITA-KUN.
PLEASE! GIVE ME BACK THAT DOLL.
SHUT UP!
SLAP
HOLD IT, HAMURO!

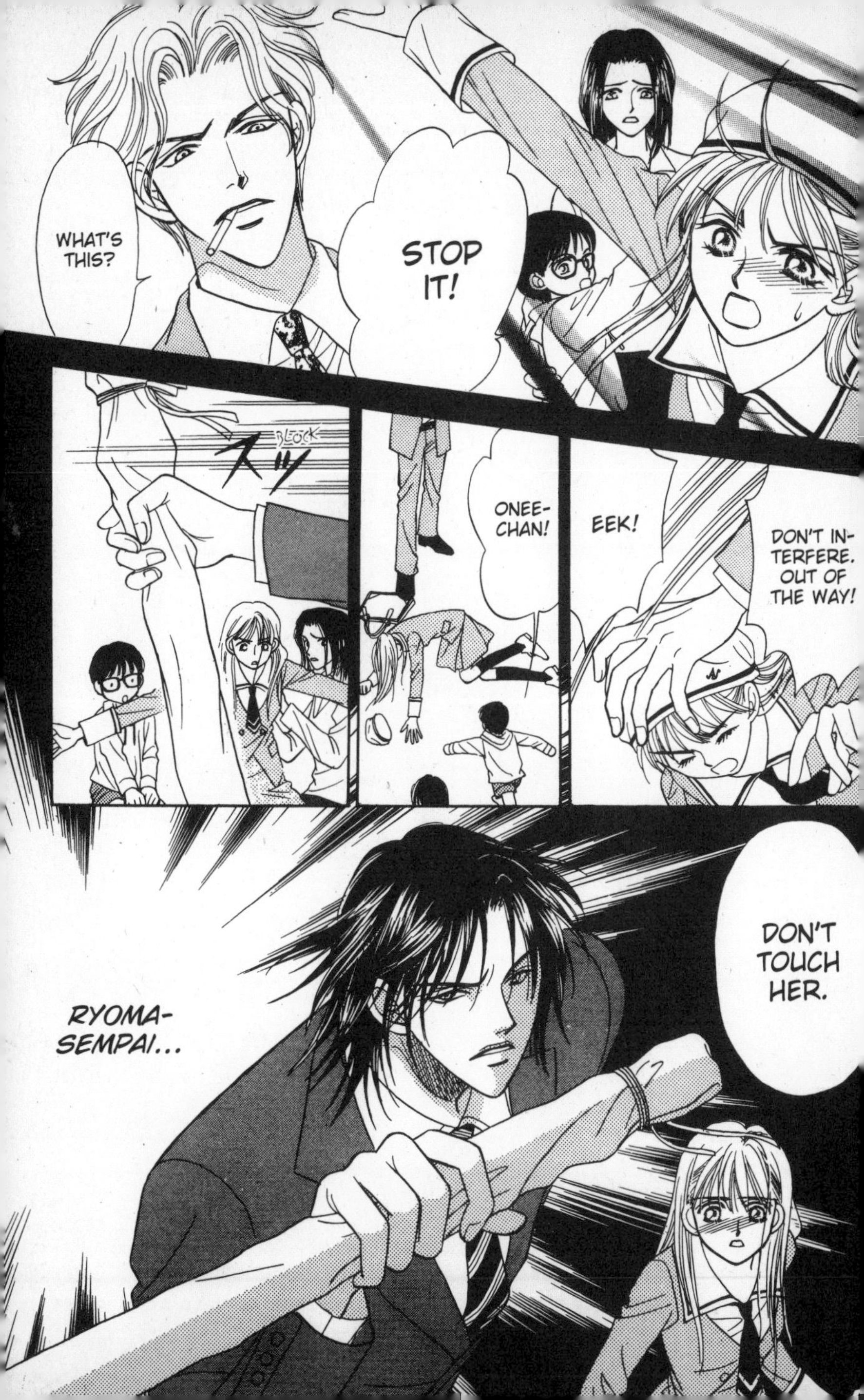
STOP IT!
WHAT'S THIS?
DON'T INTERFERE. OUT OF THE WAY!
EEK!
ONEE-CHAN!
スッ
BLOCK
DON'T TOUCH HER.
RYOMA-SEMPAI...

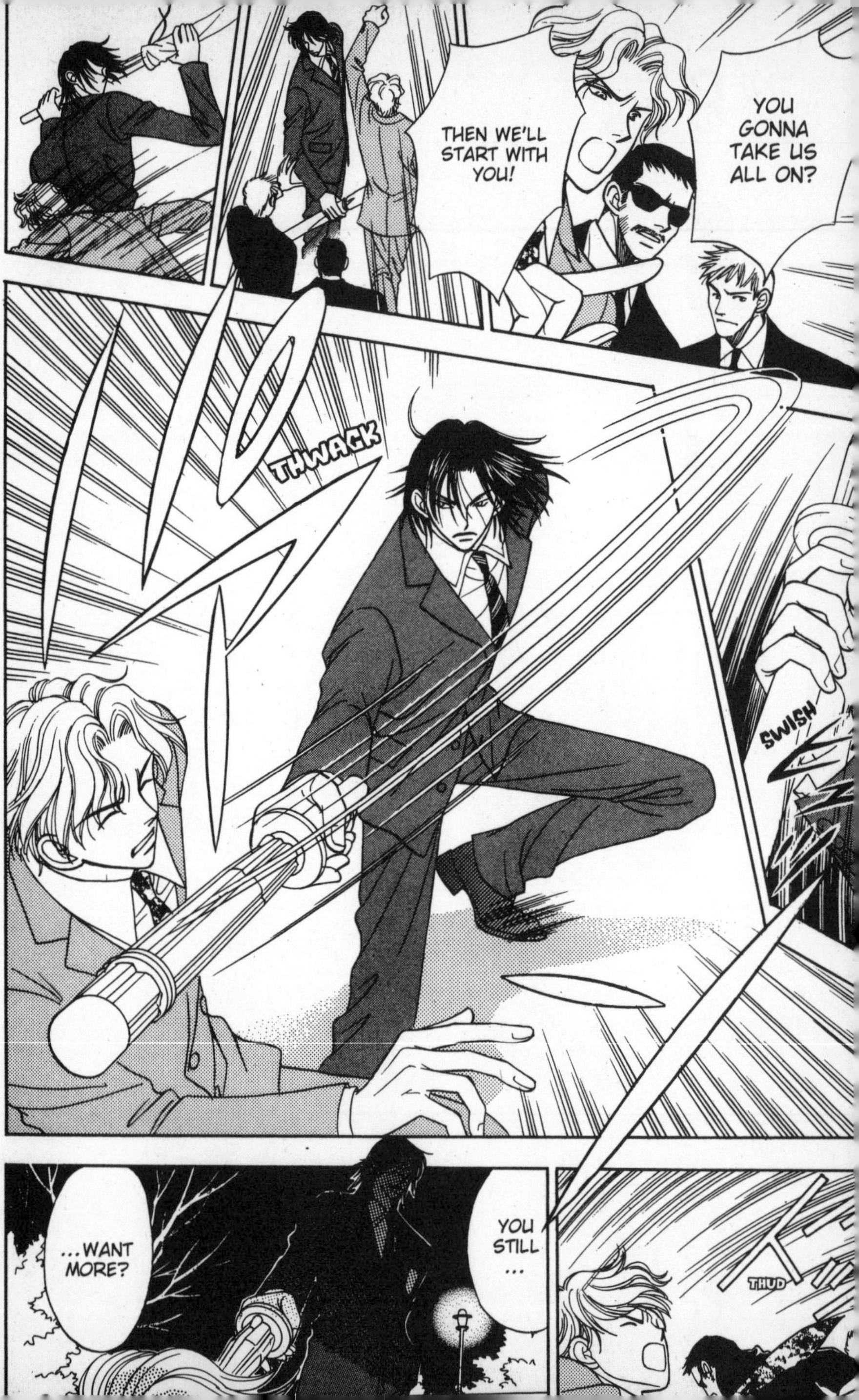
YOU GONNA TAKE US ALL ON?
THEN WE'LL START WITH YOU!
THWACK
SWISH
YOU STILL ...
...WANT MORE?
THUD

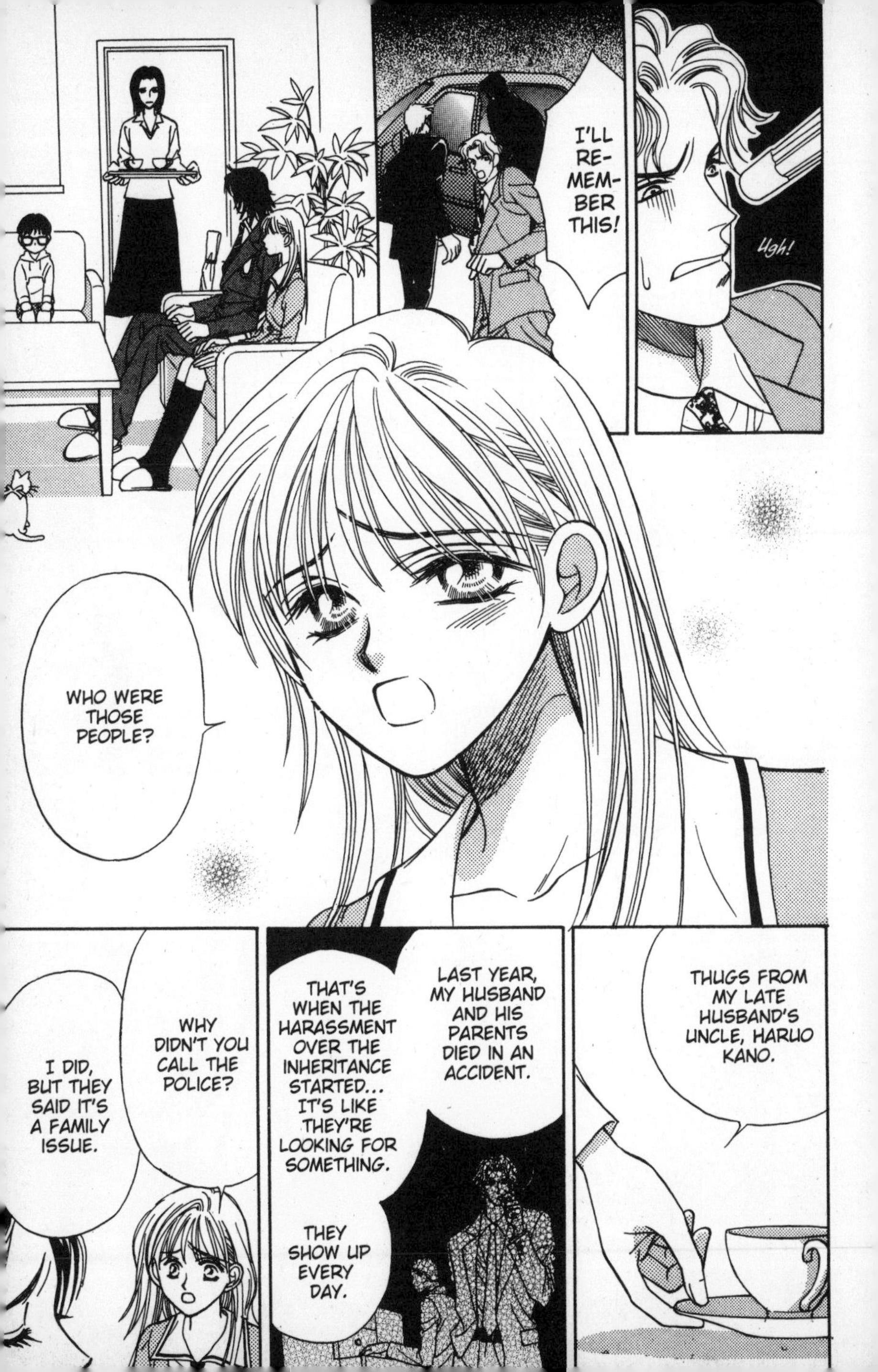
Ugh!
I'LL RE-MEM-BER THIS!
WHO WERE THOSE PEOPLE?
THUGS FROM MY LATE HUSBAND'S UNCLE, HARUO KANO.
LAST YEAR, MY HUSBAND AND HIS PARENTS DIED IN AN ACCIDENT.
THAT'S WHEN THE HARASSMENT OVER THE INHERITANCE STARTED... IT'S LIKE THEY'RE LOOKING FOR SOMETHING.
THEY SHOW UP EVERY DAY.
WHY DIDN'T YOU CALL THE POLICE?
I DID, BUT THEY SAID IT'S A FAMILY ISSUE.

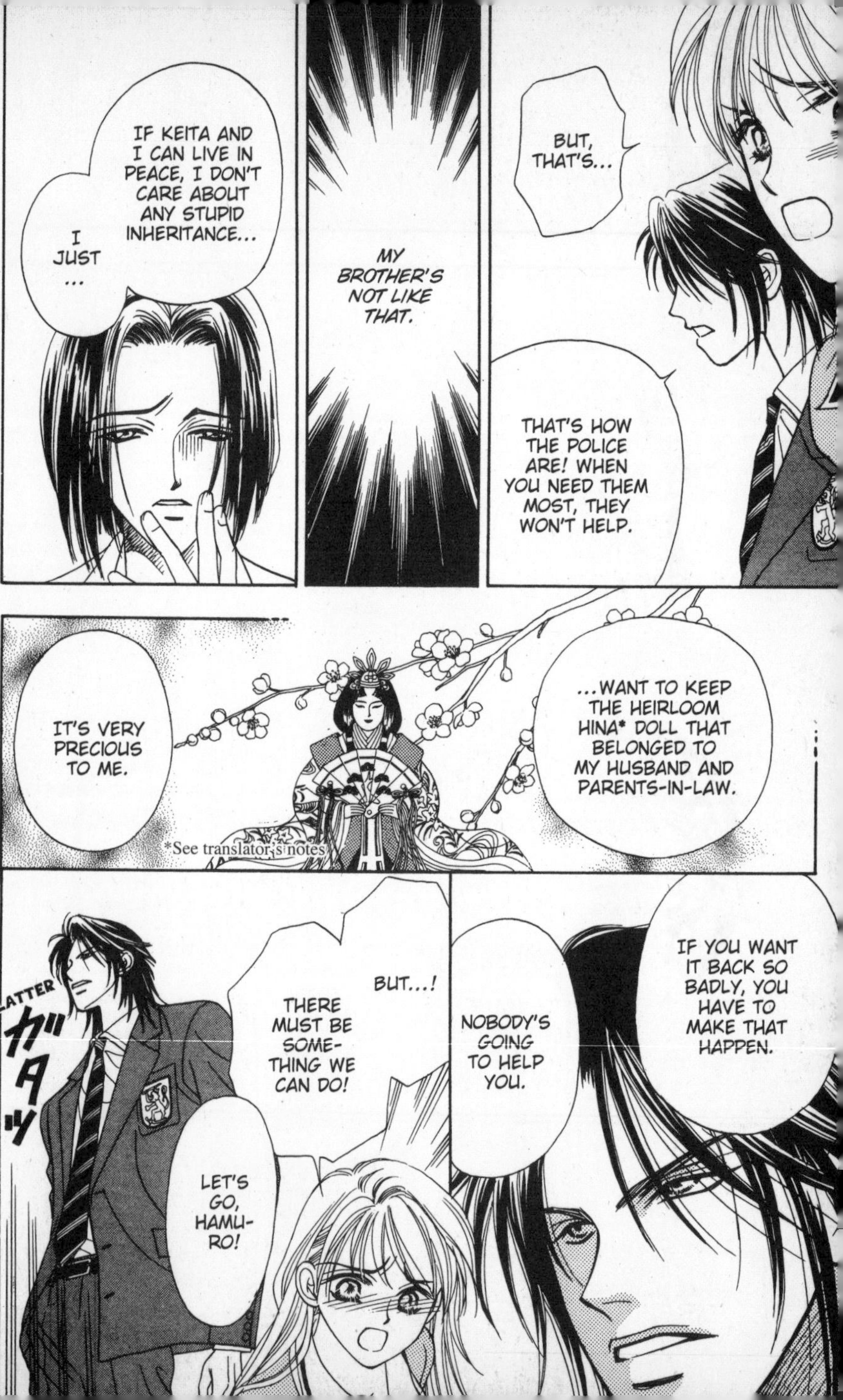
BUT, THAT'S...
THAT'S HOW THE POLICE ARE! WHEN YOU NEED THEM MOST, THEY WON'T HELP.
MY BROTHER'S NOT LIKE THAT.
IF KEITA AND I CAN LIVE IN PEACE, I DON'T CARE ABOUT ANY STUPID INHERITANCE...
I JUST ...
...WANT TO KEEP THE HEIRLOOM HINA* DOLL THAT BELONGED TO MY HUSBAND AND PARENTS-IN-LAW.
IT'S VERY PRECIOUS TO ME.
IF YOU WANT IT BACK SO BADLY, YOU HAVE TO MAKE THAT HAPPEN.
NOBODY'S GOING TO HELP YOU.
BUT...!
THERE MUST BE SOME-THING WE CAN DO!
LET'S GO, HAMU-RO!
CLATTER
ガタッ
*See translator's notes

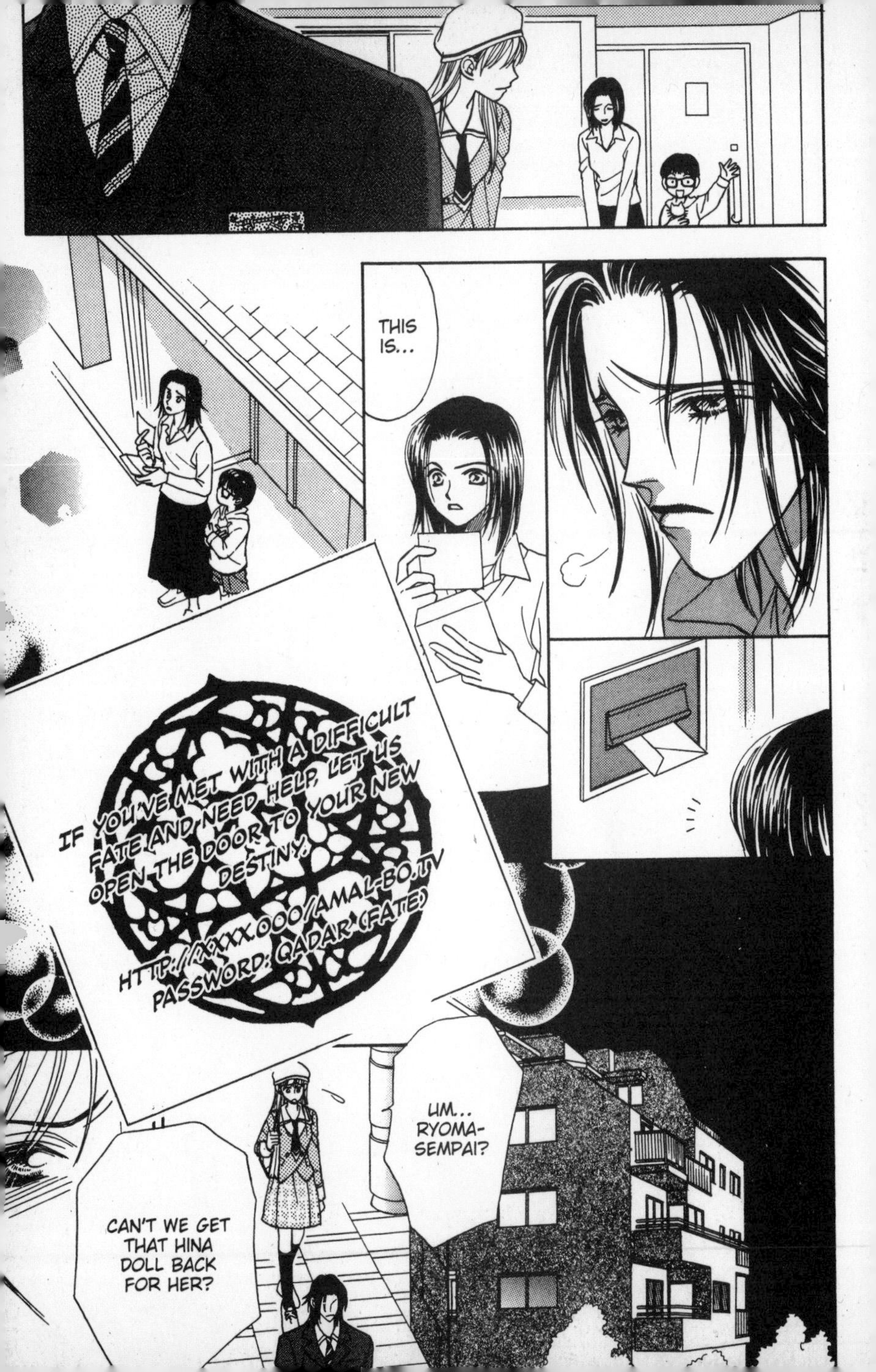
THIS IS...
IF YOU'VE MET WITH A DIFFICULT FATE AND NEED HELP, LET US OPEN THE DOOR TO YOUR NEW DESTINY.
HTTP://X.XXX.000/AMAL-BO.TV
PASSWORD: QADAR (FATE)
UM... RYOMA-SEMPAI?
CAN'T WE GET THAT HINA DOLL BACK FOR HER?

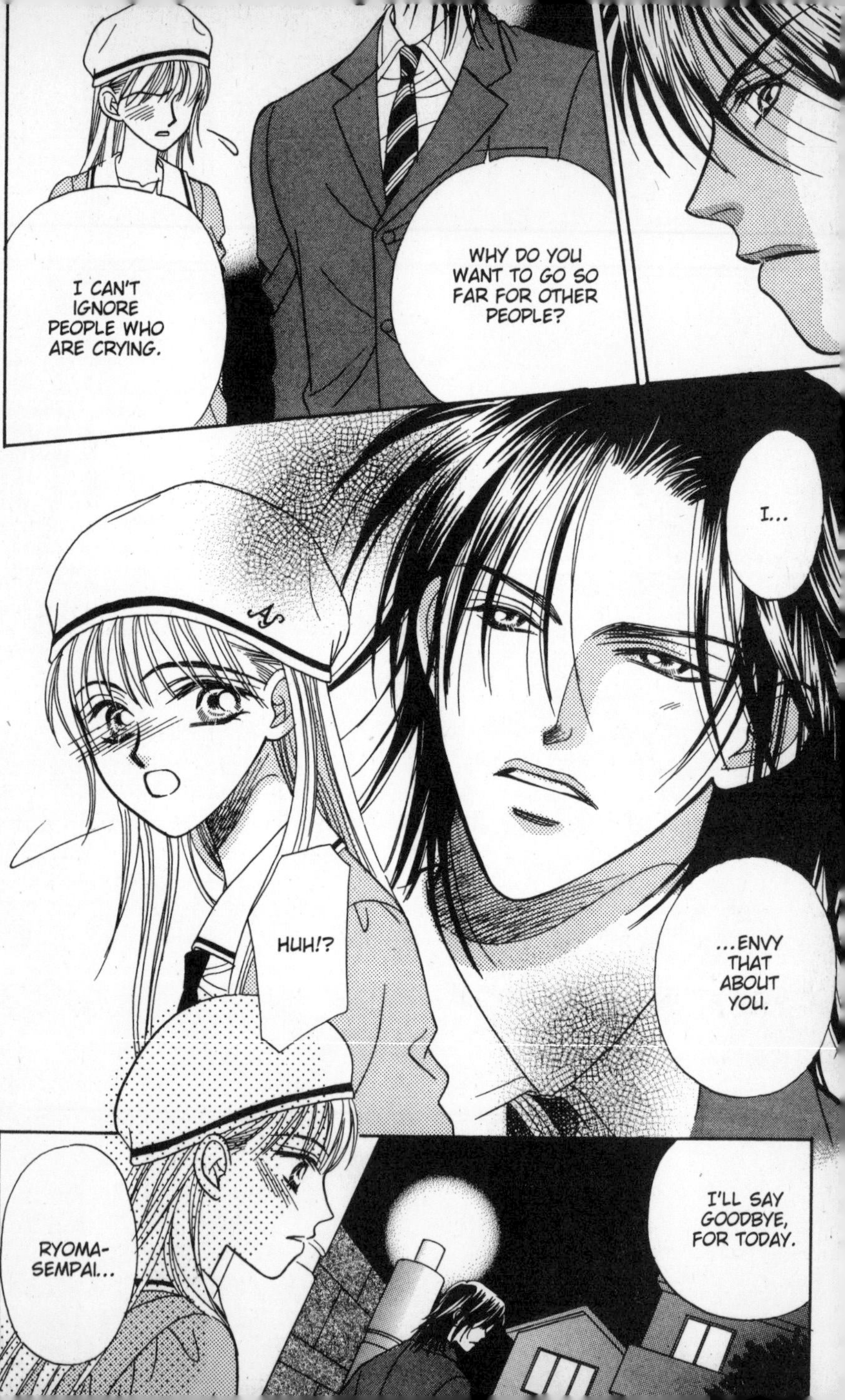
WHY DO YOU WANT TO GO SO FAR FOR OTHER PEOPLE?
I CAN'T IGNORE PEOPLE WHO ARE CRYING.
I...
...ENVY THAT ABOUT YOU.
HUH!?
I'LL SAY GOODBYE, FOR TODAY.
RYOMA-SEMPAI...

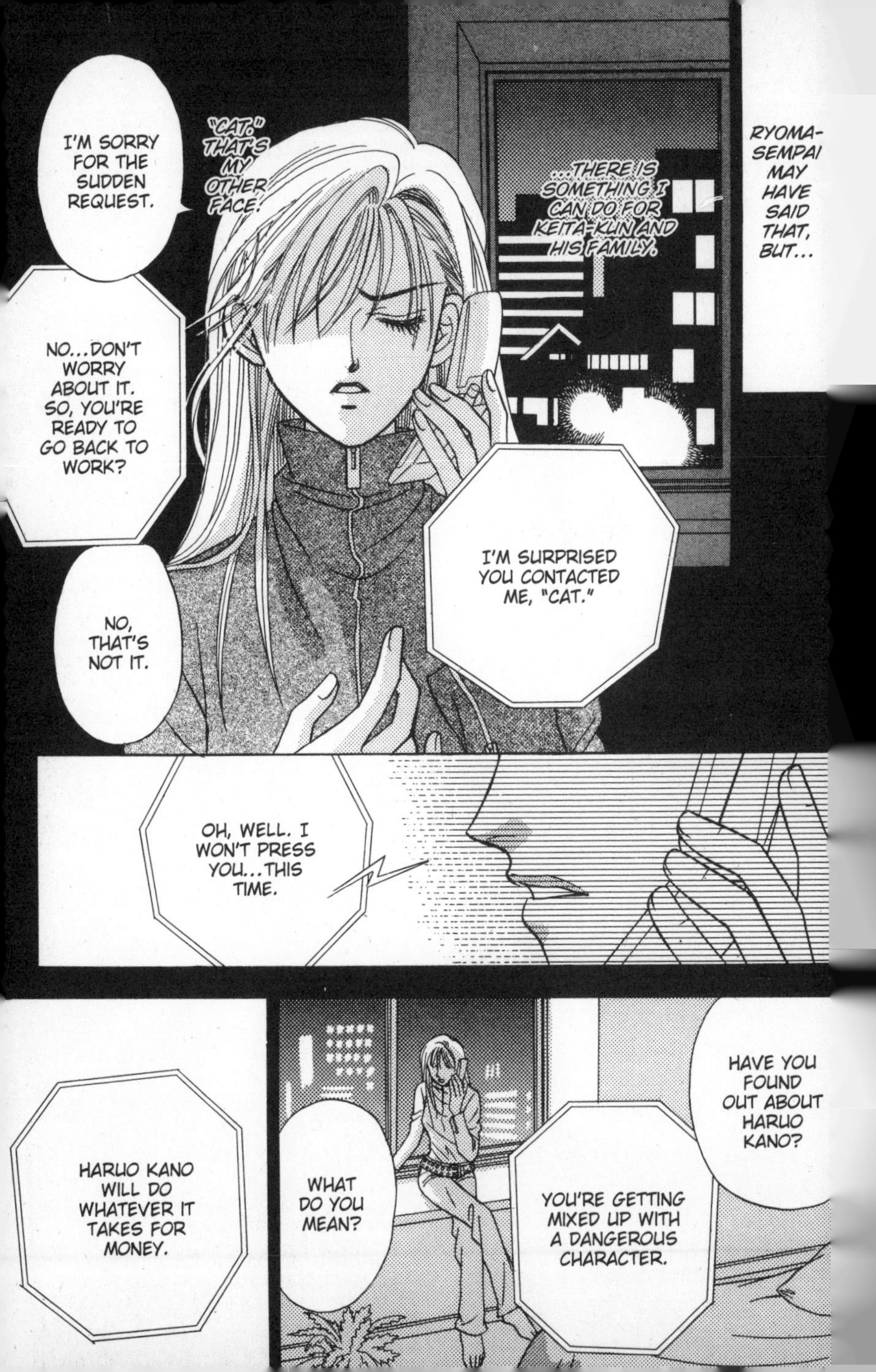
RYOMA-SEMPAI MAY HAVE SAID THAT, BUT...
...THERE IS SOMETHING I CAN DO FOR KEITA-KUN AND HIS FAMILY.
"CAT." THAT'S MY OTHER FACE.
I'M SURPRISED YOU CONTACTED ME, "CAT."
I'M SORRY FOR THE SUDDEN REQUEST.
NO...DON'T WORRY ABOUT IT. SO, YOU'RE READY TO GO BACK TO WORK?
NO, THAT'S NOT IT.
OH, WELL. I WON'T PRESS YOU...THIS TIME.
HAVE YOU FOUND OUT ABOUT HARUO KANO?
YOU'RE GETTING MIXED UP WITH A DANGEROUS CHARACTER.
WHAT DO YOU MEAN?
HARUO KANO WILL DO WHATEVER IT TAKES FOR MONEY.

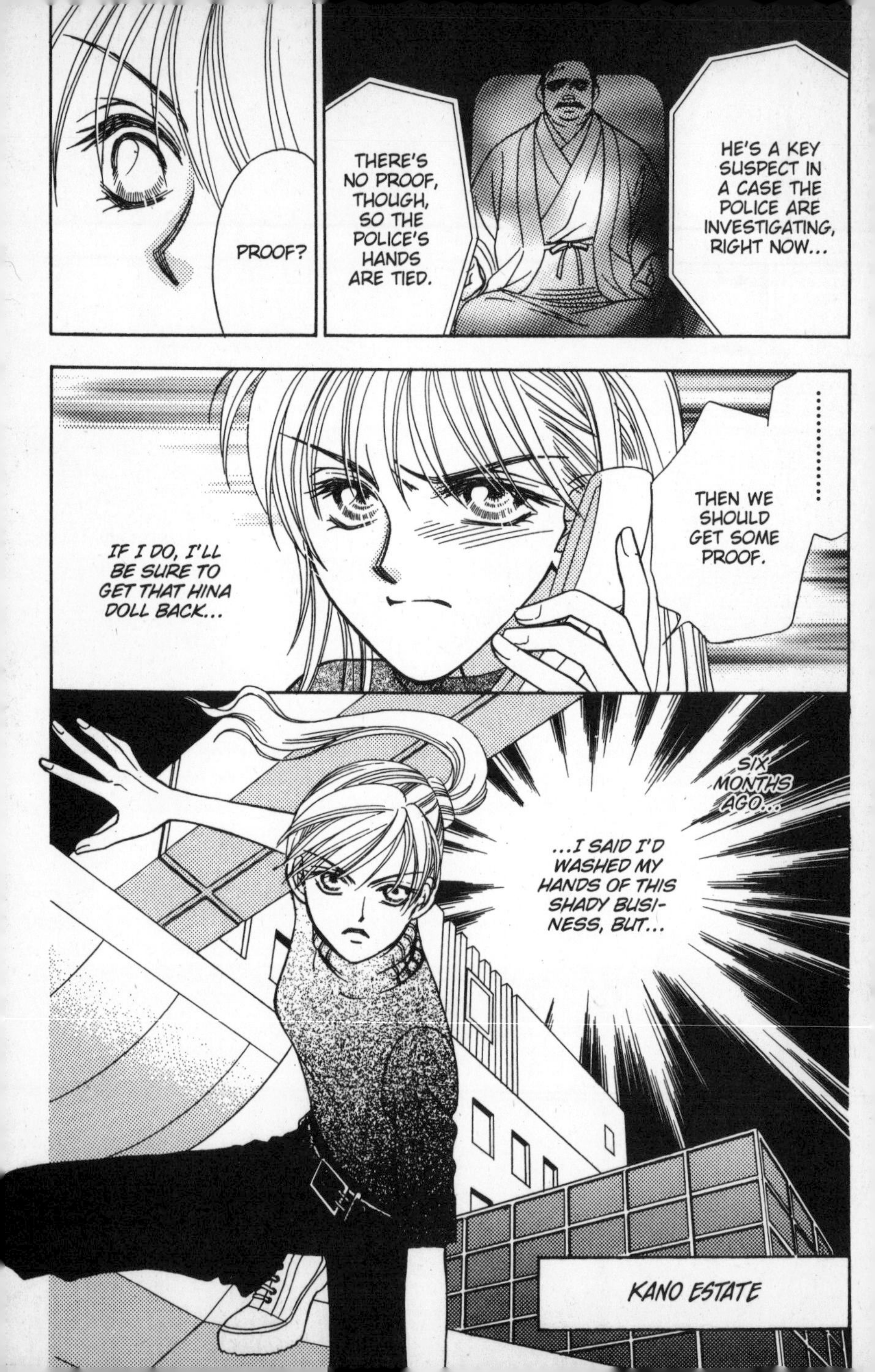
HE'S A KEY SUSPECT IN A CASE THE POLICE ARE INVESTIGATING, RIGHT NOW...
THERE'S NO PROOF, THOUGH, SO THE POLICE'S HANDS ARE TIED.
PROOF?
......
THEN WE SHOULD GET SOME PROOF.
IF I DO, I'LL BE SURE TO GET THAT HINA DOLL BACK...
SIX MONTHS AGO...
...I SAID I'D WASHED MY HANDS OF THIS SHADY BUSI-NESS, BUT...
KANO ESTATE

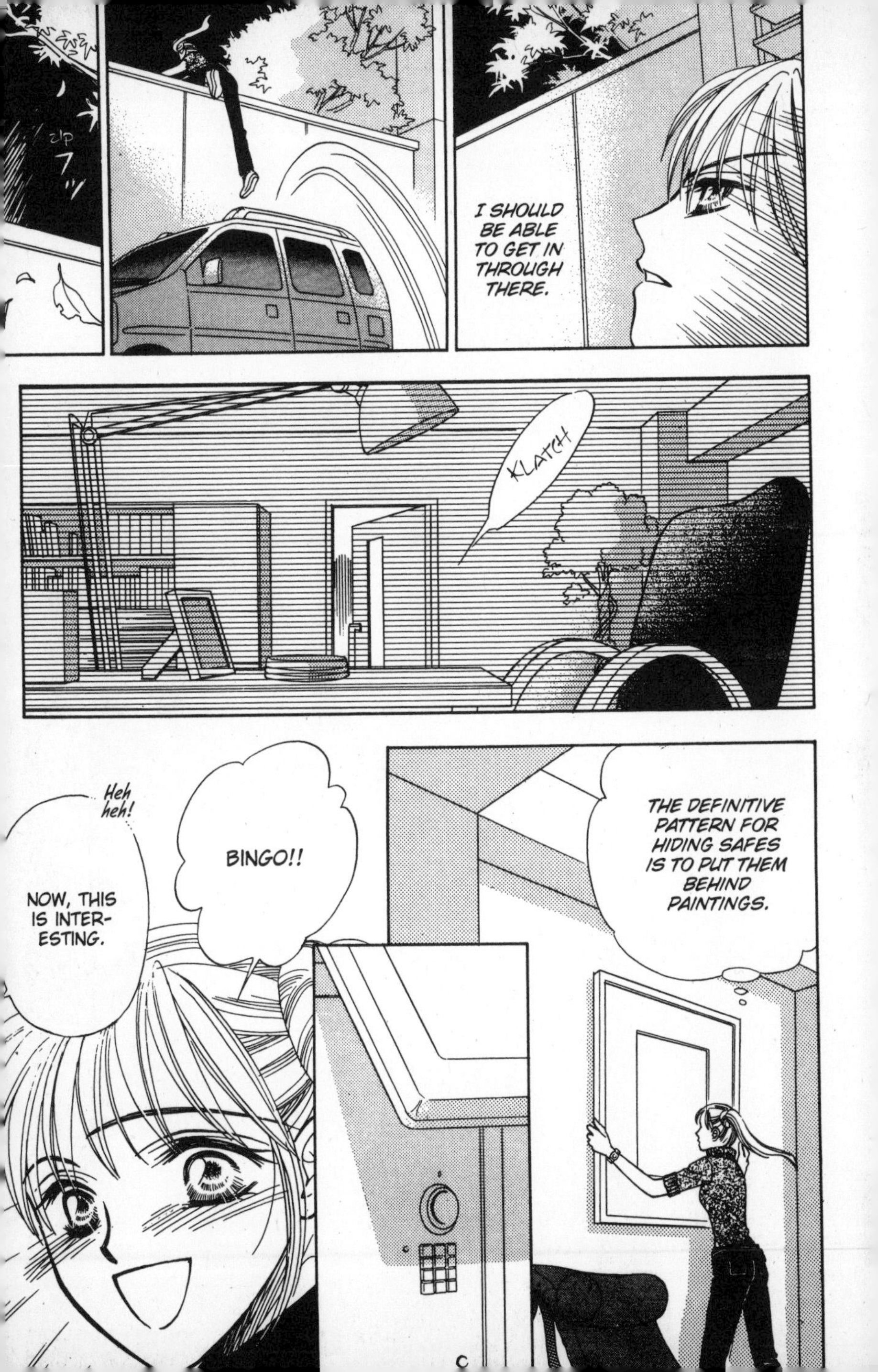
I SHOULD BE ABLE TO GET IN THROUGH THERE.
zip
フッ
KLATCH
THE DEFINITIVE PATTERN FOR HIDING SAFES IS TO PUT THEM BEHIND PAINTINGS.
BINGO!!
Heh heh!
NOW, THIS IS INTER-ESTING.

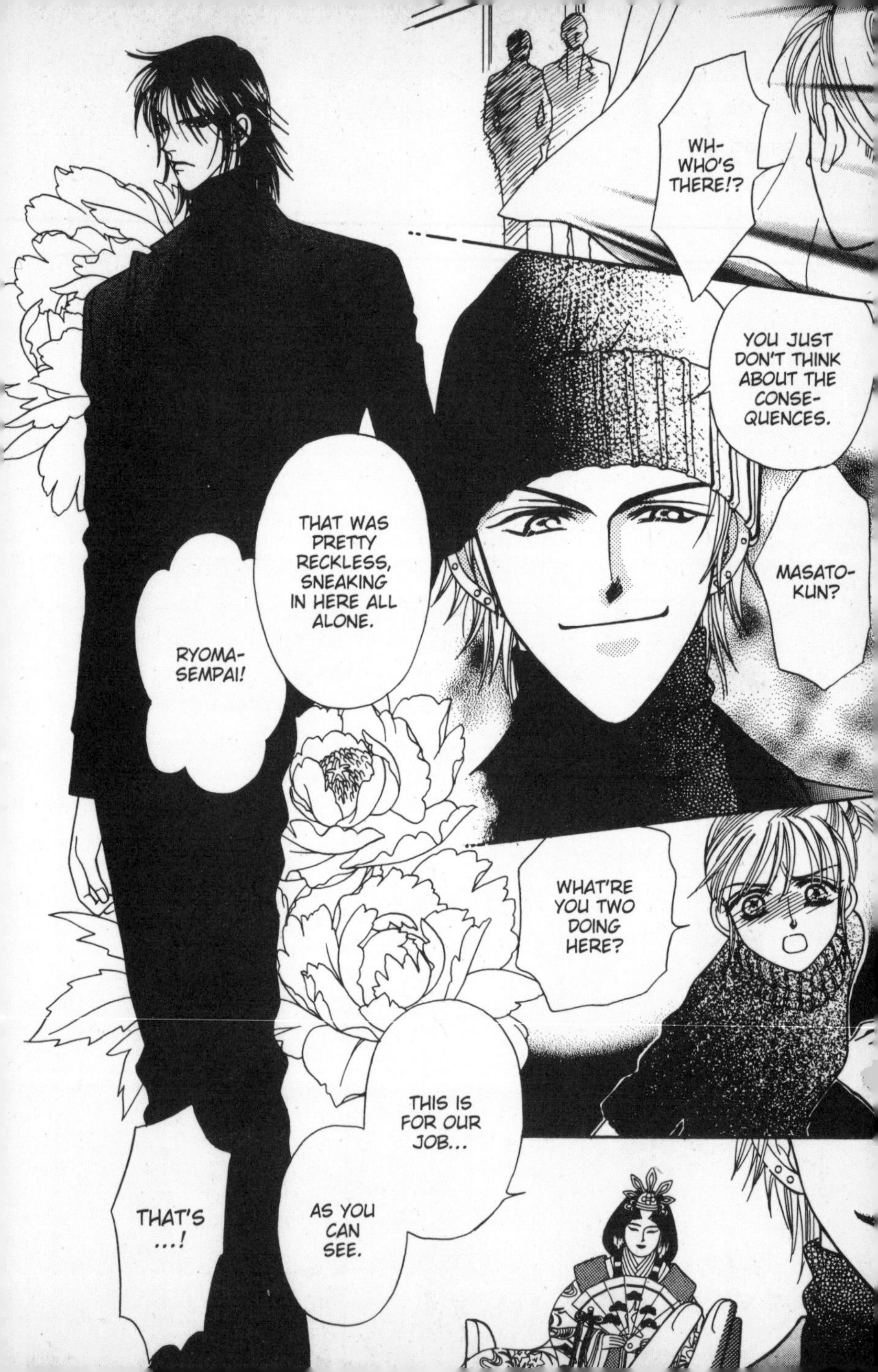
WH-
WHO'S
THERE!?
YOU JUST
DON'T THINK
ABOUT THE
CONSE-
QUENCES.
THAT WAS
PRETTY
RECKLESS,
SNEAKING
IN HERE ALL
ALONE.
MASATO-
KUN?
RYOMA-
SEMPAI!
WHAT'RE
YOU TWO
DOING
HERE?
THIS IS
FOR OUR
JOB...
AS YOU
CAN
SEE.
THAT'S
...!

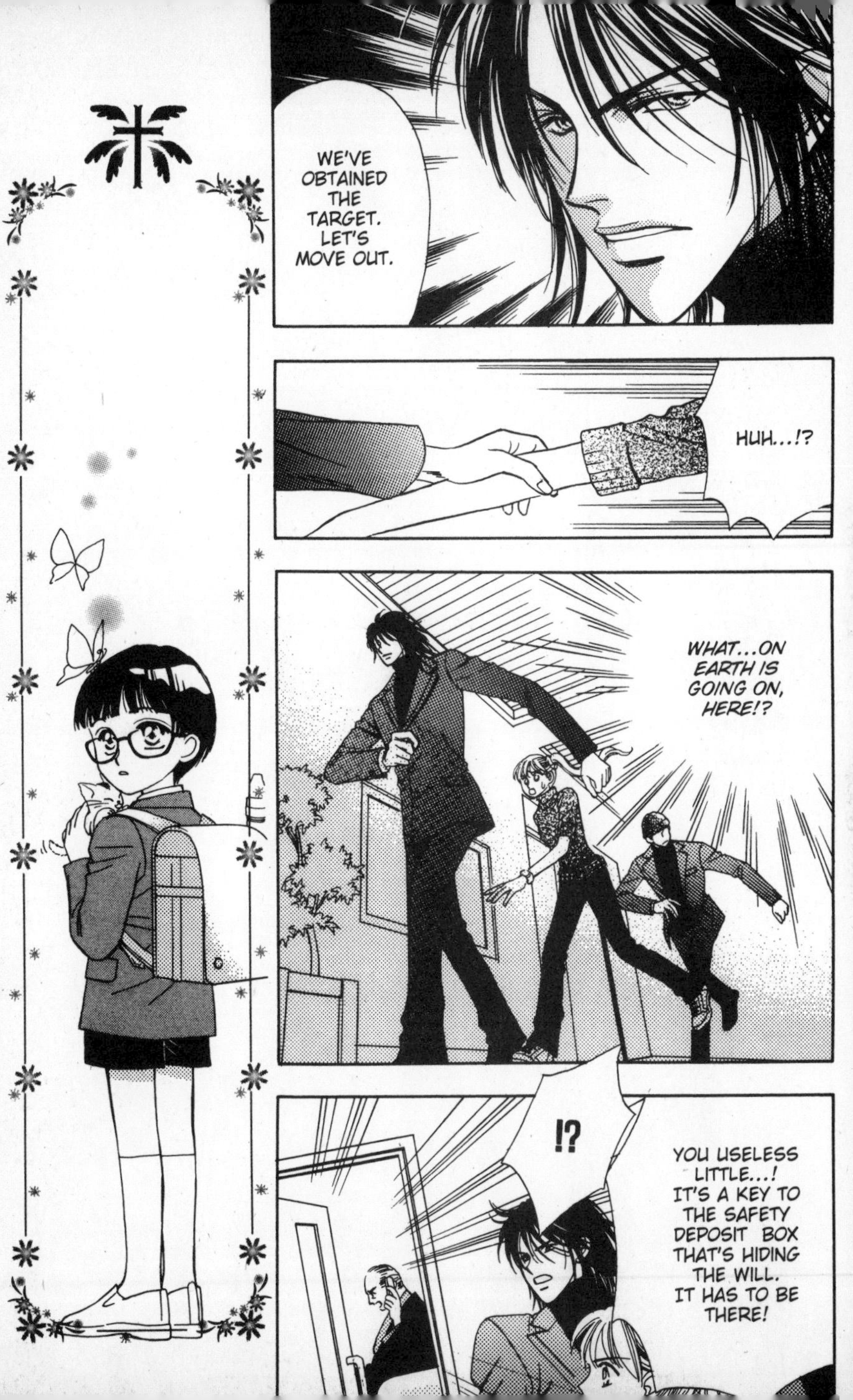
WE'VE OBTAINED THE TARGET. LET'S MOVE OUT.
HUH...!?
WHAT...ON EARTH IS GOING ON, HERE!?
!?
YOU USELESS LITTLE...! IT'S A KEY TO THE SAFETY DEPOSIT BOX THAT'S HIDING THE WILL. IT HAS TO BE THERE!

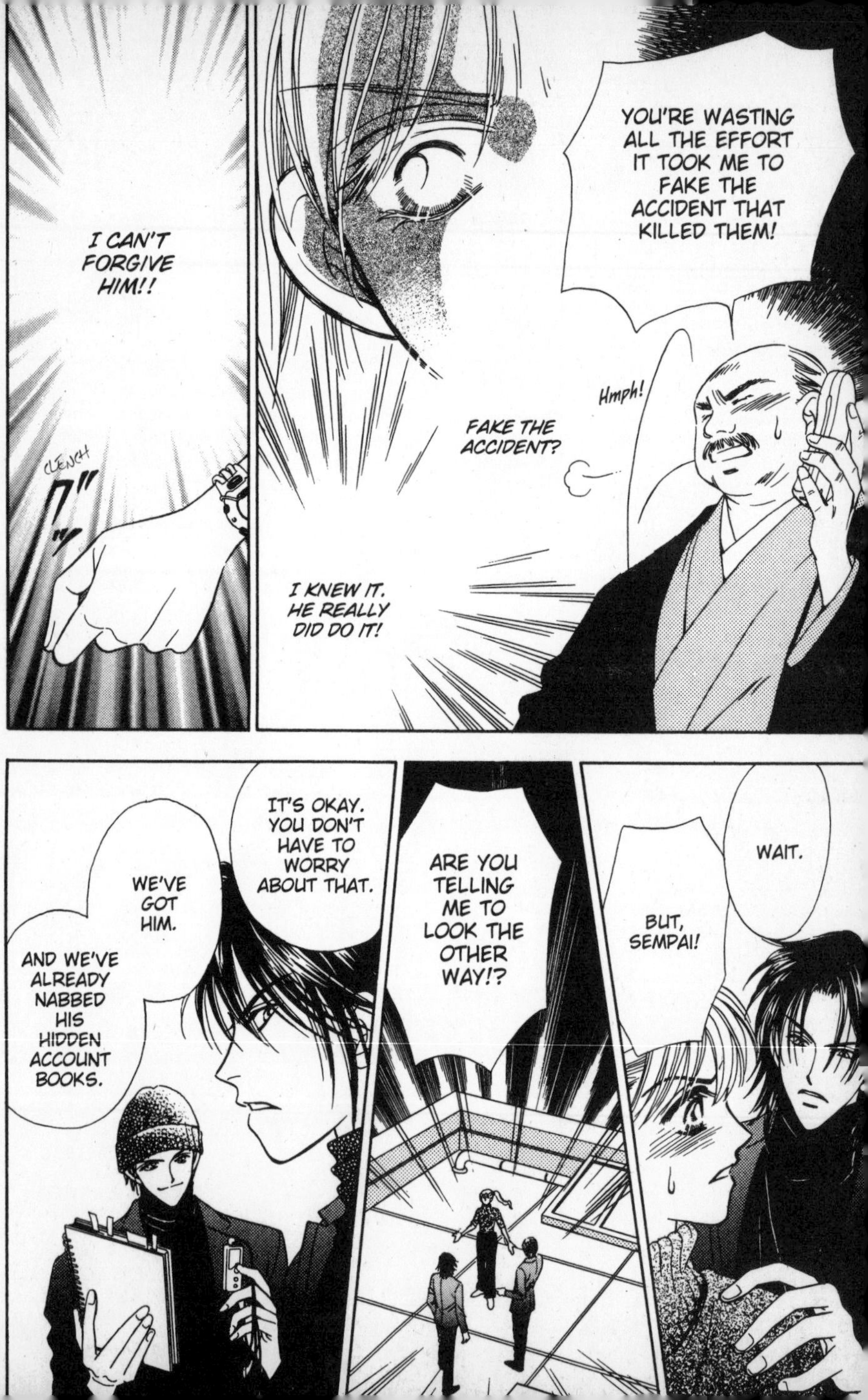
YOU'RE WASTING ALL THE EFFORT IT TOOK ME TO FAKE THE ACCIDENT THAT KILLED THEM!
Hmph!
FAKE THE ACCIDENT?
I KNEW IT. HE REALLY DID DO IT!
I CAN'T FORGIVE HIM!!
CLENCH
WAIT.
BUT, SEMPAI!
ARE YOU TELLING ME TO LOOK THE OTHER WAY!?
IT'S OKAY. YOU DON'T HAVE TO WORRY ABOUT THAT.
WE'VE GOT HIM.
AND WE'VE ALREADY NABBED HIS HIDDEN ACCOUNT BOOKS.

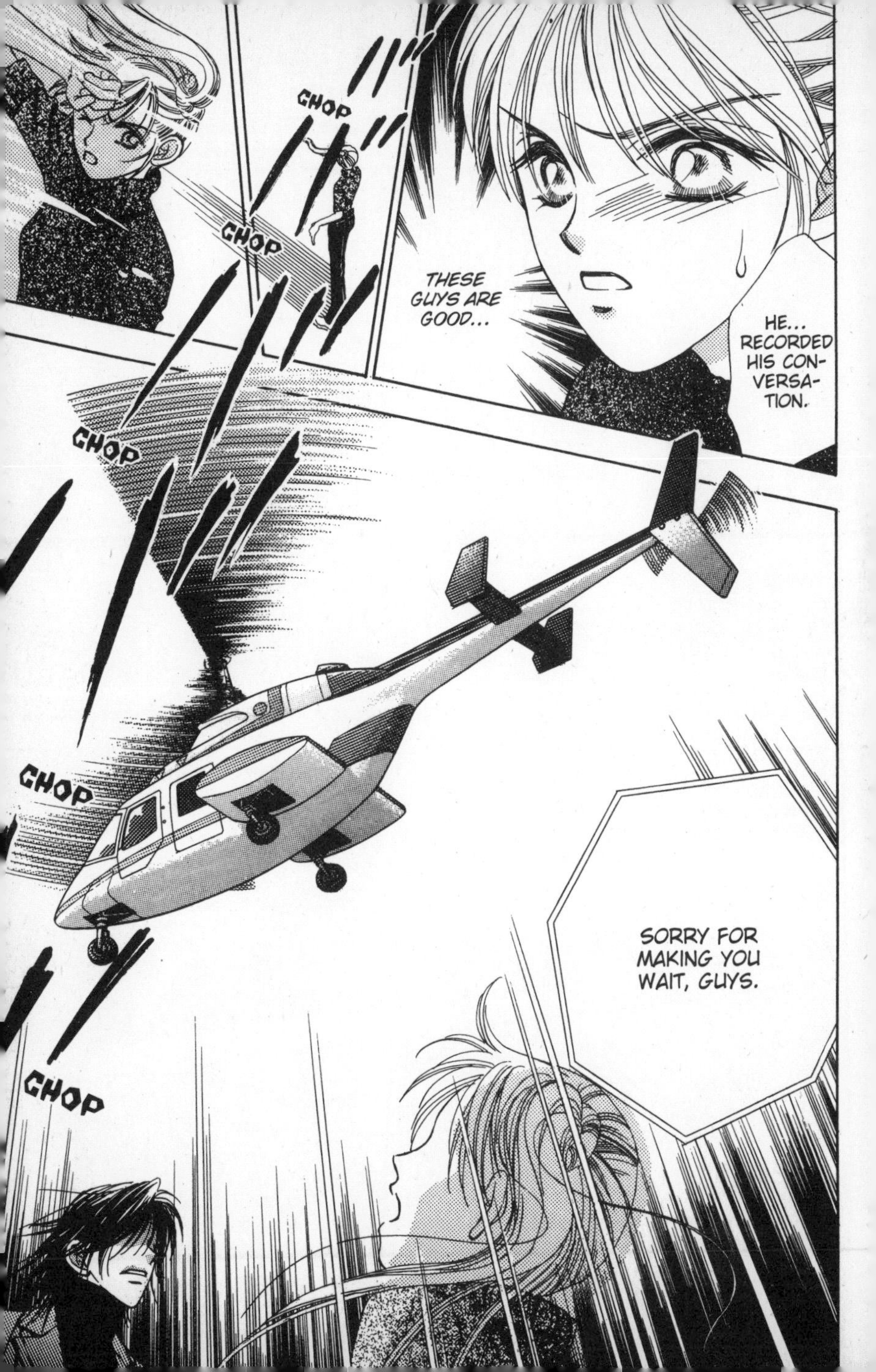
HE... RECORDED HIS CONVERSATION.
THESE GUYS ARE GOOD...
CHOP
CHOP
CHOP
CHOP
CHOP
SORRY FOR MAKING YOU WAIT, GUYS.

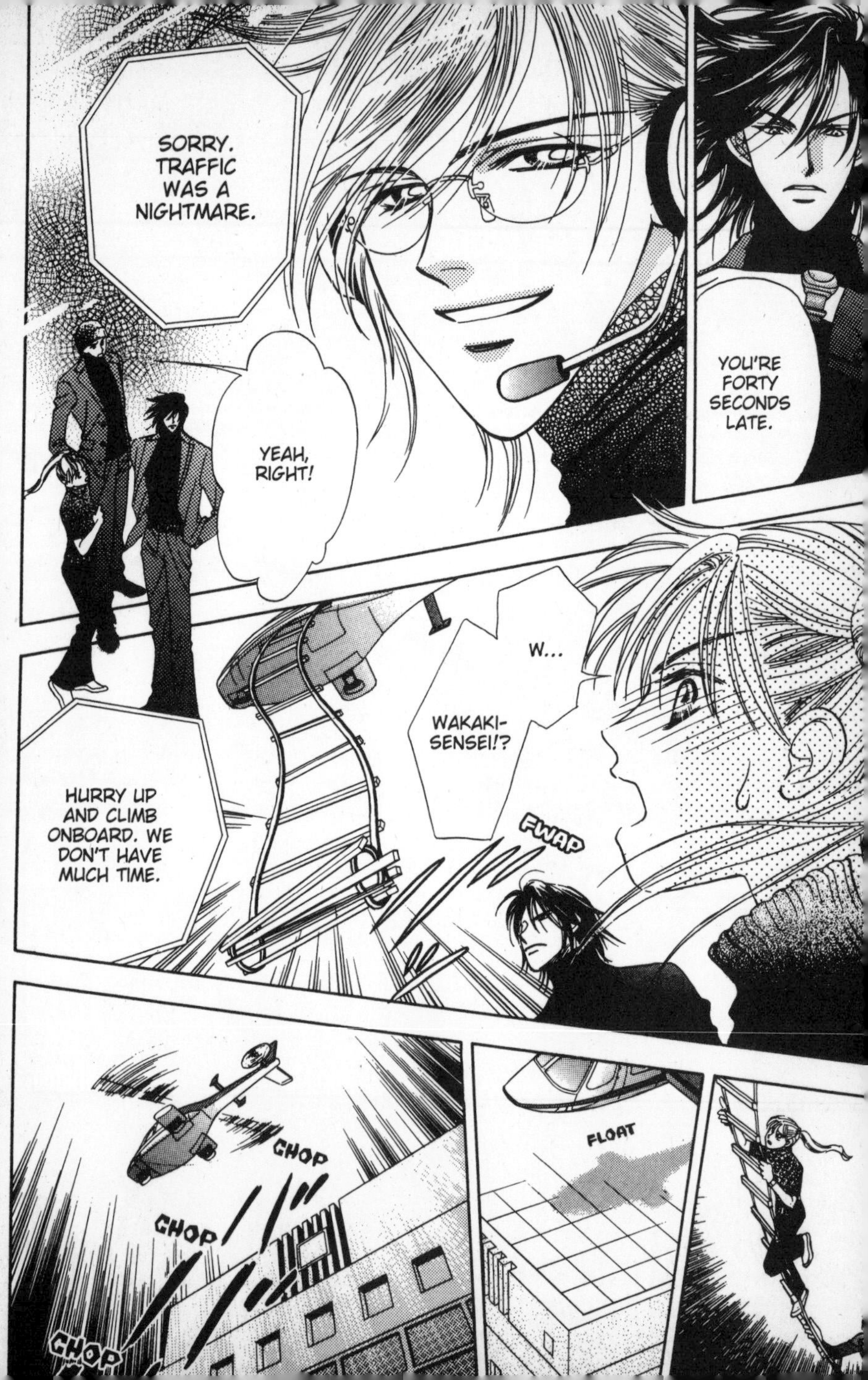
YOU'RE FORTY SECONDS LATE.
SORRY. TRAFFIC WAS A NIGHTMARE.
YEAH, RIGHT!
W...
WAKAKI-SENSEI!?
HURRY UP AND CLIMB ONBOARD. WE DON'T HAVE MUCH TIME.
FWAP
FLOAT
CHOP
CHOP
CHOP

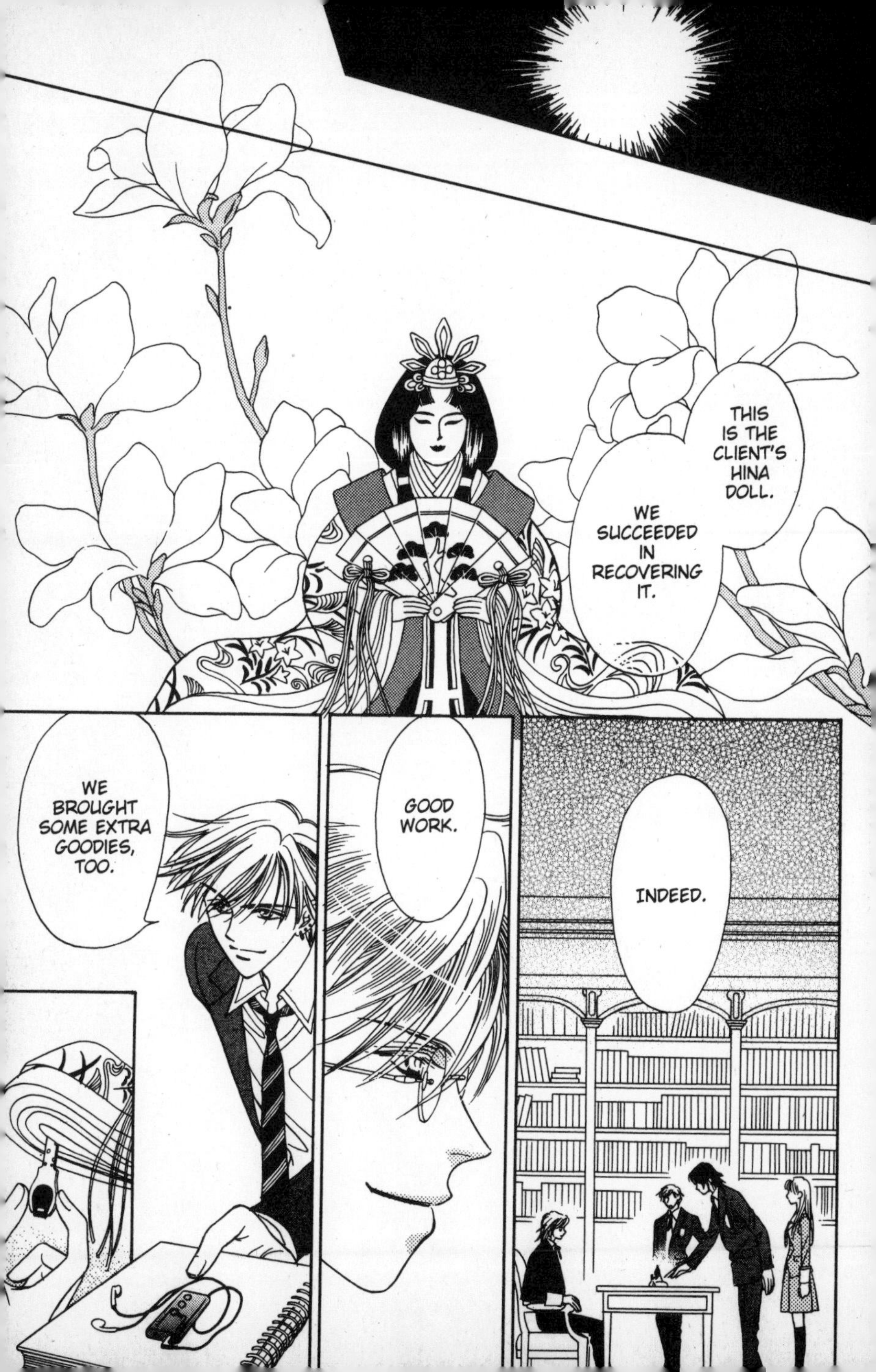

THIS IS THE CLIENT'S HINA DOLL.
WE SUCCEEDED IN RECOVERING IT.
INDEED.
GOOD WORK.
WE BROUGHT SOME EXTRA GOODIES, TOO.

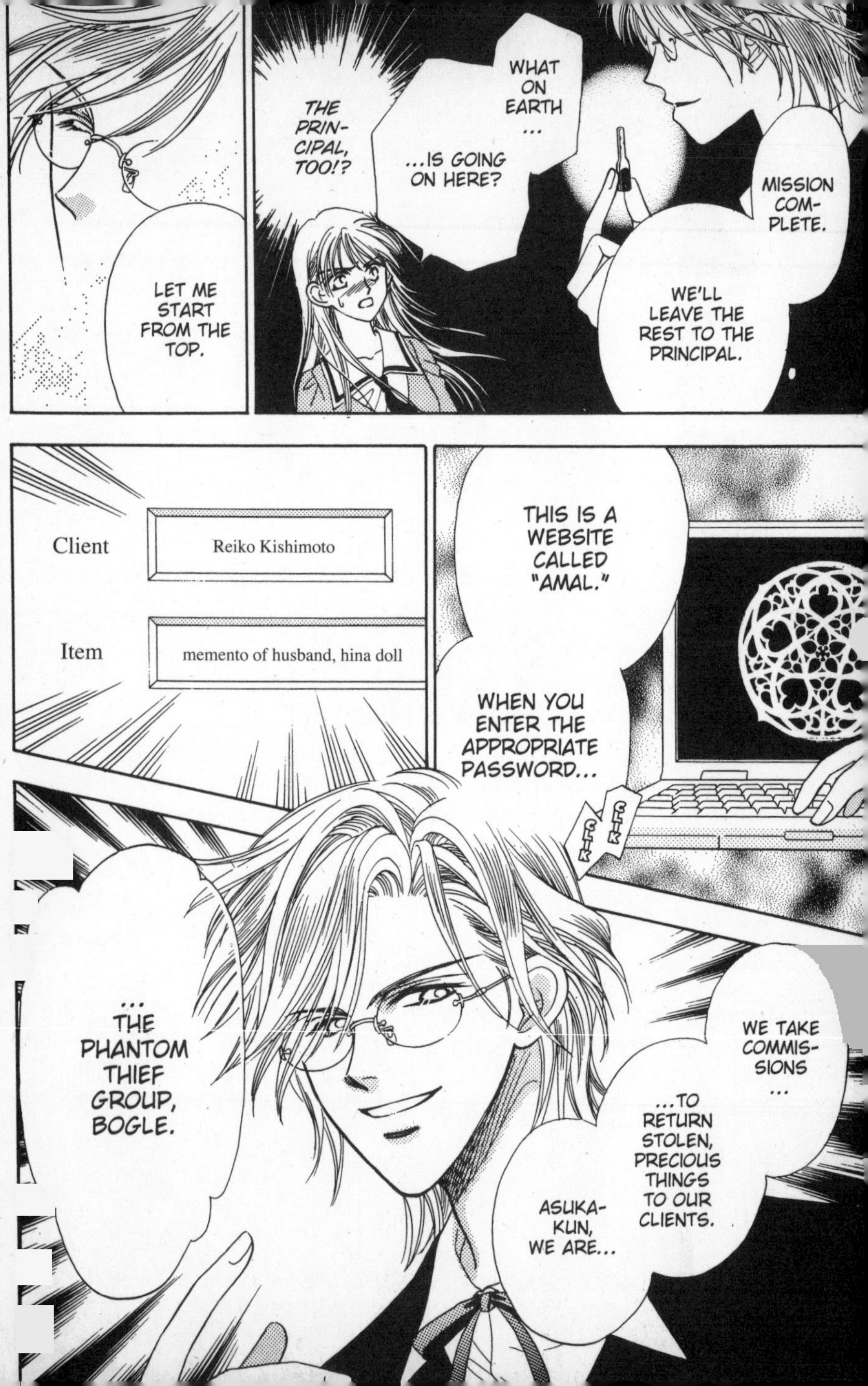
MISSION COM-PLETE.
WE'LL LEAVE THE REST TO THE PRINCIPAL.
WHAT ON EARTH ...
...IS GOING ON HERE?
THE PRIN-CIPAL, TOO!?
LET ME START FROM THE TOP.
THIS IS A WEBSITE CALLED "AMAL."
WHEN YOU ENTER THE APPROPRIATE PASSWORD...
CLIK CLIK
Client
Reiko Kishimoto
Item
memento of husband, hina doll
WE TAKE COMMIS-SIONS ...
...TO RETURN STOLEN, PRECIOUS THINGS TO OUR CLIENTS.
ASUKA-KUN, WE ARE...
... THE PHANTOM THIEF GROUP, BOGLE.

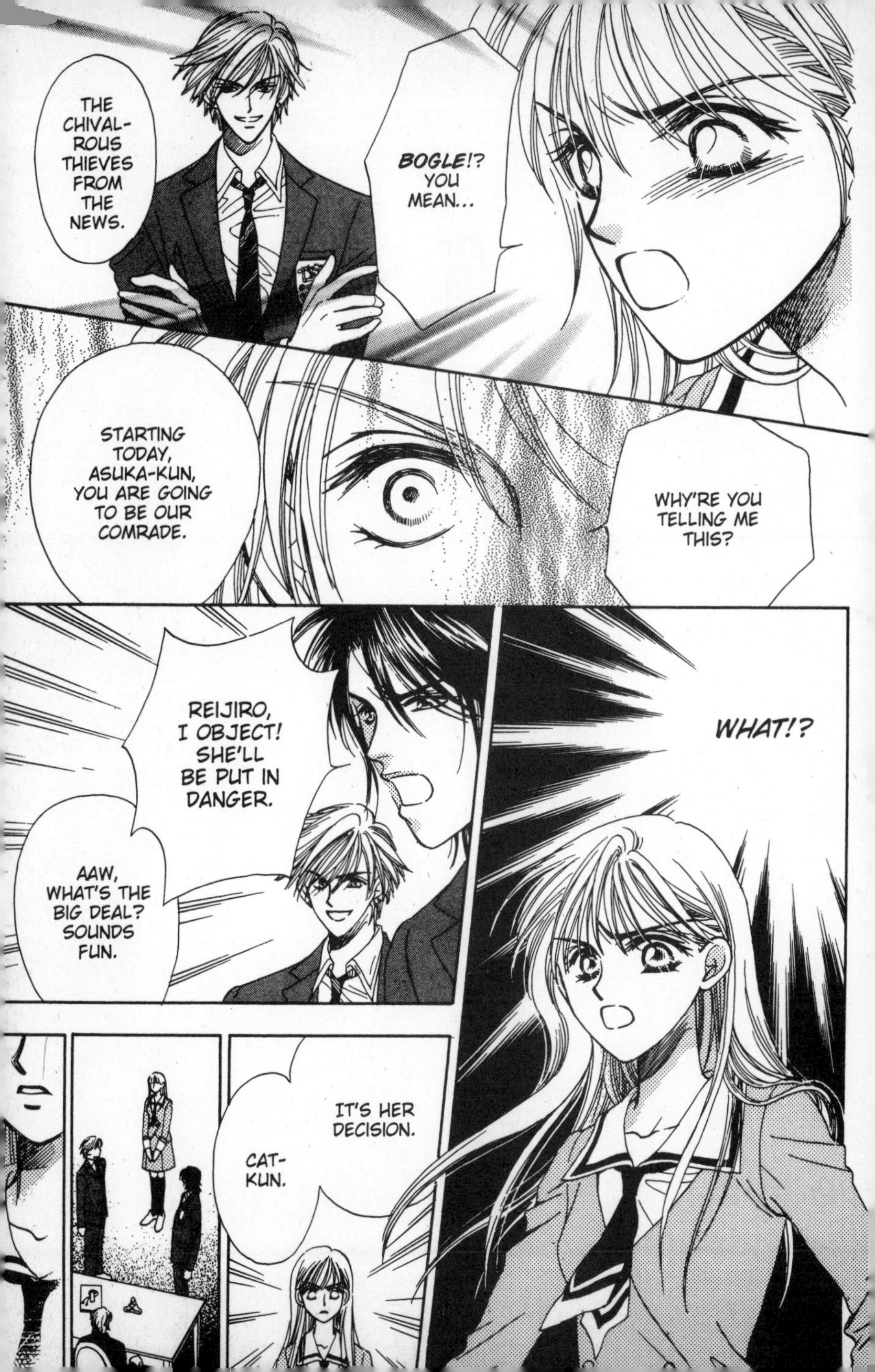
BOGLE!? YOU MEAN...
THE CHIVAL-ROUS THIEVES FROM THE NEWS.
WHY'RE YOU TELLING ME THIS?
STARTING TODAY, ASUKA-KUN, YOU ARE GOING TO BE OUR COMRADE.
WHAT!?
REIJIRO, I OBJECT! SHE'LL BE PUT IN DANGER.
AAW, WHAT'S THE BIG DEAL? SOUNDS FUN.
IT'S HER DECISION.
CAT-KUN.

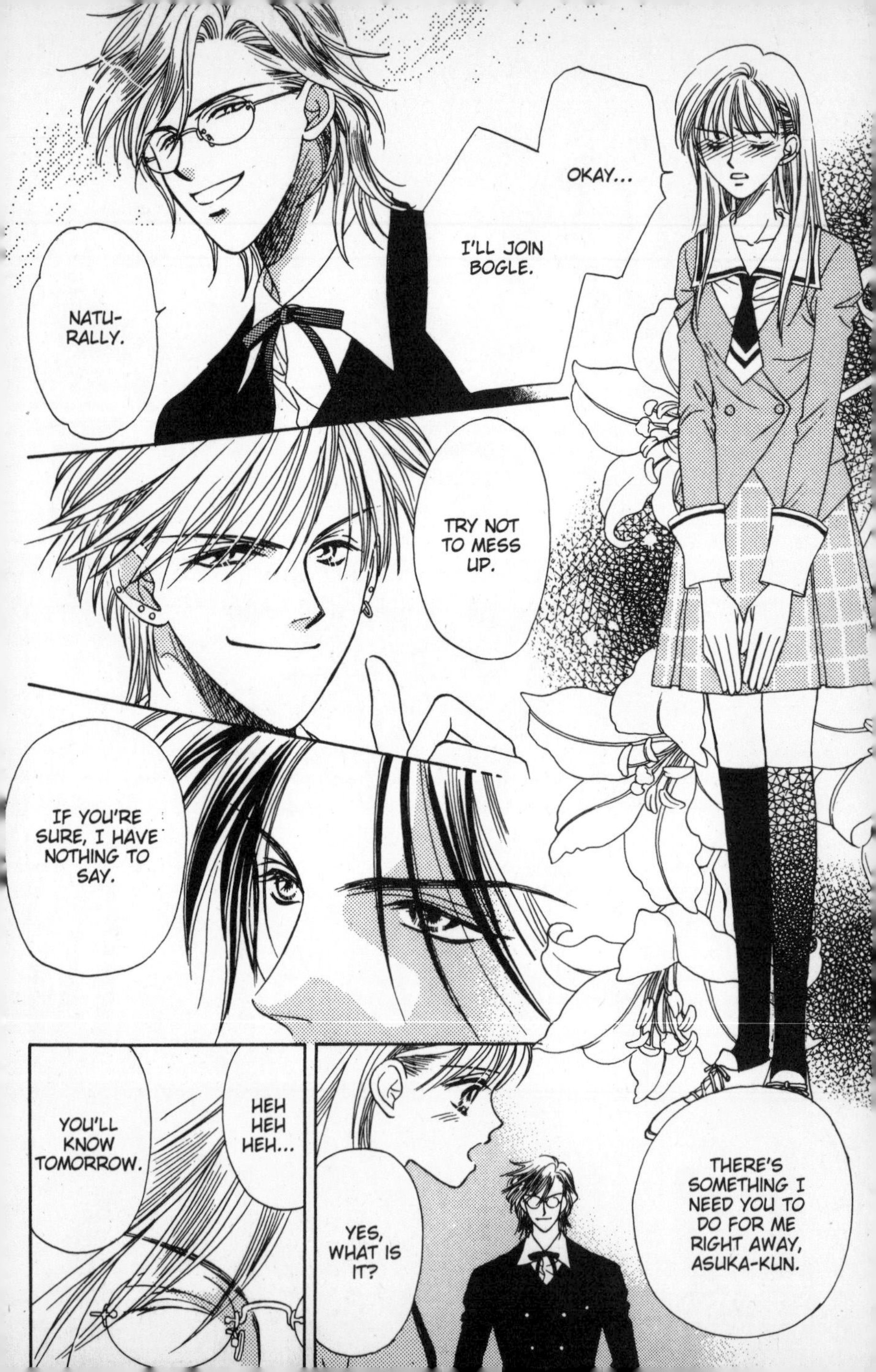
OKAY...
I'LL JOIN BOGLE.
NATU-RALLY.
TRY NOT TO MESS UP.
IF YOU'RE SURE, I HAVE NOTHING TO SAY.
THERE'S SOMETHING I NEED YOU TO DO FOR ME RIGHT AWAY, ASUKA-KUN.
YES, WHAT IS IT?
HEH HEH HEH...
YOU'LL KNOW TOMORROW.

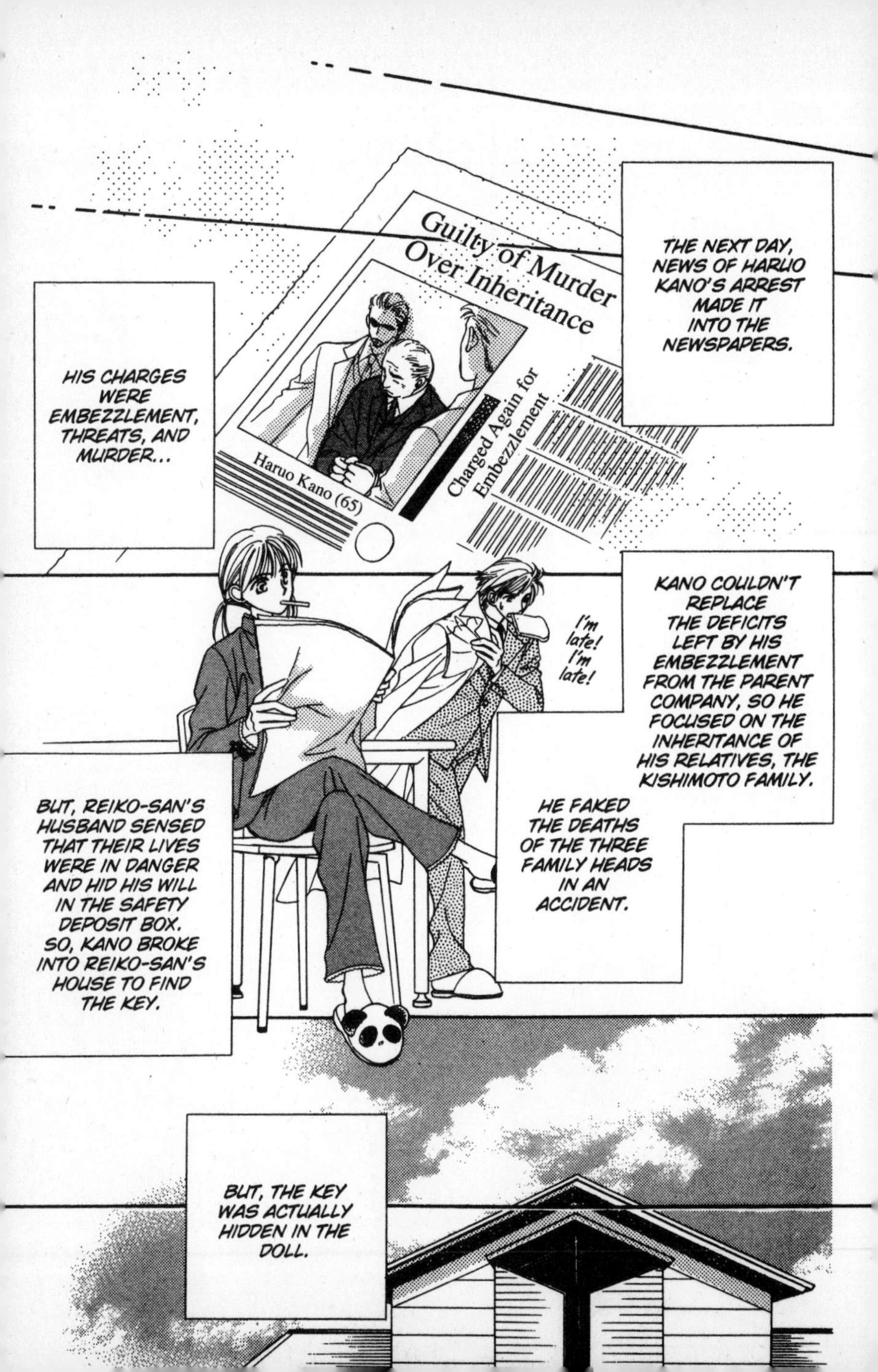
THE NEXT DAY, NEWS OF HARUO KANO'S ARREST MADE IT INTO THE NEWSPAPERS.
Guilty of Murder Over Inheritance
Charged Again for Embezzlement
Haruo Kano (65)
HIS CHARGES WERE EMBEZZLEMENT, THREATS, AND MURDER...
KANO COULDN'T REPLACE THE DEFICITS LEFT BY HIS EMBEZZLEMENT FROM THE PARENT COMPANY, SO HE FOCUSED ON THE INHERITANCE OF HIS RELATIVES, THE KISHIMOTO FAMILY.
I'm late! I'm late!
HE FAKED THE DEATHS OF THE THREE FAMILY HEADS IN AN ACCIDENT.
BUT, REIKO-SAN'S HUSBAND SENSED THAT THEIR LIVES WERE IN DANGER AND HID HIS WILL IN THE SAFETY DEPOSIT BOX. SO, KANO BROKE INTO REIKO-SAN'S HOUSE TO FIND THE KEY.
BUT, THE KEY WAS ACTUALLY HIDDEN IN THE DOLL.

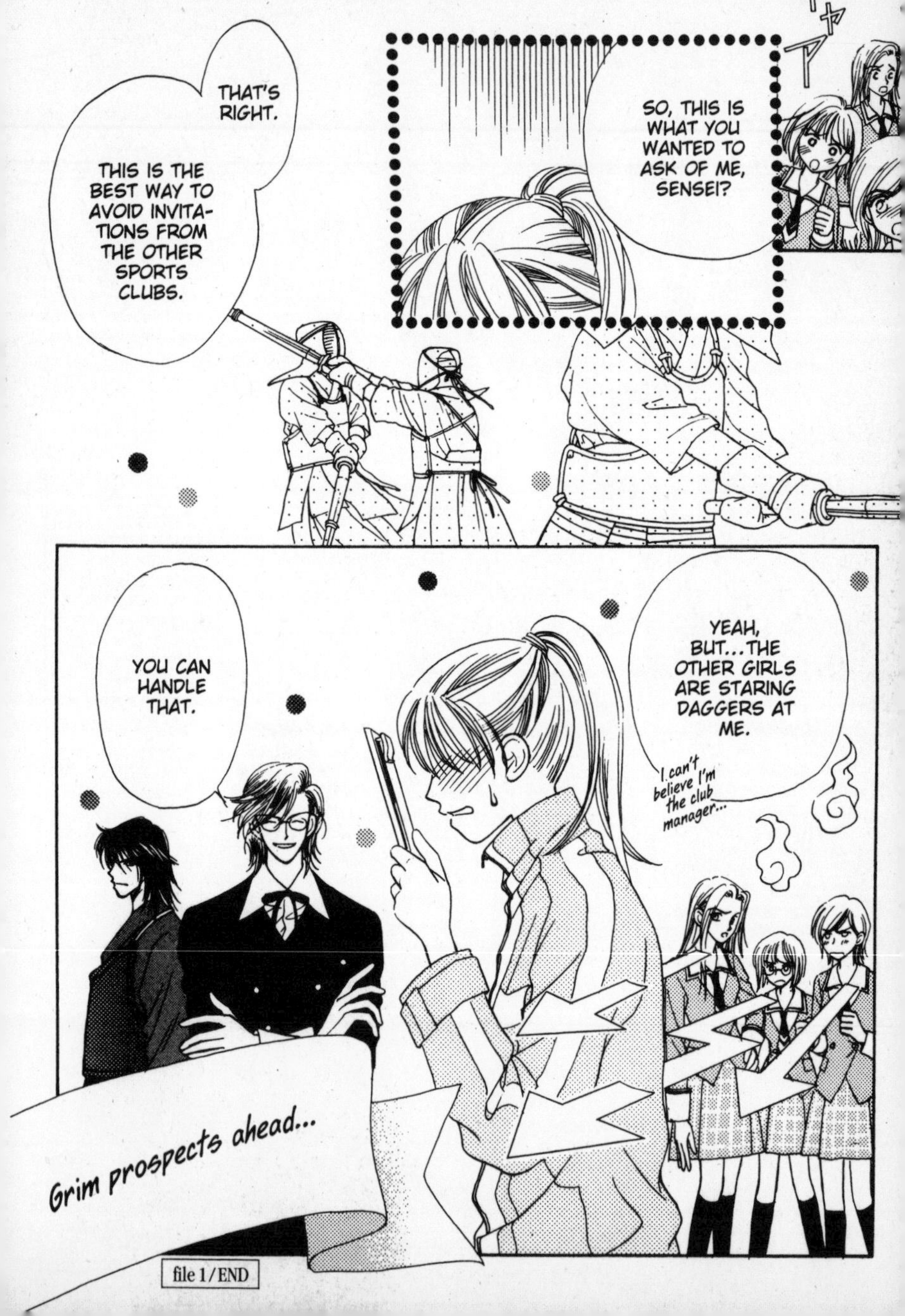
GAB
キャア
GAB
SO, THIS IS WHAT YOU WANTED TO ASK OF ME, SENSEI?
THAT'S RIGHT.
THIS IS THE BEST WAY TO AVOID INVITATIONS FROM THE OTHER SPORTS CLUBS.
YEAH, BUT...THE OTHER GIRLS ARE STARING DAGGERS AT ME.
I can't believe I'm the club manager...
YOU CAN HANDLE THAT.
Grim prospects ahead...

file 1/END

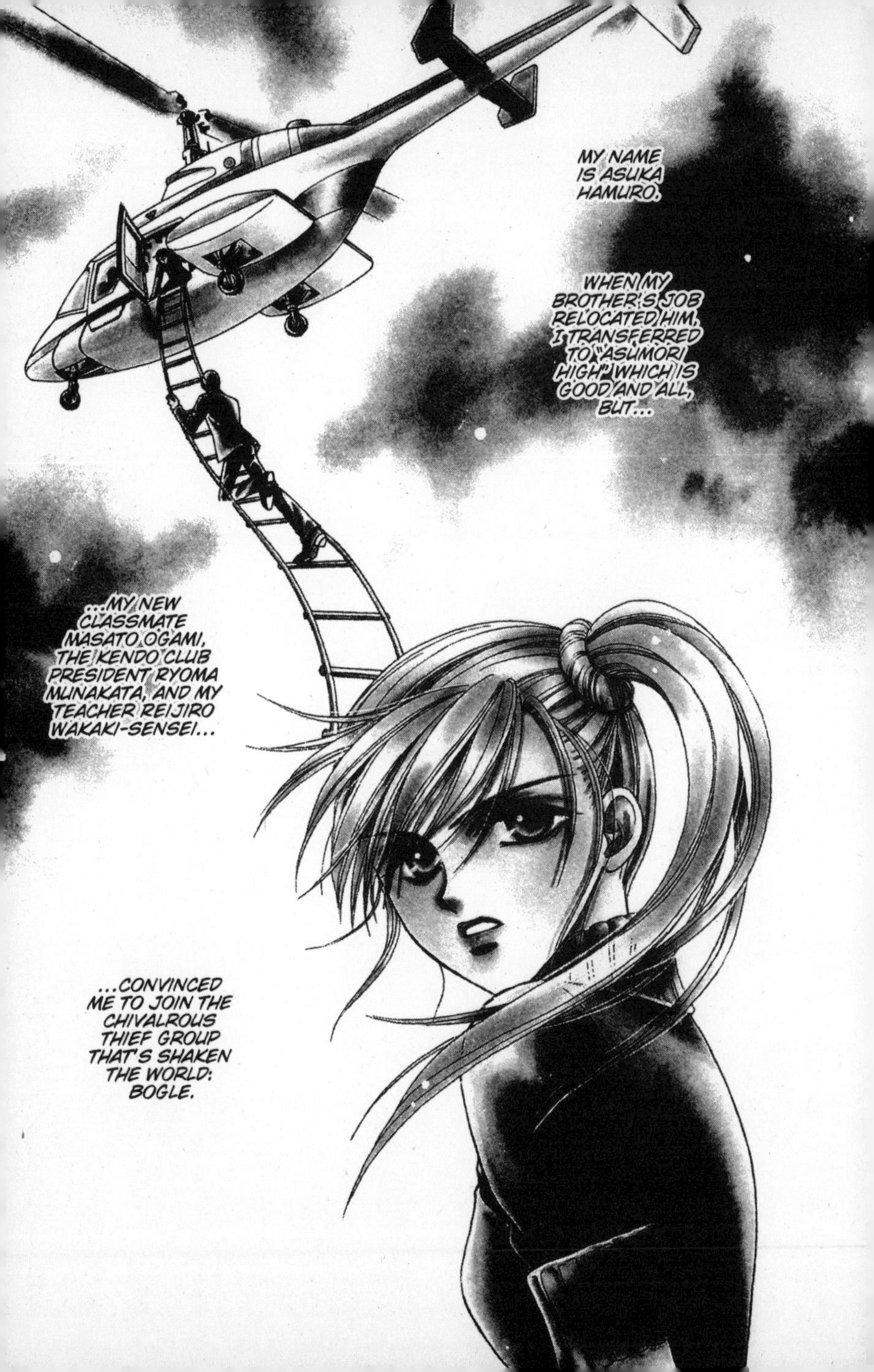
MY NAME IS ASUKA HAMURO.
WHEN MY BROTHER'S JOB RELOCATED HIM, I TRANSFERRED TO "ASUMORI HIGH" WHICH IS GOOD AND ALL, BUT...
...MY NEW CLASSMATE MASATO OGAMI, THE KENDO CLUB PRESIDENT RYOMA MUNAKATA, AND MY TEACHER REIJIRO WAKAKI-SENSEI...
...CONVINCED ME TO JOIN THE CHIVALROUS THIEF GROUP THAT'S SHAKEN THE WORLD: BOGLE.

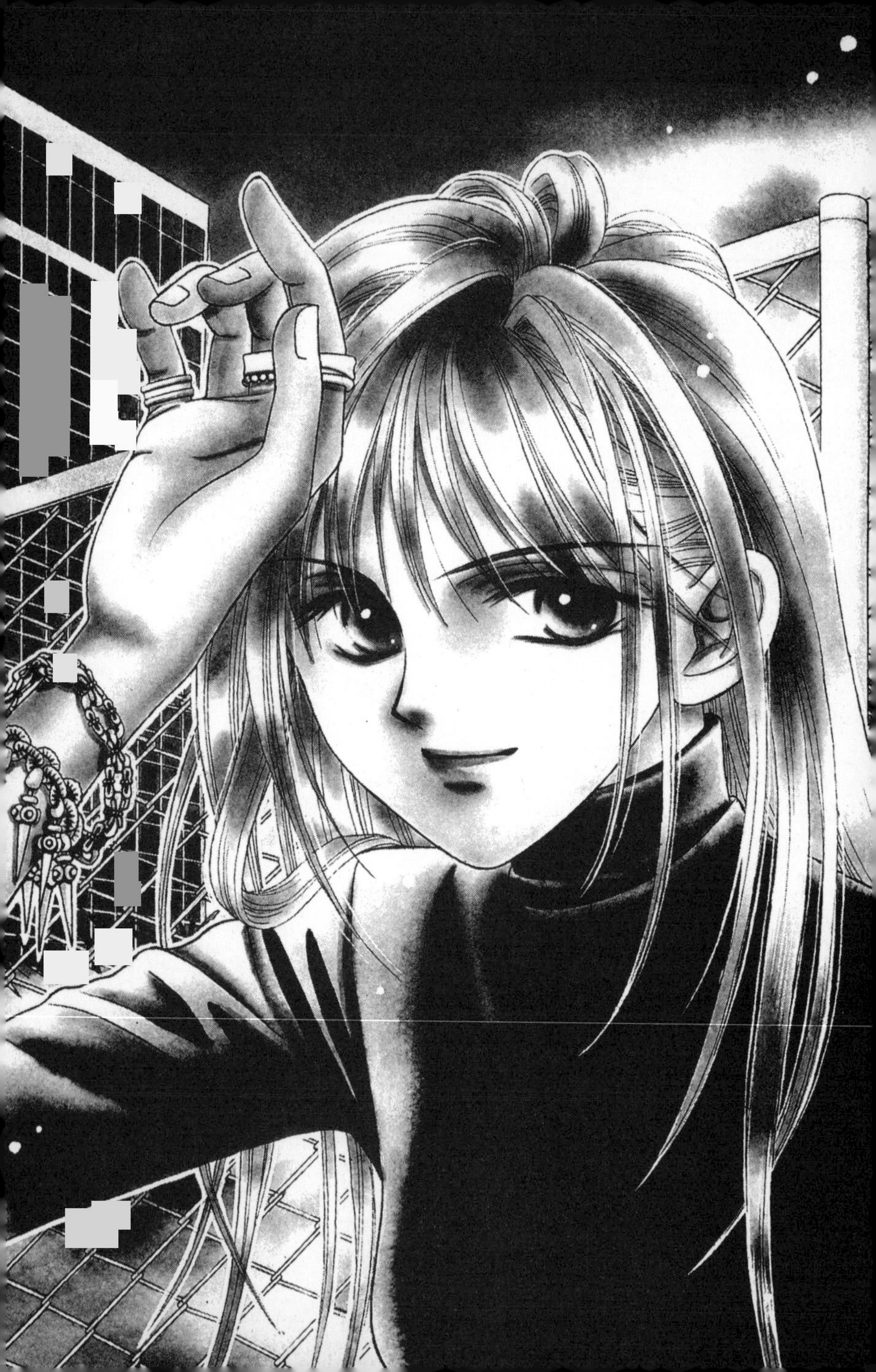

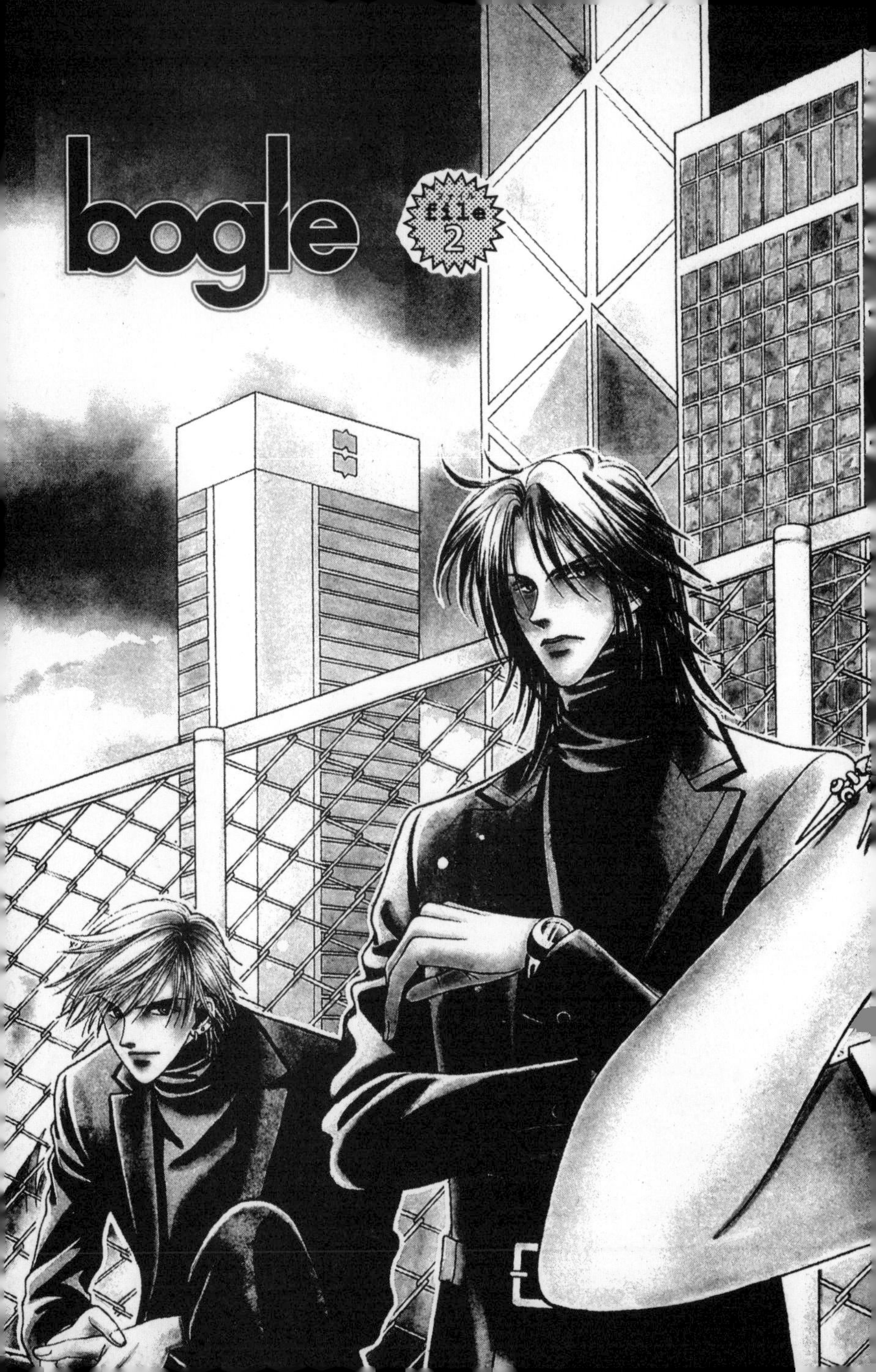
bogle
file
2

Asuka Hamuro
AGE: 16

♀

158cm tall / 42kg heavy
Birthday: May 5th
Aries
Blood Type: O

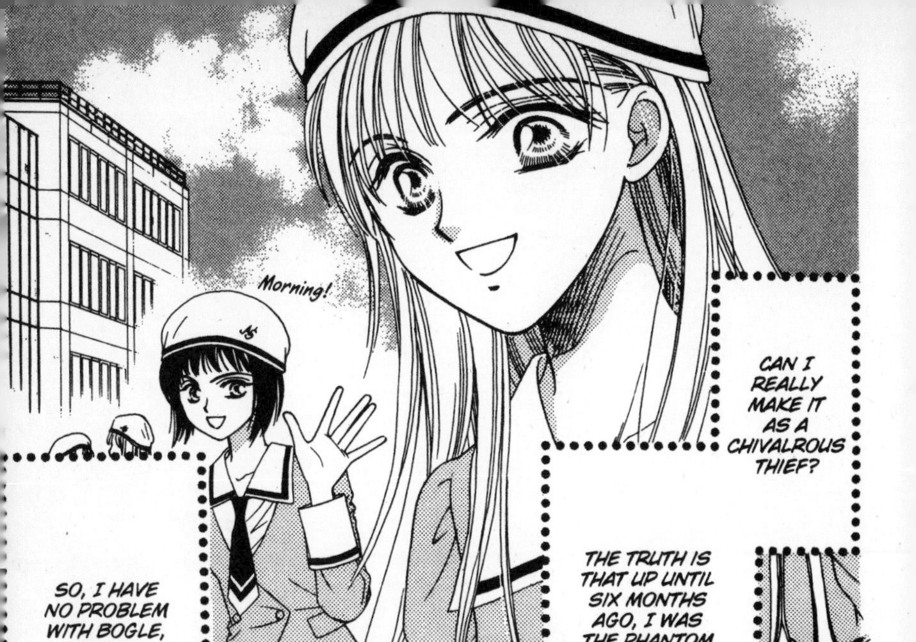

CAN I REALLY MAKE IT AS A CHIVALROUS THIEF?
THE TRUTH IS THAT UP UNTIL SIX MONTHS AGO, I WAS THE PHANTOM THIEF "CAT."
Morning!
SO, I HAVE NO PROBLEM WITH BOGLE, ITSELF...
BUT...
RATTLE

Hello, hello! This is Ichiju.
While in the middle of writing this book, I was rooted to the spot by the World Cup.
I'm so weak for pretty guys it's pathetic, but I've seriously become reduced to a Beckham watcher. Gah! I'd like to give a shout out to the passion and efforts of all the athletes out there: "You move me!"

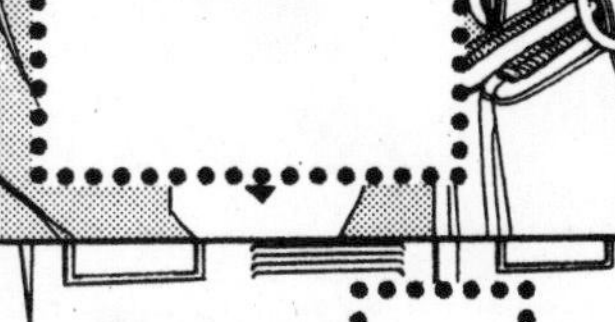

Word!

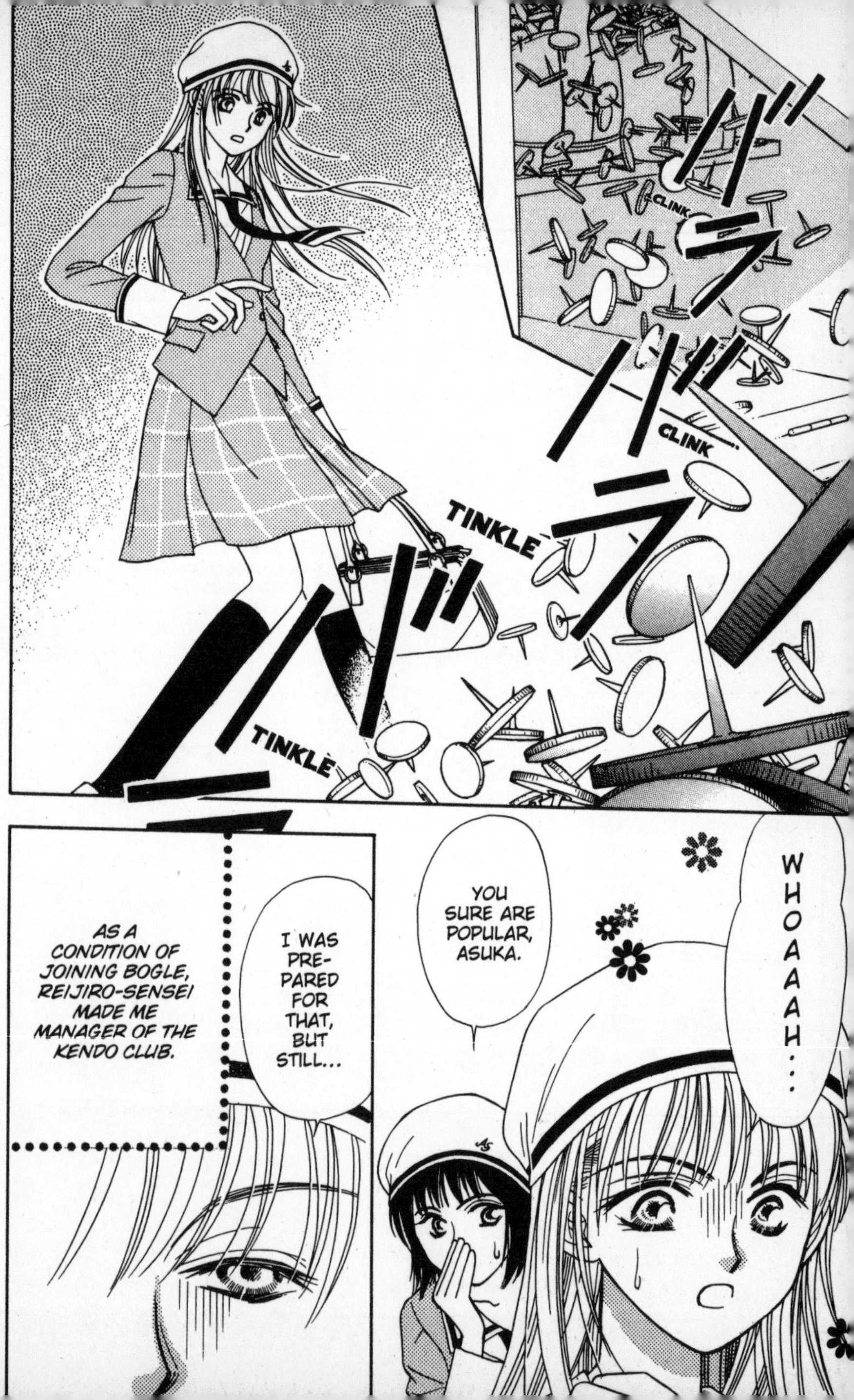

CLINK
CLINK
TINKLE
TINKLE
WHOAAAAH...
YOU SURE ARE POPULAR, ASUKA.
I WAS PRE-PARED FOR THAT, BUT STILL...
AS A CONDITION OF JOINING BOGLE, REIJIRO-SENSEI MADE ME MANAGER OF THE KENDO CLUB.

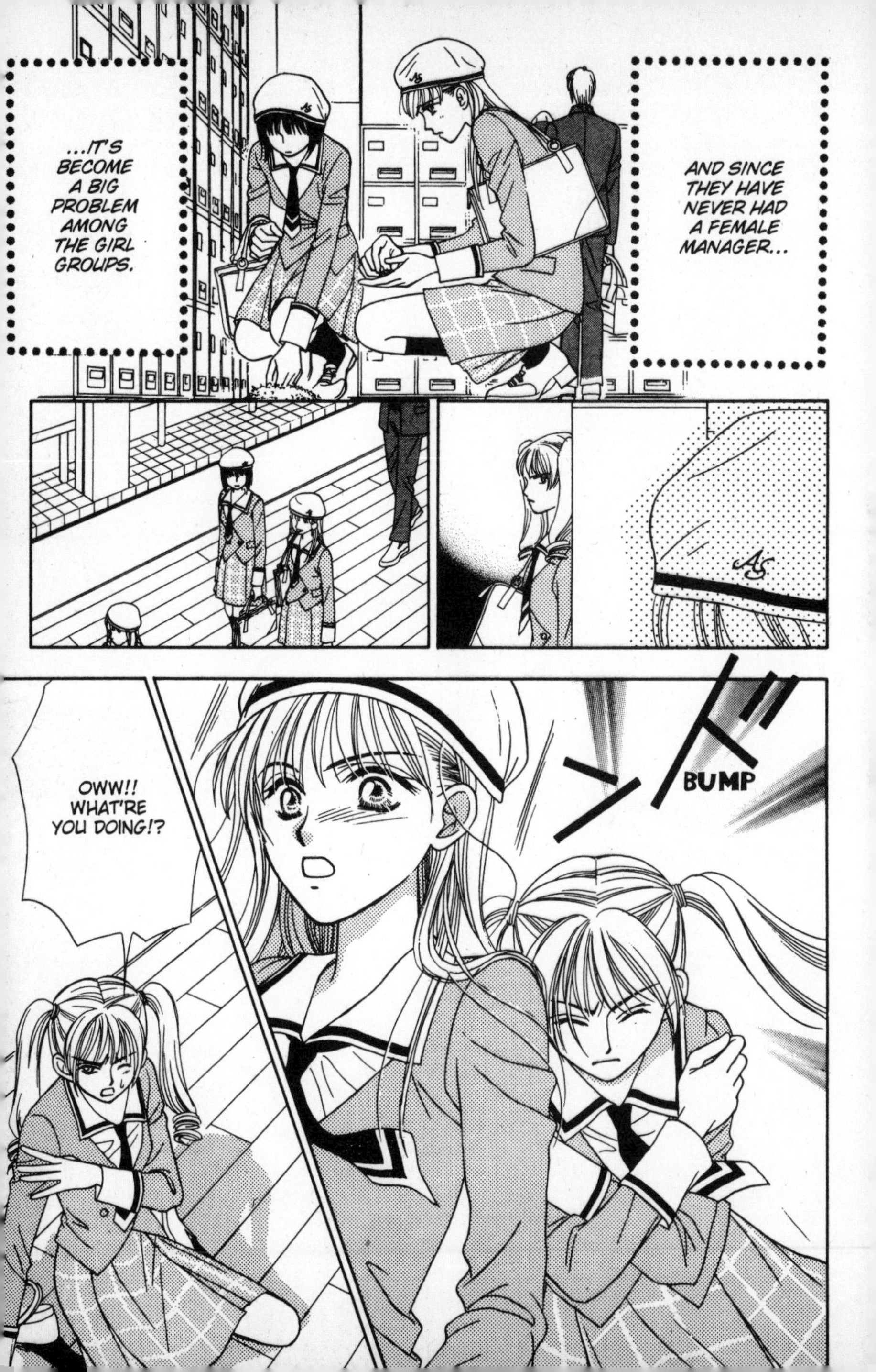
...IT'S BECOME A BIG PROBLEM AMONG THE GIRL GROUPS.
AND SINCE THEY HAVE NEVER HAD A FEMALE MANAGER...
BUMP
OWW!! WHAT'RE YOU DOING!?

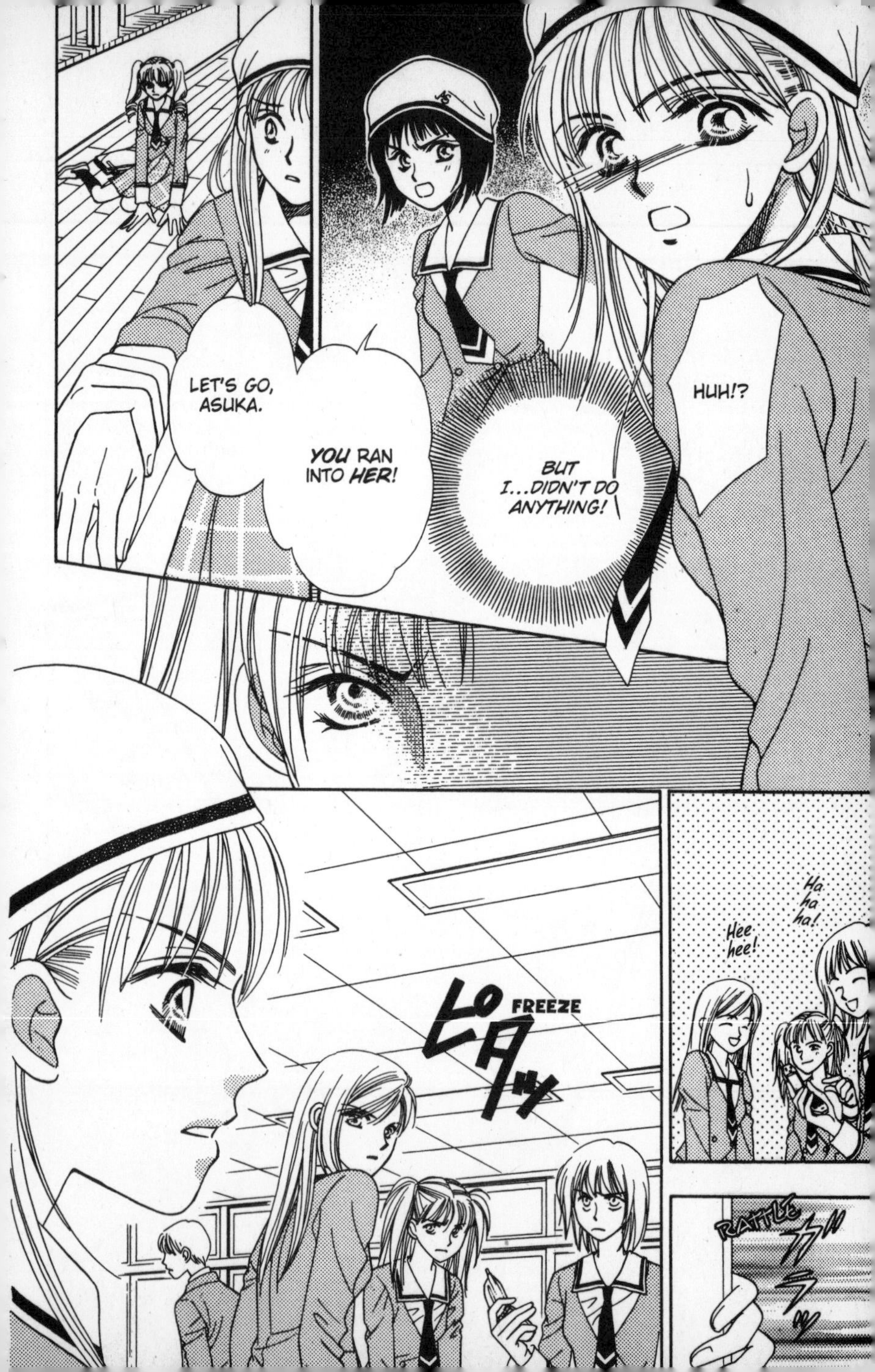
HUH!?
BUT I...DIDN'T DO ANYTHING!
YOU RAN INTO HER!
LET'S GO, ASUKA.
Ha ha ha!
Hee hee!
FREEZE
RATTLE

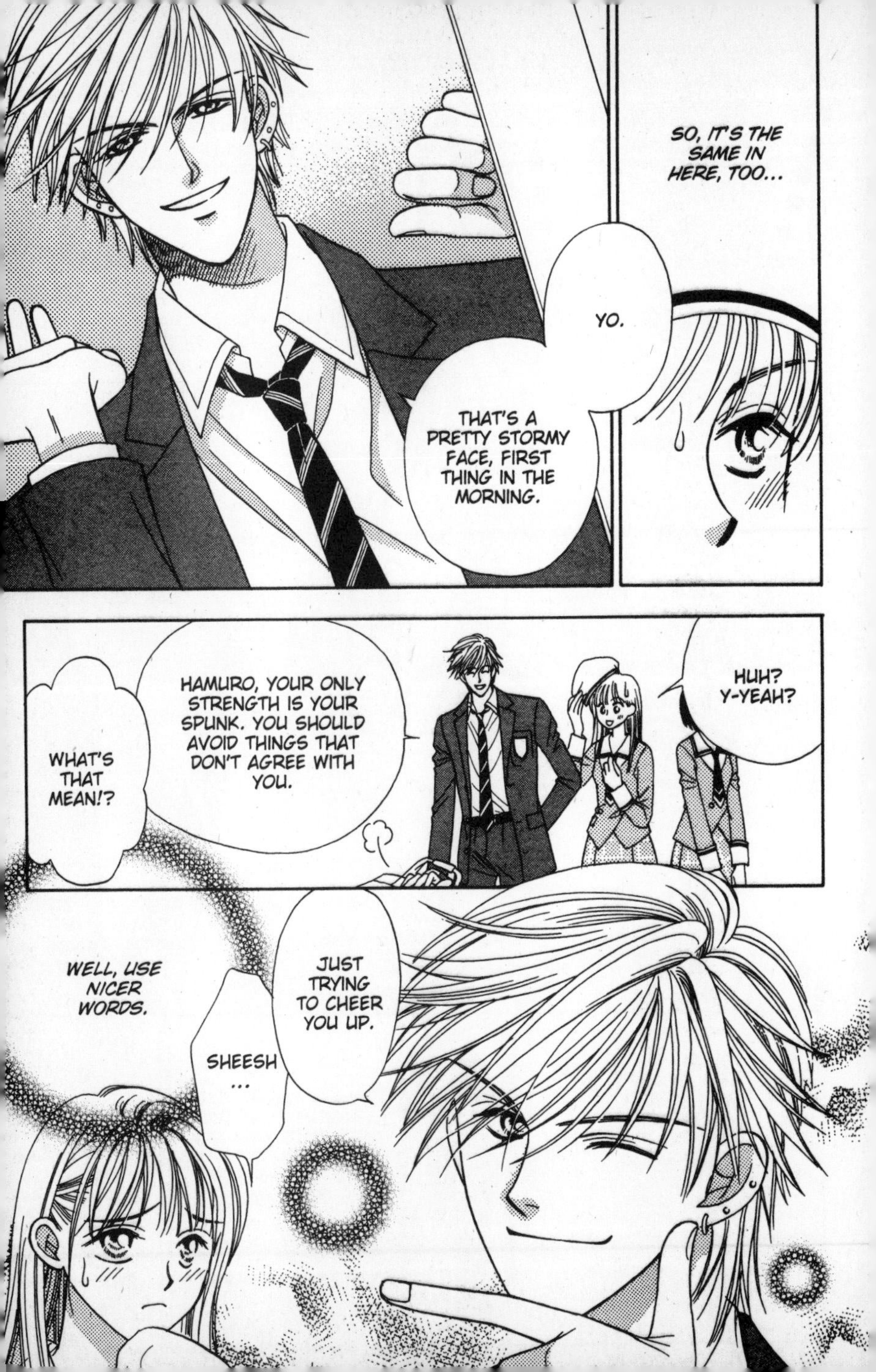
SO, IT'S THE SAME IN HERE, TOO...
YO.
THAT'S A PRETTY STORMY FACE, FIRST THING IN THE MORNING.
HUH? Y-YEAH?
HAMURO, YOUR ONLY STRENGTH IS YOUR SPUNK. YOU SHOULD AVOID THINGS THAT DON'T AGREE WITH YOU.
WHAT'S THAT MEAN!?
JUST TRYING TO CHEER YOU UP.
SHEESH...
WELL, USE NICER WORDS.

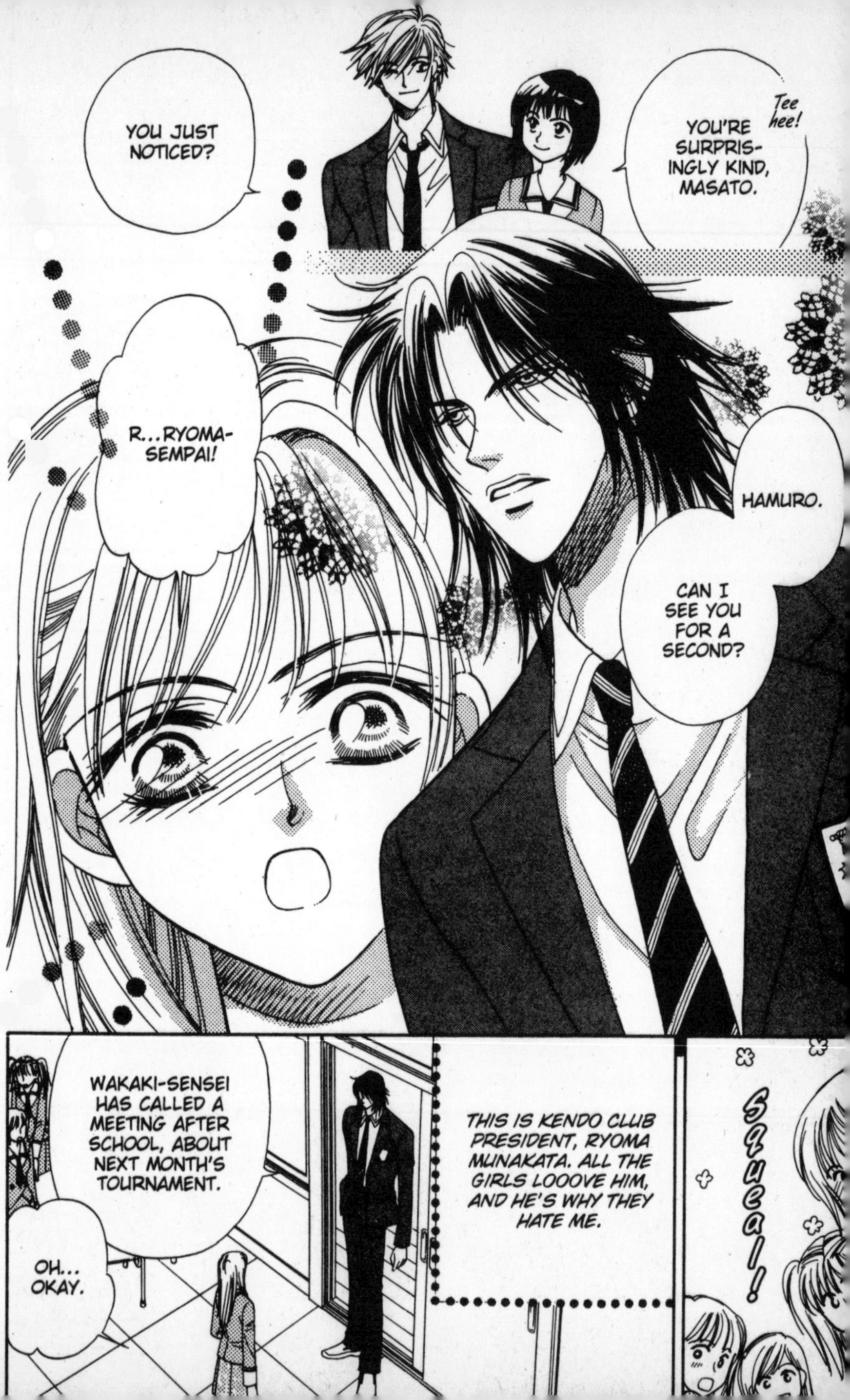
YOU'RE SURPRISINGLY KIND, MASATO.
Tee hee!
YOU JUST NOTICED?
HAMURO.
CAN I SEE YOU FOR A SECOND?
R...RYOMA-SEMPAI!
Squeal!
THIS IS KENDO CLUB PRESIDENT, RYOMA MUNAKATA. ALL THE GIRLS LOOOVE HIM, AND HE'S WHY THEY HATE ME.
WAKAKI-SENSEI HAS CALLED A MEETING AFTER SCHOOL, ABOUT NEXT MONTH'S TOURNAMENT.
OH... OKAY.

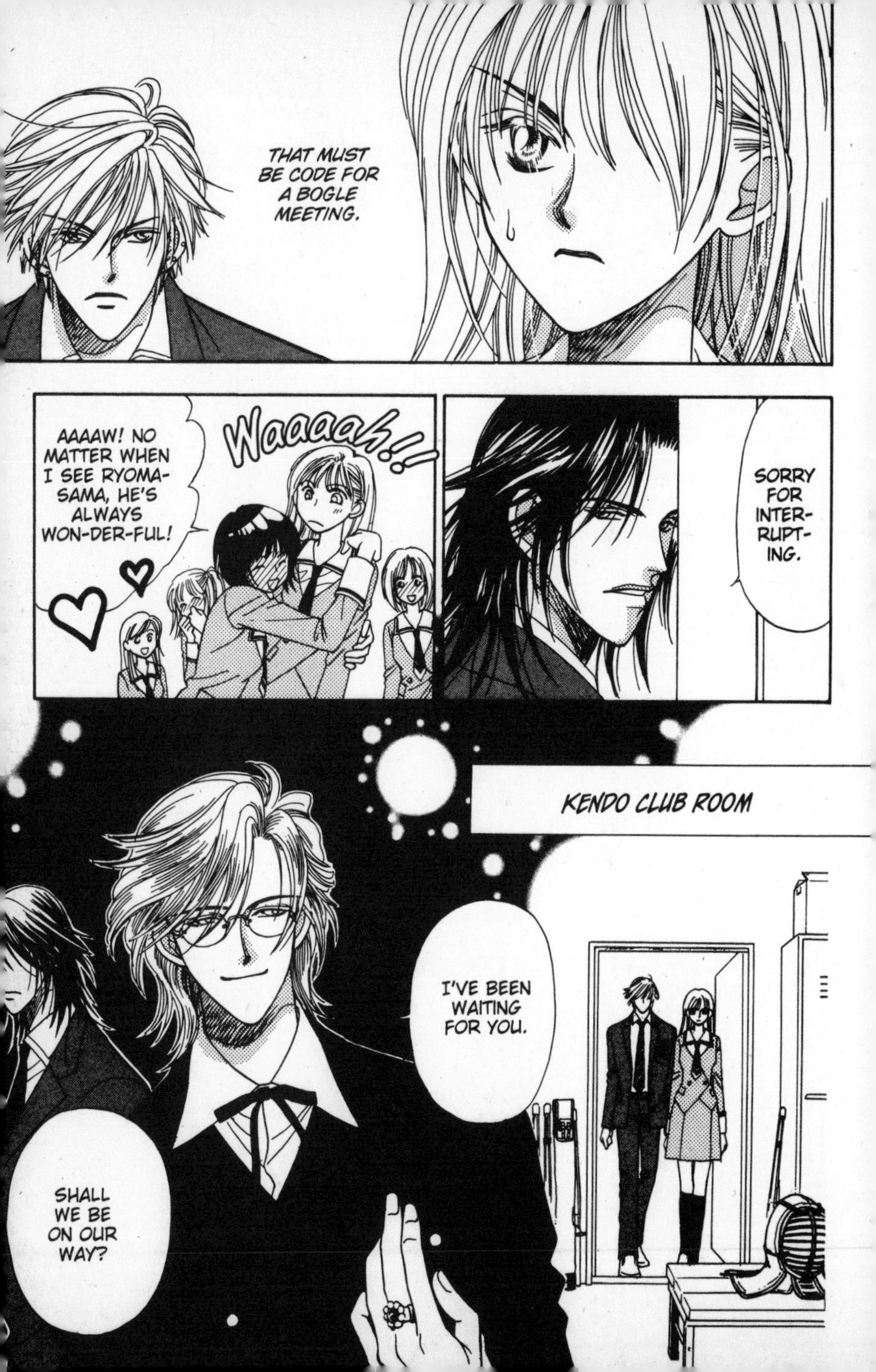
THAT MUST BE CODE FOR A BOGLE MEETING.
SORRY FOR INTER-RUPT-ING.
Waaaah!!
AAAAW! NO MATTER WHEN I SEE RYOMA-SAMA, HE'S ALWAYS WON-DER-FUL!
KENDO CLUB ROOM
I'VE BEEN WAITING FOR YOU.
SHALL WE BE ON OUR WAY?

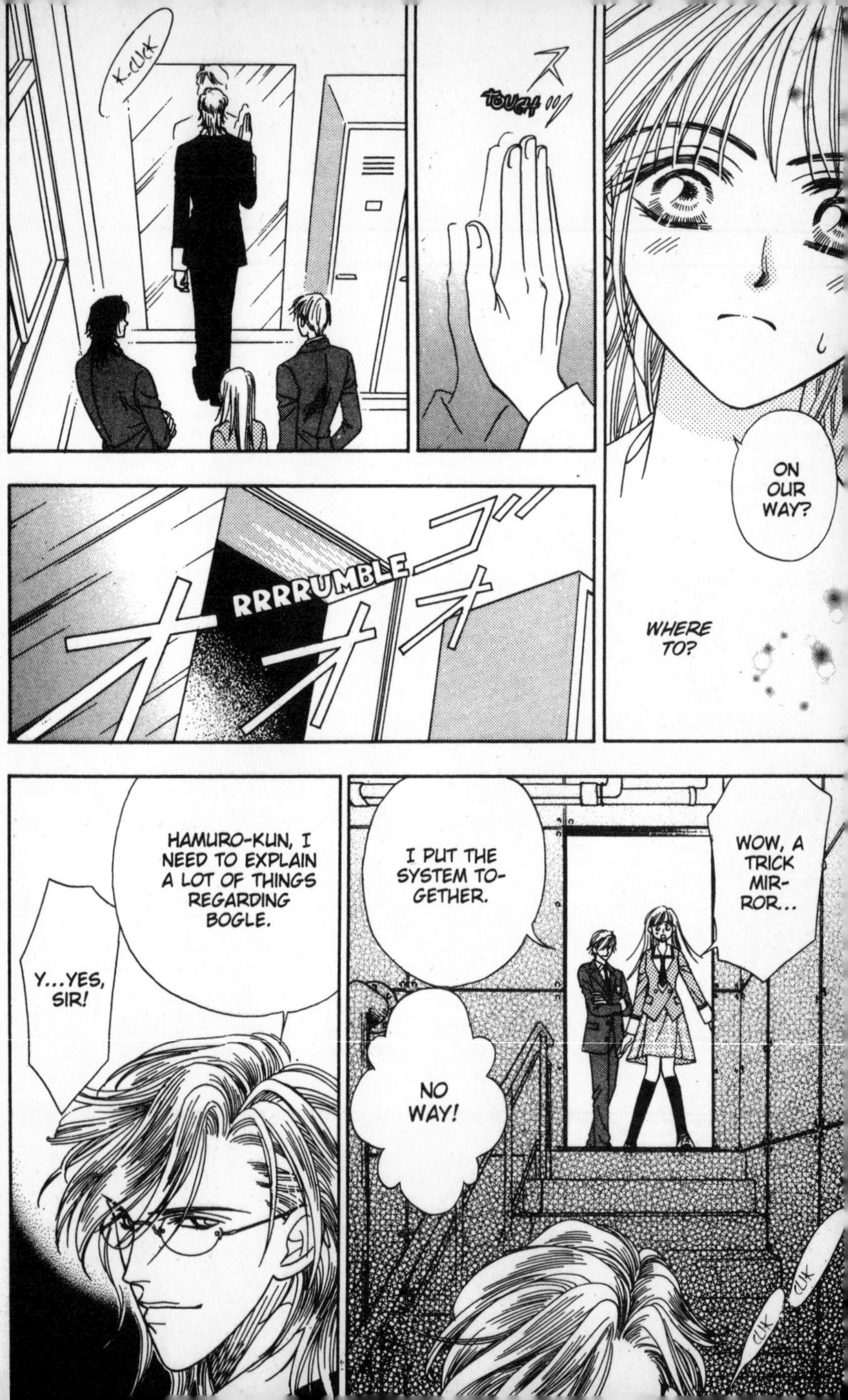

ON OUR WAY?
WHERE TO?
TOUCH
K-CLICK
RRRRUMBLE
WOW, A TRICK MIR-ROR...
I PUT THE SYSTEM TO-GETHER.
NO WAY!
CLIK
CLIK
HAMURO-KUN, I NEED TO EXPLAIN A LOT OF THINGS REGARDING BOGLE.
Y...YES, SIR!

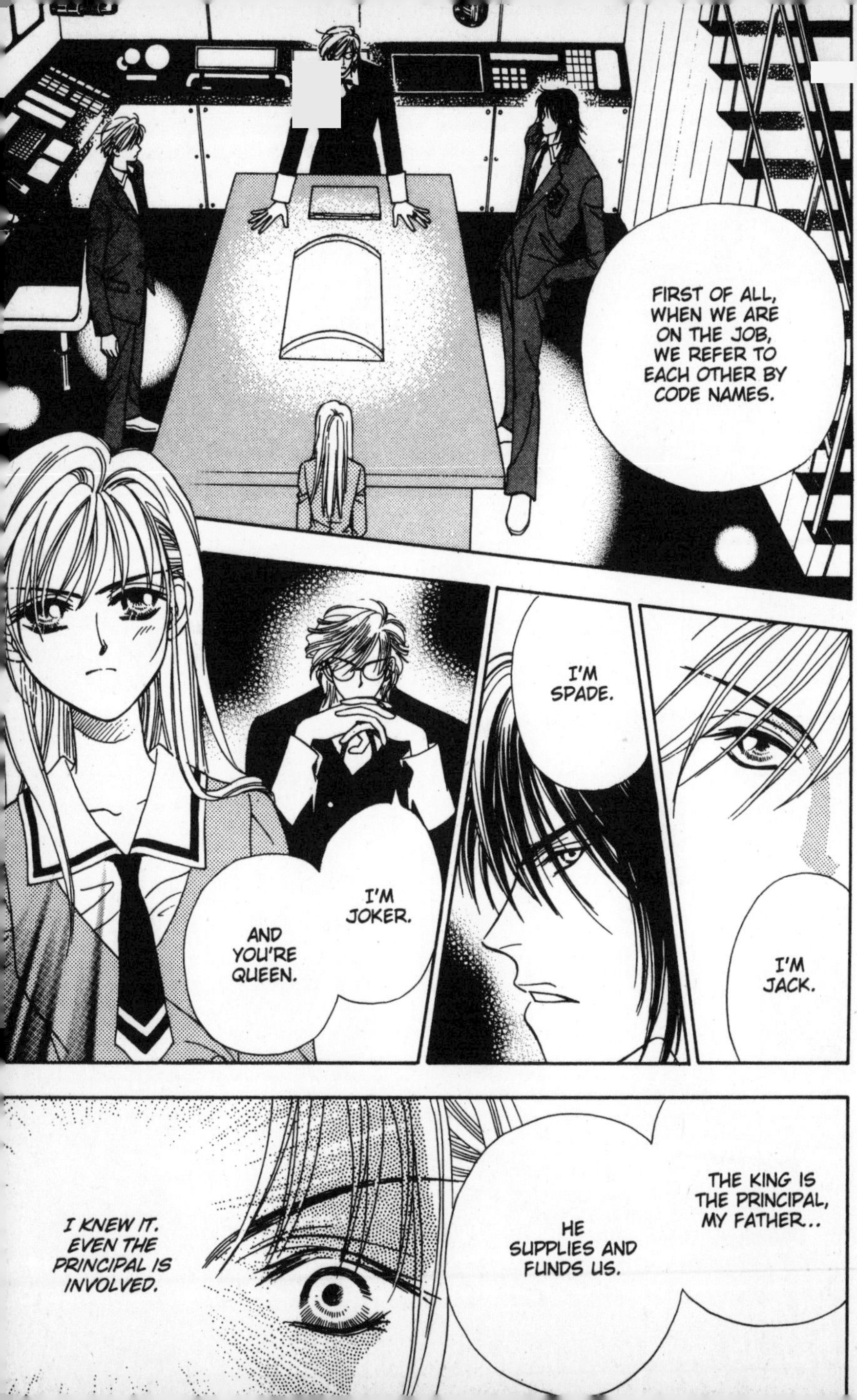
FIRST OF ALL, WHEN WE ARE ON THE JOB, WE REFER TO EACH OTHER BY CODE NAMES.
I'M JACK.
I'M SPADE.
I'M JOKER.
AND YOU'RE QUEEN.
THE KING IS THE PRINCIPAL, MY FATHER..
HE SUPPLIES AND FUNDS US.
I KNEW IT. EVEN THE PRINCIPAL IS INVOLVED.

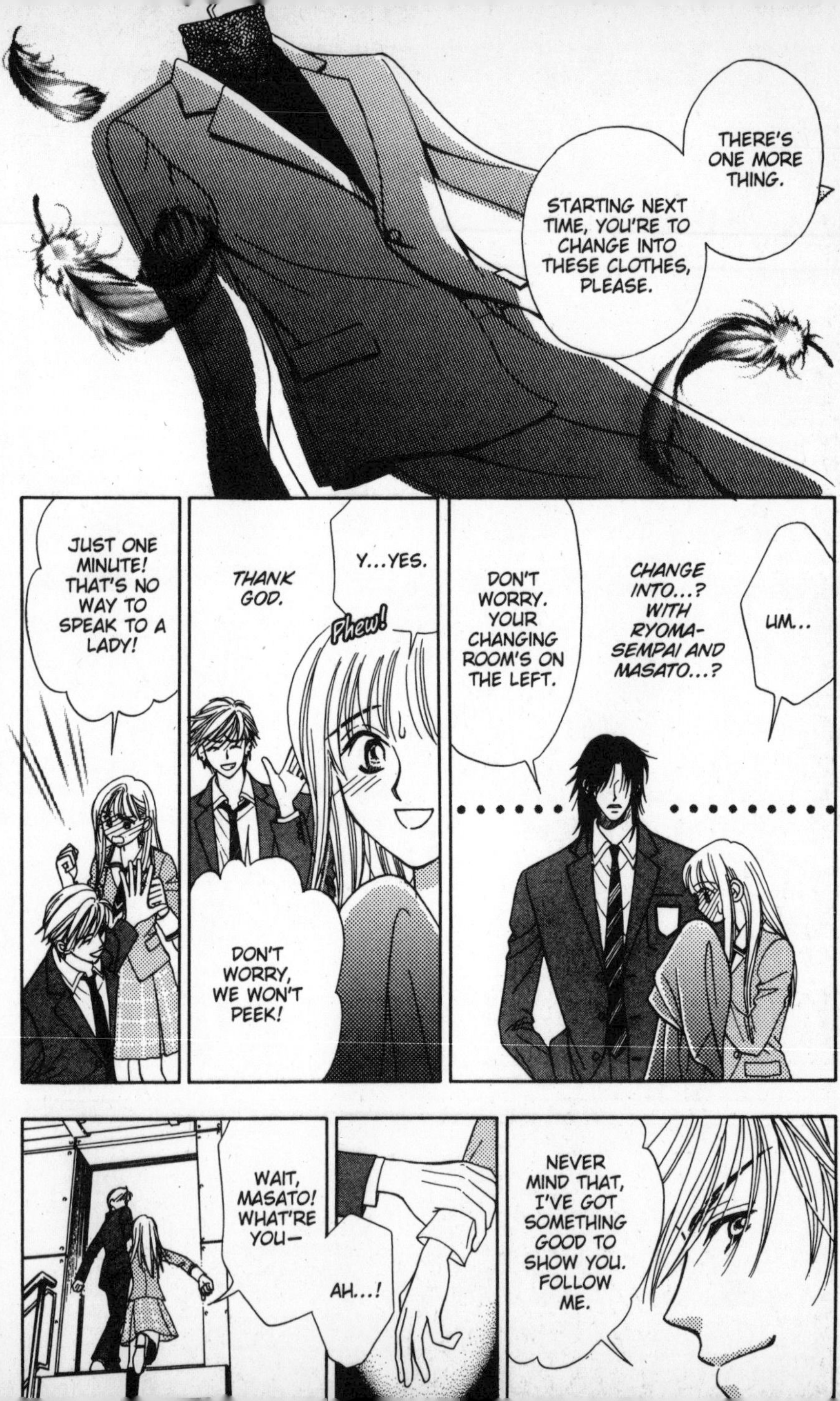
THERE'S ONE MORE THING.
STARTING NEXT TIME, YOU'RE TO CHANGE INTO THESE CLOTHES, PLEASE.
UM...
CHANGE INTO...? WITH RYOMA-SEMPAI AND MASATO...?
DON'T WORRY. YOUR CHANGING ROOM'S ON THE LEFT.
Y...YES.
THANK GOD.
Phew!
DON'T WORRY, WE WON'T PEEK!
JUST ONE MINUTE! THAT'S NO WAY TO SPEAK TO A LADY!
NEVER MIND THAT, I'VE GOT SOMETHING GOOD TO SHOW YOU. FOLLOW ME.
AH...!
WAIT, MASATO! WHAT'RE YOU—

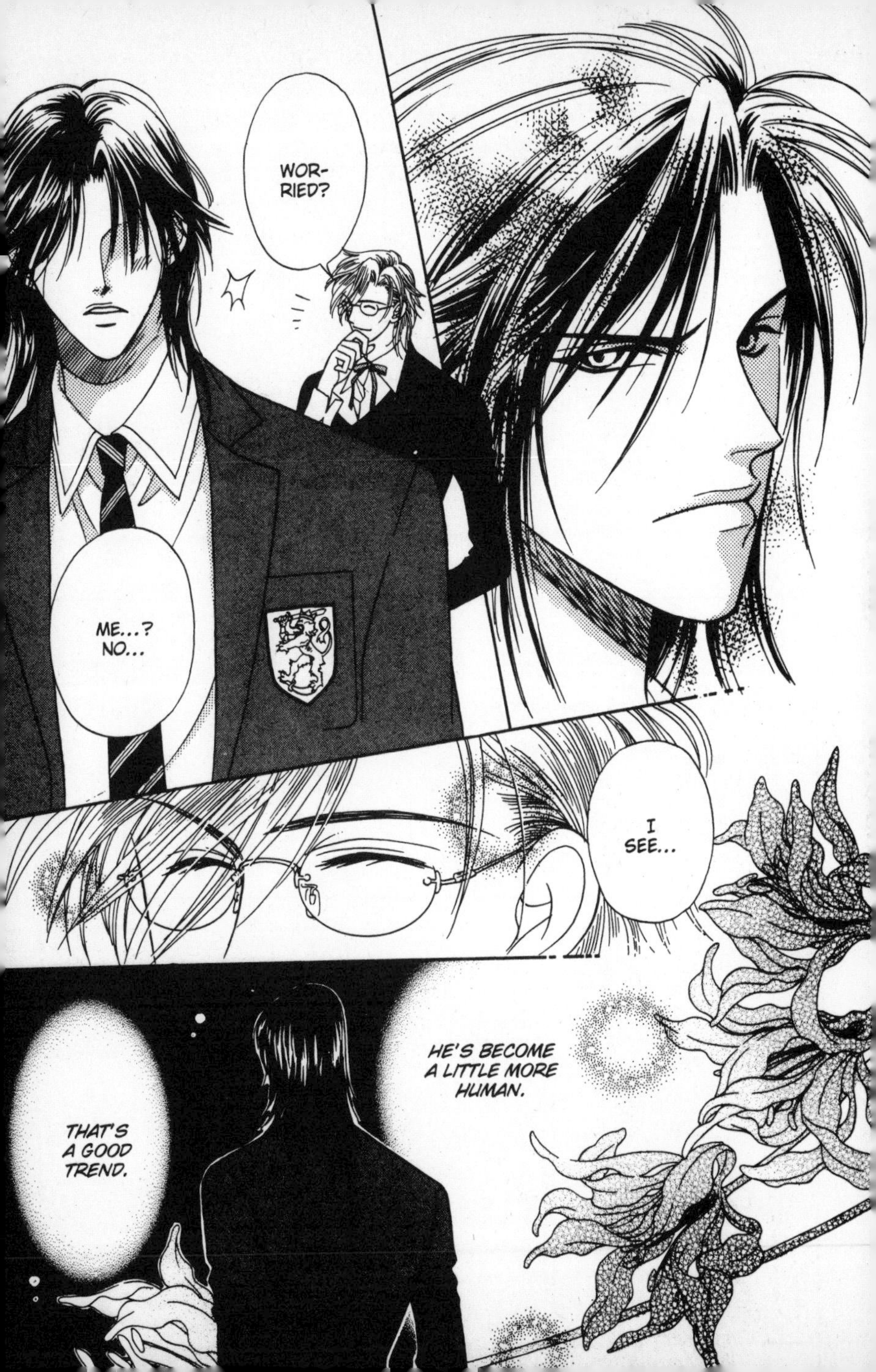
WOR-
RIED?
ME...?
NO...
I
SEE...
HE'S BECOME
A LITTLE MORE
HUMAN.
THAT'S
A GOOD
TREND.

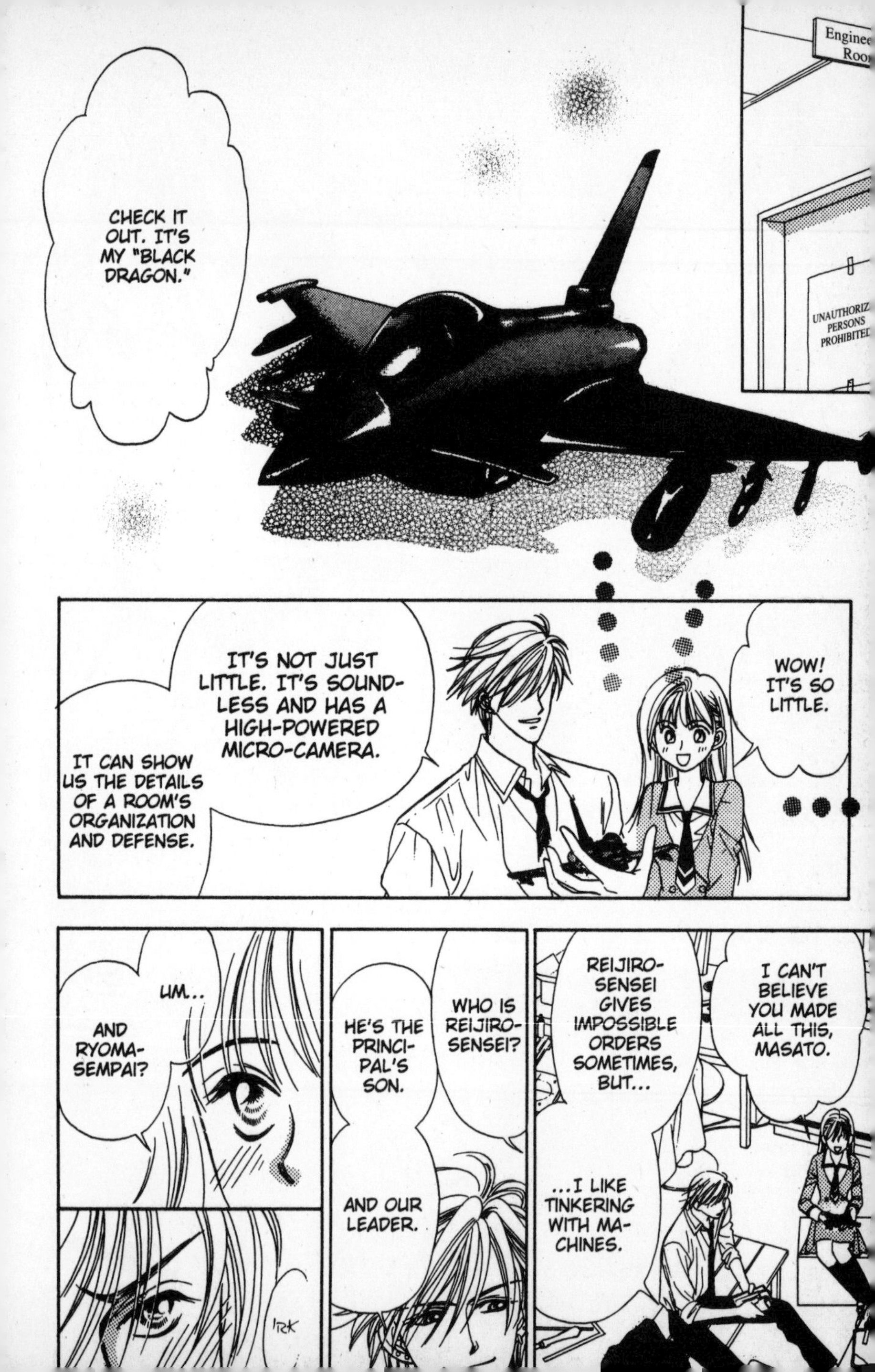
CHECK IT OUT. IT'S MY "BLACK DRAGON."
PERSONS
PROHIBITED
WOW! IT'S SO LITTLE.
...
IT'S NOT JUST LITTLE. IT'S SOUNDLESS AND HAS A HIGH-POWERED MICRO-CAMERA.
IT CAN SHOW US THE DETAILS OF A ROOM'S ORGANIZATION AND DEFENSE.
I CAN'T BELIEVE YOU MADE ALL THIS, MASATO.
REIJIRO-SENSEI GIVES IMPOSSIBLE ORDERS SOMETIMES, BUT...
...I LIKE TINKERING WITH MACHINES.
WHO IS REIJIRO-SENSEI?
HE'S THE PRINCIPAL'S SON.
AND OUR LEADER.
UM...
AND RYOMA-SEMPAI?
IRK

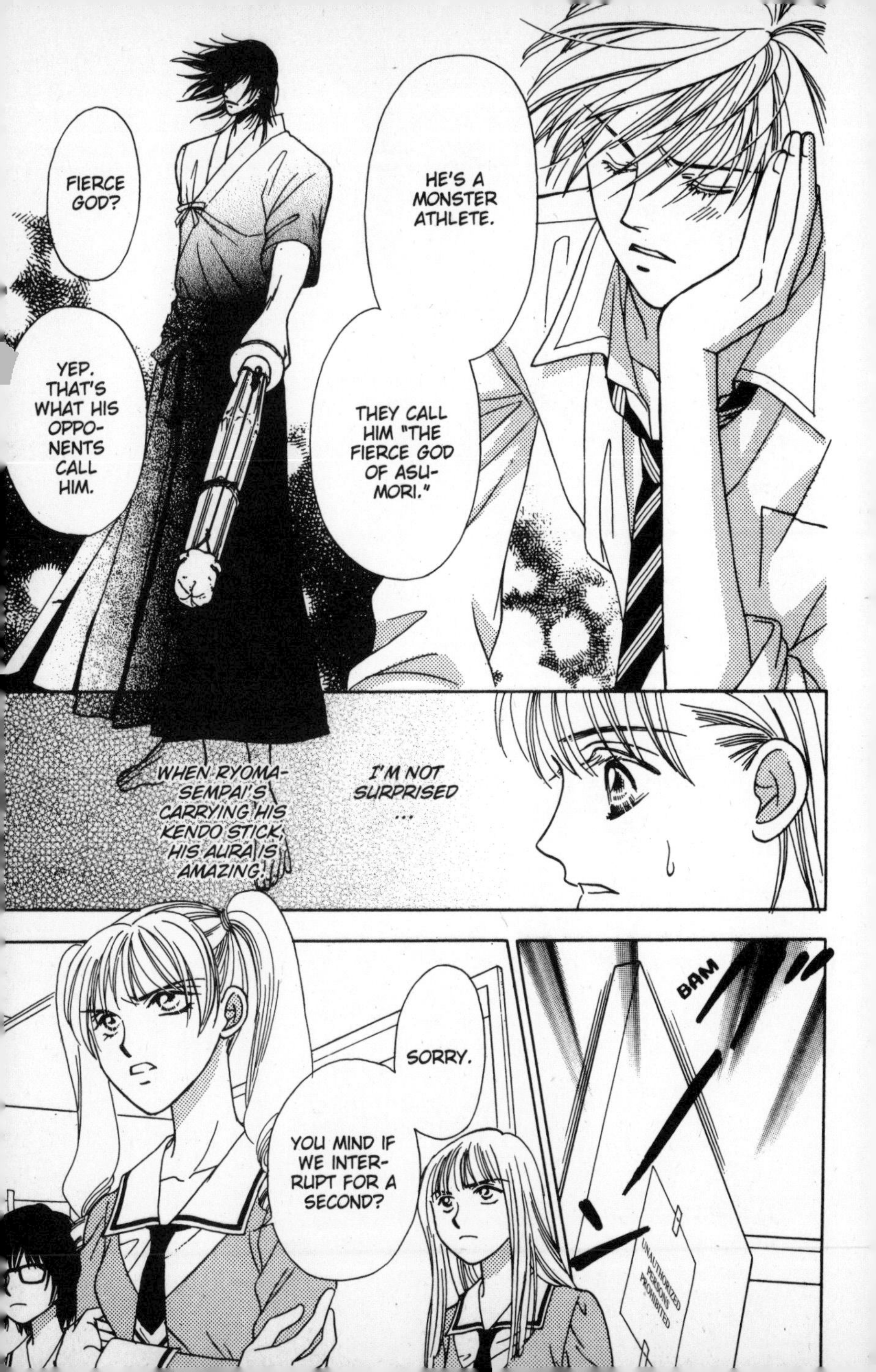
HE'S A MONSTER ATHLETE.
THEY CALL HIM "THE FIERCE GOD OF ASUMORI."
FIERCE GOD?
YEP. THAT'S WHAT HIS OPPONENTS CALL HIM.
I'M NOT SURPRISED ...
WHEN RYOMA-SEMPAI'S CARRYING HIS KENDO STICK, HIS AURA IS AMAZING!
BAM
UNAUTHORIZED PERSONS PROHIBITED
SORRY.
YOU MIND IF WE INTERRUPT FOR A SECOND?

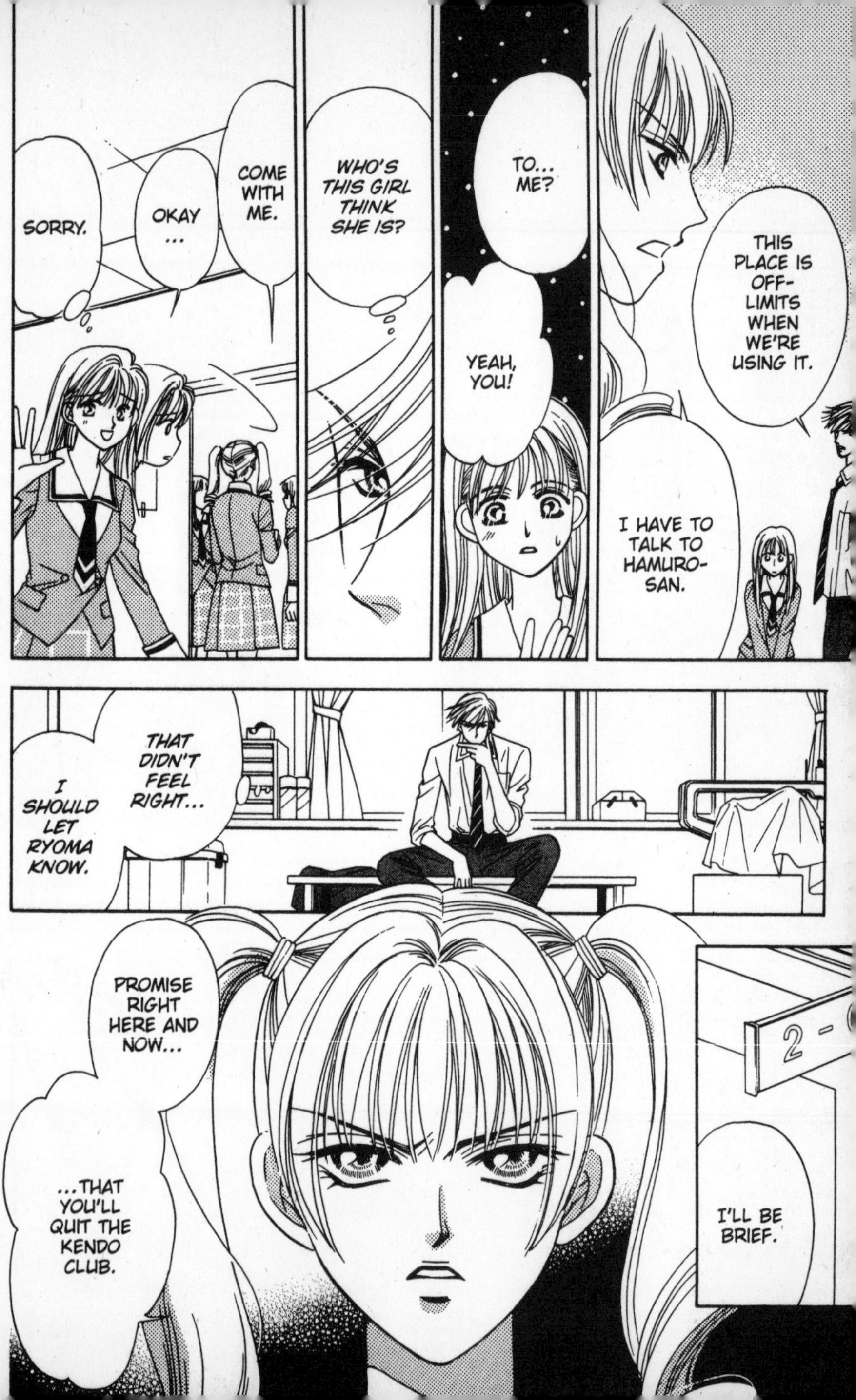
THIS PLACE IS OFF-LIMITS WHEN WE'RE USING IT.
I HAVE TO TALK TO HAMURO-SAN.
TO... ME?
YEAH, YOU!
WHO'S THIS GIRL THINK SHE IS?
COME WITH ME.
OKAY ...
SORRY.
THAT DIDN'T FEEL RIGHT...
I SHOULD LET RYOMA KNOW.
I'LL BE BRIEF.
PROMISE RIGHT HERE AND NOW...
...THAT YOU'LL QUIT THE KENDO CLUB.

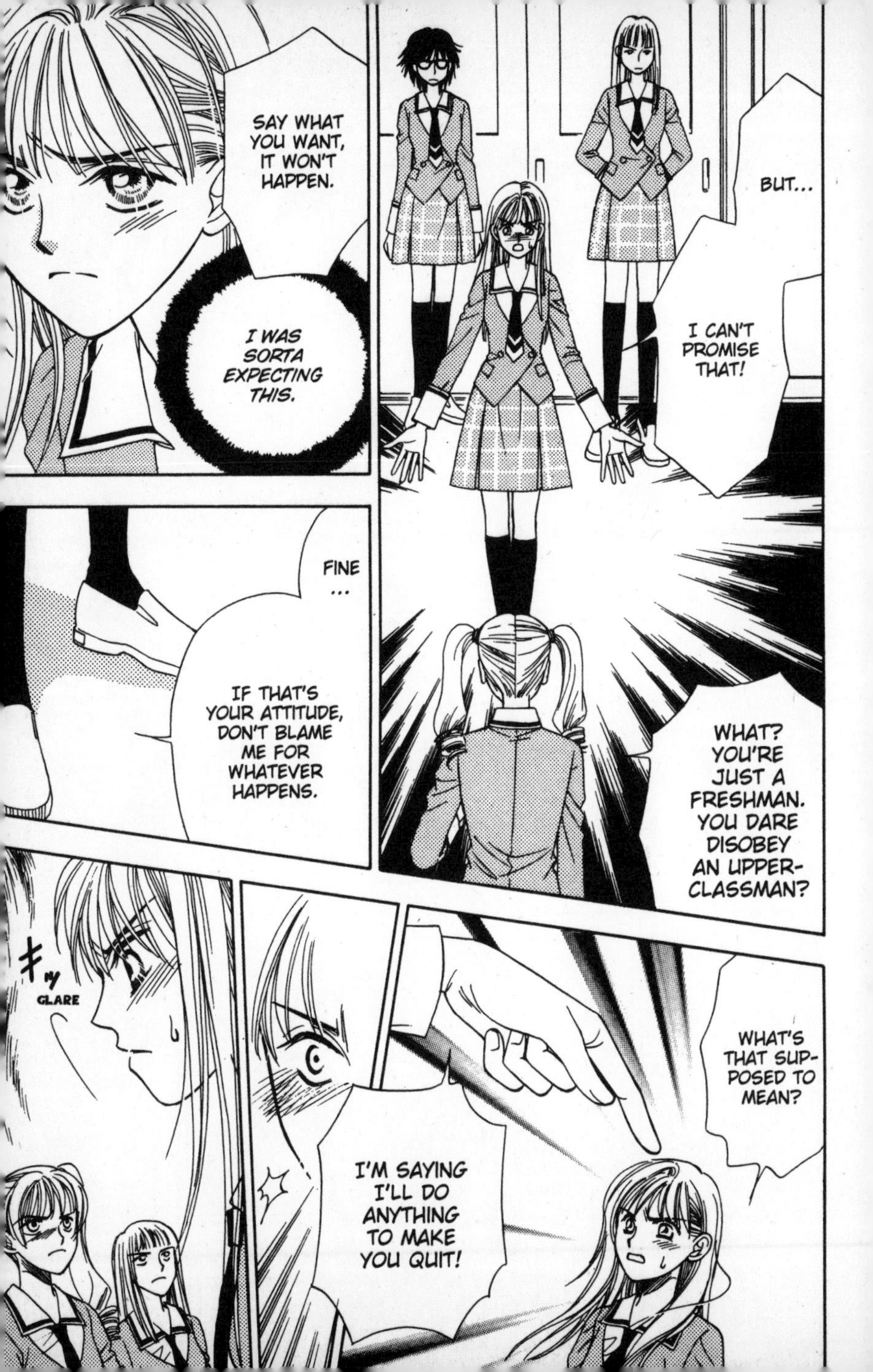
BUT...
I CAN'T PROMISE THAT!
SAY WHAT YOU WANT, IT WON'T HAPPEN.
I WAS SORTA EXPECTING THIS.
WHAT? YOU'RE JUST A FRESHMAN. YOU DARE DISOBEY AN UPPER-CLASSMAN?
FINE ...
IF THAT'S YOUR ATTITUDE, DON'T BLAME ME FOR WHATEVER HAPPENS.
WHAT'S THAT SUP-POSED TO MEAN?
I'M SAYING I'LL DO ANYTHING TO MAKE YOU QUIT!
GLARE

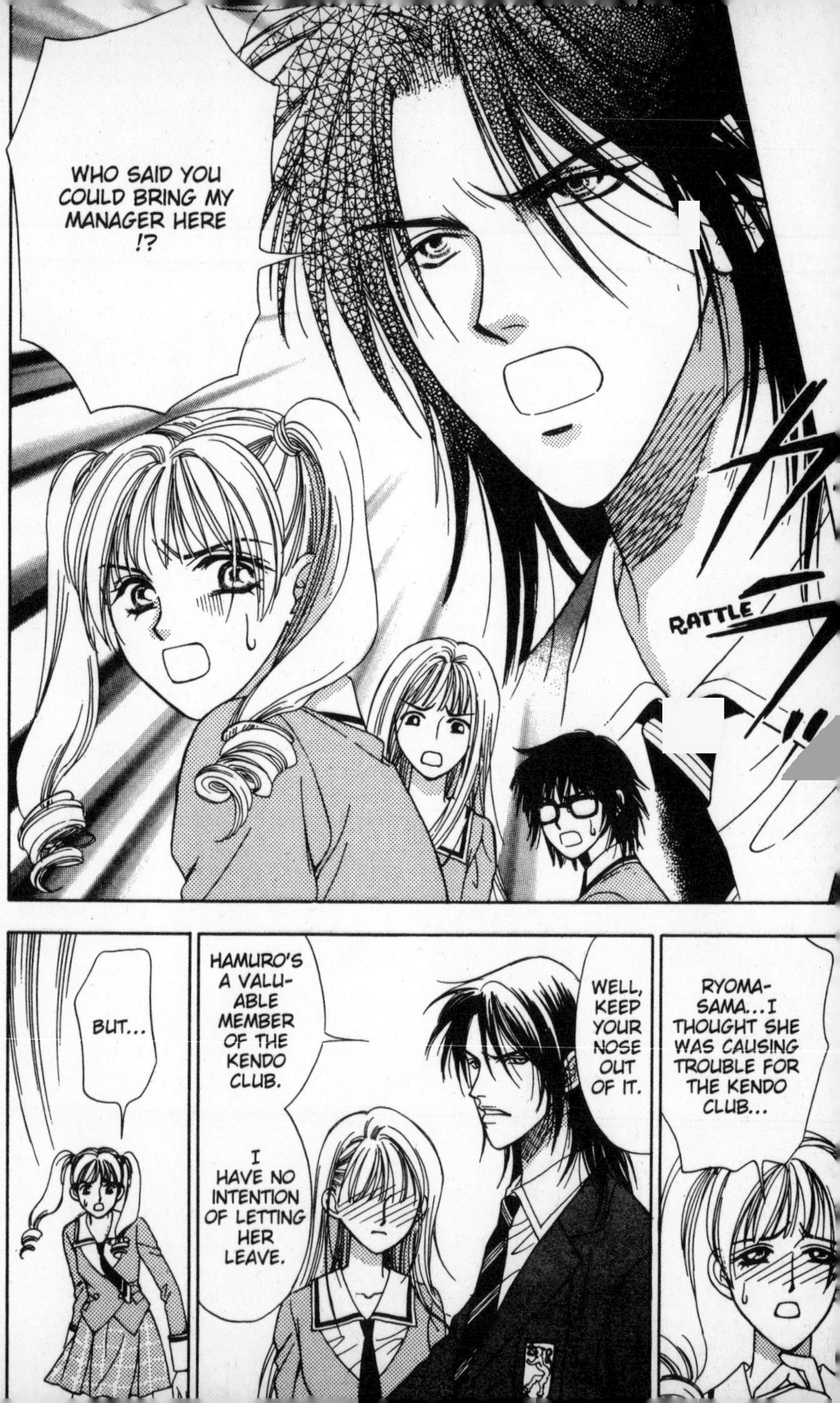
WHO SAID YOU COULD BRING MY MANAGER HERE !?
RATTLE
RYOMA-SAMA...I THOUGHT SHE WAS CAUSING TROUBLE FOR THE KENDO CLUB...
WELL, KEEP YOUR NOSE OUT OF IT.
HAMURO'S A VALU-ABLE MEMBER OF THE KENDO CLUB.
I HAVE NO INTENTION OF LETTING HER LEAVE.
BUT...

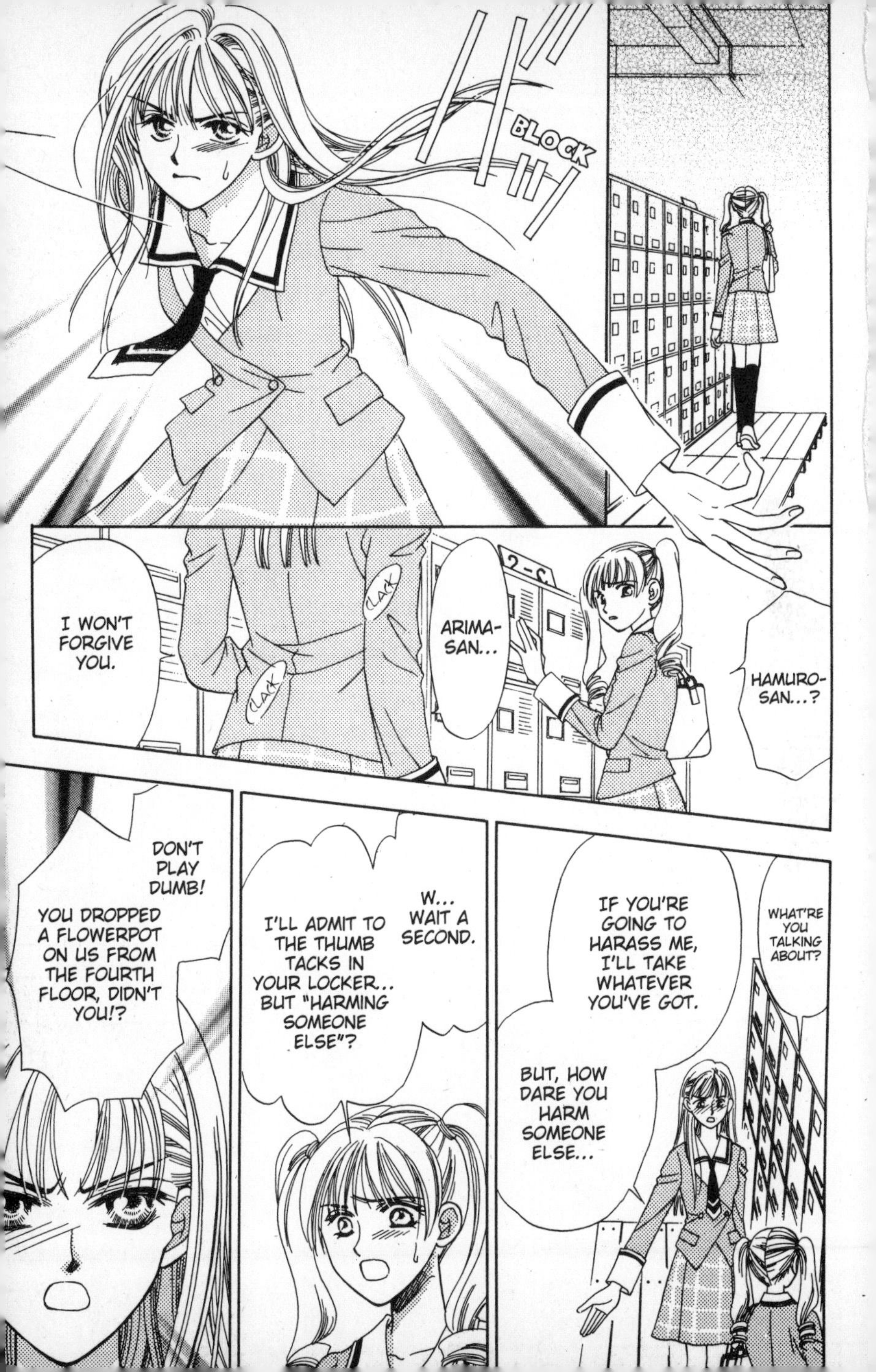
BLOCK
HAMURO-SAN...?
ARIMA-SAN...
CLACK
CLACK
I WON'T FORGIVE YOU.
WHAT'RE YOU TALKING ABOUT?
IF YOU'RE GOING TO HARASS ME, I'LL TAKE WHATEVER YOU'VE GOT.
BUT, HOW DARE YOU HARM SOMEONE ELSE...
W... WAIT A SECOND.
I'LL ADMIT TO THE THUMB TACKS IN YOUR LOCKER... BUT "HARMING SOMEONE ELSE"?
DON'T PLAY DUMB!
YOU DROPPED A FLOWERPOT ON US FROM THE FOURTH FLOOR, DIDN'T YOU!?

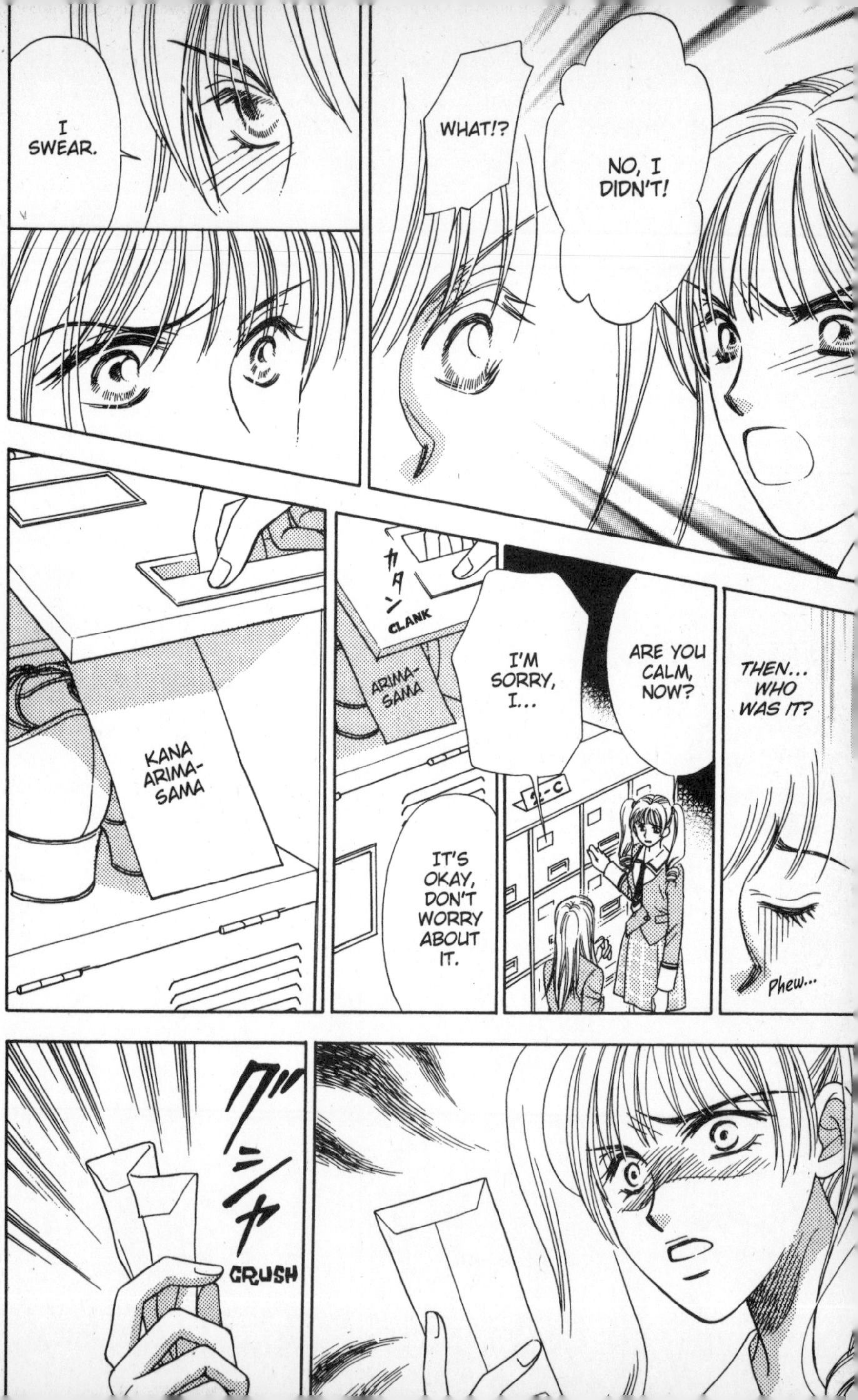
WHAT!?
NO, I DIDN'T!
I SWEAR.
THEN... WHO WAS IT?
Phew...
ARE YOU CALM, NOW?
I'M SORRY, I...
IT'S OKAY, DON'T WORRY ABOUT IT.
カタン
CLANK
ARIMA-SAMA
KANA ARIMA-SAMA
グシャ
GRUSH

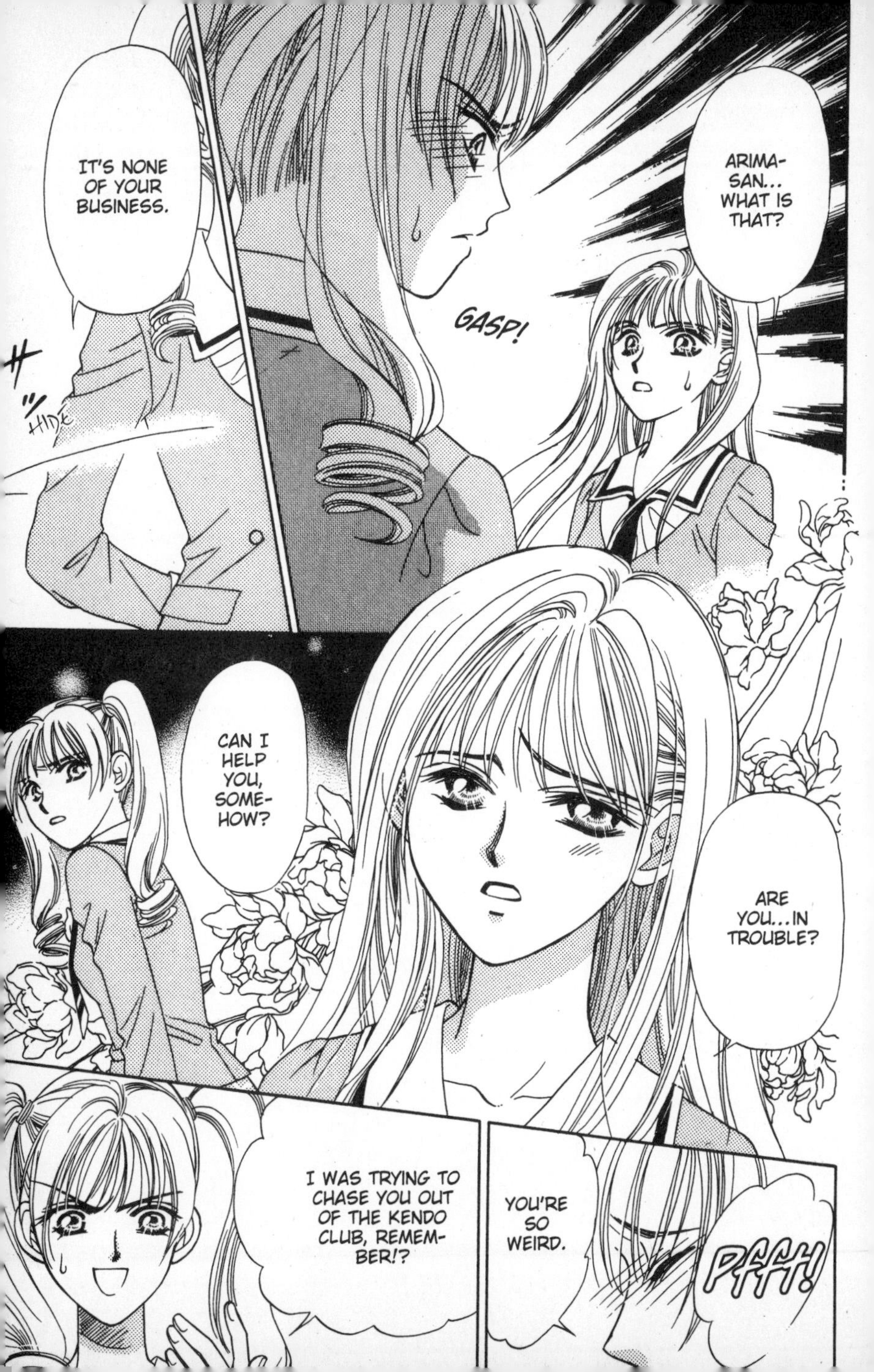
ARIMA-SAN... WHAT IS THAT?
GASP!
IT'S NONE OF YOUR BUSINESS.
HIDE
ARE YOU...IN TROUBLE?
CAN I HELP YOU, SOMEHOW?
Pfft!
YOU'RE SO WEIRD.
I WAS TRYING TO CHASE YOU OUT OF THE KENDO CLUB, REMEMBER!?

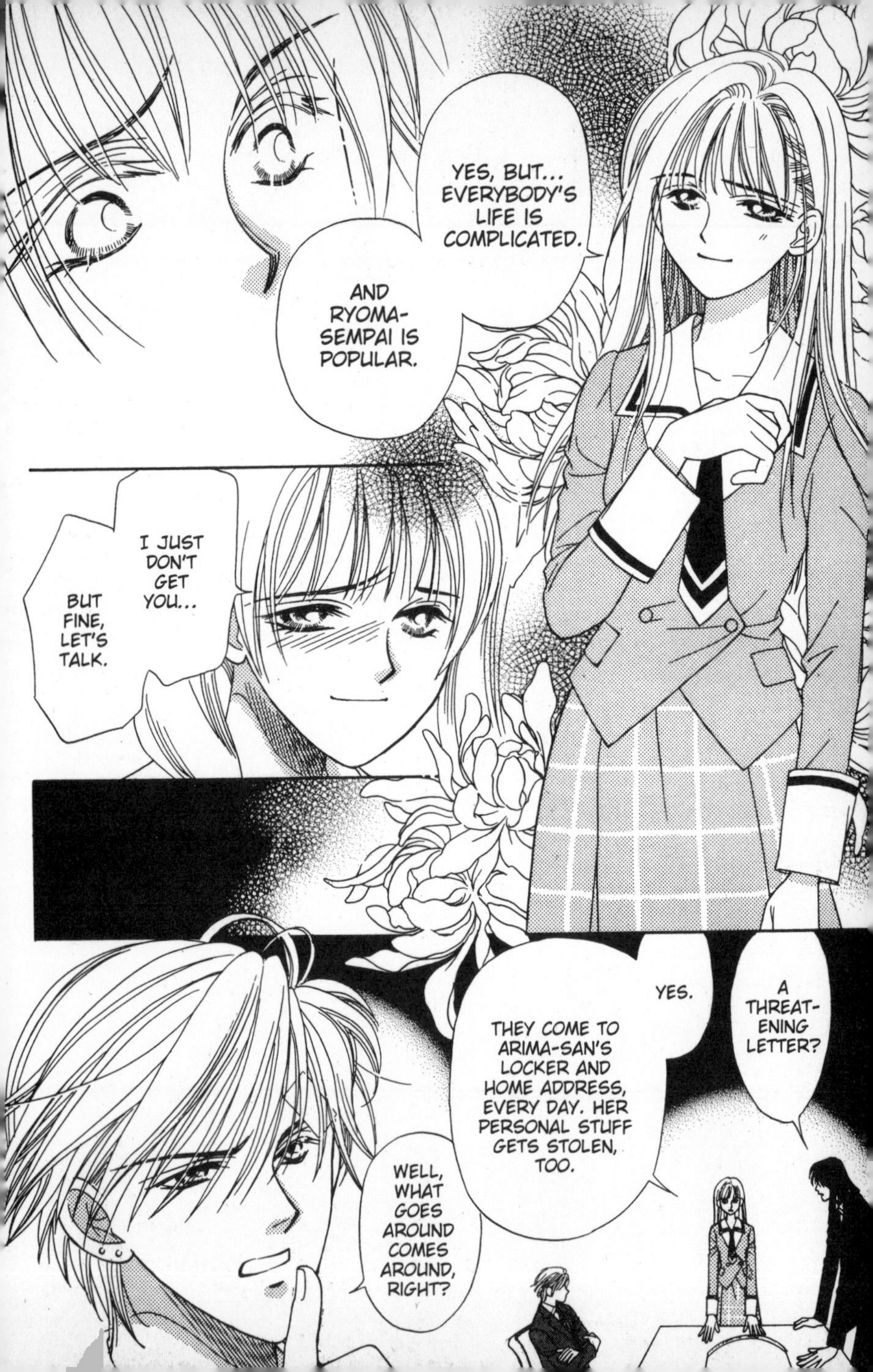
YES, BUT... EVERYBODY'S LIFE IS COMPLICATED.
AND RYOMA-SEMPAI IS POPULAR.
I JUST DON'T GET YOU...
BUT FINE, LET'S TALK.
A THREAT-ENING LETTER?
YES.
THEY COME TO ARIMA-SAN'S LOCKER AND HOME ADDRESS, EVERY DAY. HER PERSONAL STUFF GETS STOLEN, TOO.
WELL, WHAT GOES AROUND COMES AROUND, RIGHT?

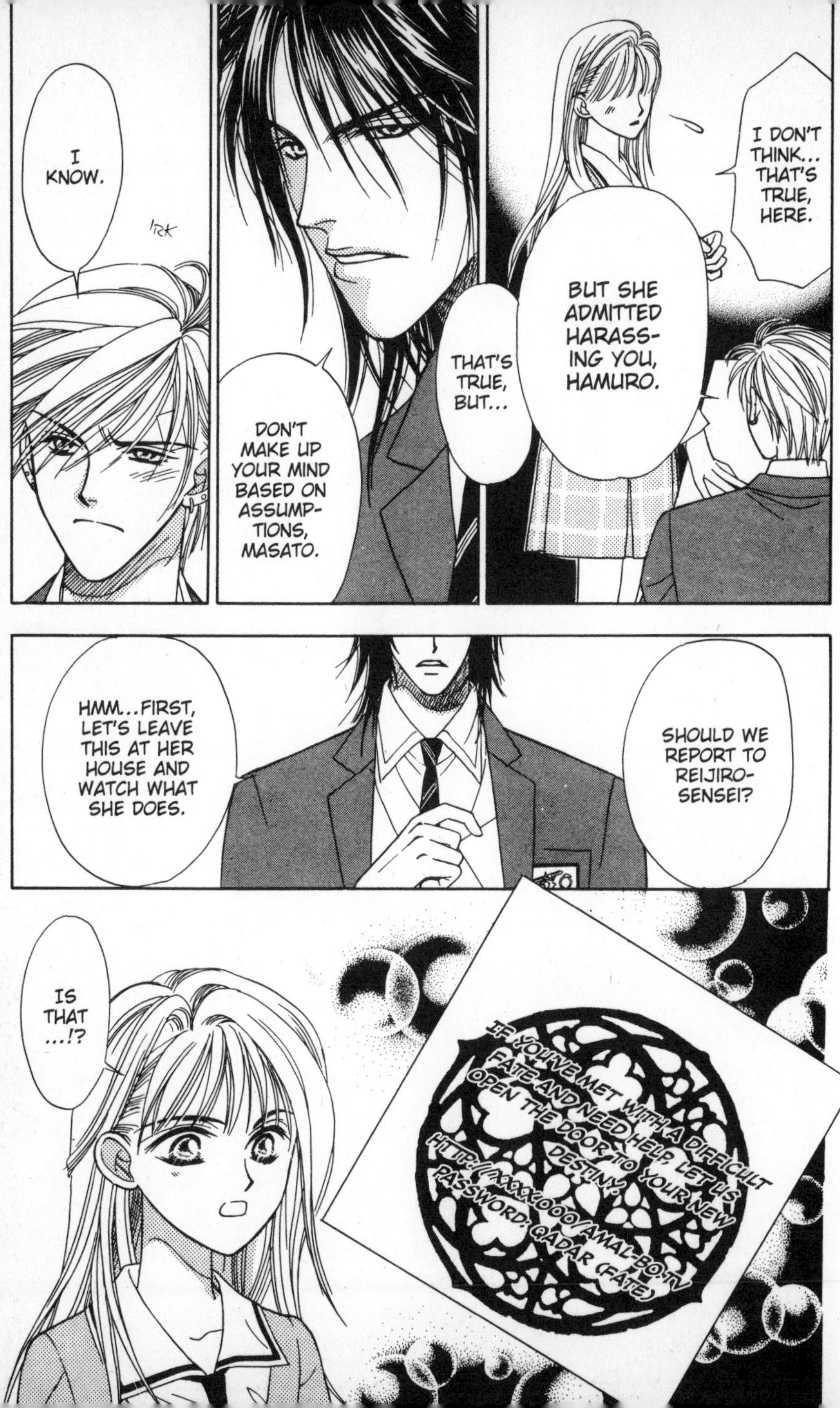
I DON'T THINK... THAT'S TRUE, HERE.
BUT SHE ADMITTED HARASS-ING YOU, HAMURO.
THAT'S TRUE, BUT...
DON'T MAKE UP YOUR MIND BASED ON ASSUMP-TIONS, MASATO.
IRK
I KNOW.
SHOULD WE REPORT TO REIJIRO-SENSEI?
HMM...FIRST, LET'S LEAVE THIS AT HER HOUSE AND WATCH WHAT SHE DOES.
IF YOU'VE MET WITH A DIFFICULT FATE AND NEED HELP, LET US OPEN THE DOOR TO YOUR NEW DESTINY.
HTTP://XXX.OOO/AMAL-BO.TV
PASSWORD: QADAR (FATE)
IS THAT ...!?

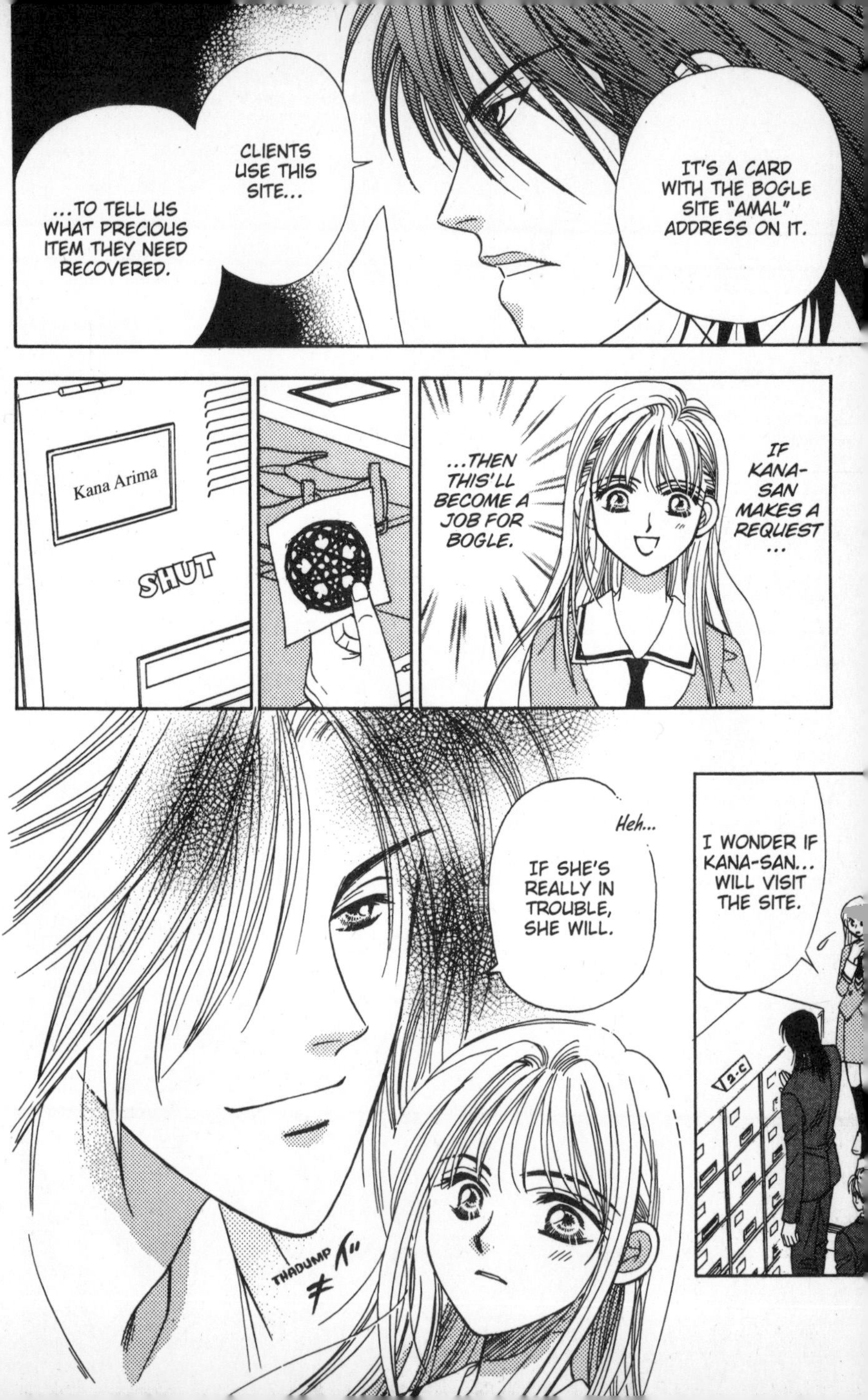

IT'S A CARD WITH THE BOGLE SITE "AMAL" ADDRESS ON IT.
CLIENTS USE THIS SITE...
...TO TELL US WHAT PRECIOUS ITEM THEY NEED RECOVERED.
IF KANA-SAN MAKES A REQUEST...
...THEN THIS'LL BECOME A JOB FOR BOGLE.
Kana Arima
SHUT
I WONDER IF KANA-SAN... WILL VISIT THE SITE.
Heh...
IF SHE'S REALLY IN TROUBLE, SHE WILL.
THADUMP

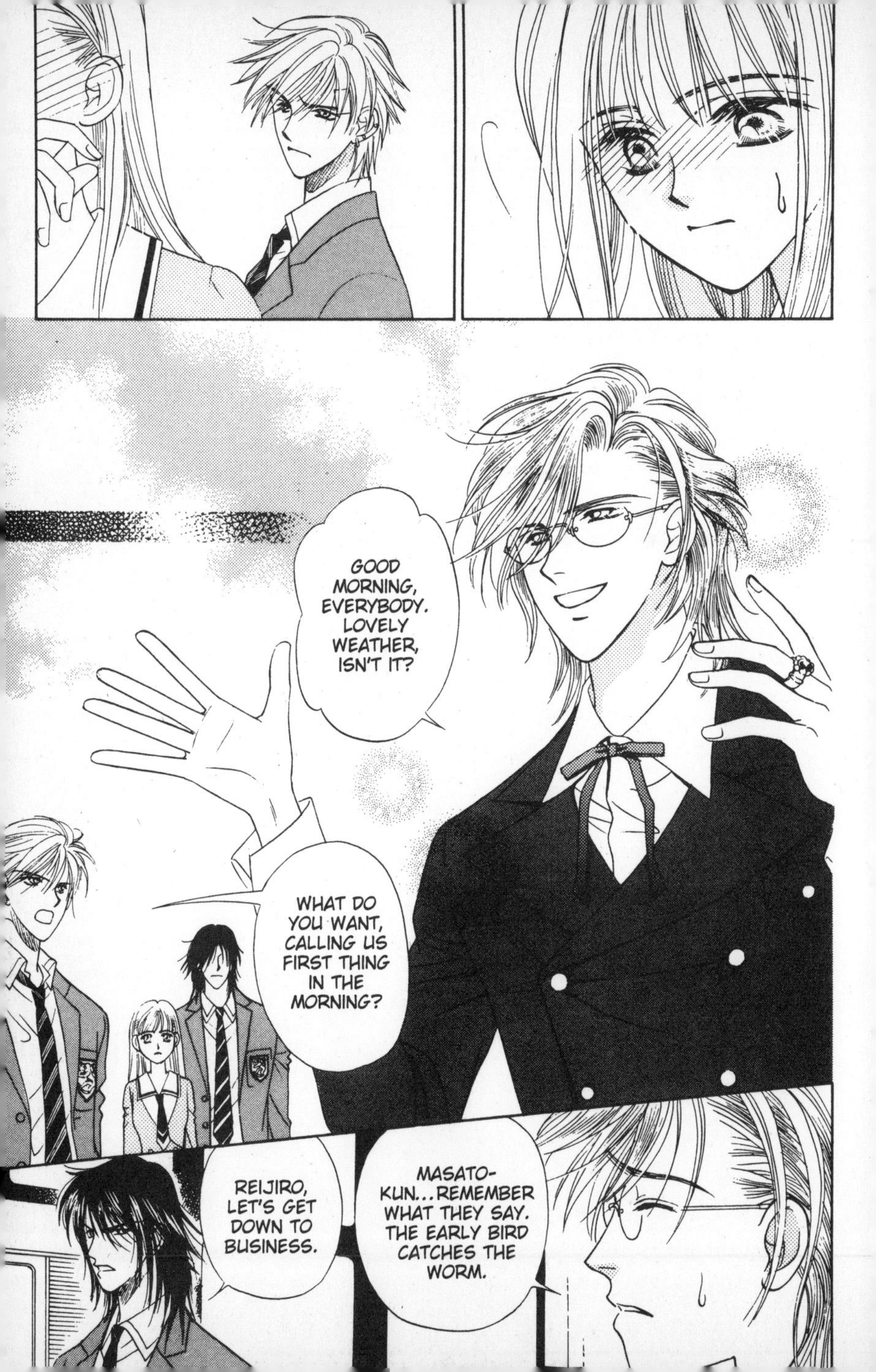
GOOD MORNING, EVERYBODY. LOVELY WEATHER, ISN'T IT?
WHAT DO YOU WANT, CALLING US FIRST THING IN THE MORNING?
MASATO-KUN... REMEMBER WHAT THEY SAY. THE EARLY BIRD CATCHES THE WORM.
REIJIRO, LET'S GET DOWN TO BUSINESS.

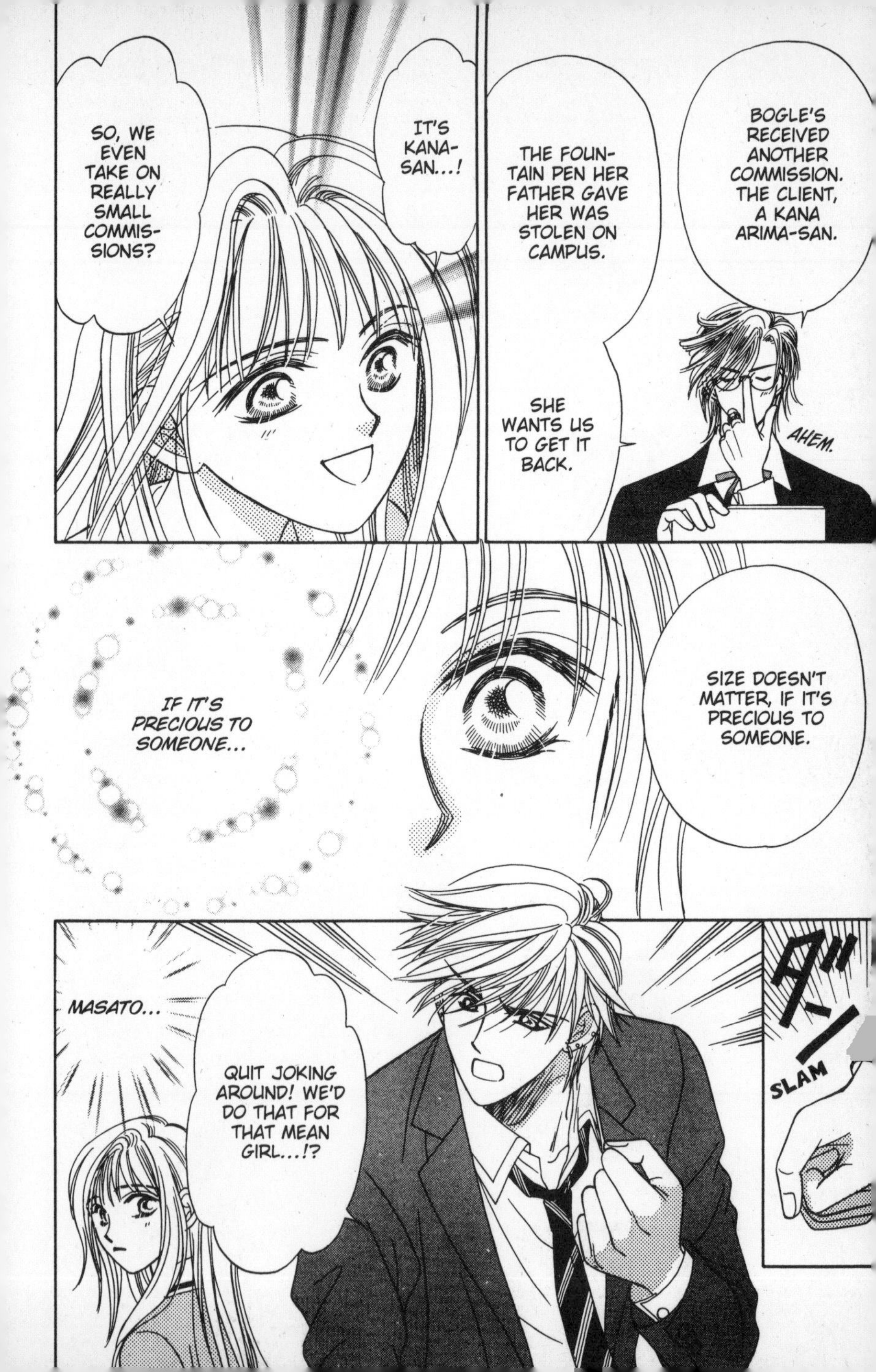
BOGLE'S RECEIVED ANOTHER COMMISSION. THE CLIENT, A KANA ARIMA-SAN.
THE FOUN-TAIN PEN HER FATHER GAVE HER WAS STOLEN ON CAMPUS.
SHE WANTS US TO GET IT BACK.
AHEM.
IT'S KANA-SAN...!
SO, WE EVEN TAKE ON REALLY SMALL COMMIS-SIONS?
SIZE DOESN'T MATTER, IF IT'S PRECIOUS TO SOMEONE.
IF IT'S PRECIOUS TO SOMEONE...
SLAM
QUIT JOKING AROUND! WE'D DO THAT FOR THAT MEAN GIRL...!?
MASATO...

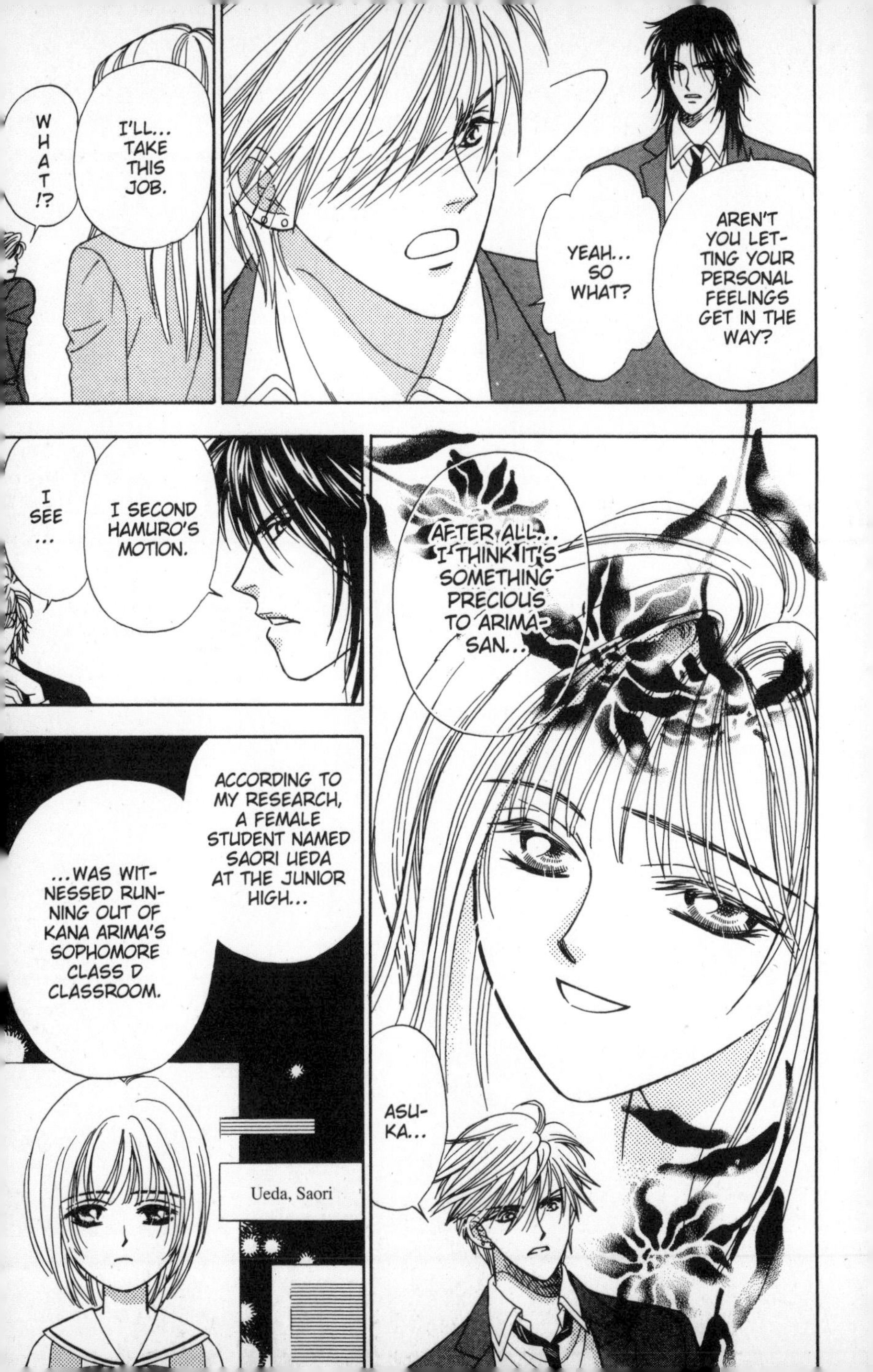
AREN'T YOU LET-TING YOUR PERSONAL FEELINGS GET IN THE WAY?
YEAH... SO WHAT?
I'LL... TAKE THIS JOB.
WHAT!?
AFTER ALL... I THINK IT'S SOMETHING PRECIOUS TO ARIMA-SAN...
I SECOND HAMURO'S MOTION.
I SEE...
ASU-KA...
ACCORDING TO MY RESEARCH, A FEMALE STUDENT NAMED SAORI UEDA AT THE JUNIOR HIGH...
...WAS WIT-NESSED RUN-NING OUT OF KANA ARIMA'S SOPHOMORE CLASS D CLASSROOM.
Ueda, Saori

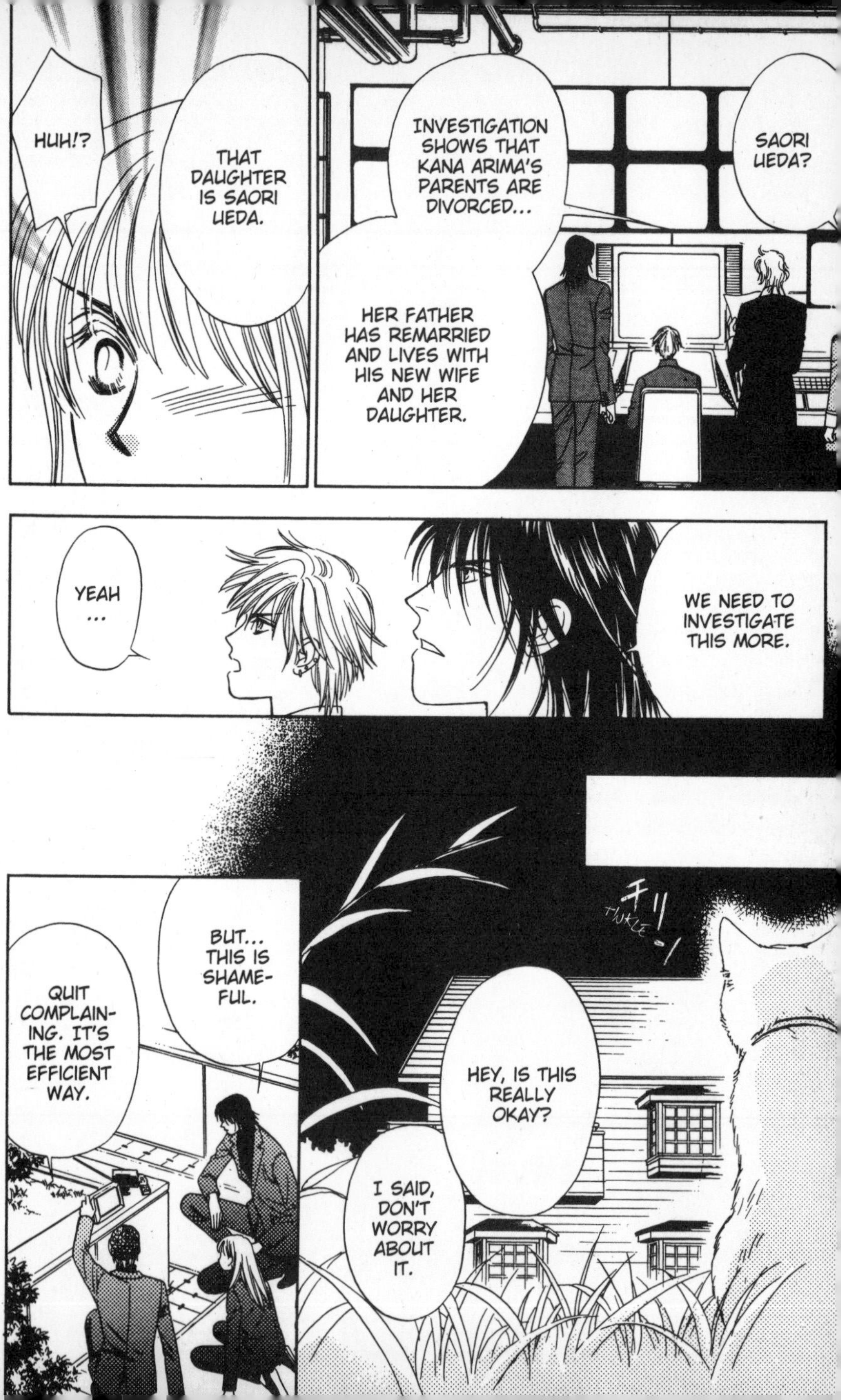
SAORI UEDA?
INVESTIGATION SHOWS THAT KANA ARIMA'S PARENTS ARE DIVORCED...
HER FATHER HAS REMARRIED AND LIVES WITH HIS NEW WIFE AND HER DAUGHTER.
THAT DAUGHTER IS SAORI UEDA.
HUH!?
WE NEED TO INVESTIGATE THIS MORE.
YEAH ...
チリ TINKLE
HEY, IS THIS REALLY OKAY?
I SAID, DON'T WORRY ABOUT IT.
BUT... THIS IS SHAME-FUL.
QUIT COMPLAIN-ING. IT'S THE MOST EFFICIENT WAY.

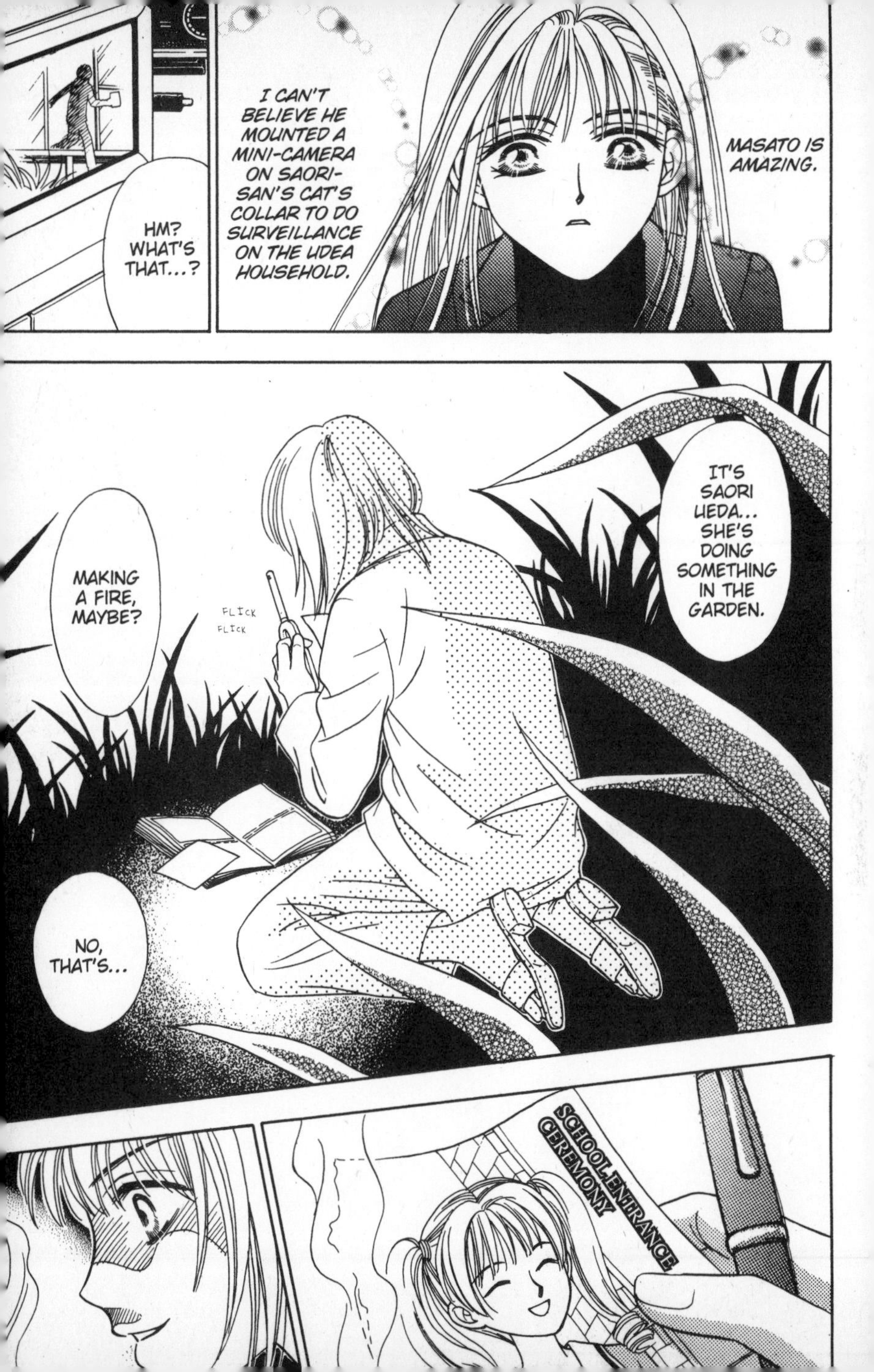
MASATO IS AMAZING.
I CAN'T BELIEVE HE MOUNTED A MINI-CAMERA ON SAORI-SAN'S CAT'S COLLAR TO DO SURVEILLANCE ON THE UDEA HOUSEHOLD.
HM? WHAT'S THAT...?
IT'S SAORI UEDA... SHE'S DOING SOMETHING IN THE GARDEN.
FLICK
FLICK
MAKING A FIRE, MAYBE?
NO, THAT'S...
SCHOOL ENTRANCE CEREMONY

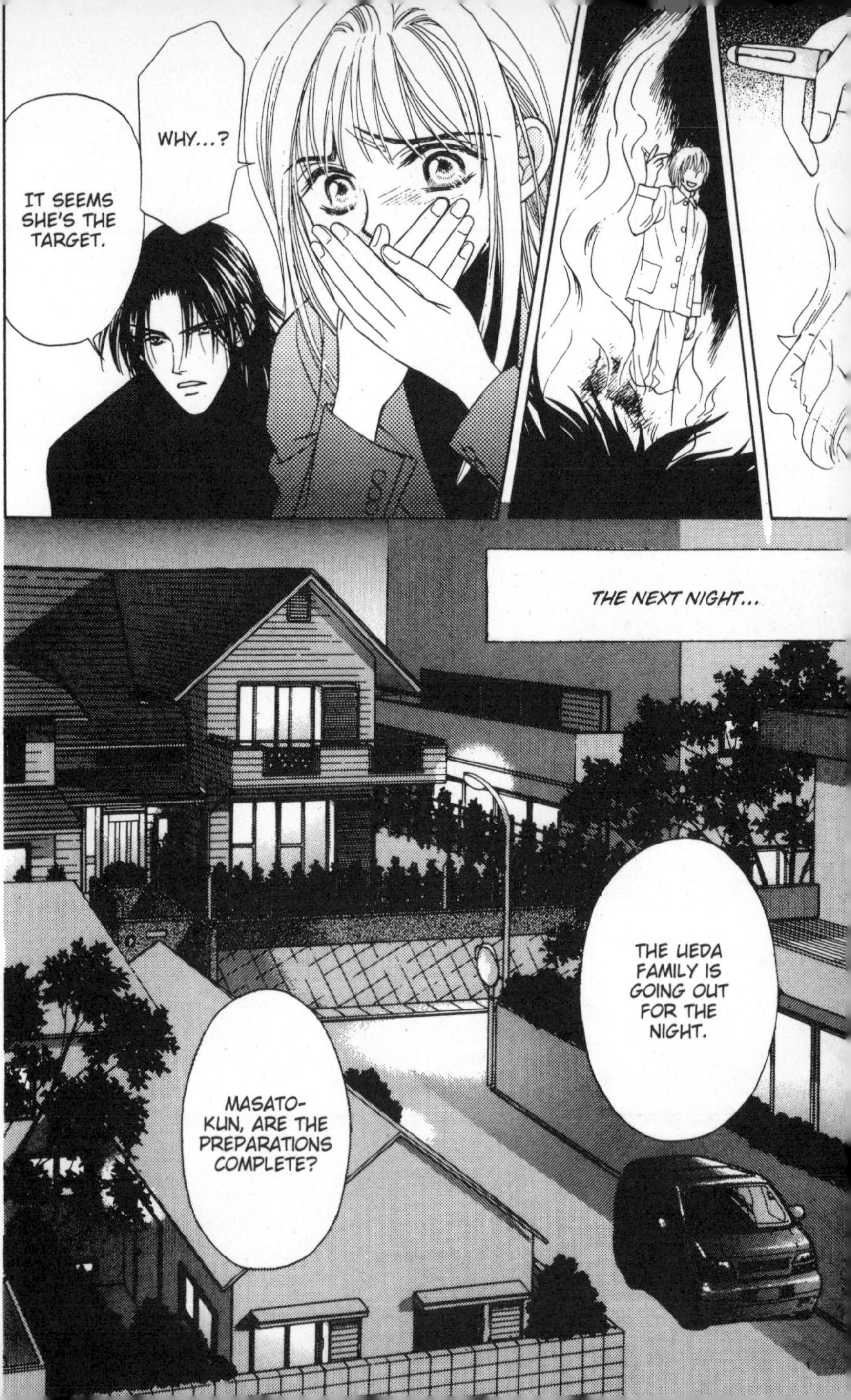
WHY...?
IT SEEMS SHE'S THE TARGET.
THE NEXT NIGHT...
THE UEDA FAMILY IS GOING OUT FOR THE NIGHT.
MASATO-KUN, ARE THE PREPARATIONS COMPLETE?

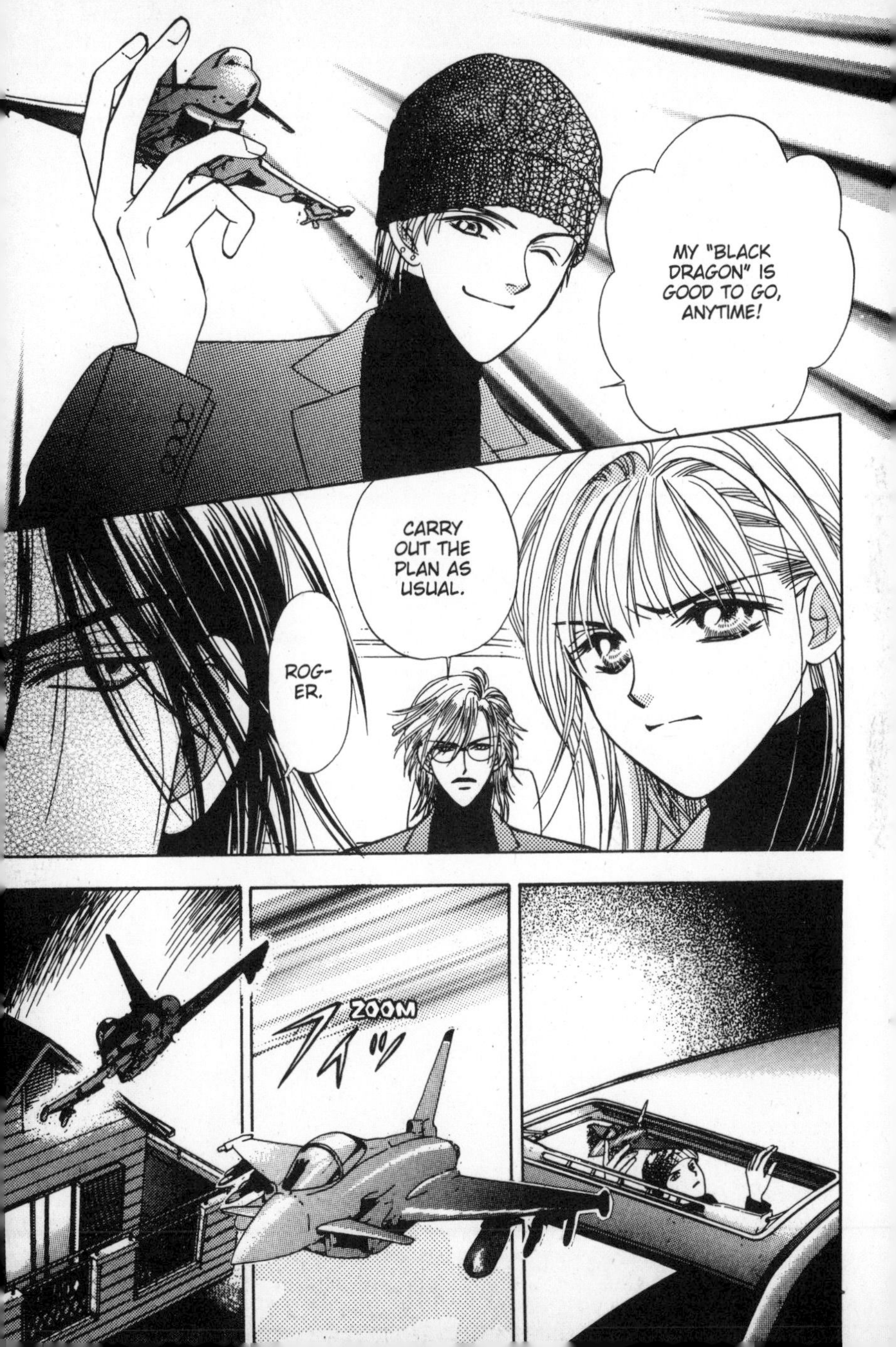
MY "BLACK DRAGON" IS GOOD TO GO, ANYTIME!
CARRY OUT THE PLAN AS USUAL.
ROG-ER.
ZOOM

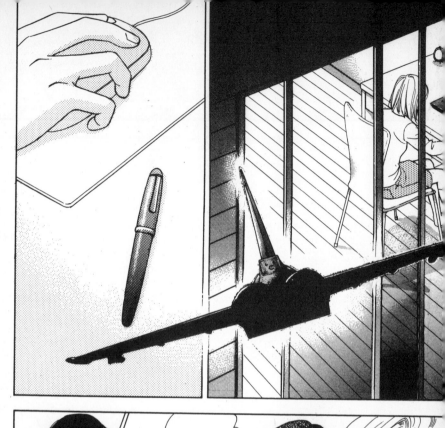

GOT IT!

AH...!

BUMP
トズッ

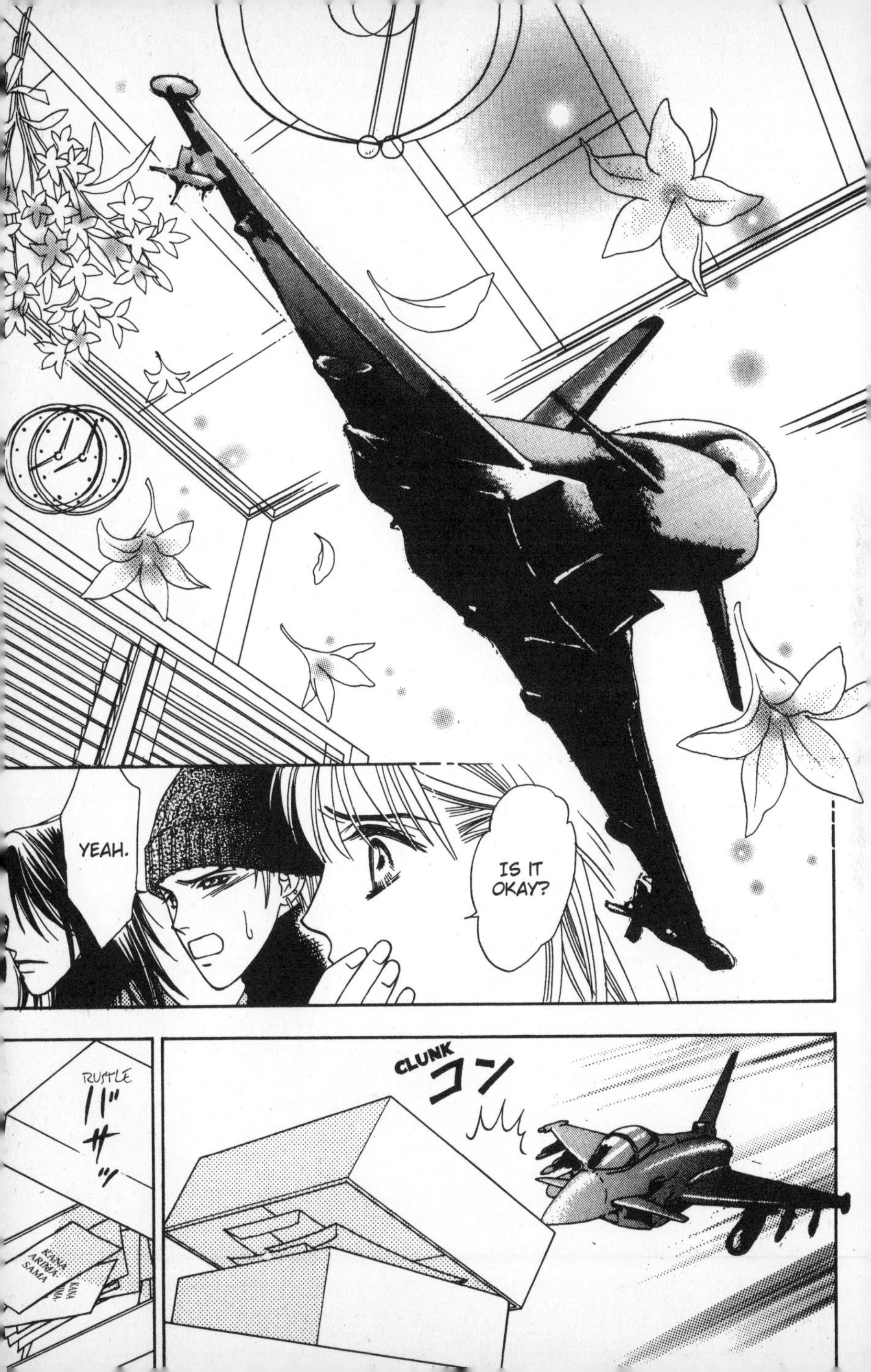
IS IT OKAY?
YEAH.
CLUNK
コン
RUSTLE
バサッ
KANA ARIMA SAMA

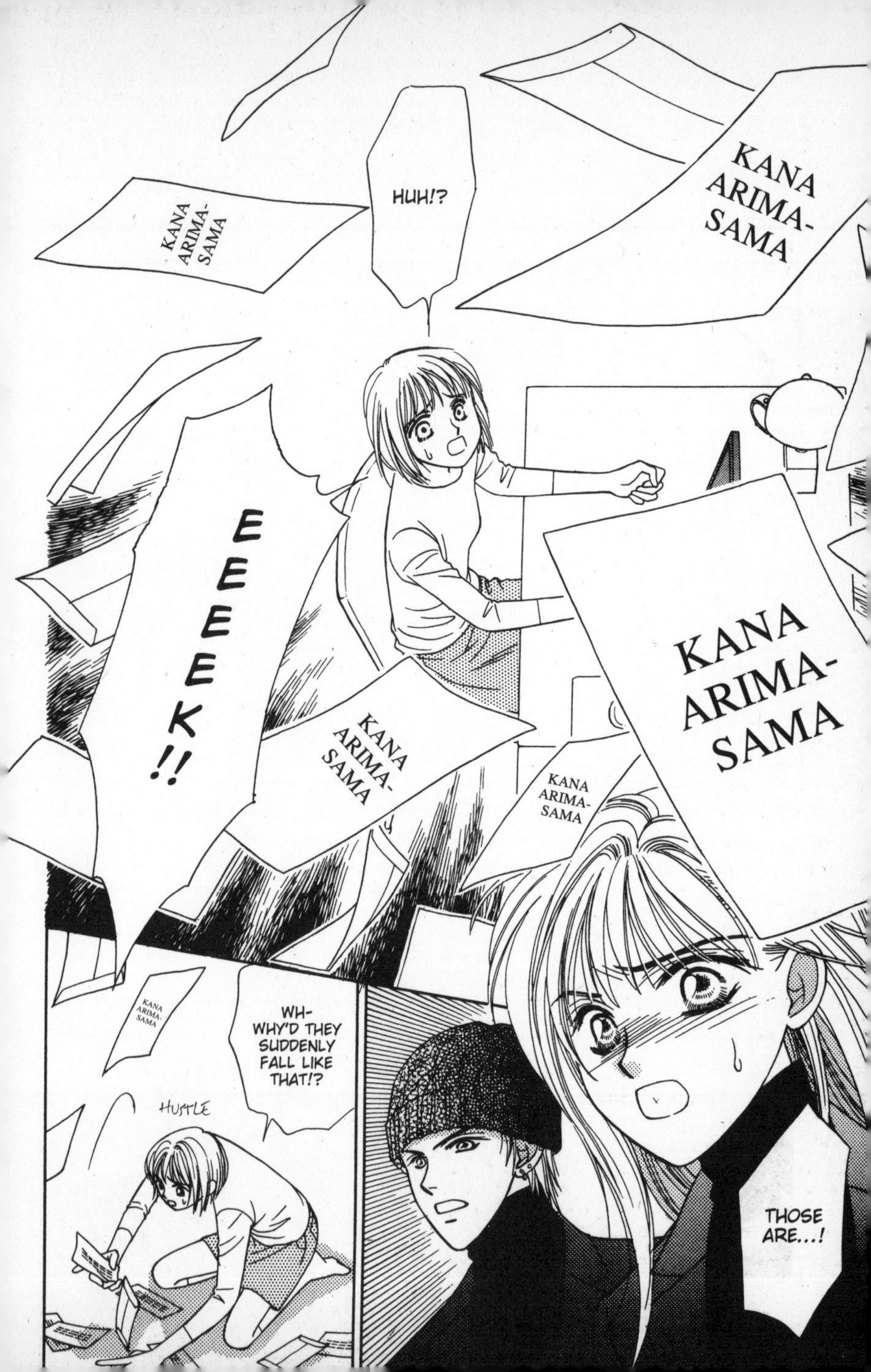
KANA
ARIMA-
SAMA
HUH!?
KANA
ARIMA-
SAMA
KANA
ARIMA-
SAMA
EEEEK!!
KANA
ARIMA-
SAMA
KANA
ARIMA-
SAMA
KANA
ARIMA-
SAMA
THOSE
ARE...!
KANA
ARIMA-
SAMA
WH-
WHY'D THEY
SUDDENLY
FALL LIKE
THAT!?
HUSTLE

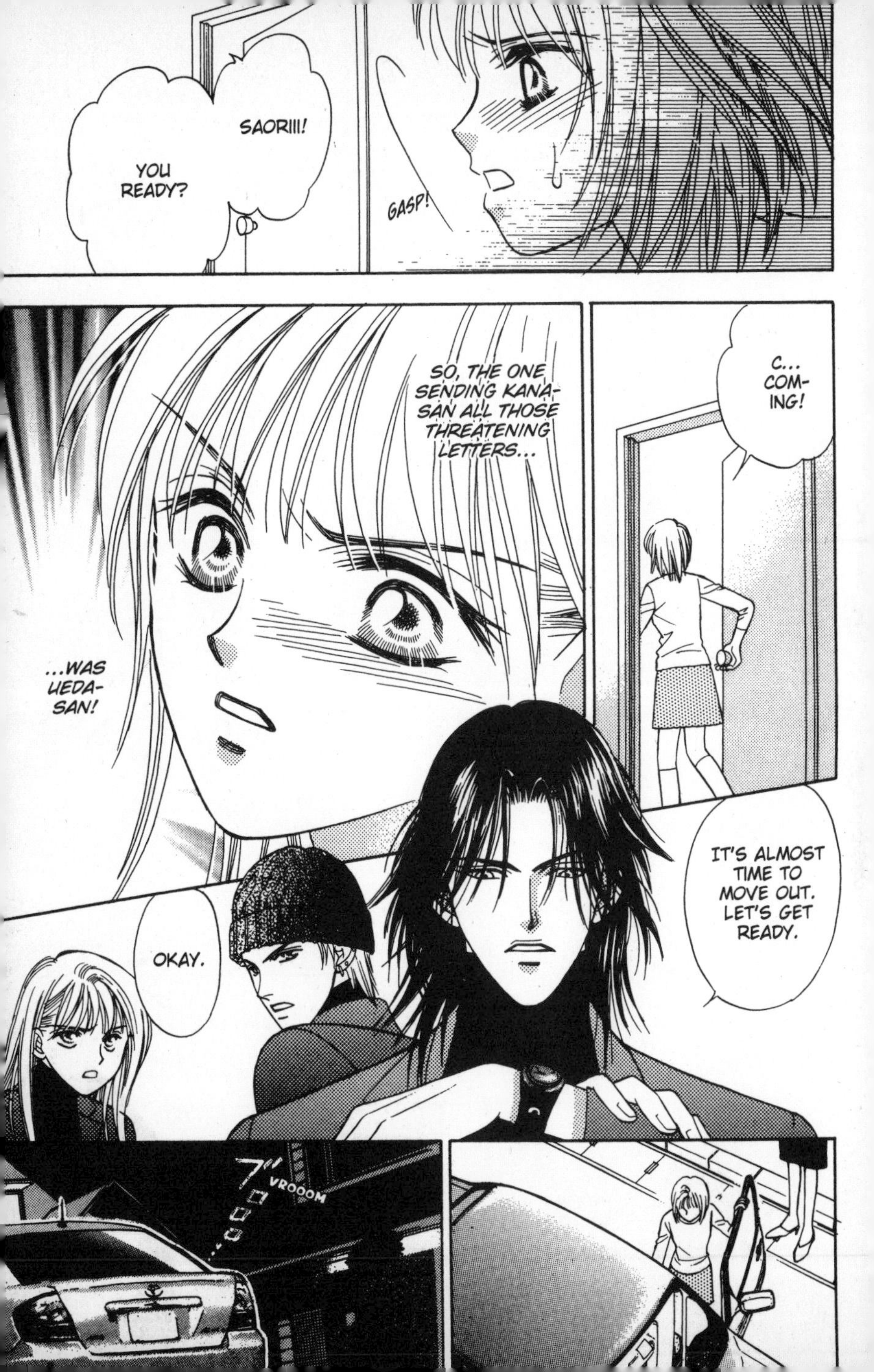
GASP!
SAORIII!
YOU READY?
C... COMING!
SO, THE ONE SENDING KANA-SAN ALL THOSE THREATENING LETTERS...
...WAS UEDA-SAN!
IT'S ALMOST TIME TO MOVE OUT. LET'S GET READY.
OKAY.
VROOOM

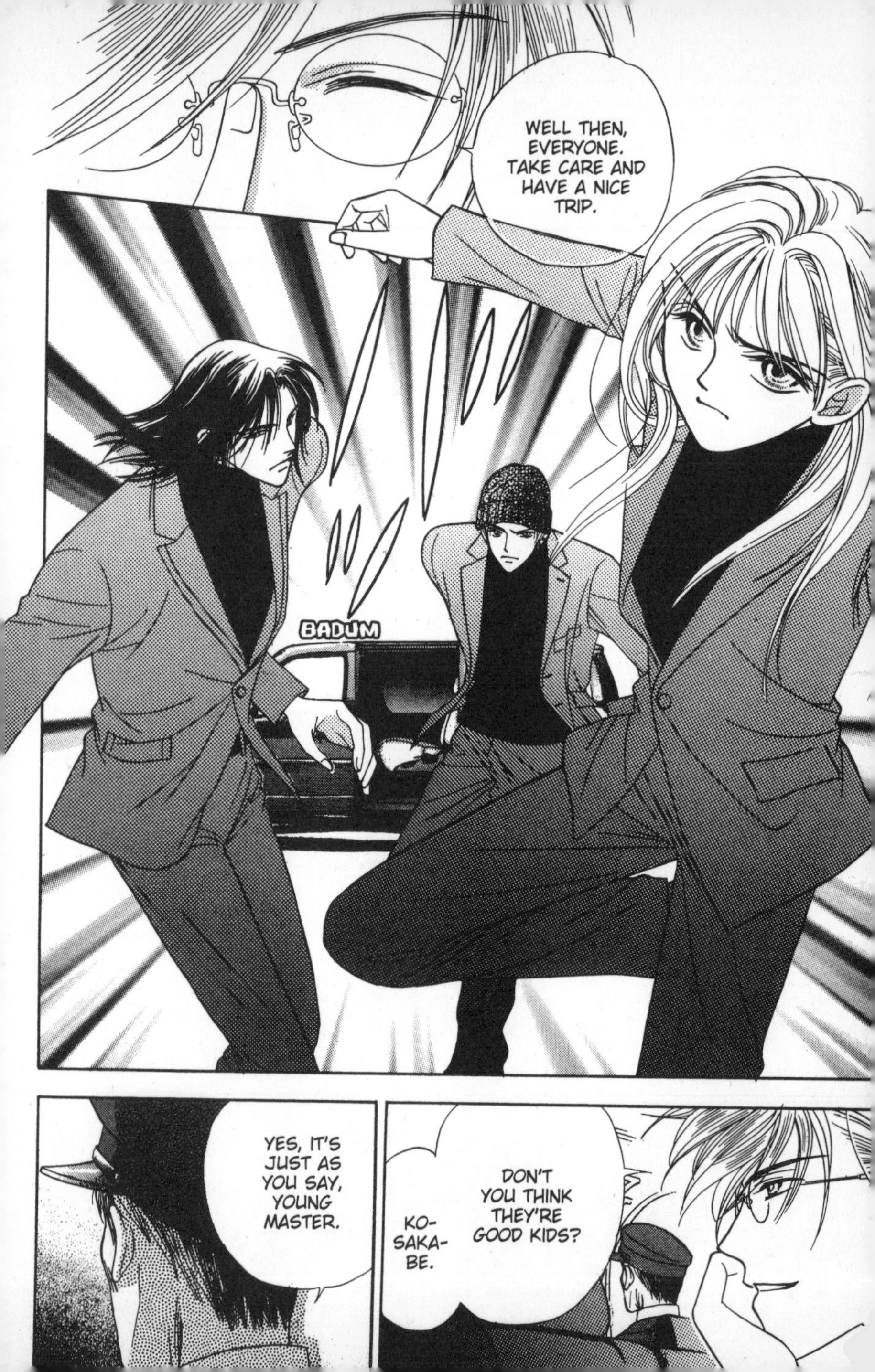
WELL THEN, EVERYONE. TAKE CARE AND HAVE A NICE TRIP.
BADUM
DON'T YOU THINK THEY'RE GOOD KIDS?
KO-SAKA-BE.
YES, IT'S JUST AS YOU SAY, YOUNG MASTER.

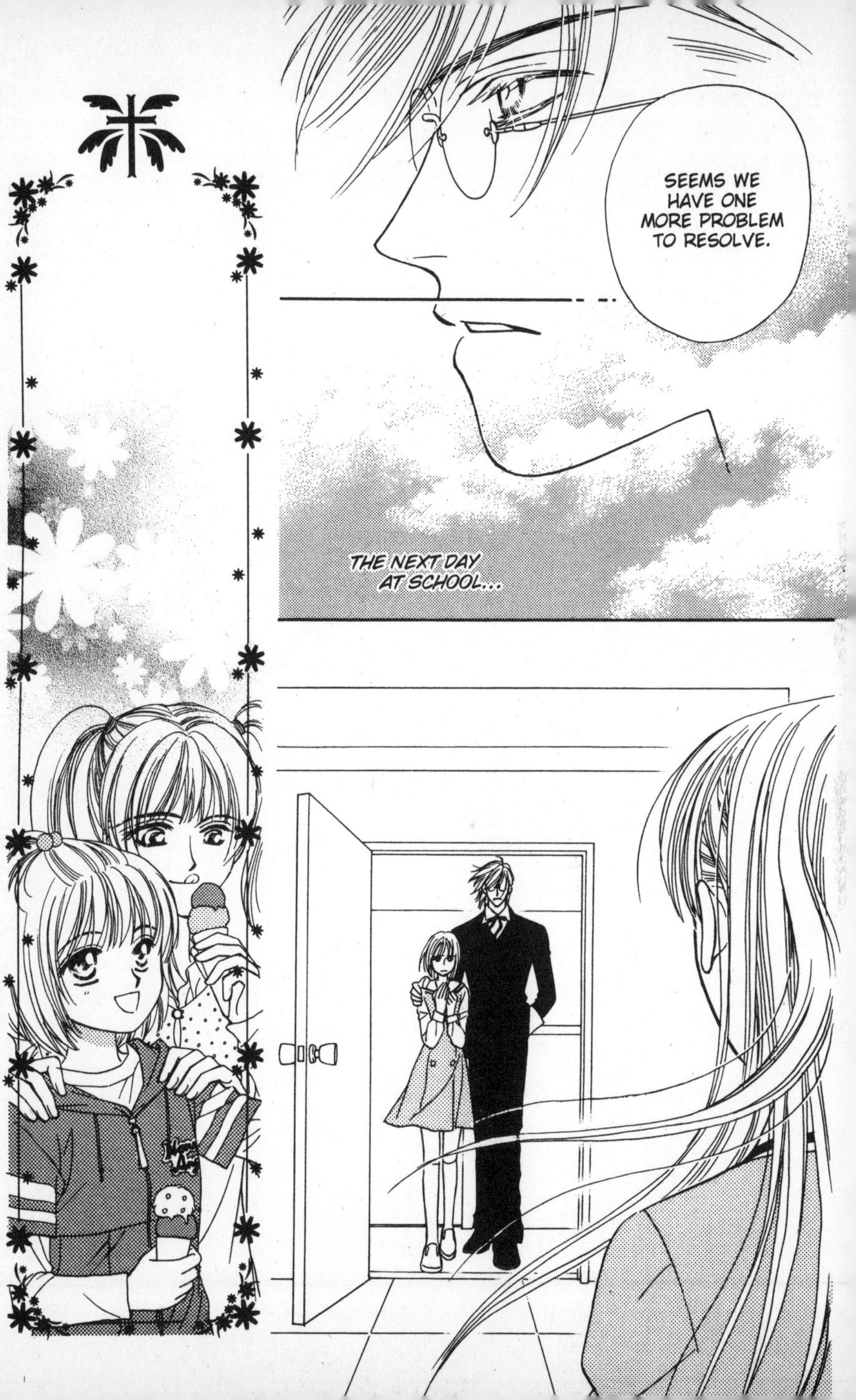
SEEMS WE HAVE ONE MORE PROBLEM TO RESOLVE.
THE NEXT DAY AT SCHOOL...

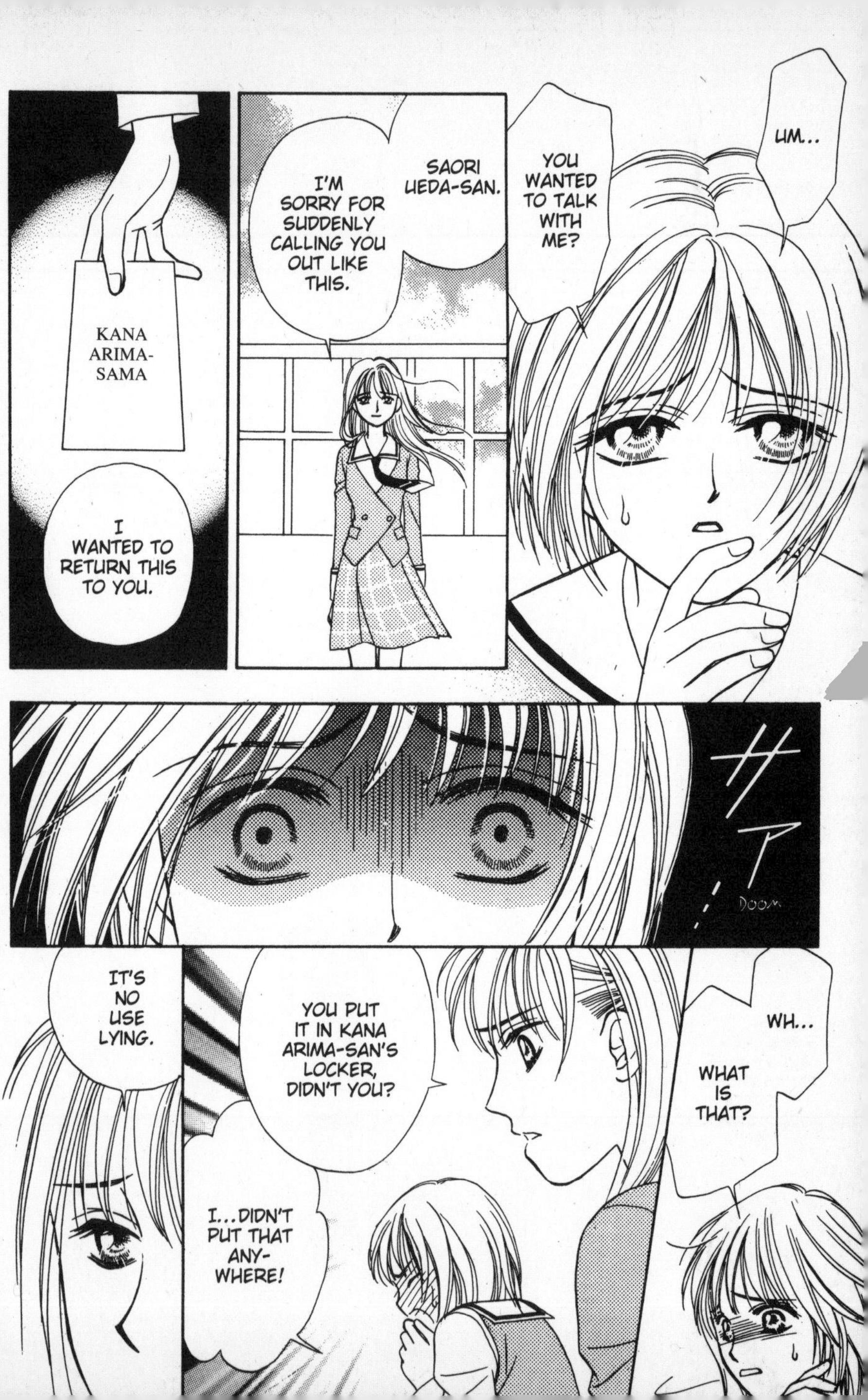
UM...
YOU WANTED TO TALK WITH ME?
SAORI UEDA-SAN.
I'M SORRY FOR SUDDENLY CALLING YOU OUT LIKE THIS.
KANA ARIMA-SAMA
I WANTED TO RETURN THIS TO YOU.
DOOM
WH...
WHAT IS THAT?
YOU PUT IT IN KANA ARIMA-SAN'S LOCKER, DIDN'T YOU?
IT'S NO USE LYING.
I...DIDN'T PUT THAT ANY-WHERE!

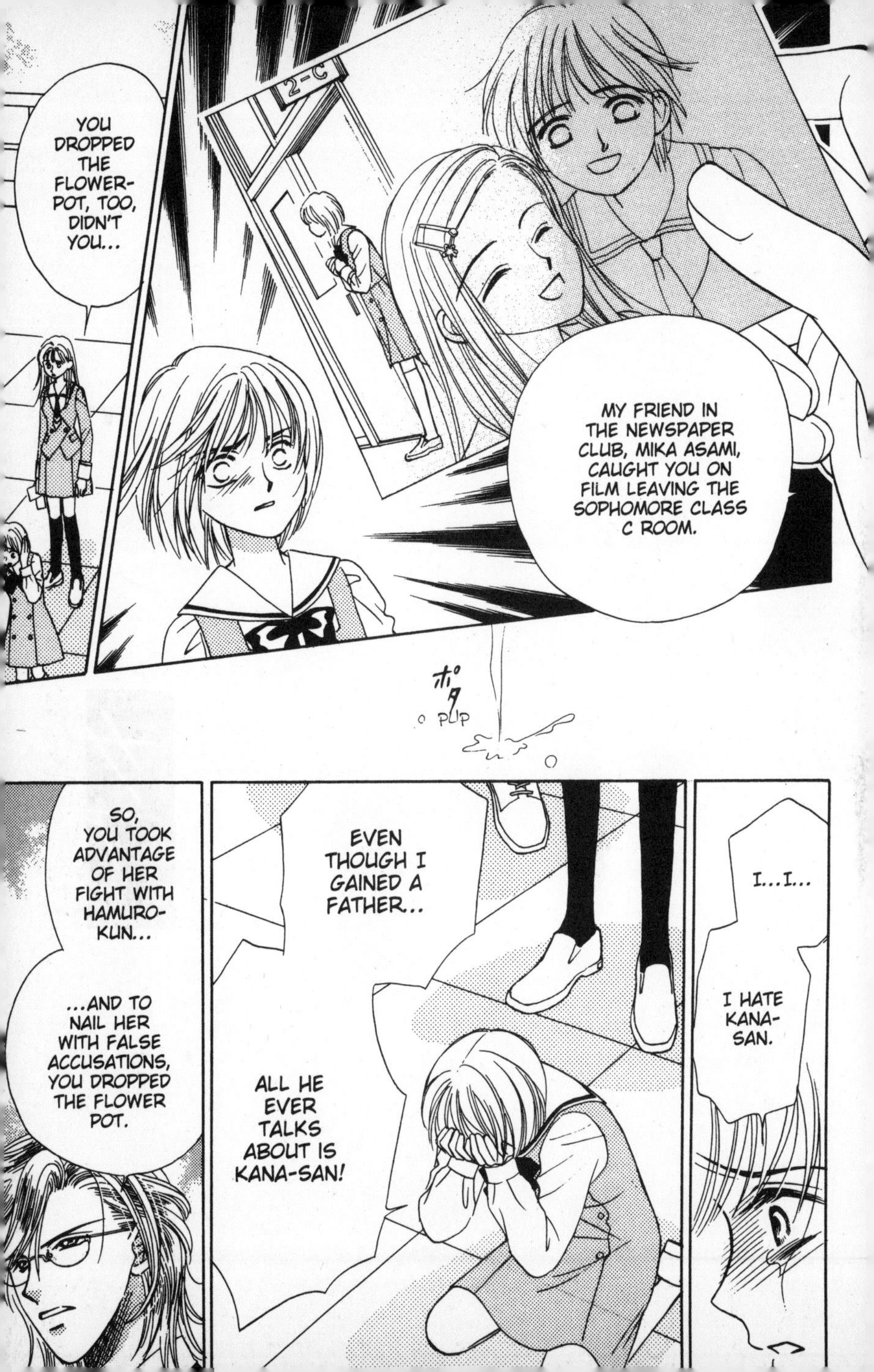
MY FRIEND IN THE NEWSPAPER CLUB, MIKA ASAMI, CAUGHT YOU ON FILM LEAVING THE SOPHOMORE CLASS C ROOM.
YOU DROPPED THE FLOWER-POT, TOO, DIDN'T YOU...
2-C
ポタ
PLIP
I...I...
I HATE KANA-SAN.
EVEN THOUGH I GAINED A FATHER...
ALL HE EVER TALKS ABOUT IS KANA-SAN!
SO, YOU TOOK ADVANTAGE OF HER FIGHT WITH HAMURO-KUN...
...AND TO NAIL HER WITH FALSE ACCUSATIONS, YOU DROPPED THE FLOWER POT.

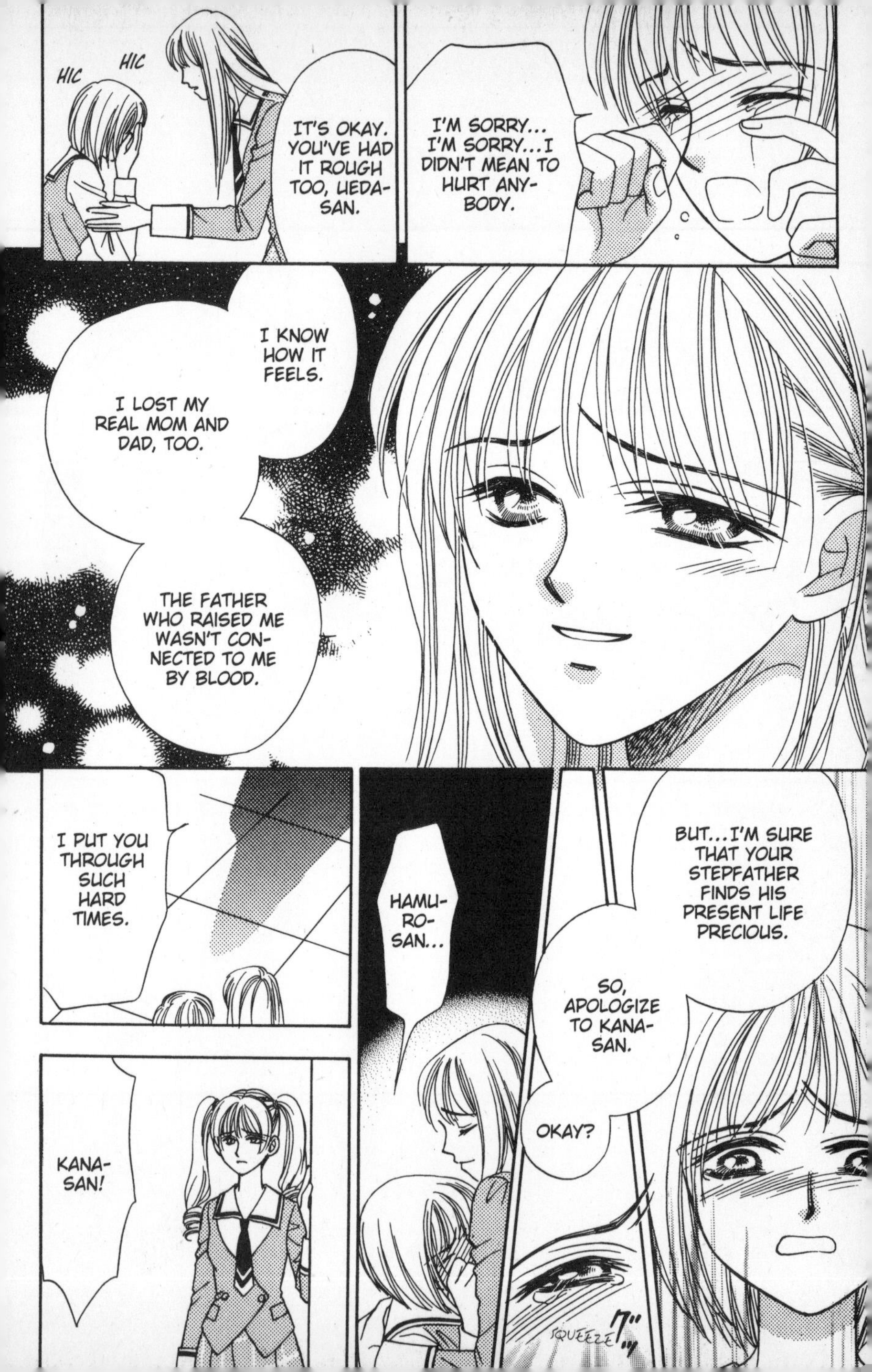
I'M SORRY... I'M SORRY... I DIDN'T MEAN TO HURT ANYBODY.
HIC
HIC
IT'S OKAY. YOU'VE HAD IT ROUGH TOO, UEDA-SAN.
I KNOW HOW IT FEELS.
I LOST MY REAL MOM AND DAD, TOO.
THE FATHER WHO RAISED ME WASN'T CONNECTED TO ME BY BLOOD.
BUT... I'M SURE THAT YOUR STEPFATHER FINDS HIS PRESENT LIFE PRECIOUS.
SO, APOLOGIZE TO KANA-SAN.
OKAY?
SQUEEZE
HAMURO-SAN...
I PUT YOU THROUGH SUCH HARD TIMES.
KANA-SAN!

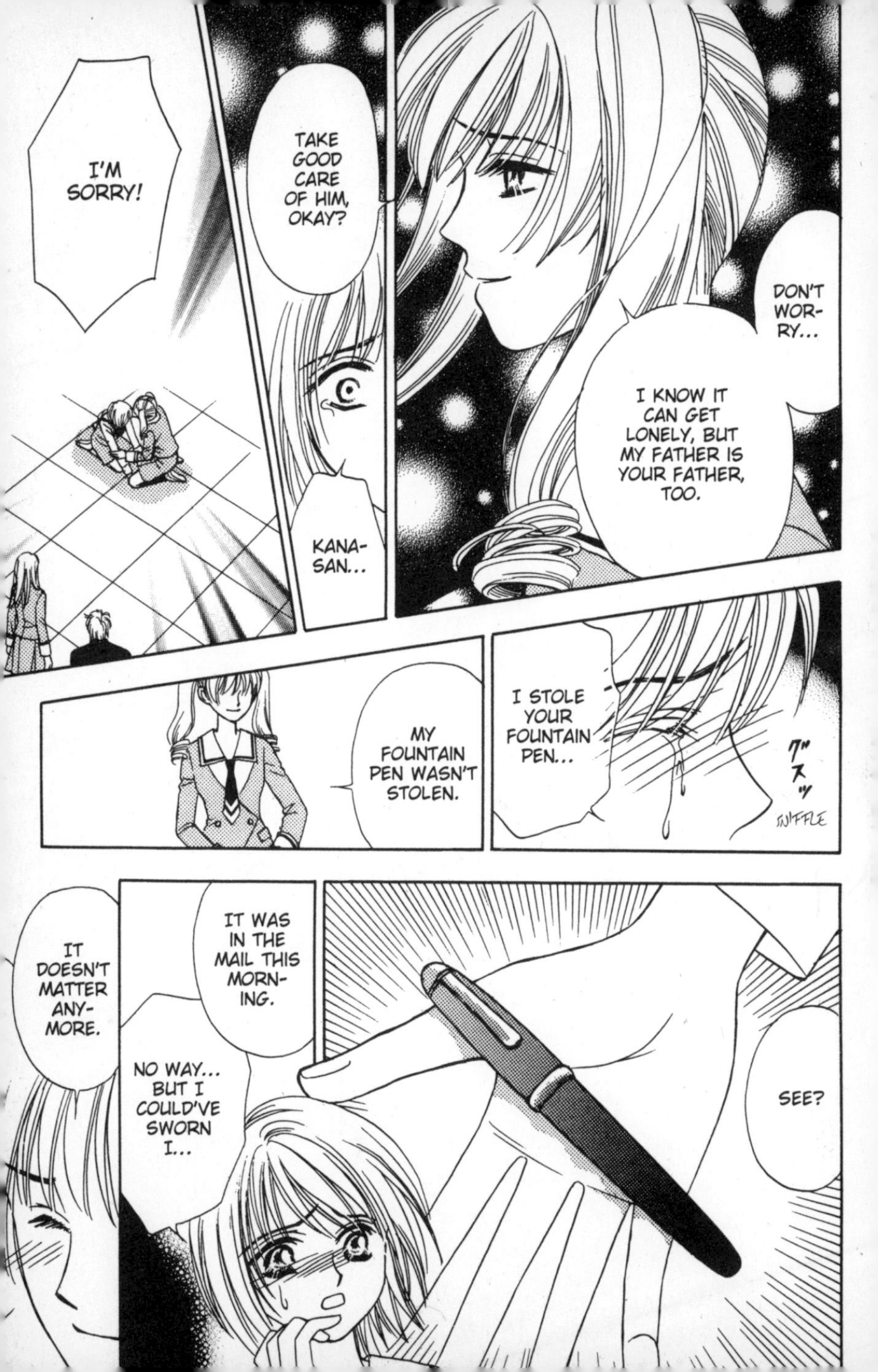
DON'T WORRY...
I KNOW IT CAN GET LONELY, BUT MY FATHER IS YOUR FATHER, TOO.
TAKE GOOD CARE OF HIM, OKAY?
KANA-SAN...
I'M SORRY!
グスッ
SNIFFLE
I STOLE YOUR FOUNTAIN PEN...
MY FOUNTAIN PEN WASN'T STOLEN.
SEE?
IT WAS IN THE MAIL THIS MORNING.
NO WAY... BUT I COULD'VE SWORN I...
IT DOESN'T MATTER ANYMORE.

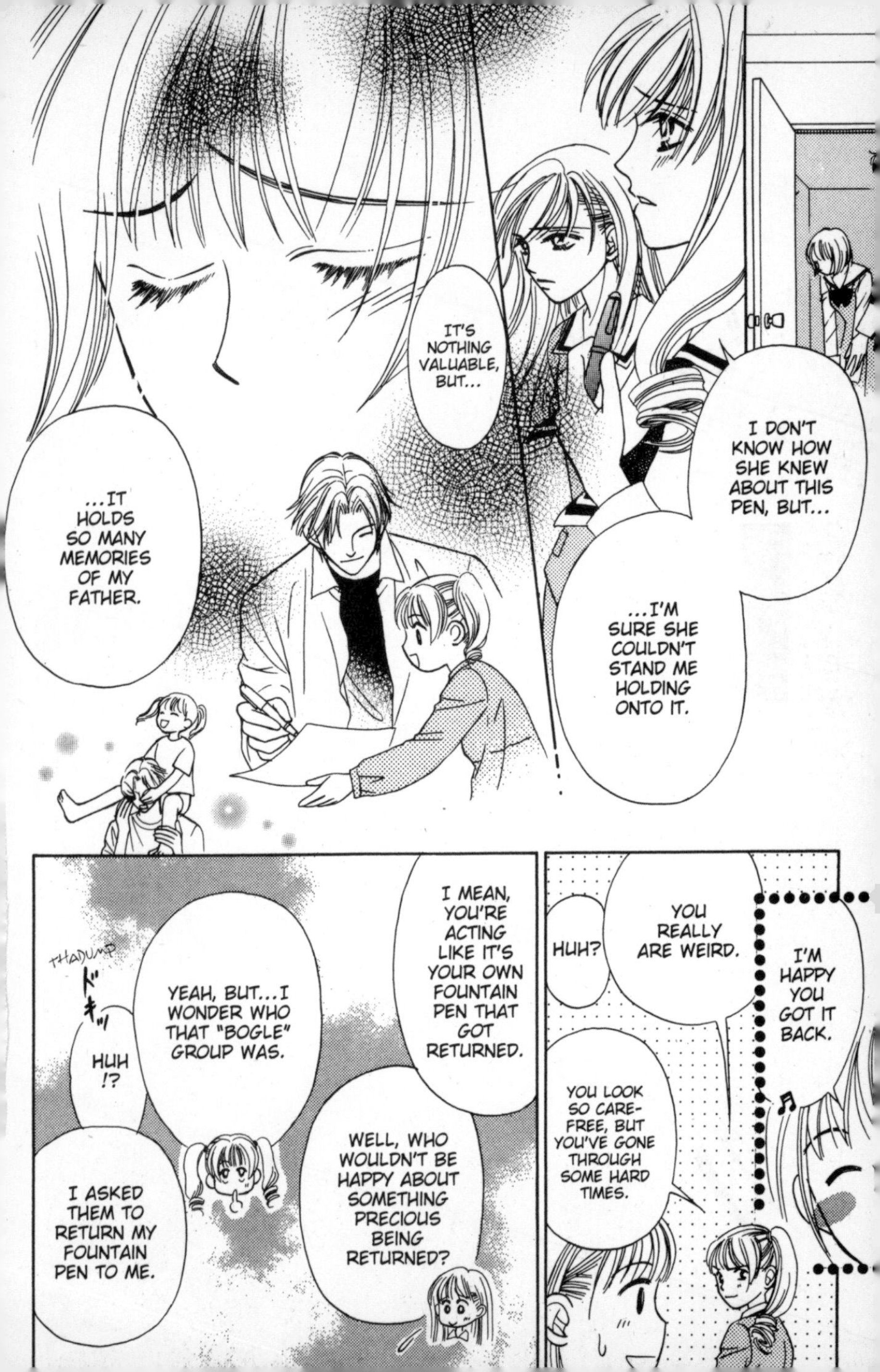
I DON'T KNOW HOW SHE KNEW ABOUT THIS PEN, BUT...
...I'M SURE SHE COULDN'T STAND ME HOLDING ONTO IT.
IT'S NOTHING VALUABLE, BUT...
...IT HOLDS SO MANY MEMORIES OF MY FATHER.
I'M HAPPY YOU GOT IT BACK.
YOU REALLY ARE WEIRD.
HUH?
YOU LOOK SO CARE-FREE, BUT YOU'VE GONE THROUGH SOME HARD TIMES.
I MEAN, YOU'RE ACTING LIKE IT'S YOUR OWN FOUNTAIN PEN THAT GOT RETURNED.
WELL, WHO WOULDN'T BE HAPPY ABOUT SOMETHING PRECIOUS BEING RETURNED?
YEAH, BUT...I WONDER WHO THAT "BOGLE" GROUP WAS.
THADUMP
ドキッ
HUH!?
I ASKED THEM TO RETURN MY FOUNTAIN PEN TO ME.

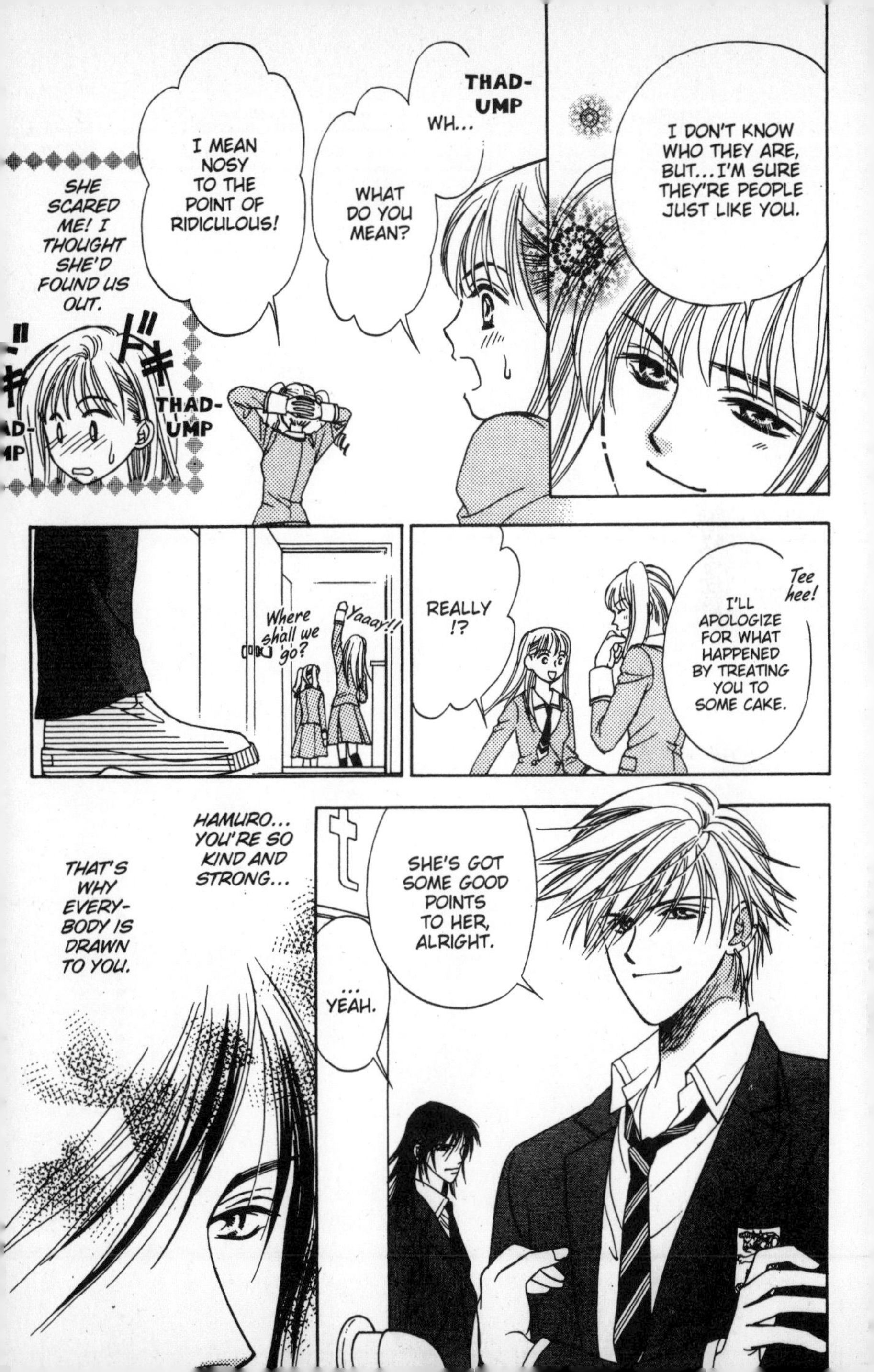
I DON'T KNOW WHO THEY ARE, BUT...I'M SURE THEY'RE PEOPLE JUST LIKE YOU.
THAD-UMP
WH...
WHAT DO YOU MEAN?
I MEAN NOSY TO THE POINT OF RIDICULOUS!
SHE SCARED ME! I THOUGHT SHE'D FOUND US OUT.
THAD-UMP
Tee hee!
I'LL APOLOGIZE FOR WHAT HAPPENED BY TREATING YOU TO SOME CAKE.
REALLY !?
Yaaay!!
Where shall we go?
SHE'S GOT SOME GOOD POINTS TO HER, ALRIGHT.
...YEAH.
HAMURO... YOU'RE SO KIND AND STRONG...
THAT'S WHY EVERY-BODY IS DRAWN TO YOU.

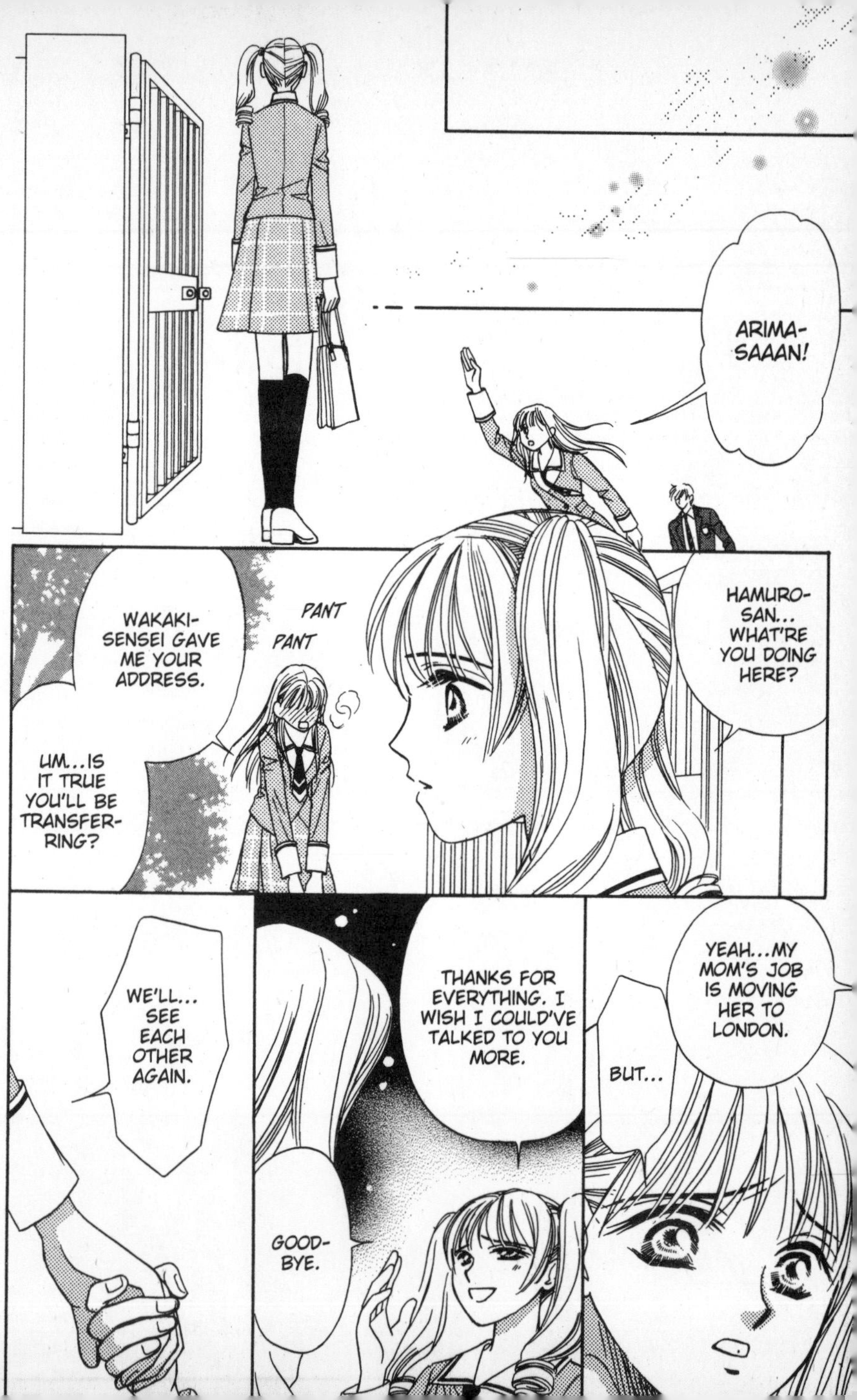
ARIMA-SAAAN!
HAMURO-SAN... WHAT'RE YOU DOING HERE?
PANT PANT
WAKAKI-SENSEI GAVE ME YOUR ADDRESS.
UM...IS IT TRUE YOU'LL BE TRANSFERRING?
YEAH...MY MOM'S JOB IS MOVING HER TO LONDON.
BUT...
THANKS FOR EVERYTHING. I WISH I COULD'VE TALKED TO YOU MORE.
GOOD-BYE.
WE'LL... SEE EACH OTHER AGAIN.

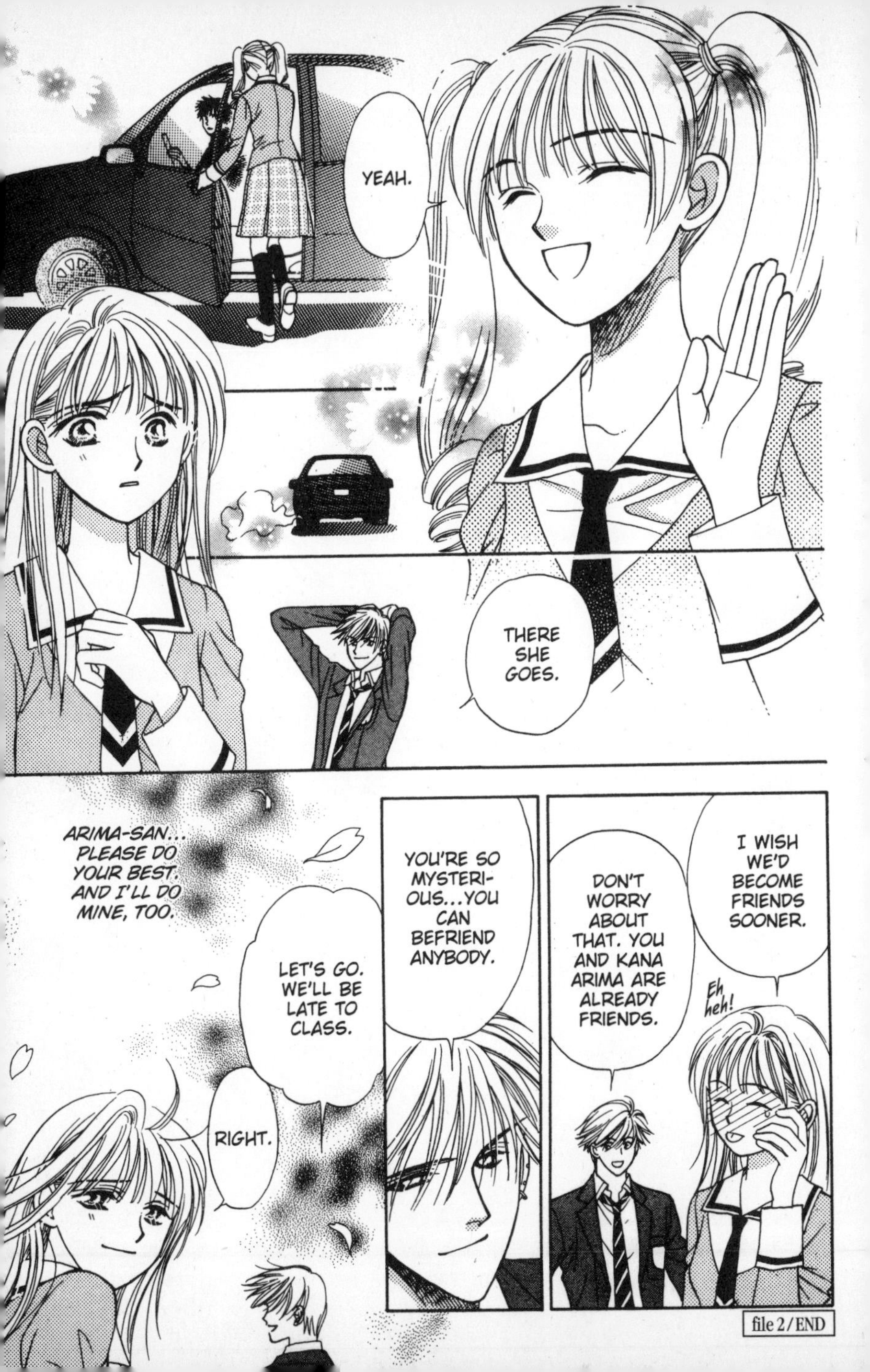
YEAH.
THERE SHE GOES.
I WISH WE'D BECOME FRIENDS SOONER.
Eh heh!
DON'T WORRY ABOUT THAT. YOU AND KANA ARIMA ARE ALREADY FRIENDS.
YOU'RE SO MYSTERI-OUS...YOU CAN BEFRIEND ANYBODY.
LET'S GO. WE'LL BE LATE TO CLASS.
RIGHT.
ARIMA-SAN... PLEASE DO YOUR BEST. AND I'LL DO MINE, TOO.
file 2/END

Thank you for buying Bogle volume 1, today.
I'm Shino Taira who wrote the script for it.
I planned this story when I was 27 years old.
Since then, six years have passed.
At the initial stage, it was a story about four boys.
But since then, I've rewritten it so many times that now it is Asuka-chan...

Shino Taira

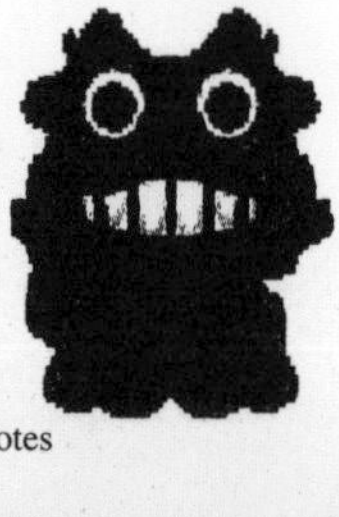

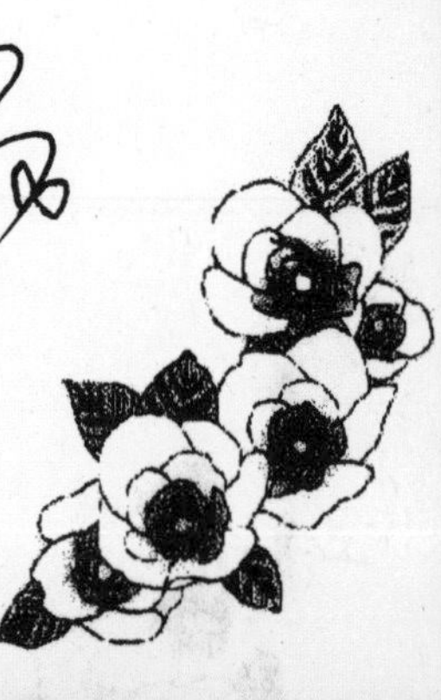

*See translator's notes

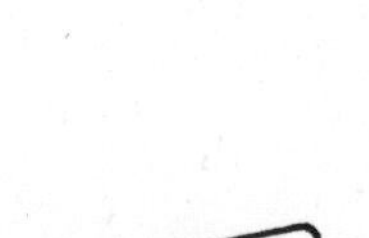

...who has been established as the main character.
Not only did I get to have Yuko Ichiju-sensei draw me some wonderful characters, but it even eventually went on sale as a comic!!
 I'm sure that when I'm not looking, the bogle fairy* is working his magic. ★ ★
At least, sometimes I think that.
I want to work even harder after this, to write a fun story.
So best wishes and regards hereafter.

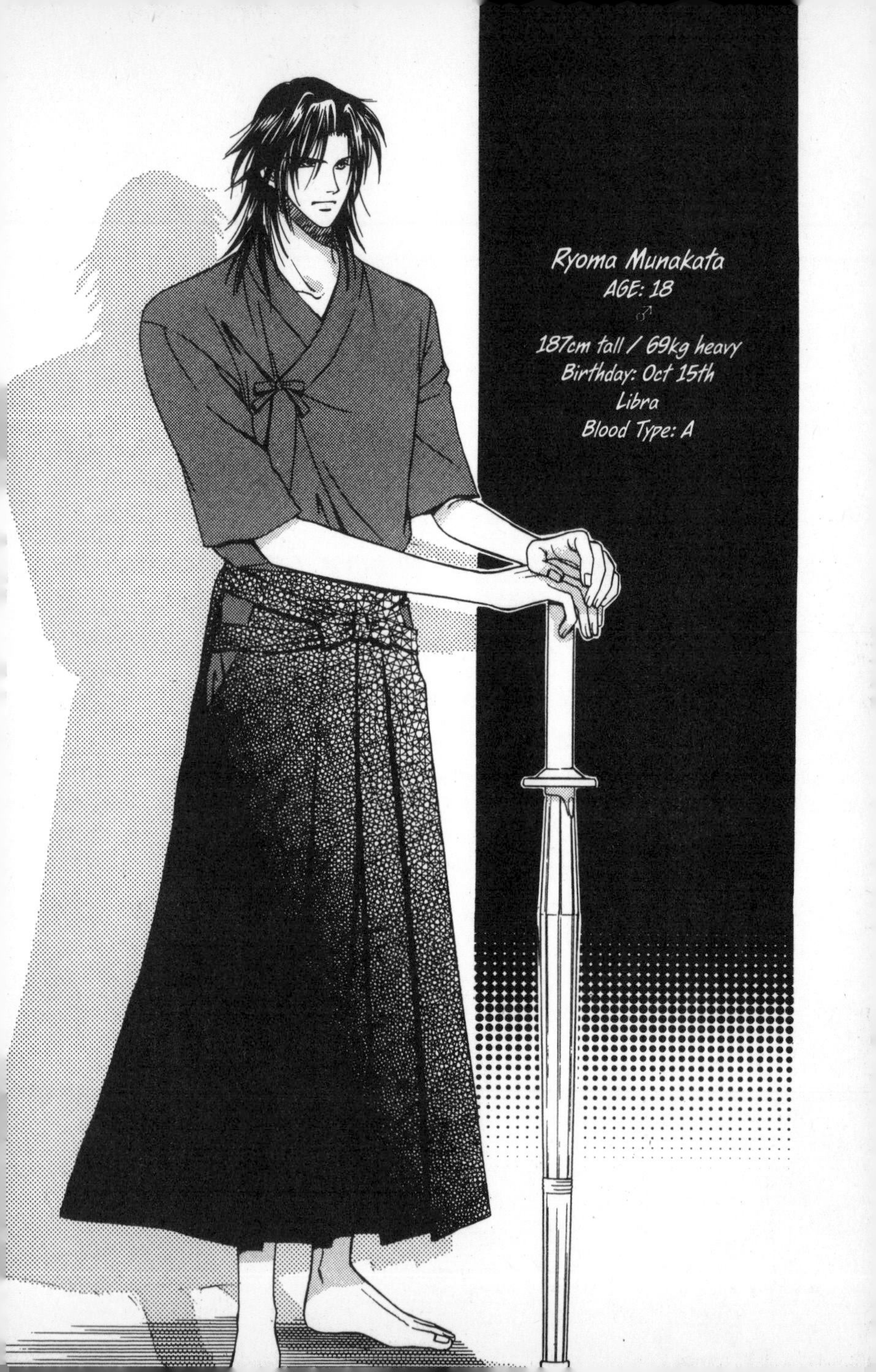
Ryoma Munakata
AGE: 18
♂
187cm tall / 69kg heavy
Birthday: Oct 15th
Libra
Blood Type: A

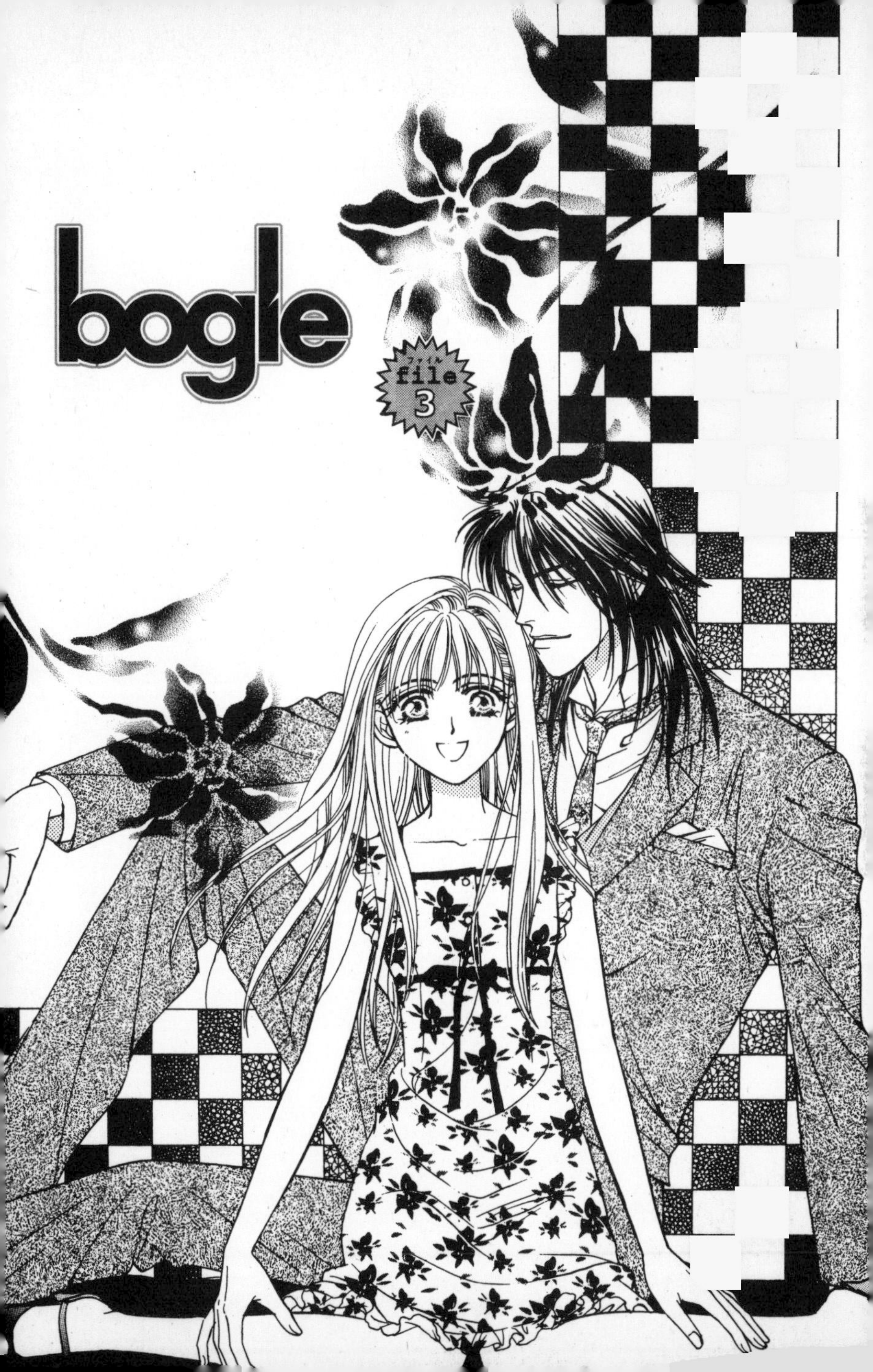
bogle
file
3

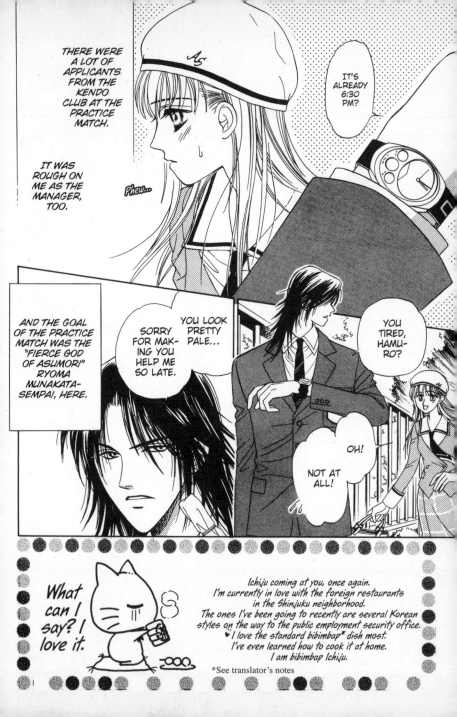

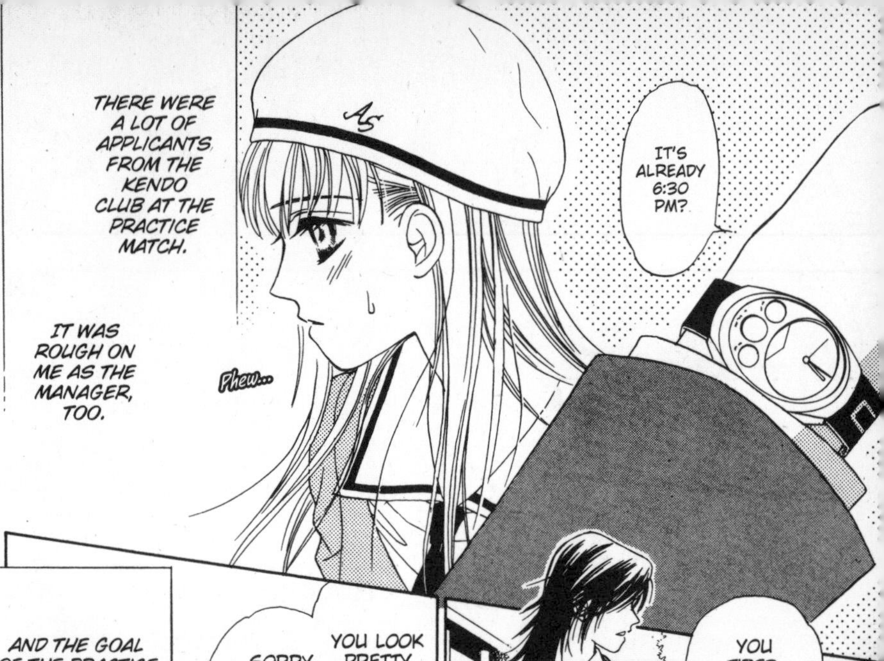
IT'S ALREADY 6:30 PM?
THERE WERE A LOT OF APPLICANTS FROM THE KENDO CLUB AT THE PRACTICE MATCH.
IT WAS ROUGH ON ME AS THE MANAGER, TOO.
Phew...
YOU TIRED, HAMURO?
OH!
NOT AT ALL!
YOU LOOK PRETTY PALE...
SORRY FOR MAKING YOU HELP ME SO LATE.
AND THE GOAL OF THE PRACTICE MATCH WAS THE "FIERCE GOD OF ASUMORI" RYOMA MUNAKATA-SEMPAI, HERE.

What can I say? I love it.

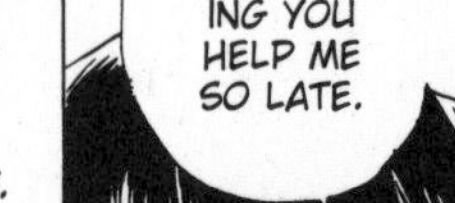

Ichiju coming at you, once again.
I'm currently in love with the foreign restaurants in the Shinjuku neighborhood.
The ones I've been going to recently are several Korean styles on the way to the public employment security office.
♥ I love the standard bibimbap dish most.*
I've even learned how to cook it at home.
I am bibimbap Ichiju.

*See translator's notes

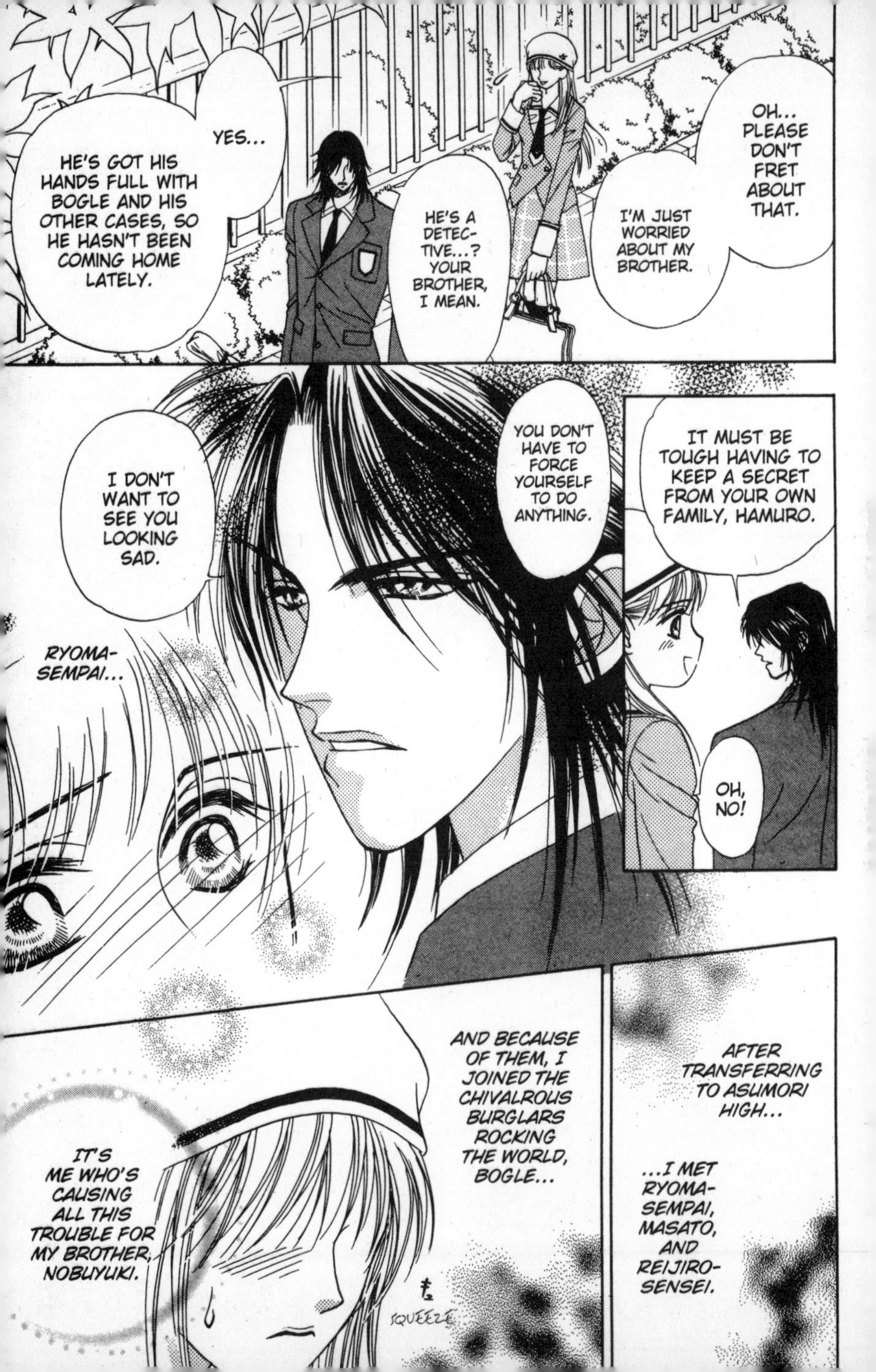
OH... PLEASE DON'T FRET ABOUT THAT.
I'M JUST WORRIED ABOUT MY BROTHER.
HE'S A DETECTIVE...? YOUR BROTHER, I MEAN.
YES...
HE'S GOT HIS HANDS FULL WITH BOGLE AND HIS OTHER CASES, SO HE HASN'T BEEN COMING HOME LATELY.
IT MUST BE TOUGH HAVING TO KEEP A SECRET FROM YOUR OWN FAMILY, HAMURO.
OH, NO!
YOU DON'T HAVE TO FORCE YOURSELF TO DO ANYTHING.
I DON'T WANT TO SEE YOU LOOKING SAD.
RYOMA-SEMPAI...
AFTER TRANSFERRING TO ASUMORI HIGH...
...I MET RYOMA-SEMPAI, MASATO, AND REIJIRO-SENSEI.
AND BECAUSE OF THEM, I JOINED THE CHIVALROUS BURGLARS ROCKING THE WORLD, BOGLE...
IT'S ME WHO'S CAUSING ALL THIS TROUBLE FOR MY BROTHER, NOBUYUKI.
SQUEEZE

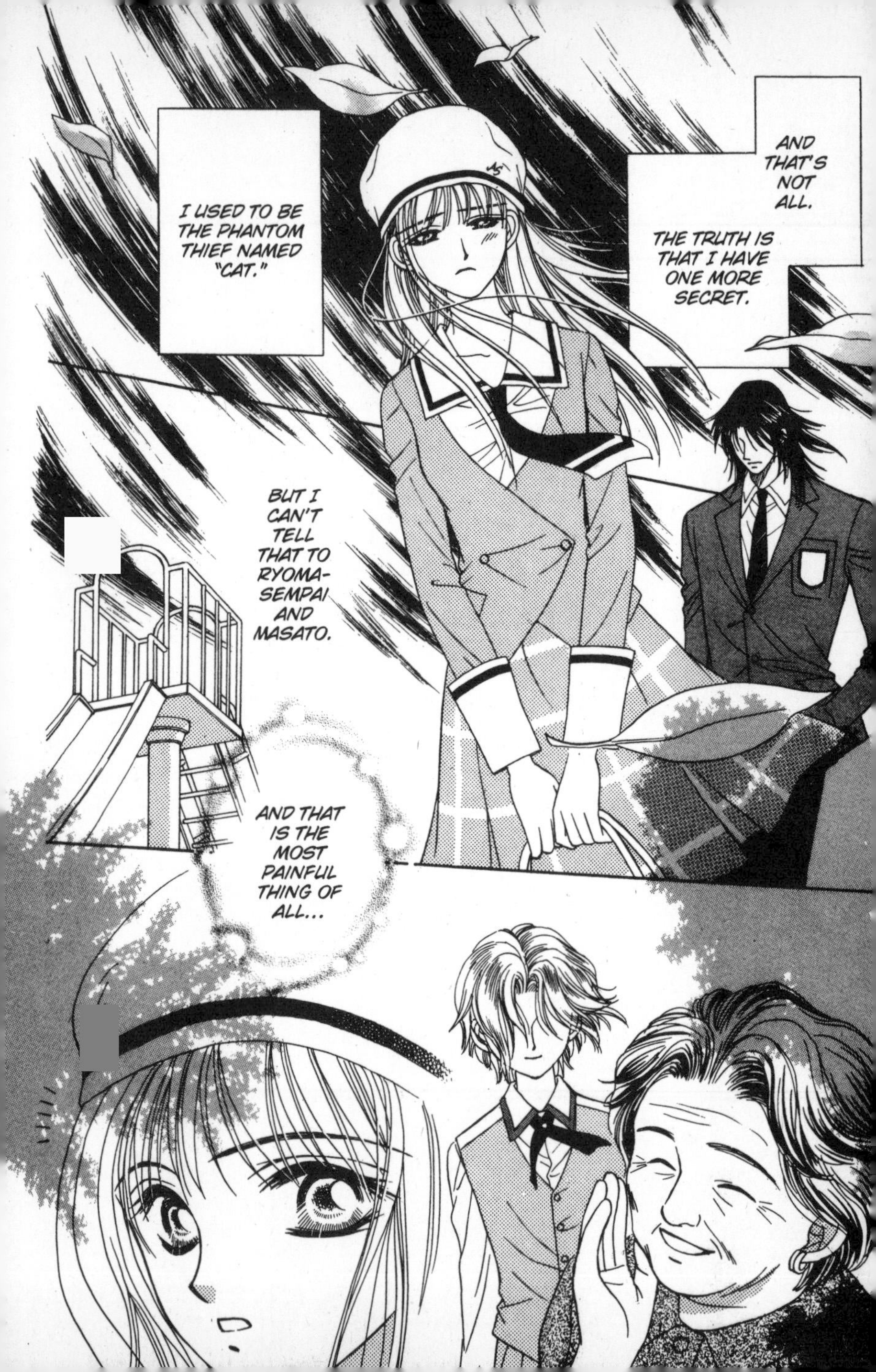
AND THAT'S NOT ALL.
THE TRUTH IS THAT I HAVE ONE MORE SECRET.
I USED TO BE THE PHANTOM THIEF NAMED "CAT."
BUT I CAN'T TELL THAT TO RYOMA-SEMPAI AND MASATO.
AND THAT IS THE MOST PAINFUL THING OF ALL...

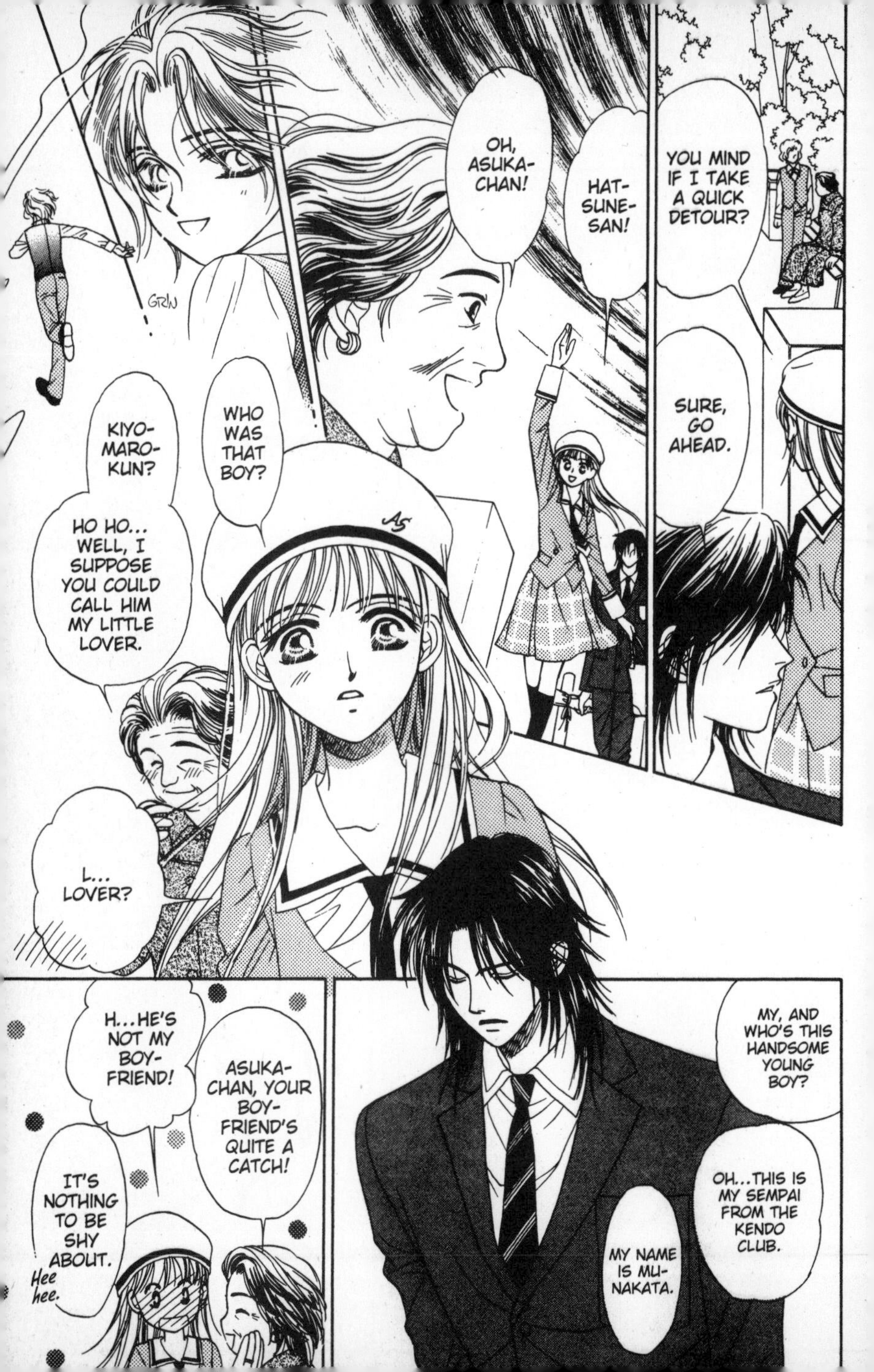
YOU MIND IF I TAKE A QUICK DETOUR?
SURE, GO AHEAD.
HAT-SUNE-SAN!
OH, ASUKA-CHAN!
GRIN
WHO WAS THAT BOY?
KIYO-MARO-KUN?
HO HO... WELL, I SUPPOSE YOU COULD CALL HIM MY LITTLE LOVER.
L... LOVER?
MY, AND WHO'S THIS HANDSOME YOUNG BOY?
OH...THIS IS MY SEMPAI FROM THE KENDO CLUB.
MY NAME IS MU-NAKATA.
ASUKA-CHAN, YOUR BOY-FRIEND'S QUITE A CATCH!
H...HE'S NOT MY BOY-FRIEND!
IT'S NOTHING TO BE SHY ABOUT.
Hee hee.

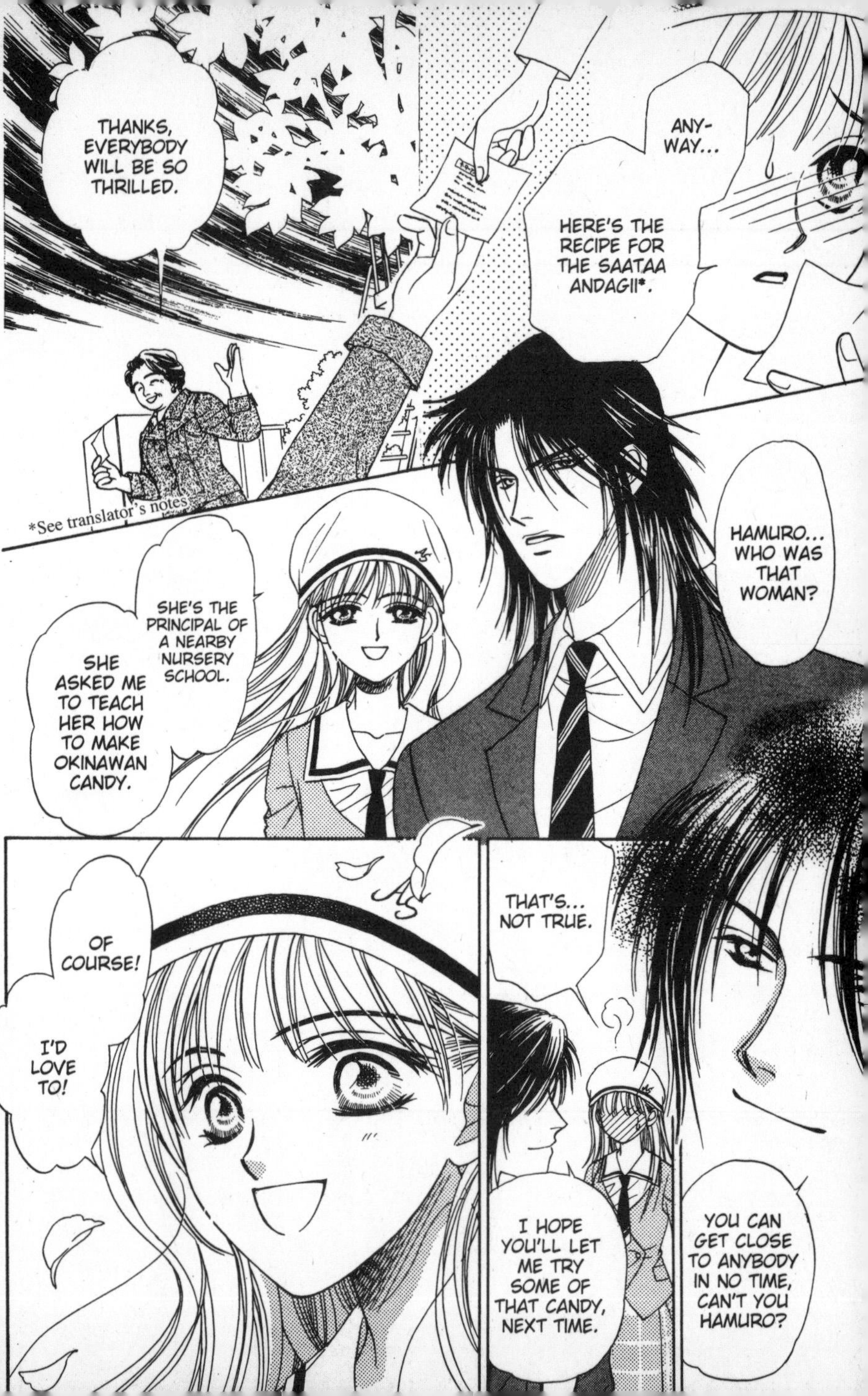
ANY-WAY...
HERE'S THE RECIPE FOR THE SAATAA ANDAGII*.
THANKS, EVERYBODY WILL BE SO THRILLED.
HAMURO... WHO WAS THAT WOMAN?
SHE'S THE PRINCIPAL OF A NEARBY NURSERY SCHOOL.
SHE ASKED ME TO TEACH HER HOW TO MAKE OKINAWAN CANDY.
YOU CAN GET CLOSE TO ANYBODY IN NO TIME, CAN'T YOU HAMURO?
THAT'S... NOT TRUE.
I HOPE YOU'LL LET ME TRY SOME OF THAT CANDY, NEXT TIME.
OF COURSE!
I'D LOVE TO!
*See translator's notes

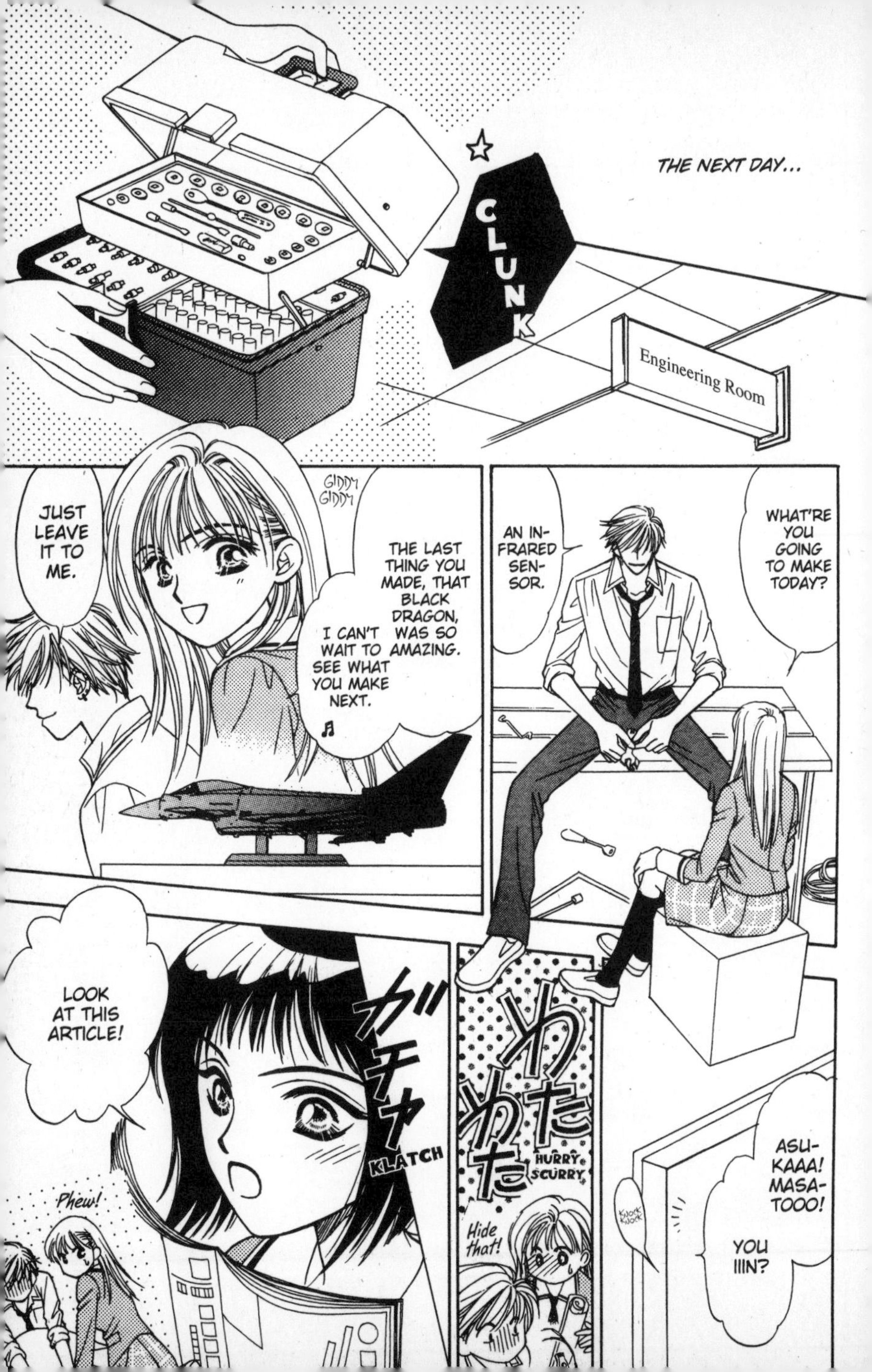
THE NEXT DAY...
CLUNK
Engineering Room
WHAT'RE YOU GOING TO MAKE TODAY?
AN IN-FRARED SEN-SOR.
GIDDY GIDDY
THE LAST THING YOU MADE, THAT BLACK DRAGON, WAS SO AMAZING.
I CAN'T WAIT TO SEE WHAT YOU MAKE NEXT.
JUST LEAVE IT TO ME.
ASU-KAAA! MASA-TOOO!
YOU IIIN?
Knock Knock
HURRY SCURRY
Hide that!
KLATCH
LOOK AT THIS ARTICLE!
Phew!

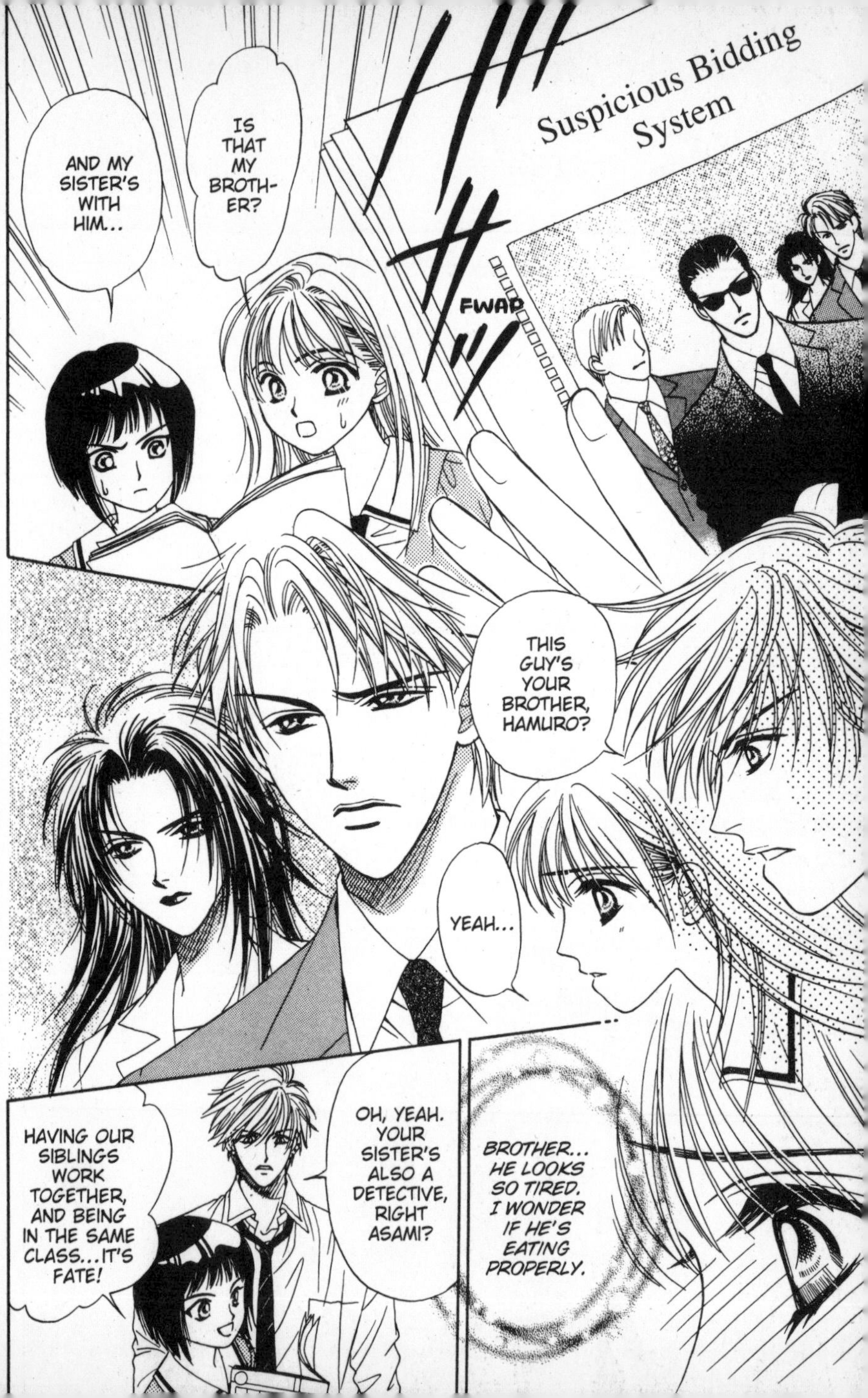
Suspicious Bidding System
FWAP
IS THAT MY BROTHER?
AND MY SISTER'S WITH HIM...
THIS GUY'S YOUR BROTHER, HAMURO?
YEAH...
BROTHER... HE LOOKS SO TIRED. I WONDER IF HE'S EATING PROPERLY.
OH, YEAH. YOUR SISTER'S ALSO A DETECTIVE, RIGHT ASAMI?
HAVING OUR SIBLINGS WORK TOGETHER, AND BEING IN THE SAME CLASS...IT'S FATE!

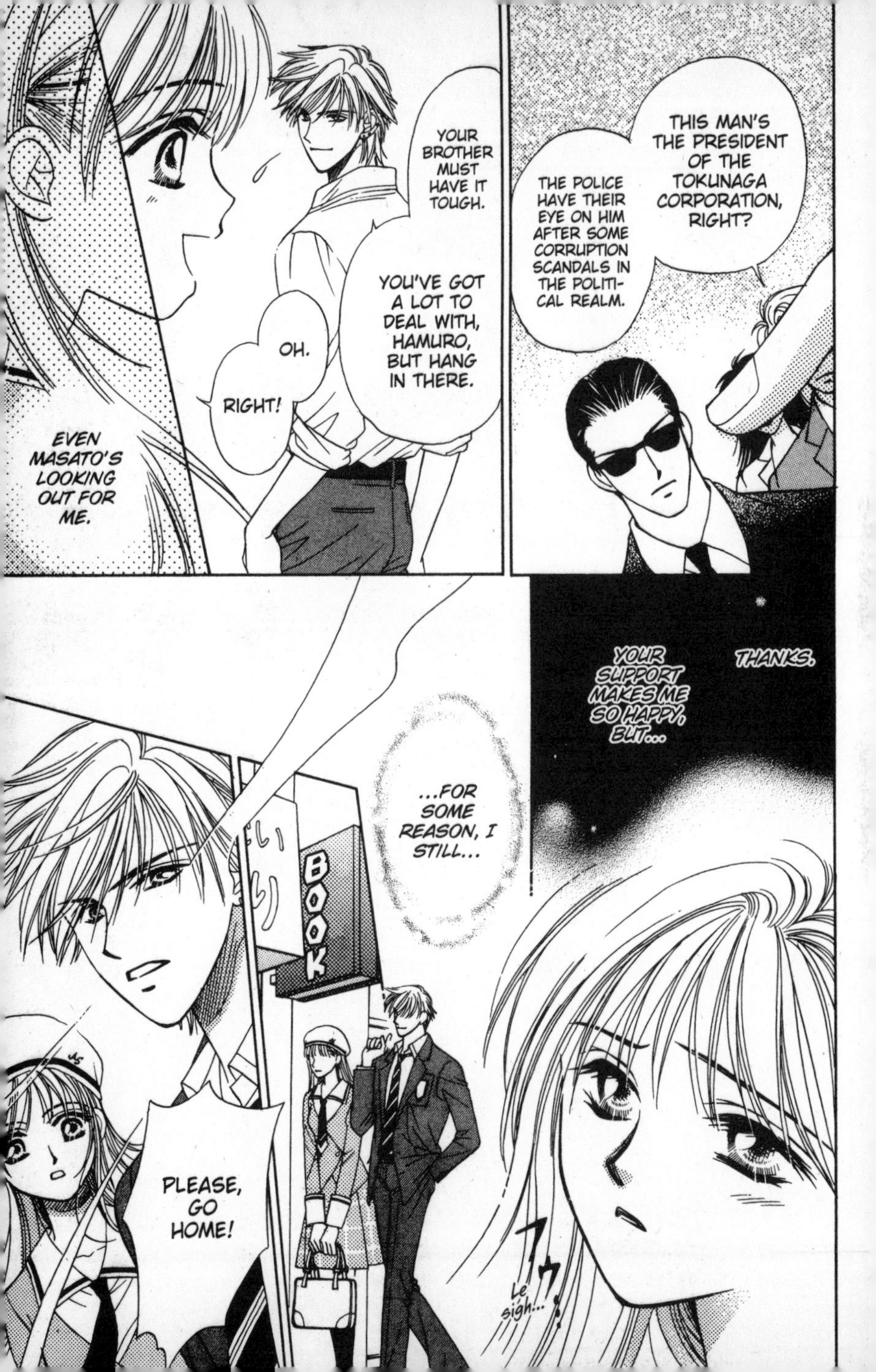
THIS MAN'S THE PRESIDENT OF THE TOKUNAGA CORPORATION, RIGHT?
THE POLICE HAVE THEIR EYE ON HIM AFTER SOME CORRUPTION SCANDALS IN THE POLITI-CAL REALM.
YOUR BROTHER MUST HAVE IT TOUGH.
YOU'VE GOT A LOT TO DEAL WITH, HAMURO, BUT HANG IN THERE.
OH.
RIGHT!
EVEN MASATO'S LOOKING OUT FOR ME.
THANKS.
YOUR SUPPORT MAKES ME SO HAPPY, BUT...
...FOR SOME REASON, I STILL...
Le sigh...
BOOK
PLEASE, GO HOME!

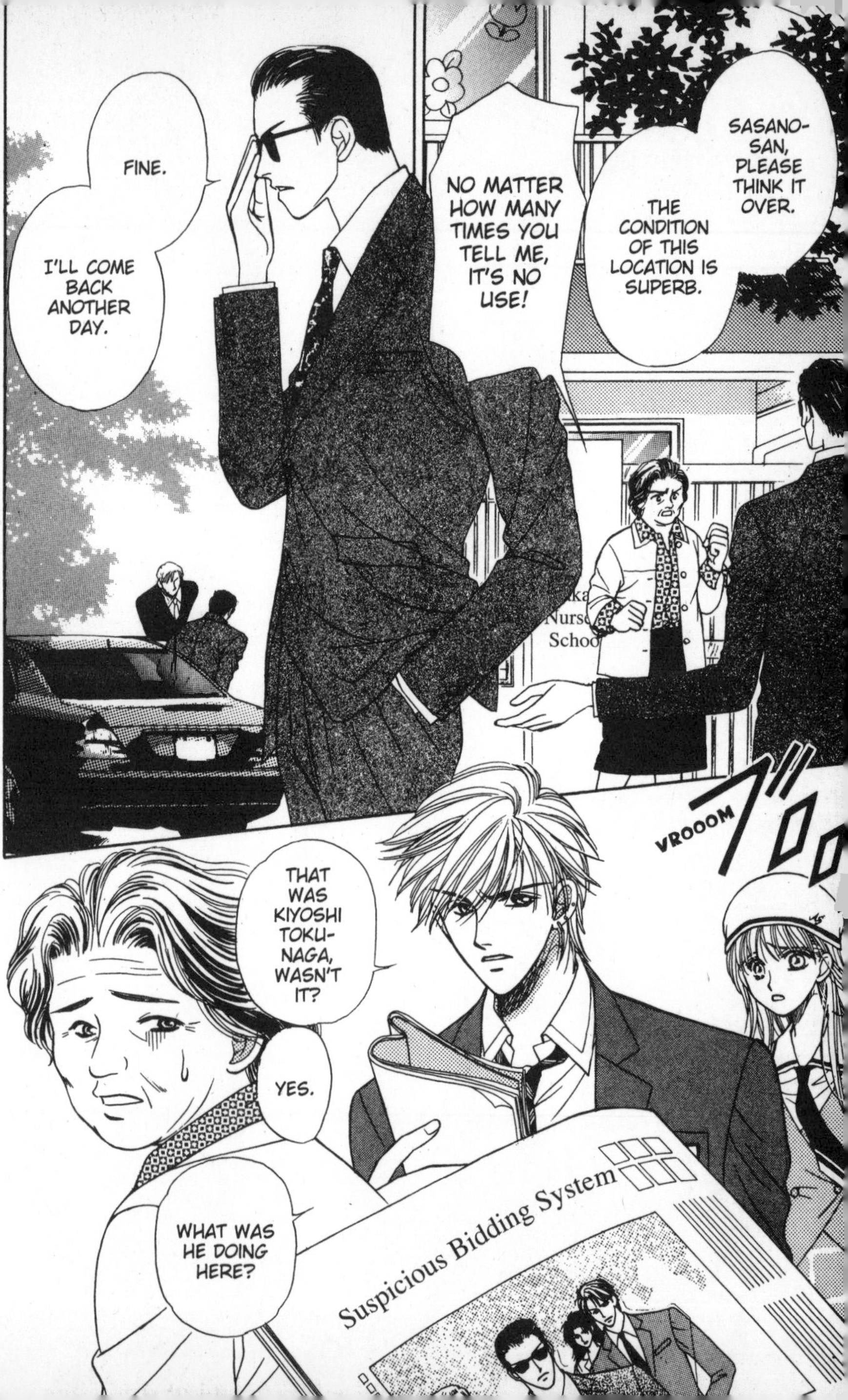
SASANO-SAN, PLEASE THINK IT OVER.
THE CONDITION OF THIS LOCATION IS SUPERB.
NO MATTER HOW MANY TIMES YOU TELL ME, IT'S NO USE!
FINE.
I'LL COME BACK ANOTHER DAY.
Nurse
Schoo
VROOOM
THAT WAS KIYOSHI TOKU-NAGA, WASN'T IT?
YES.
WHAT WAS HE DOING HERE?
Suspicious Bidding System

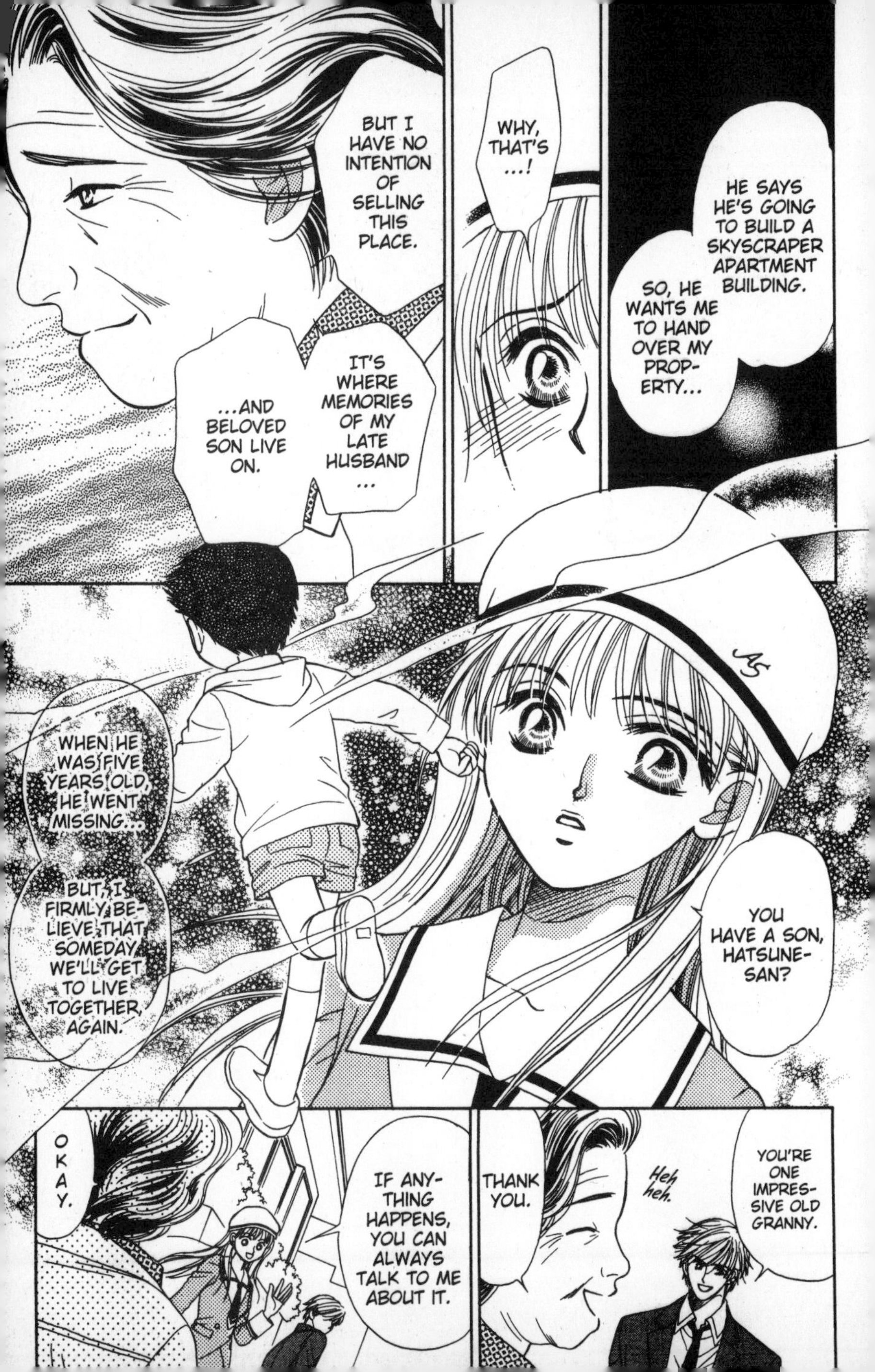
HE SAYS HE'S GOING TO BUILD A SKYSCRAPER APARTMENT BUILDING.
SO, HE WANTS ME TO HAND OVER MY PROP-ERTY...
WHY, THAT'S ...!
BUT I HAVE NO INTENTION OF SELLING THIS PLACE.
IT'S WHERE MEMORIES OF MY LATE HUSBAND ...
...AND BELOVED SON LIVE ON.
YOU HAVE A SON, HATSUNE-SAN?
WHEN HE WAS FIVE YEARS OLD, HE WENT MISSING...
BUT, I FIRMLY BE-LIEVE THAT SOMEDAY WE'LL GET TO LIVE TOGETHER, AGAIN.
YOU'RE ONE IMPRES-SIVE OLD GRANNY.
Heh heh.
THANK YOU.
IF ANY-THING HAPPENS, YOU CAN ALWAYS TALK TO ME ABOUT IT.
OKAY.

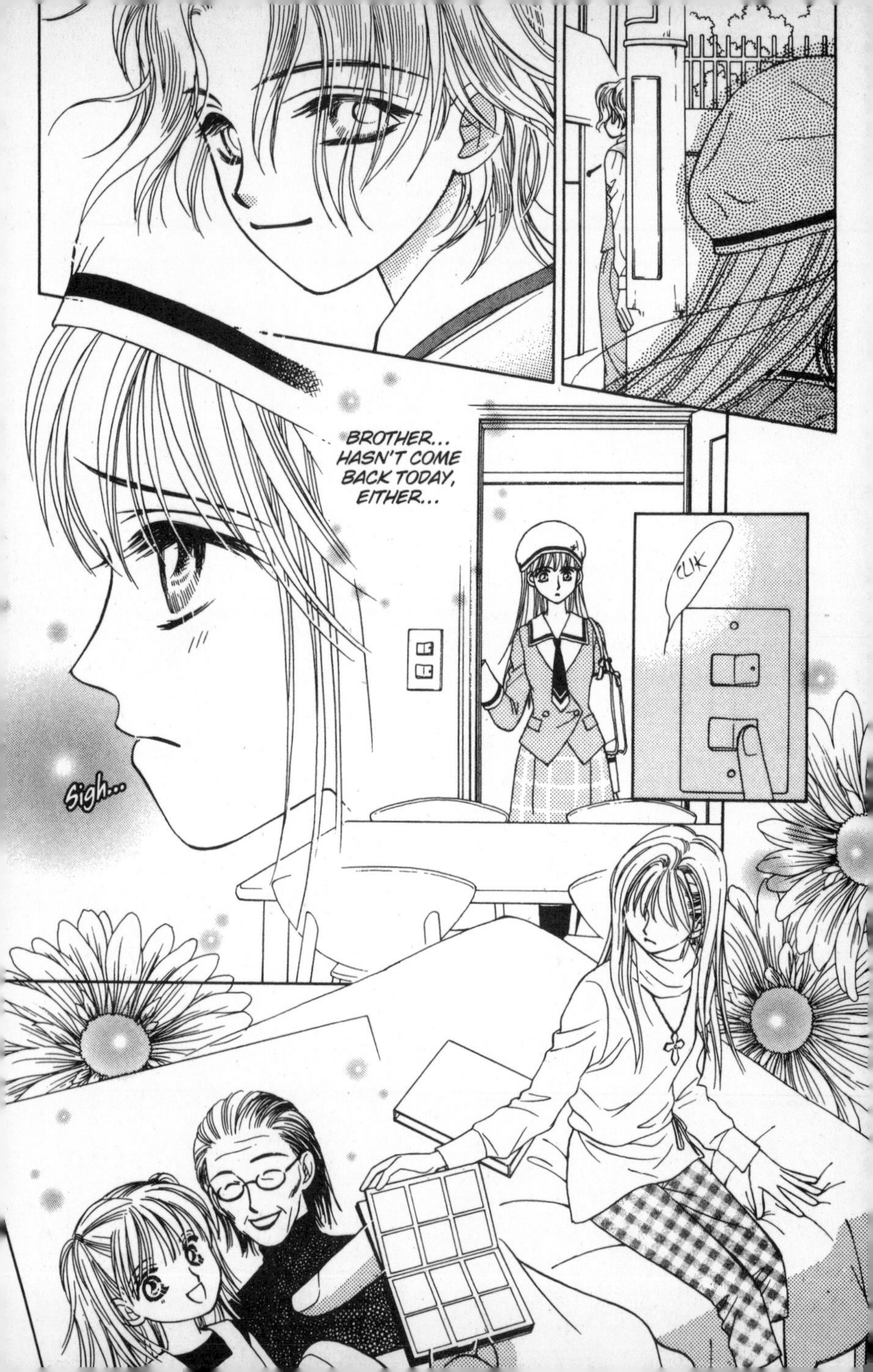

BROTHER... HASN'T COME BACK TODAY, EITHER...
CLIK
Sigh...

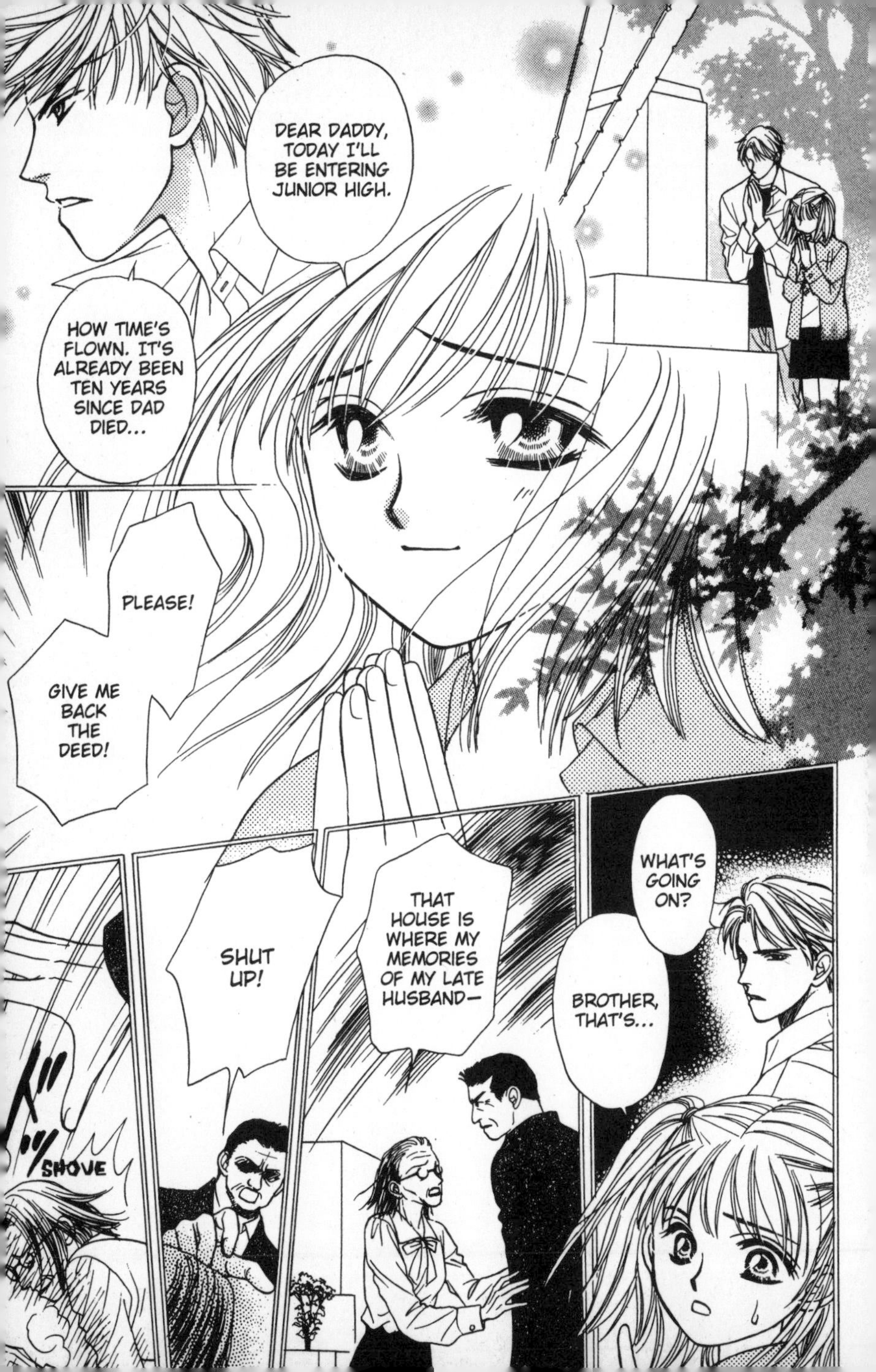
DEAR DADDY, TODAY I'LL BE ENTERING JUNIOR HIGH.
HOW TIME'S FLOWN. IT'S ALREADY BEEN TEN YEARS SINCE DAD DIED...
PLEASE!
GIVE ME BACK THE DEED!
WHAT'S GOING ON?
BROTHER, THAT'S...
THAT HOUSE IS WHERE MY MEMORIES OF MY LATE HUSBAND—
SHUT UP!
SHOVE

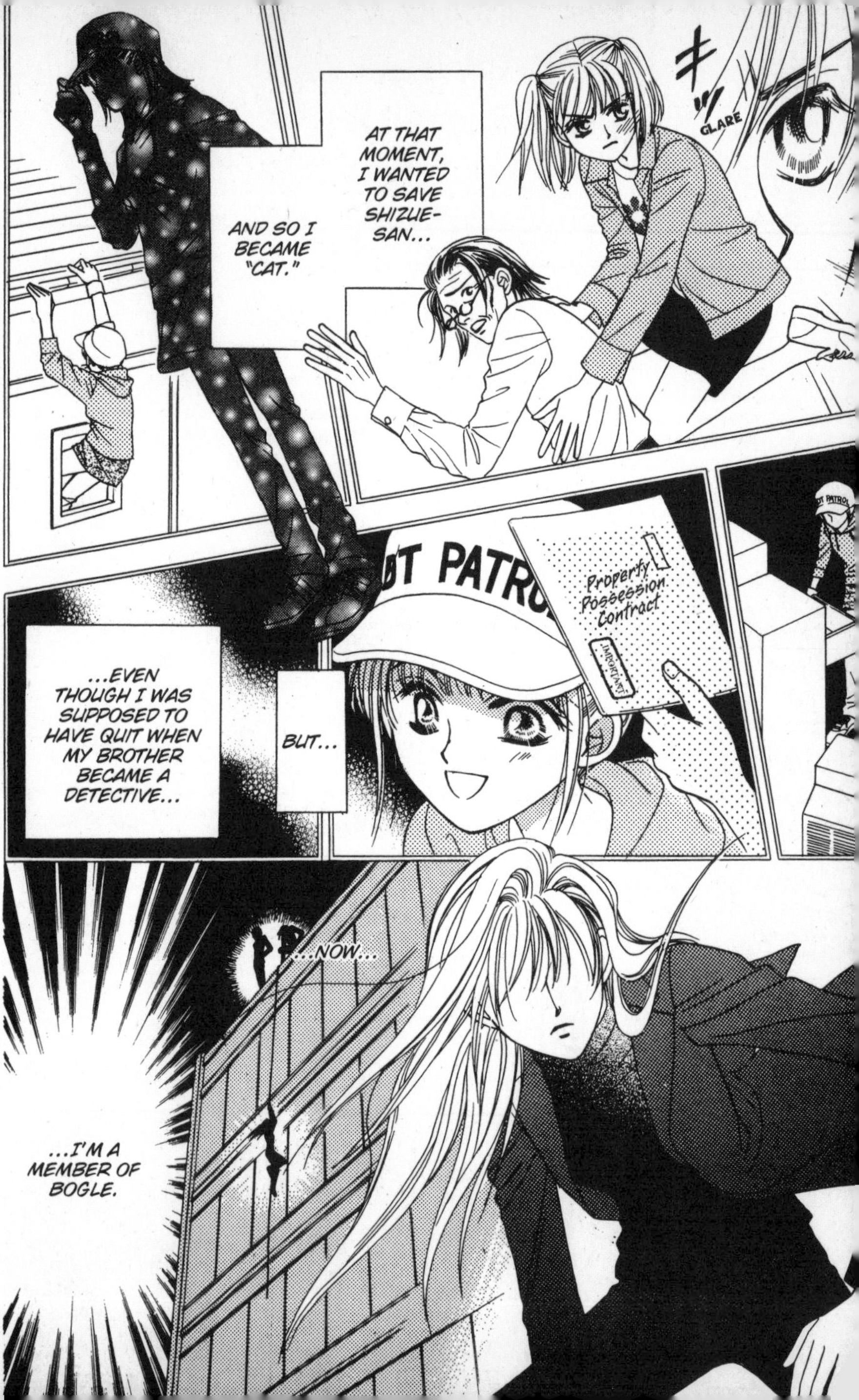
GLARE
AT THAT MOMENT, I WANTED TO SAVE SHIZUE-SAN...
AND SO I BECAME "CAT."
Property Possession Contract
IMPORTANT
BUT...
...EVEN THOUGH I WAS SUPPOSED TO HAVE QUIT WHEN MY BROTHER BECAME A DETECTIVE...
...NOW...
...I'M A MEMBER OF BOGLE.

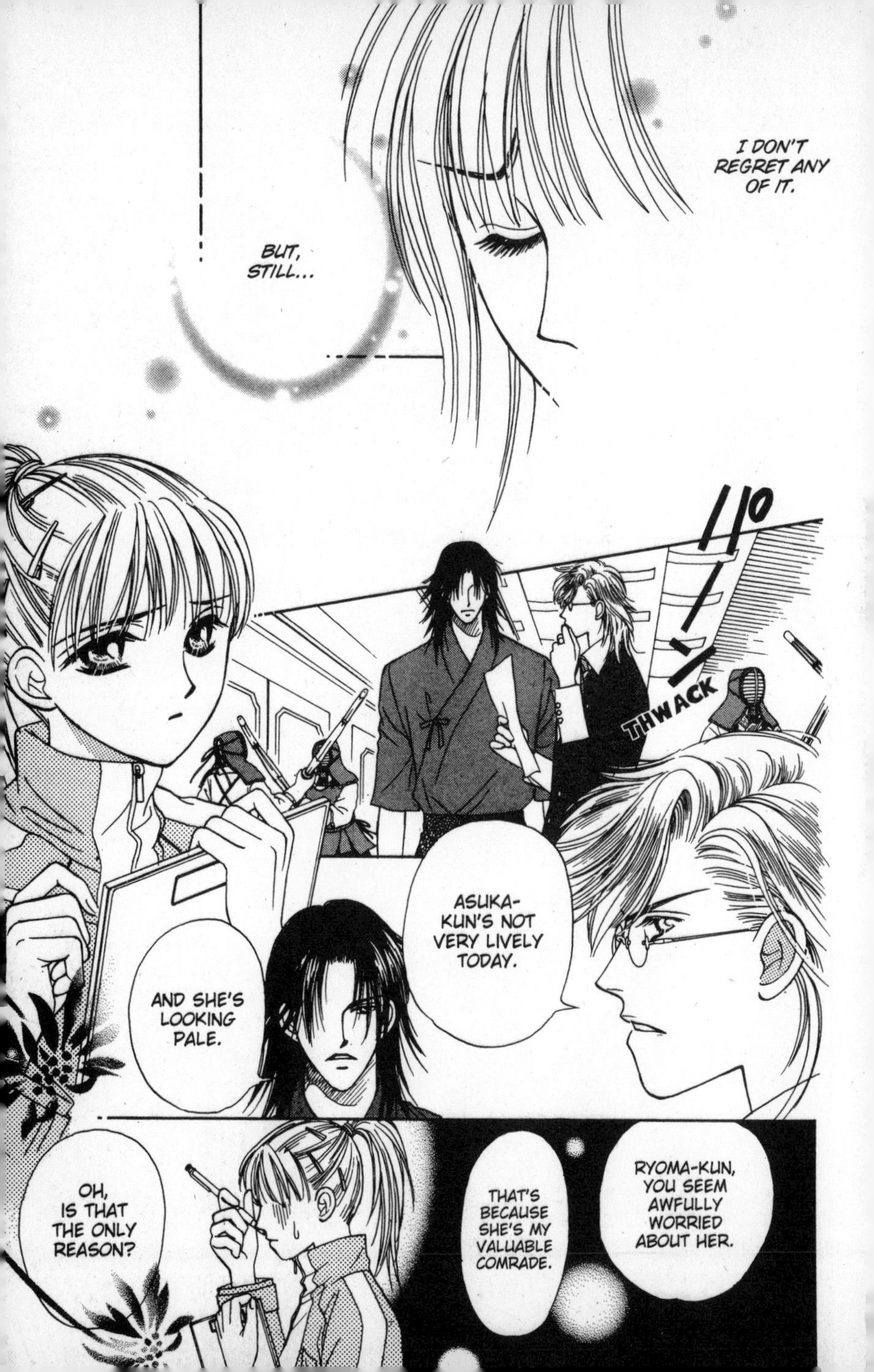
I DON'T REGRET ANY OF IT.
BUT, STILL...
THWACK
ASUKA-KUN'S NOT VERY LIVELY TODAY.
AND SHE'S LOOKING PALE.
RYOMA-KUN, YOU SEEM AWFULLY WORRIED ABOUT HER.
THAT'S BECAUSE SHE'S MY VALUABLE COMRADE.
OH, IS THAT THE ONLY REASON?

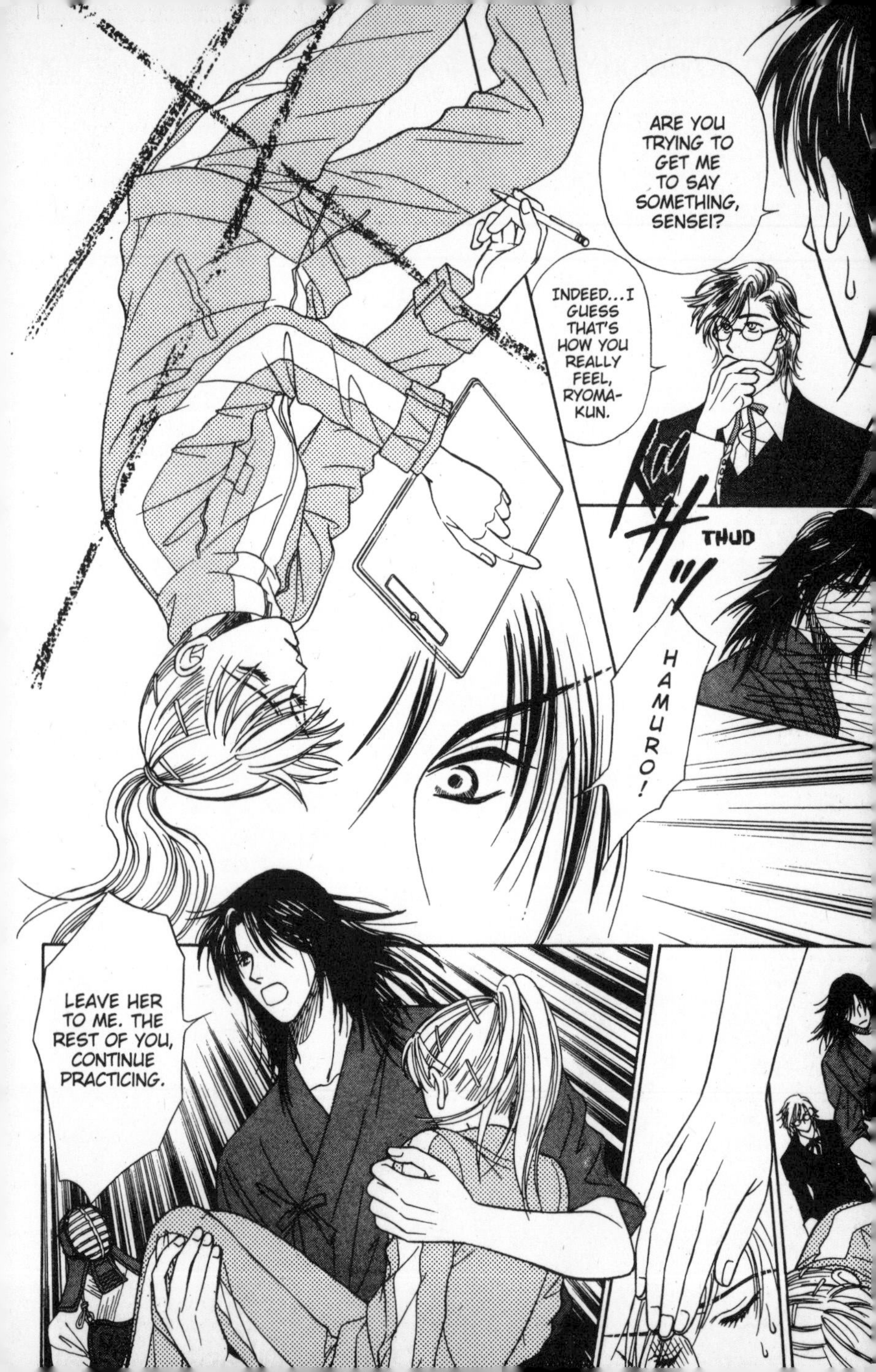
ARE YOU TRYING TO GET ME TO SAY SOMETHING, SENSEI?
INDEED...I GUESS THAT'S HOW YOU REALLY FEEL, RYOMA-KUN.
THUD
HAMURO!
LEAVE HER TO ME. THE REST OF YOU, CONTINUE PRACTICING.

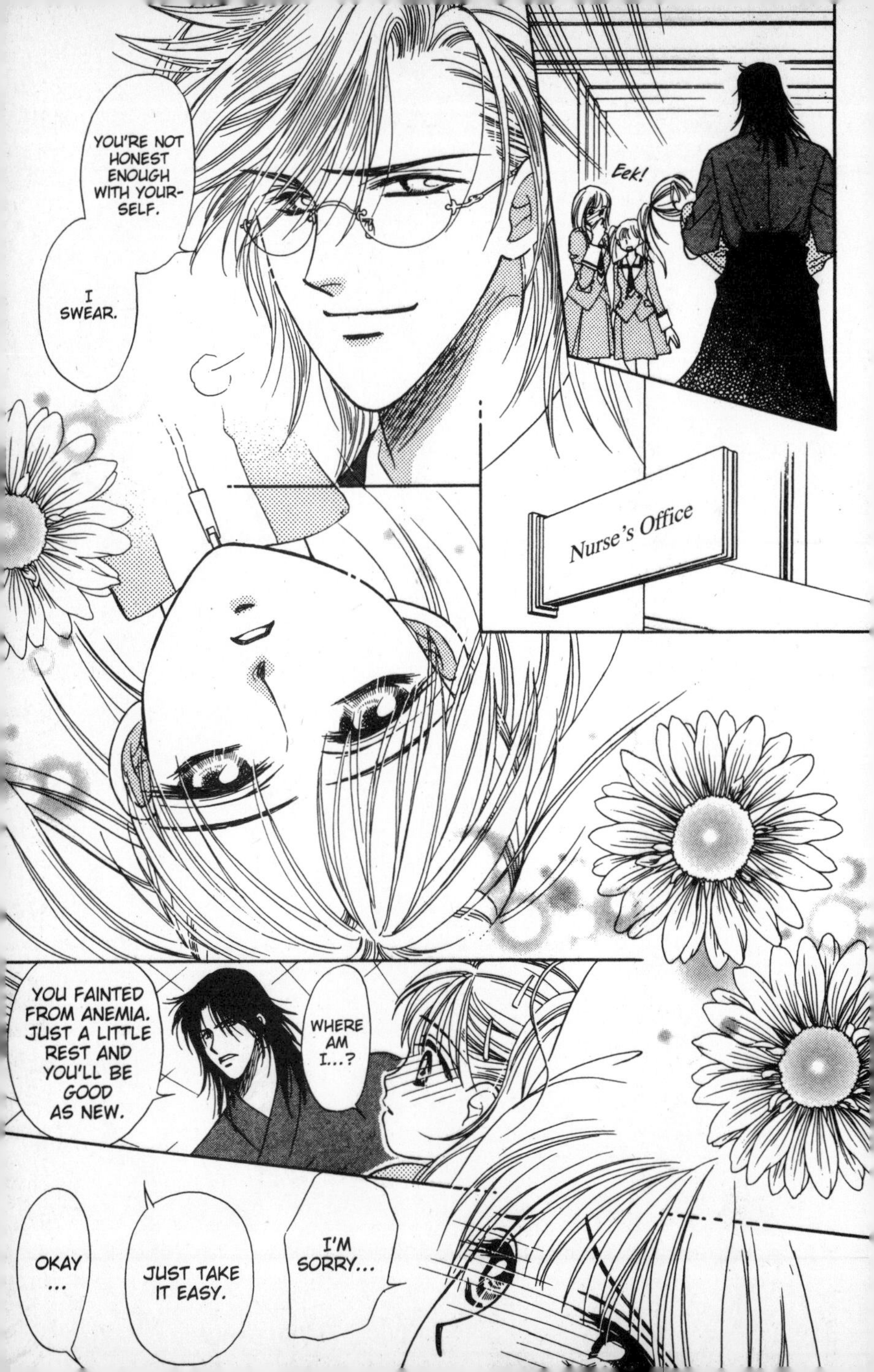
Eek!
Nurse's Office
YOU'RE NOT HONEST ENOUGH WITH YOURSELF.
I SWEAR.
WHERE AM I...?
YOU FAINTED FROM ANEMIA. JUST A LITTLE REST AND YOU'LL BE GOOD AS NEW.
I'M SORRY...
JUST TAKE IT EASY.
OKAY ...

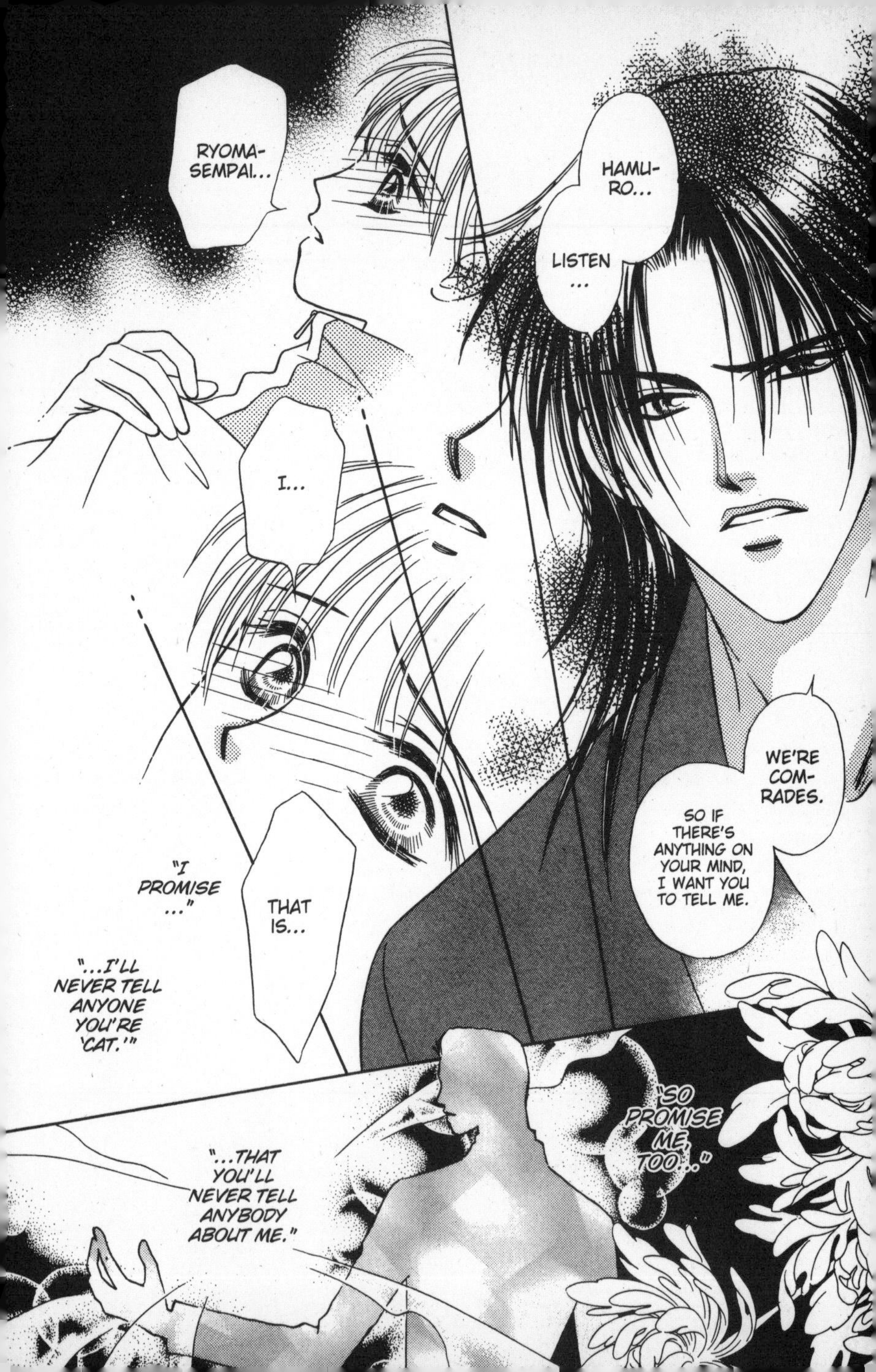
HAMU-RO...
LISTEN ...
RYOMA-SEMPAI...
WE'RE COM-RADES.
SO IF THERE'S ANYTHING ON YOUR MIND, I WANT YOU TO TELL ME.
I...
THAT IS...
"I PROMISE ..."
"...I'LL NEVER TELL ANYONE YOU'RE 'CAT.'"
"SO PROMISE ME, TOO..."
"...THAT YOU'LL NEVER TELL ANYBODY ABOUT ME."

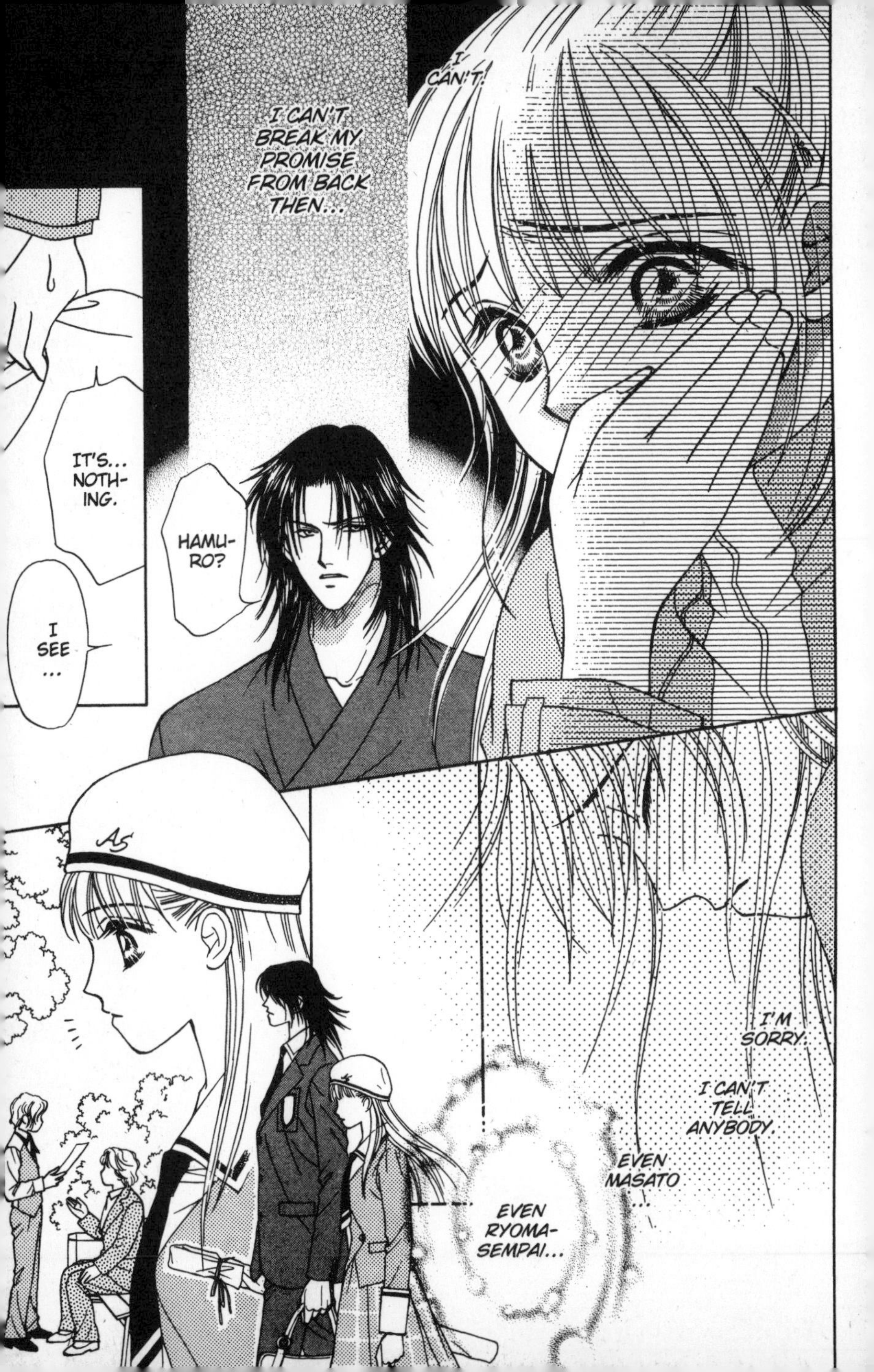
I CAN'T!
I CAN'T BREAK MY PROMISE FROM BACK THEN...
IT'S... NOTHING.
HAMURO?
I SEE...
I'M SORRY.
I CAN'T TELL ANYBODY.
EVEN MASATO...
EVEN RYOMA-SEMPAI...

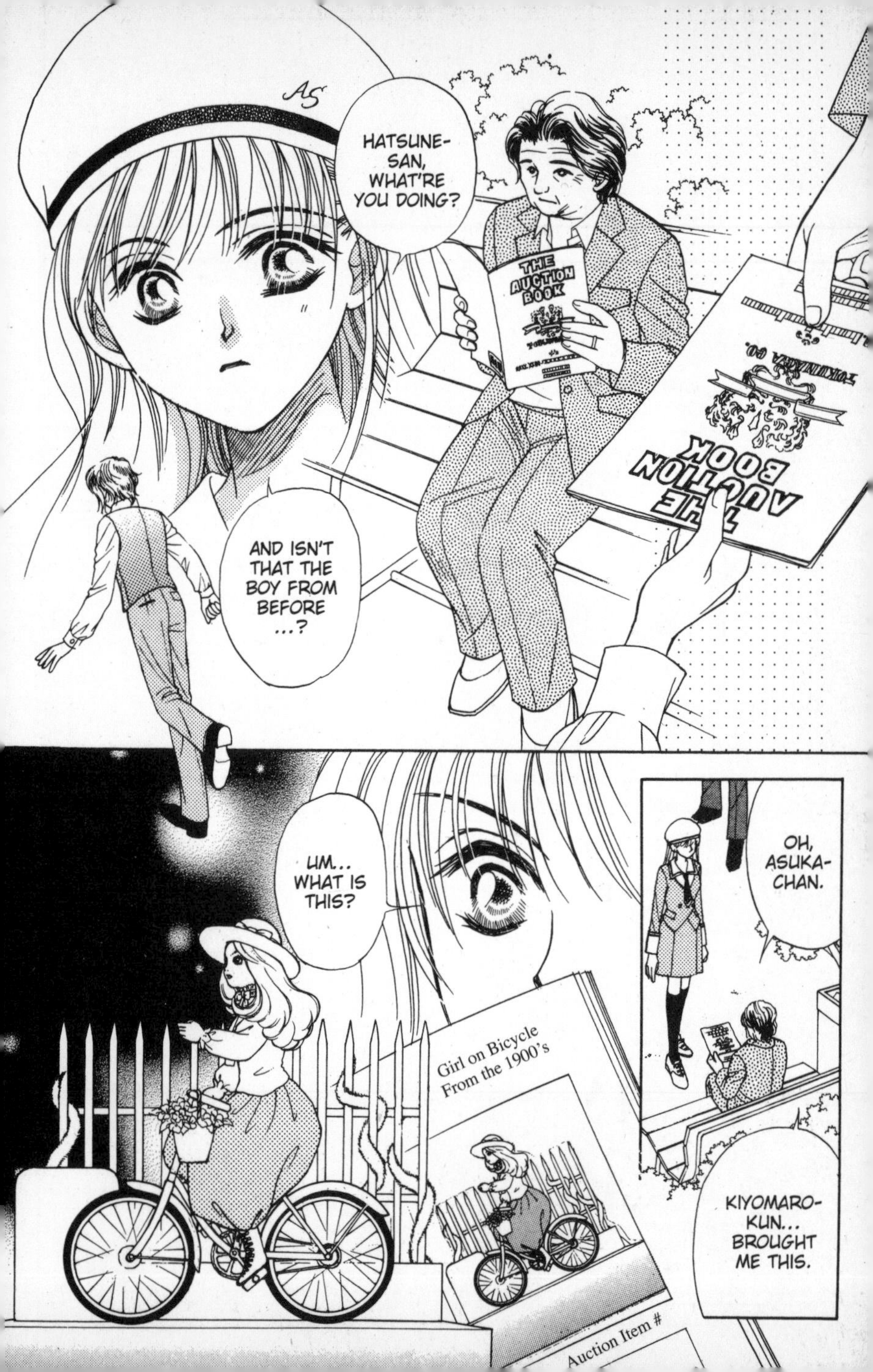

HATSUNE-SAN, WHAT'RE YOU DOING?
AND ISN'T THAT THE BOY FROM BEFORE ...?
THE AUCTION BOOK
OH, ASUKA-CHAN.
UM... WHAT IS THIS?
KIYOMARO-KUN... BROUGHT ME THIS.
Girl on Bicycle From the 1900's
Auction Item #

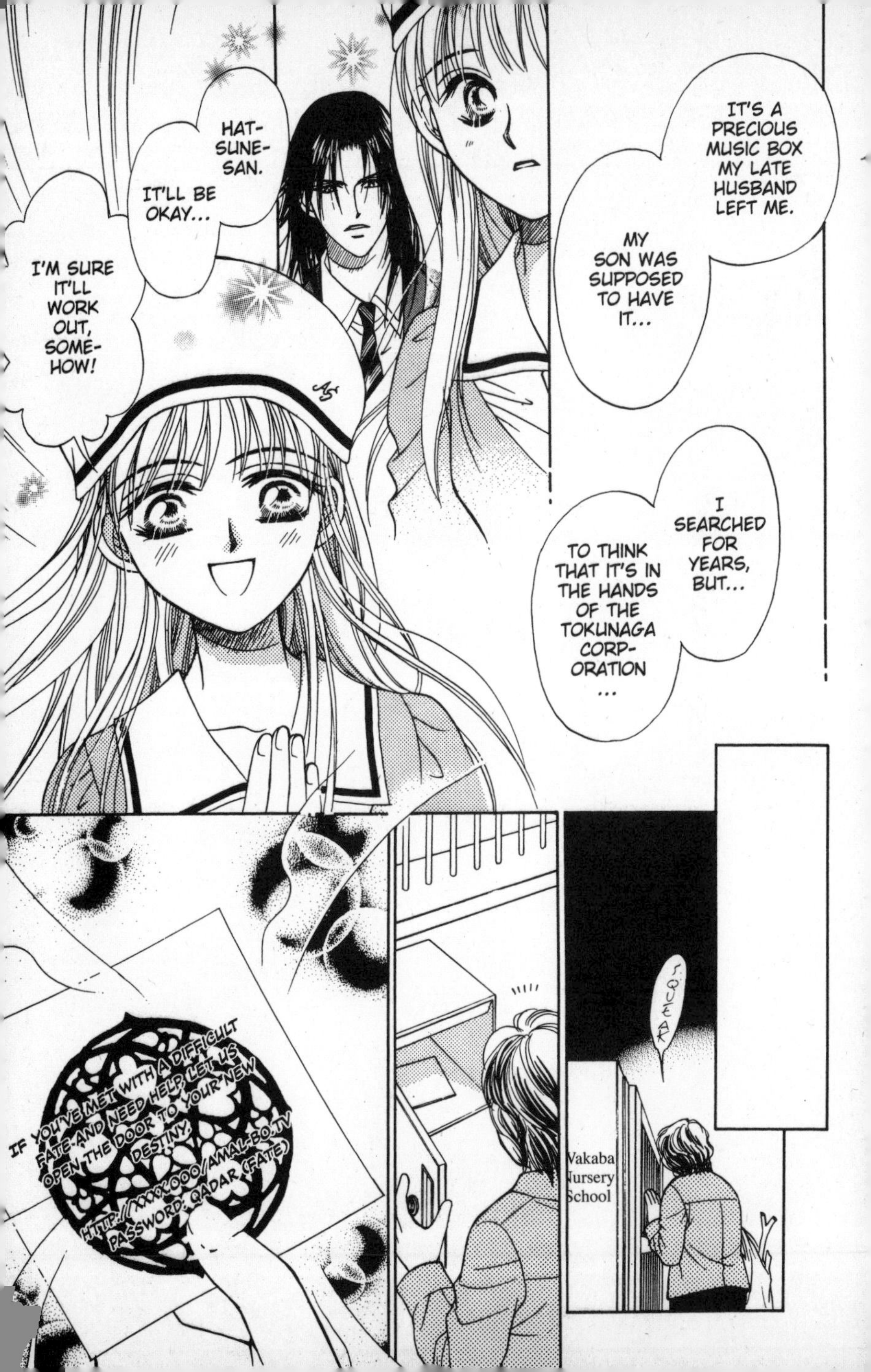

IT'S A PRECIOUS MUSIC BOX MY LATE HUSBAND LEFT ME.
MY SON WAS SUPPOSED TO HAVE IT...
HAT-SUNE-SAN.
IT'LL BE OKAY...
I'M SURE IT'LL WORK OUT, SOME-HOW!
I SEARCHED FOR YEARS, BUT...
TO THINK THAT IT'S IN THE HANDS OF THE TOKUNAGA CORP-ORATION ...
SQUEAK
Wakaba Nursery School
...
IF YOU'VE MET WITH A DIFFICULT FATE AND NEED HELP, LET US OPEN THE DOOR TO YOUR NEW DESTINY.
HTTP://XXXX000/AMAL-BO.TV
PASSWORD: QADAR (FATE)

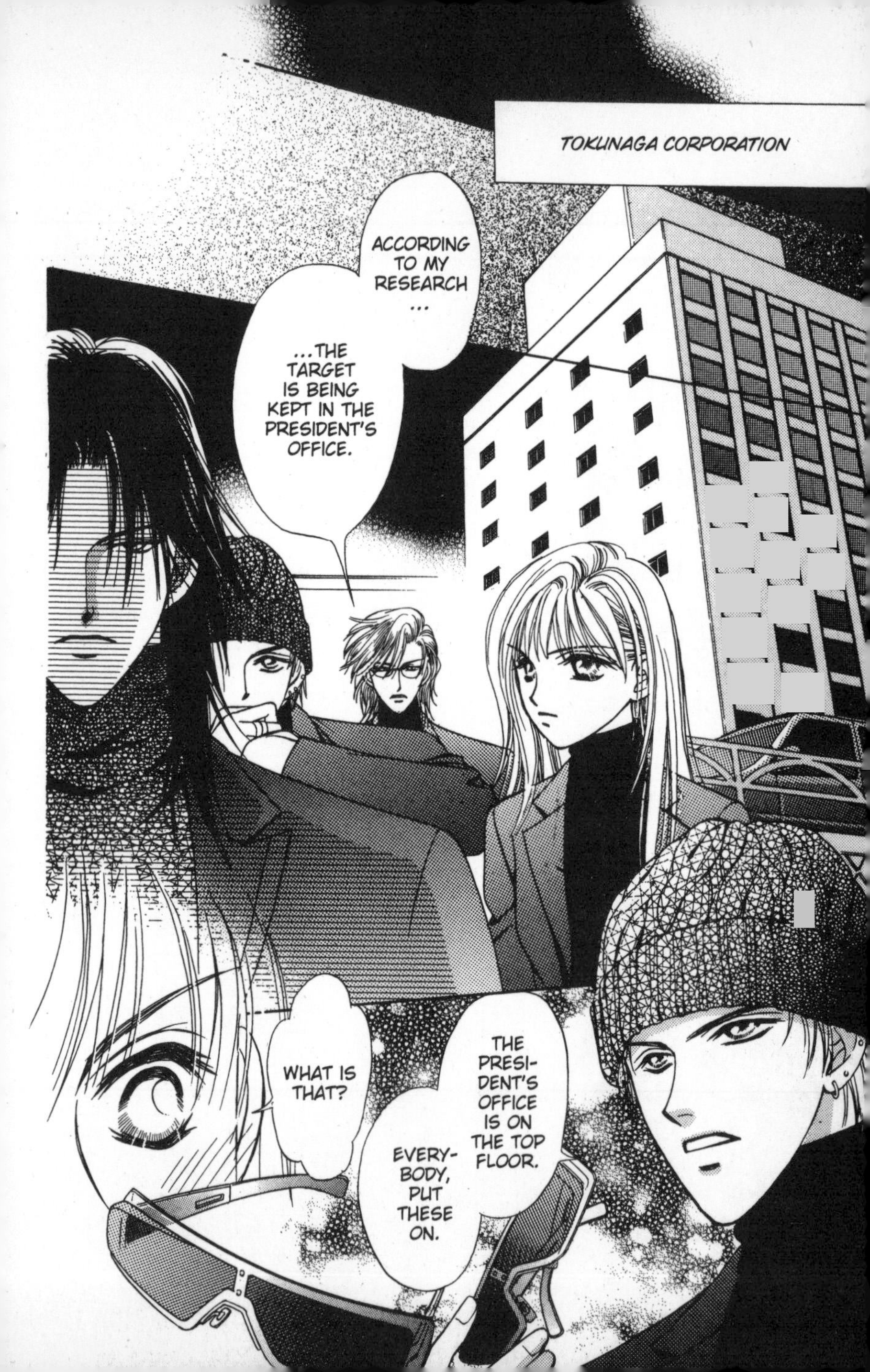
TOKUNAGA CORPORATION
ACCORDING TO MY RESEARCH ...
...THE TARGET IS BEING KEPT IN THE PRESIDENT'S OFFICE.
THE PRESI-DENT'S OFFICE IS ON THE TOP FLOOR.
EVERY-BODY, PUT THESE ON.
WHAT IS THAT?

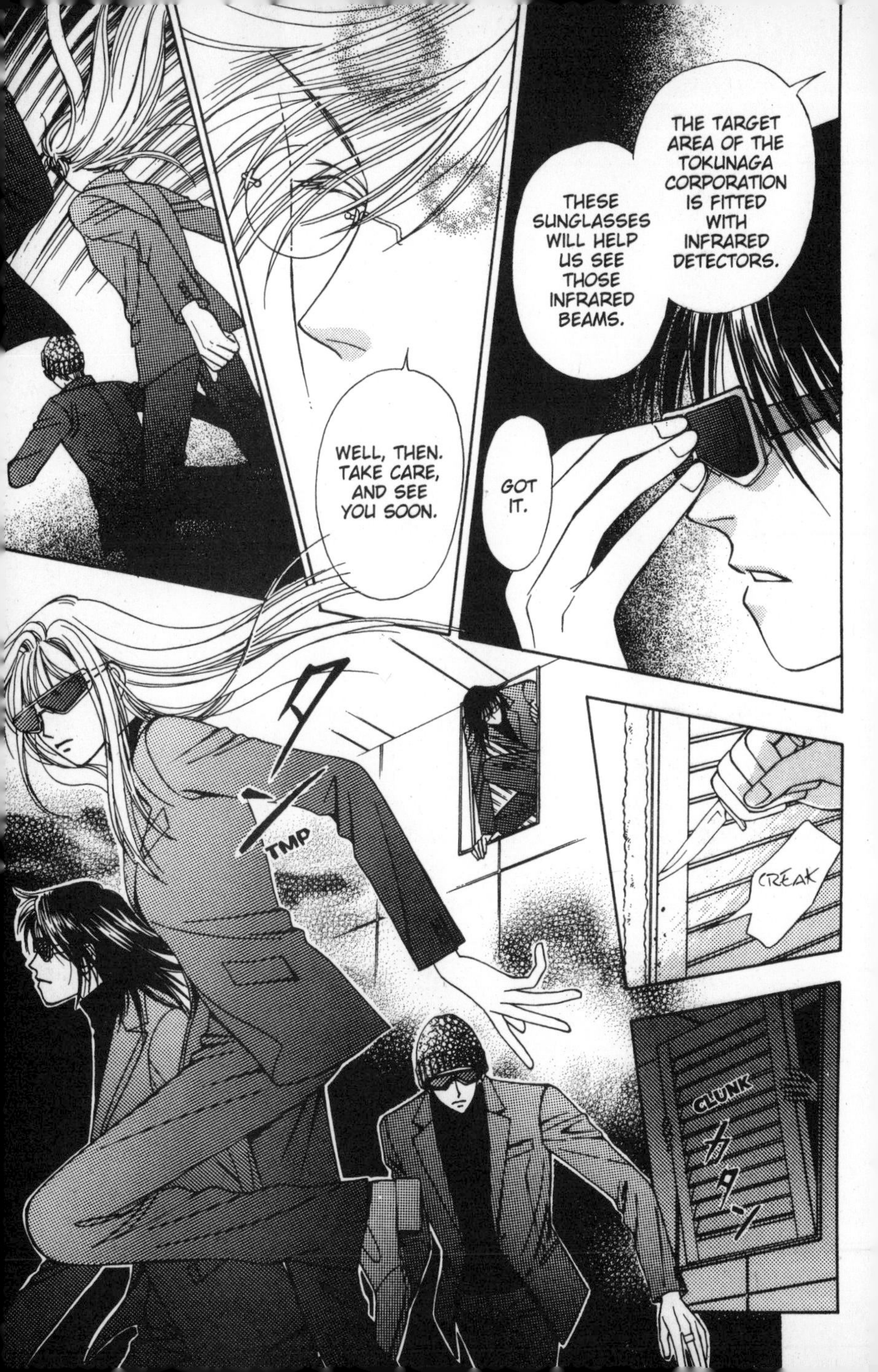
THE TARGET AREA OF THE TOKUNAGA CORPORATION IS FITTED WITH INFRARED DETECTORS.
THESE SUNGLASSES WILL HELP US SEE THOSE INFRARED BEAMS.
GOT IT.
WELL, THEN. TAKE CARE, AND SEE YOU SOON.
CREAK
TMP
CLUNK

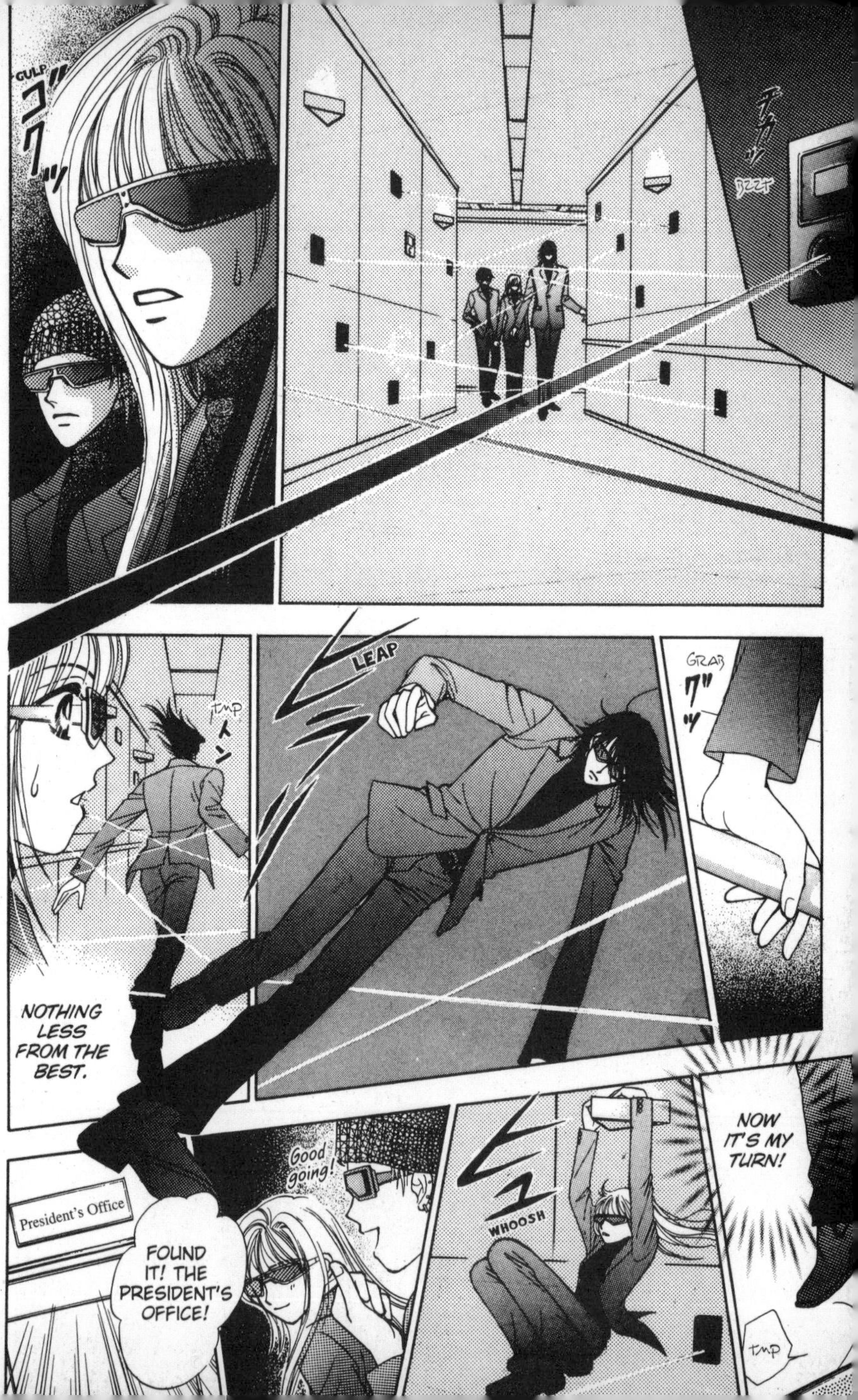
DZZT
GULP
ゴクッ
GRAB
グッ
LEAP
TMP
トン
NOTHING LESS FROM THE BEST.
NOW IT'S MY TURN!
TMP
WHOOSH
Good going!
President's Office
FOUND IT! THE PRESIDENT'S OFFICE!

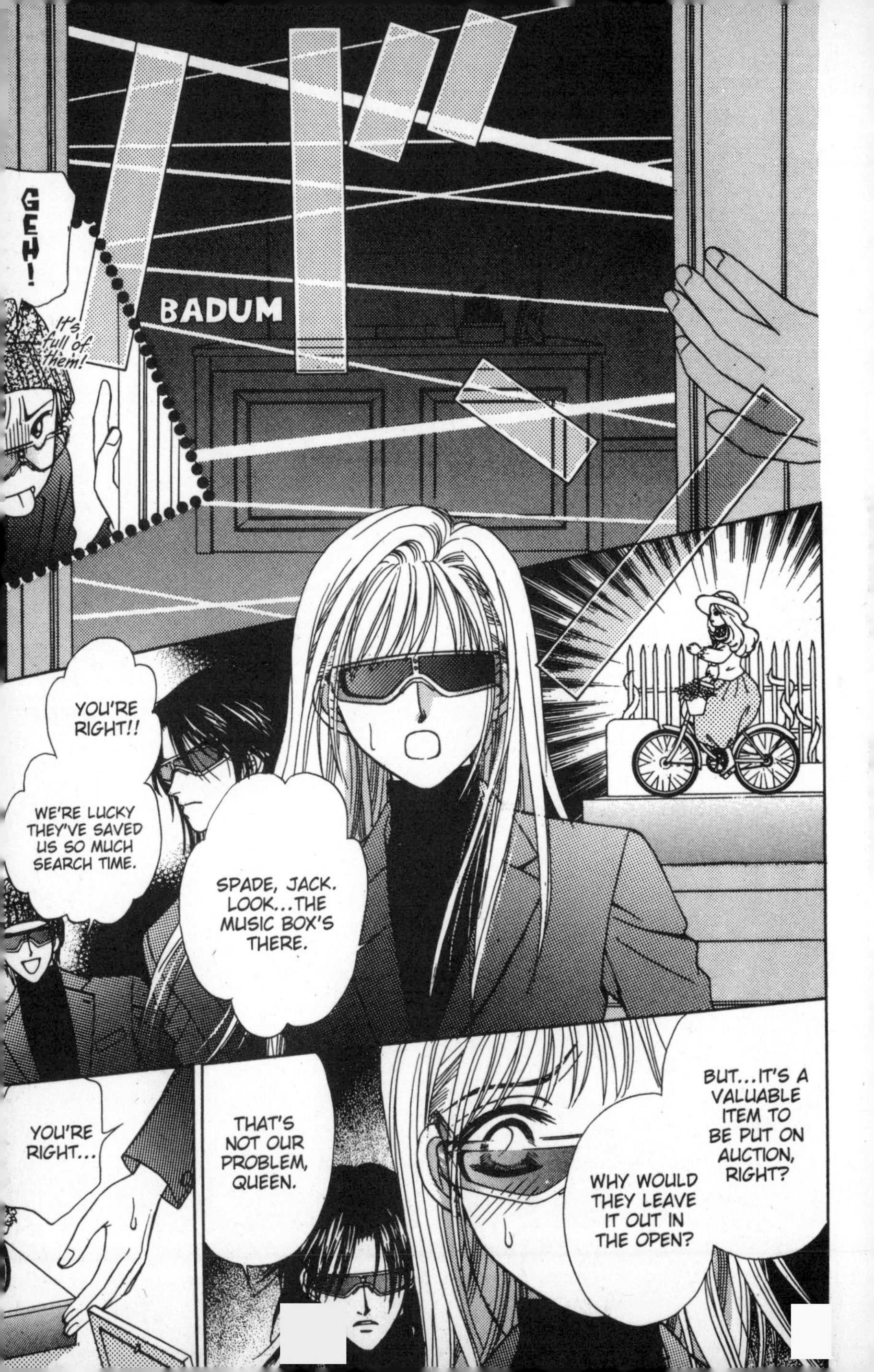
GEH!
It's full of them!
BADUM
YOU'RE RIGHT!!
WE'RE LUCKY THEY'VE SAVED US SO MUCH SEARCH TIME.
SPADE, JACK. LOOK...THE MUSIC BOX'S THERE.
BUT...IT'S A VALUABLE ITEM TO BE PUT ON AUCTION, RIGHT?
WHY WOULD THEY LEAVE IT OUT IN THE OPEN?
THAT'S NOT OUR PROBLEM, QUEEN.
YOU'RE RIGHT...

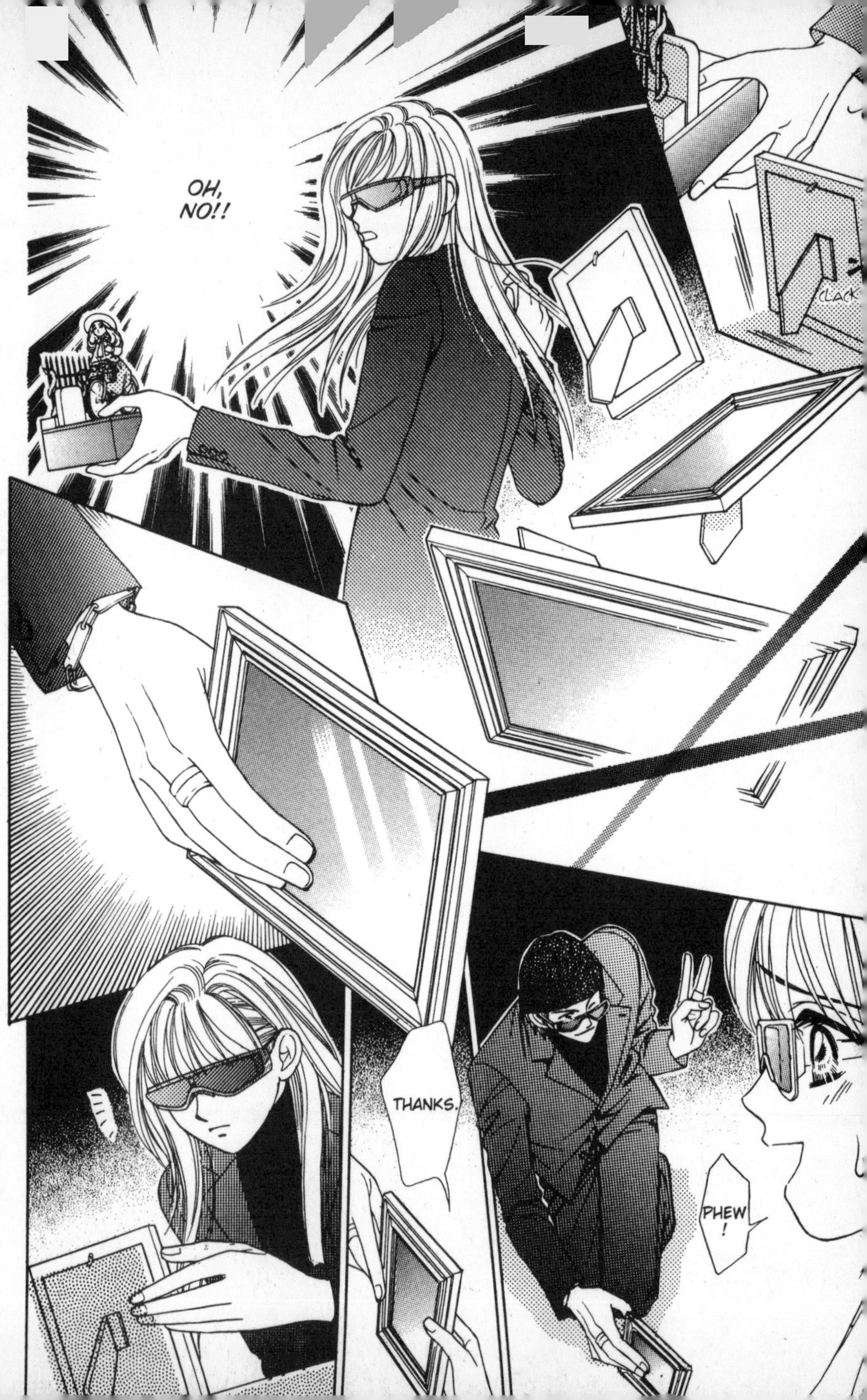
CLACK
OH, NO!!
THANKS.
PHEW!

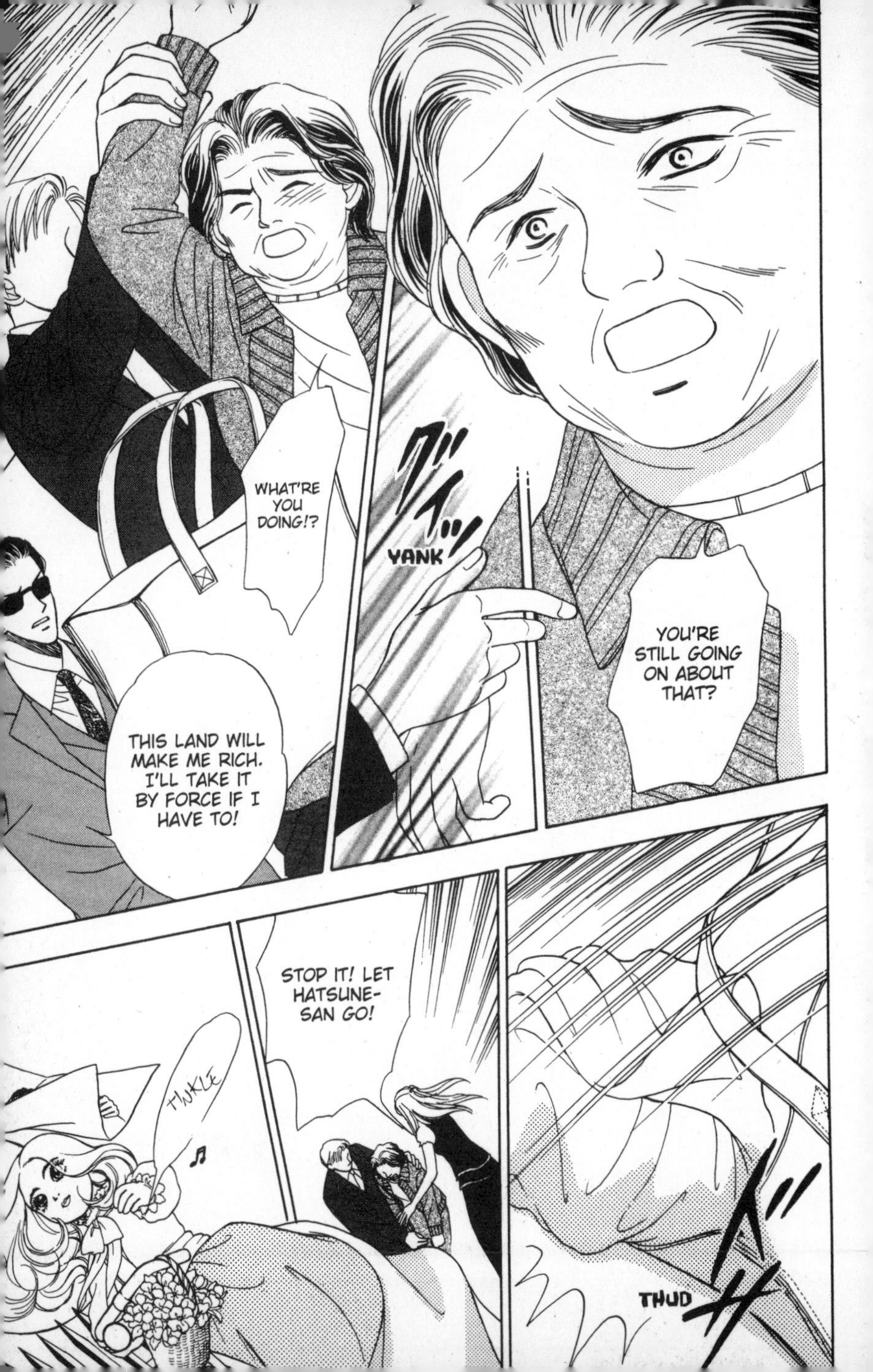

YOU'RE STILL GOING ON ABOUT THAT?
YANK
WHAT'RE YOU DOING!?
THIS LAND WILL MAKE ME RICH. I'LL TAKE IT BY FORCE IF I HAVE TO!
THUD
STOP IT! LET HATSUNE-SAN GO!
TINKLE

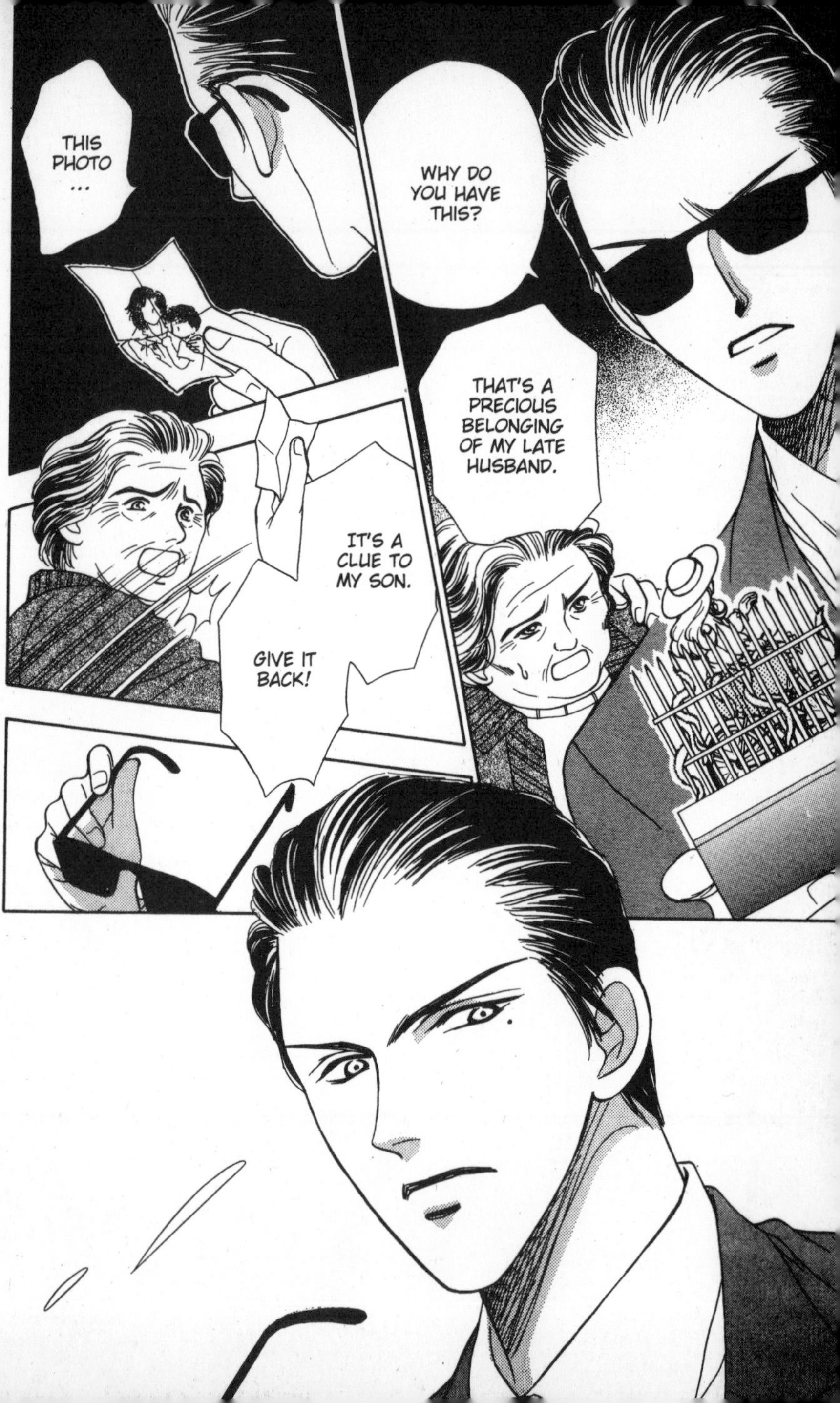
THIS PHOTO ...
WHY DO YOU HAVE THIS?
THAT'S A PRECIOUS BELONGING OF MY LATE HUSBAND.
IT'S A CLUE TO MY SON.
GIVE IT BACK!

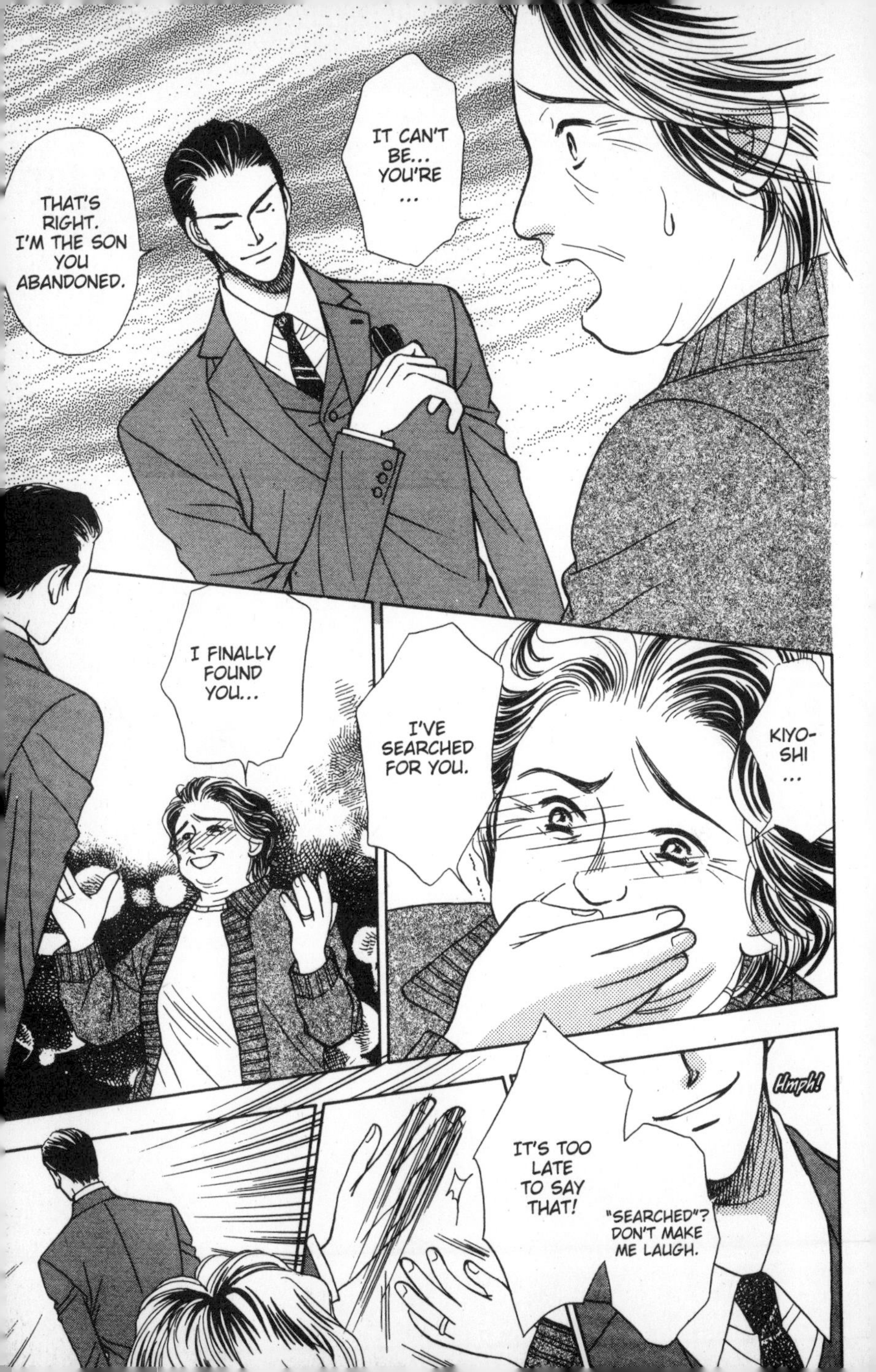
IT CAN'T BE... YOU'RE ...
THAT'S RIGHT. I'M THE SON YOU ABANDONED.
KIYO-SHI ...
I'VE SEARCHED FOR YOU.
I FINALLY FOUND YOU...
Hmph!
"SEARCHED"? DON'T MAKE ME LAUGH.
IT'S TOO LATE TO SAY THAT!

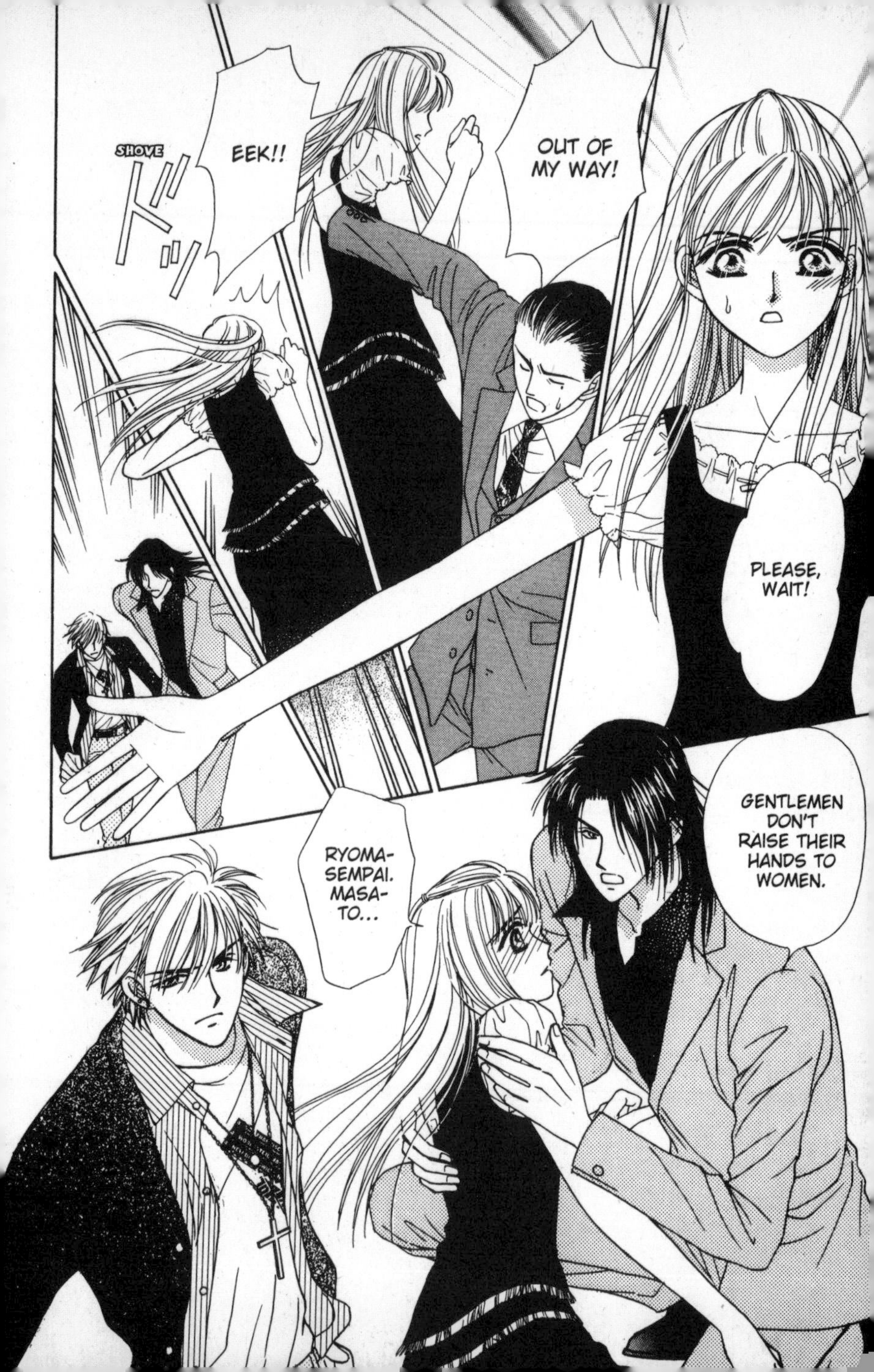
OUT OF MY WAY!
EEK!!
SHOVE
PLEASE, WAIT!
GENTLEMEN DON'T RAISE THEIR HANDS TO WOMEN.
RYOMA-SEMPAI. MASA-TO...

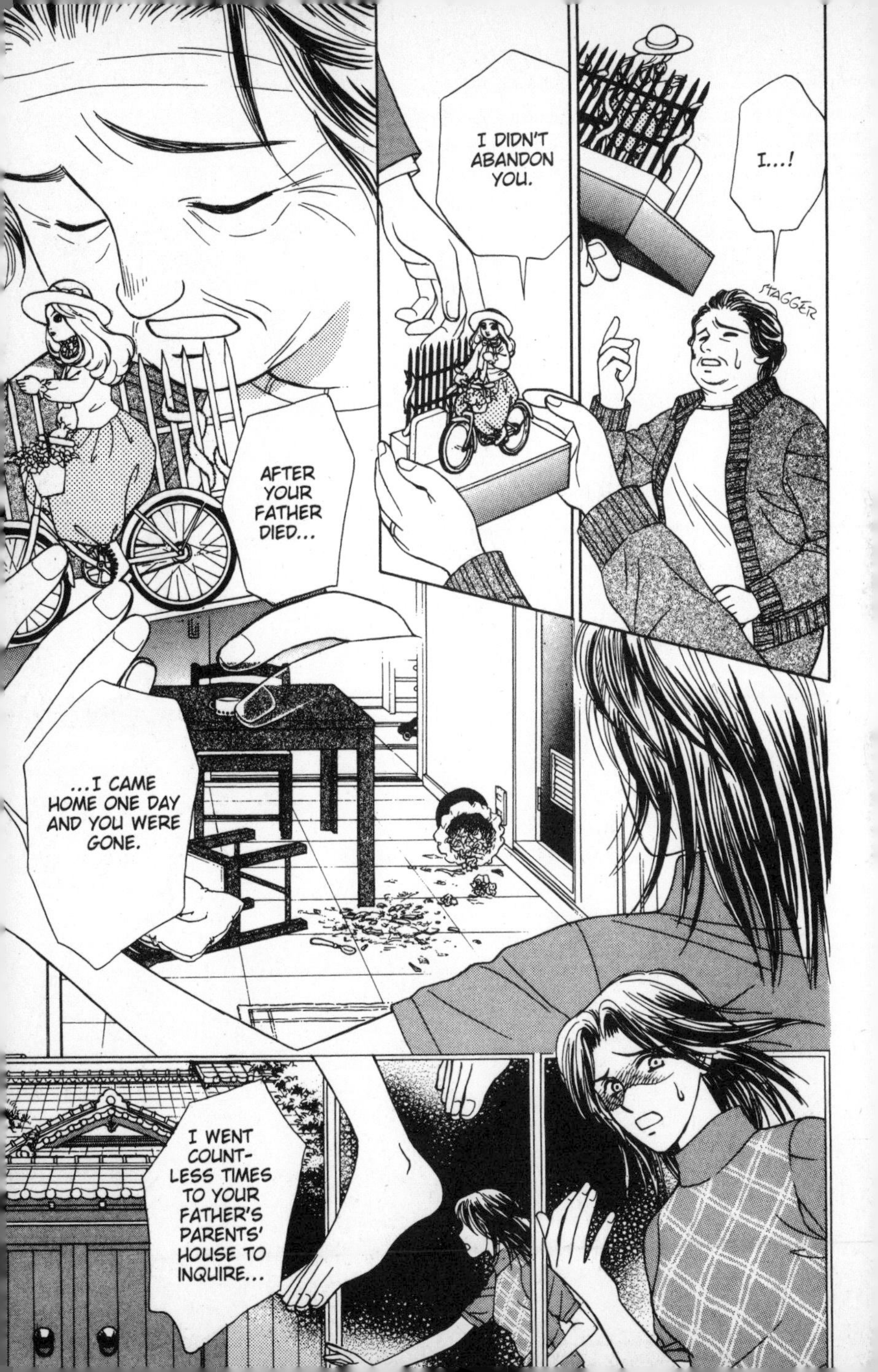
I...!
STAGGER
I DIDN'T ABANDON YOU.
AFTER YOUR FATHER DIED...
...I CAME HOME ONE DAY AND YOU WERE GONE.
I WENT COUNT-LESS TIMES TO YOUR FATHER'S PARENTS' HOUSE TO INQUIRE...

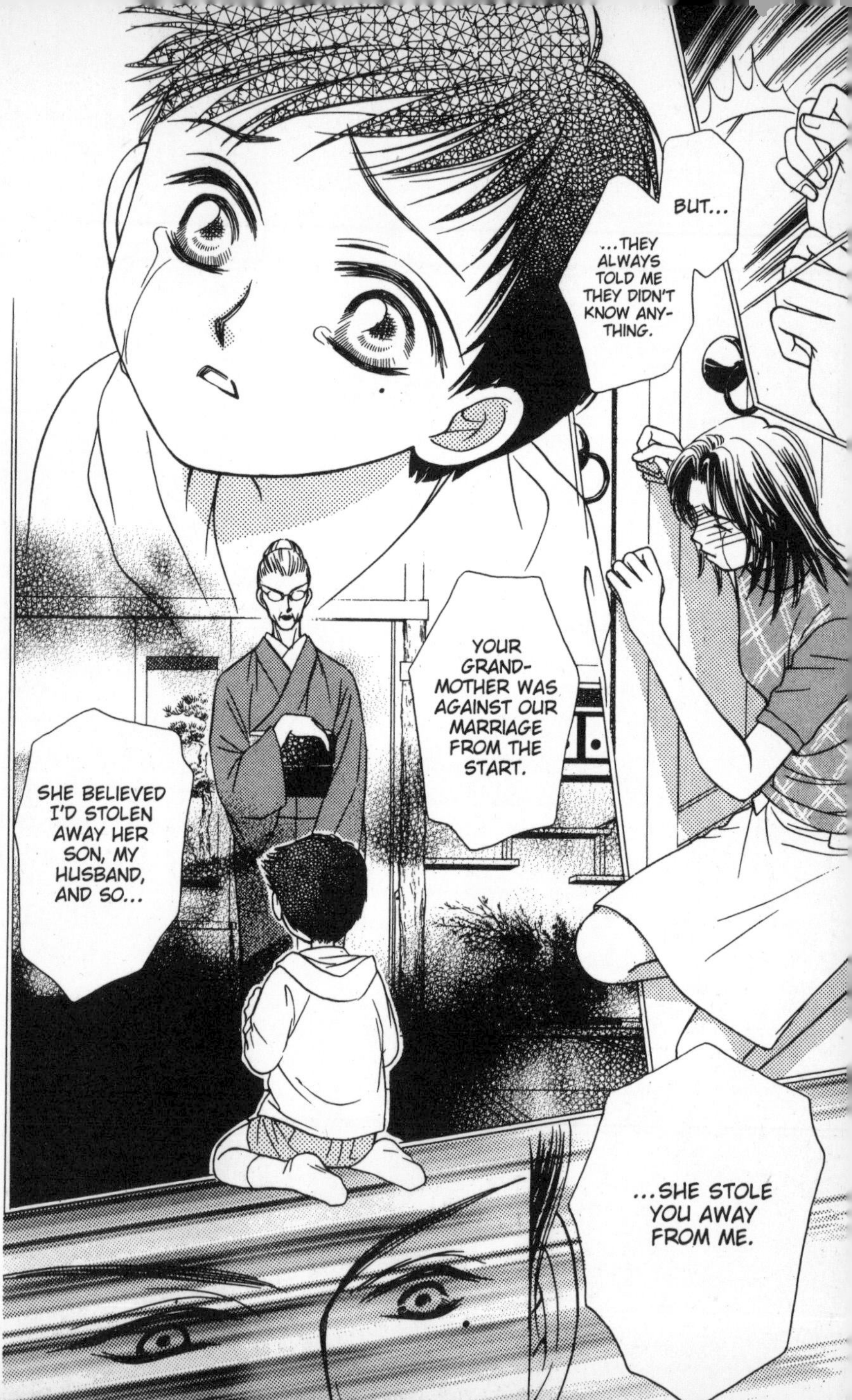
BUT...
...THEY ALWAYS TOLD ME THEY DIDN'T KNOW ANY-THING.
YOUR GRAND-MOTHER WAS AGAINST OUR MARRIAGE FROM THE START.
SHE BELIEVED I'D STOLEN AWAY HER SON, MY HUSBAND, AND SO...
...SHE STOLE YOU AWAY FROM ME.

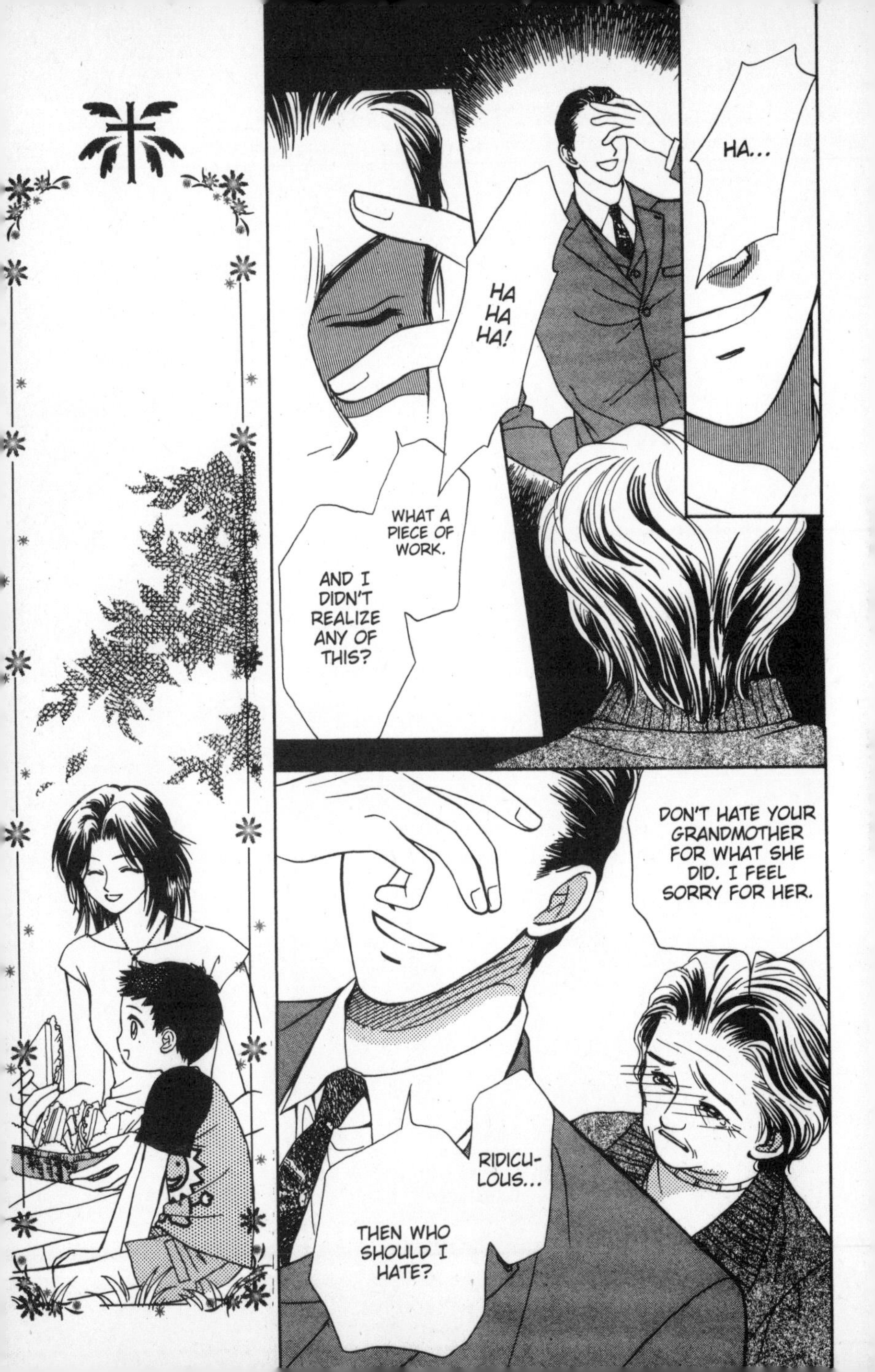
HA...
HA HA HA!
WHAT A PIECE OF WORK.
AND I DIDN'T REALIZE ANY OF THIS?
DON'T HATE YOUR GRANDMOTHER FOR WHAT SHE DID. I FEEL SORRY FOR HER.
RIDICU-LOUS...
THEN WHO SHOULD I HATE?

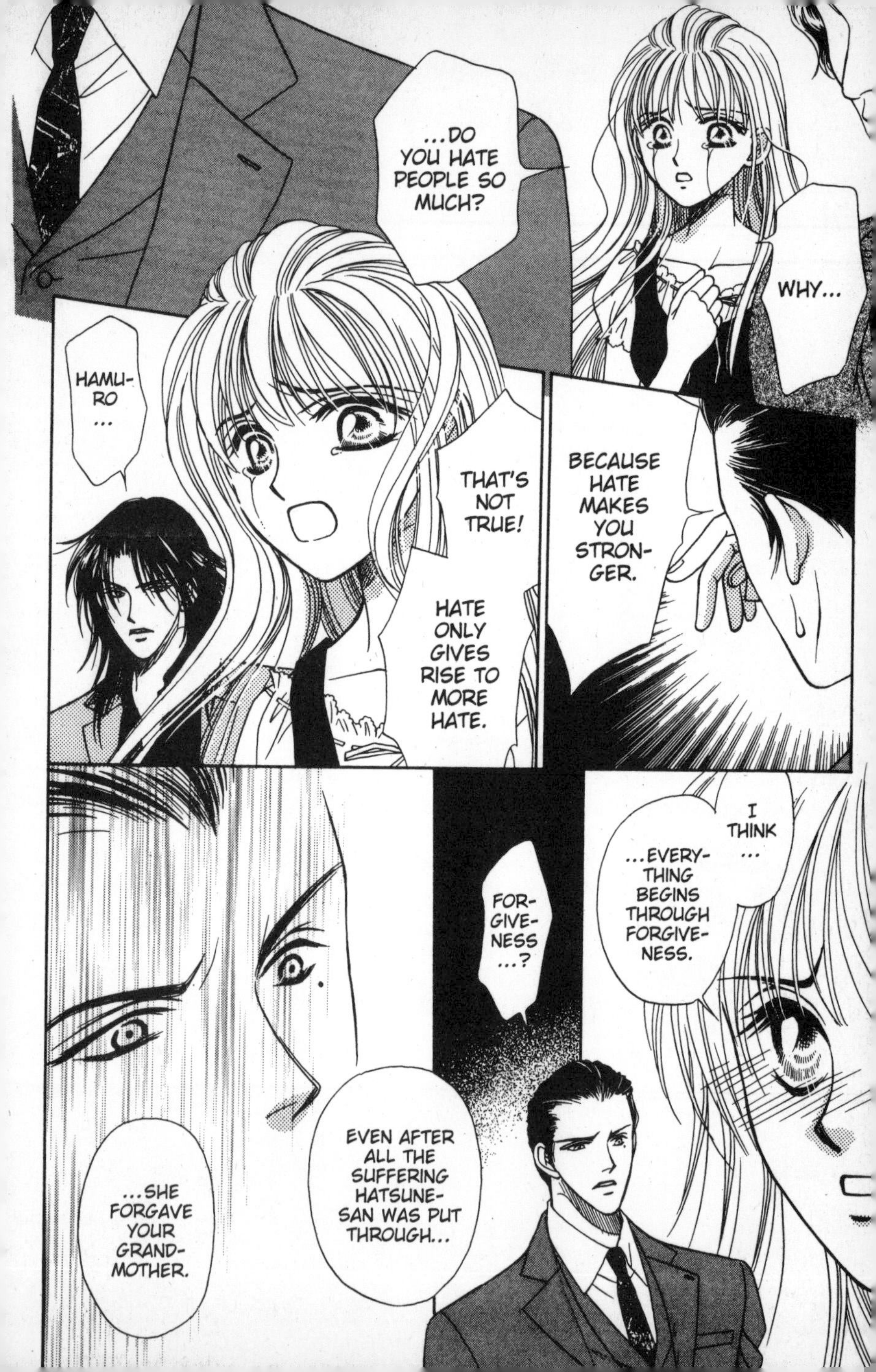
WHY...
...DO YOU HATE PEOPLE SO MUCH?
BECAUSE HATE MAKES YOU STRON-GER.
THAT'S NOT TRUE!
HATE ONLY GIVES RISE TO MORE HATE.
HAMU-RO...
I THINK...
...EVERY-THING BEGINS THROUGH FORGIVE-NESS.
FOR-GIVE-NESS...?
EVEN AFTER ALL THE SUFFERING HATSUNE-SAN WAS PUT THROUGH...
...SHE FORGAVE YOUR GRAND-MOTHER.

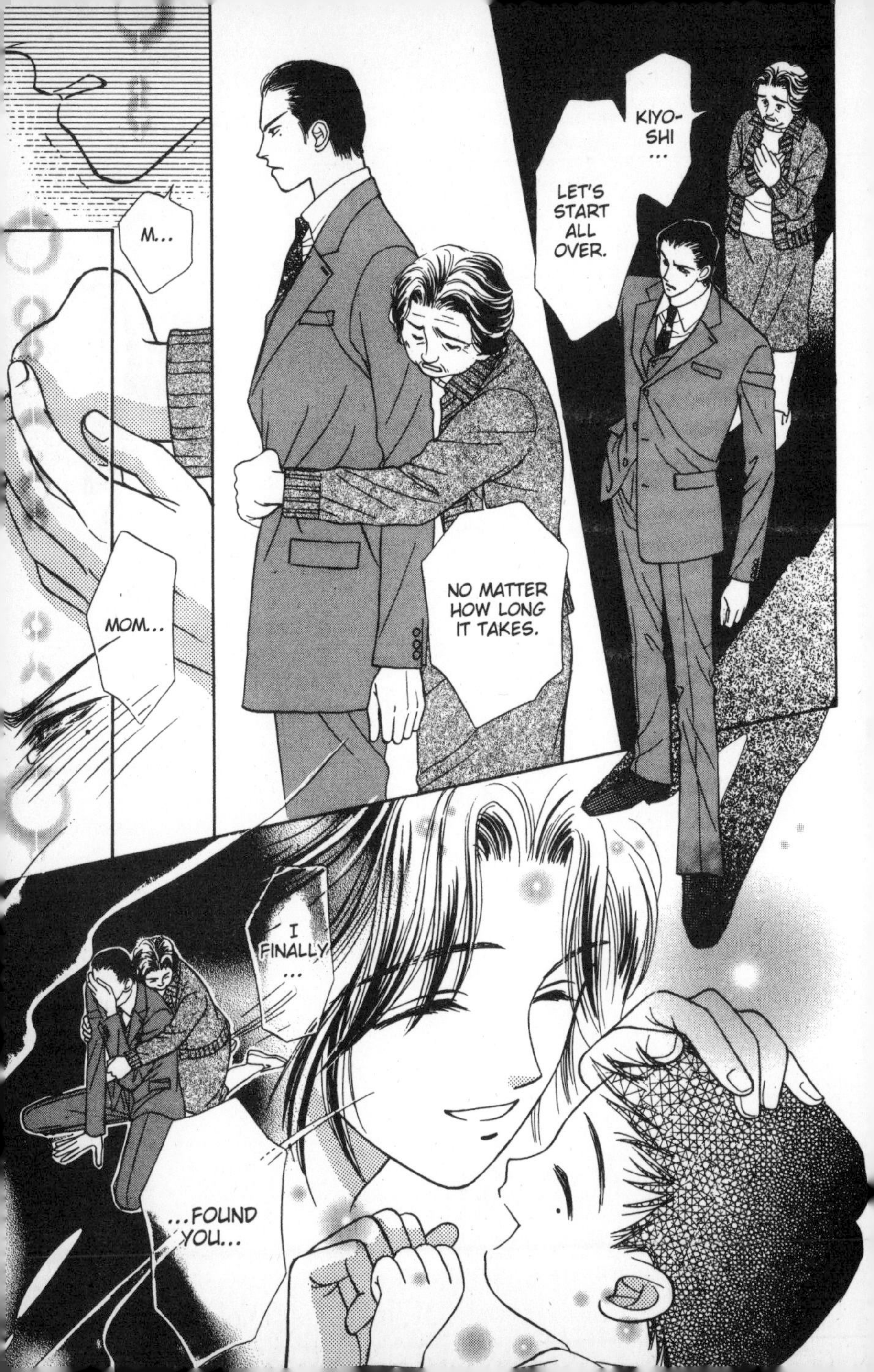
KIYO-SHI ...
LET'S START ALL OVER.
M...
NO MATTER HOW LONG IT TAKES.
MOM...
I FINALLY ...
...FOUND YOU...

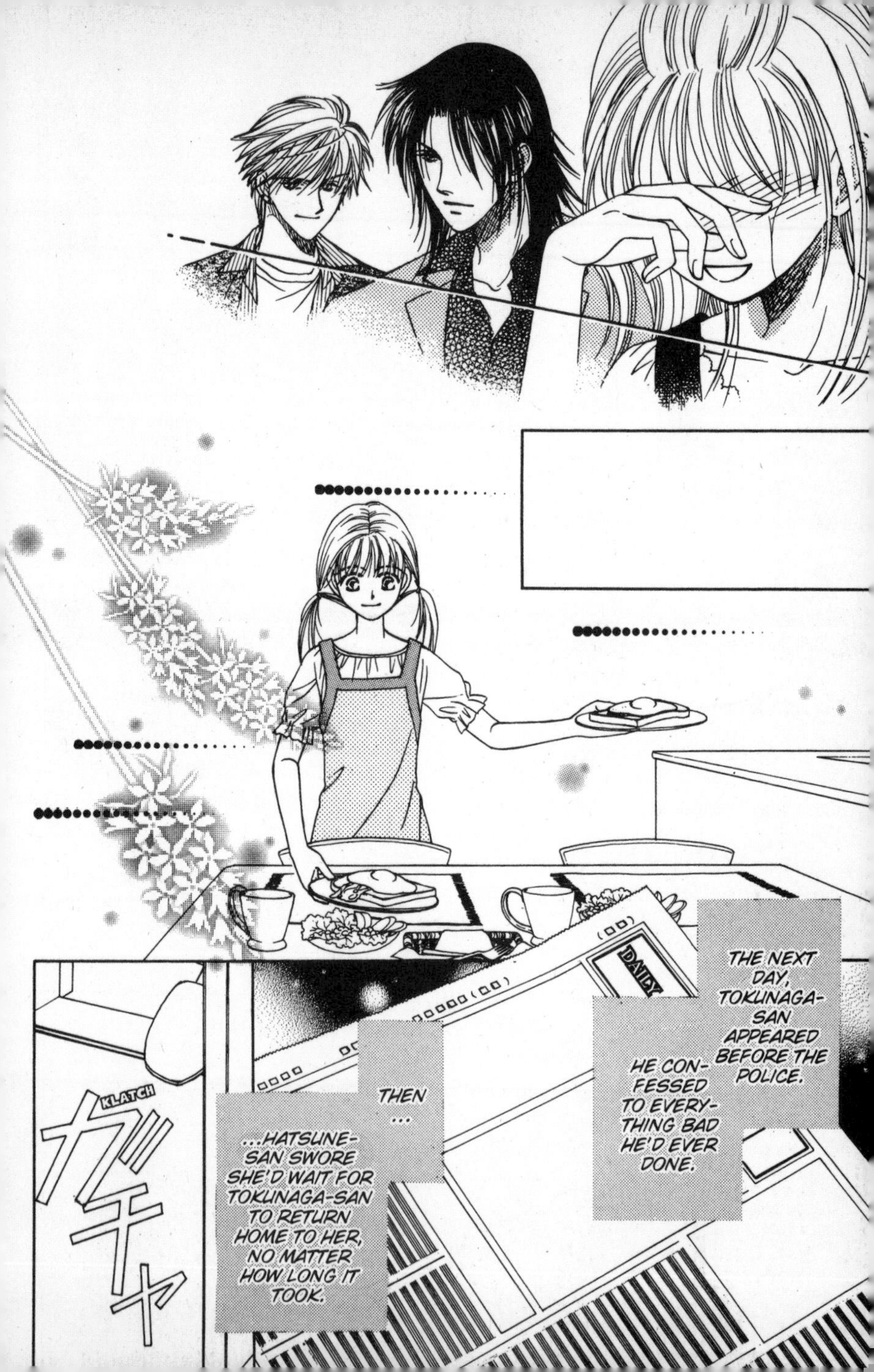
THE NEXT DAY, TOKUNAGA-SAN APPEARED BEFORE THE POLICE.
HE CONFESSED TO EVERYTHING BAD HE'D EVER DONE.
THEN ...
...HATSUNE-SAN SWORE SHE'D WAIT FOR TOKUNAGA-SAN TO RETURN HOME TO HER, NO MATTER HOW LONG IT TOOK.
KLATCH
DAILY

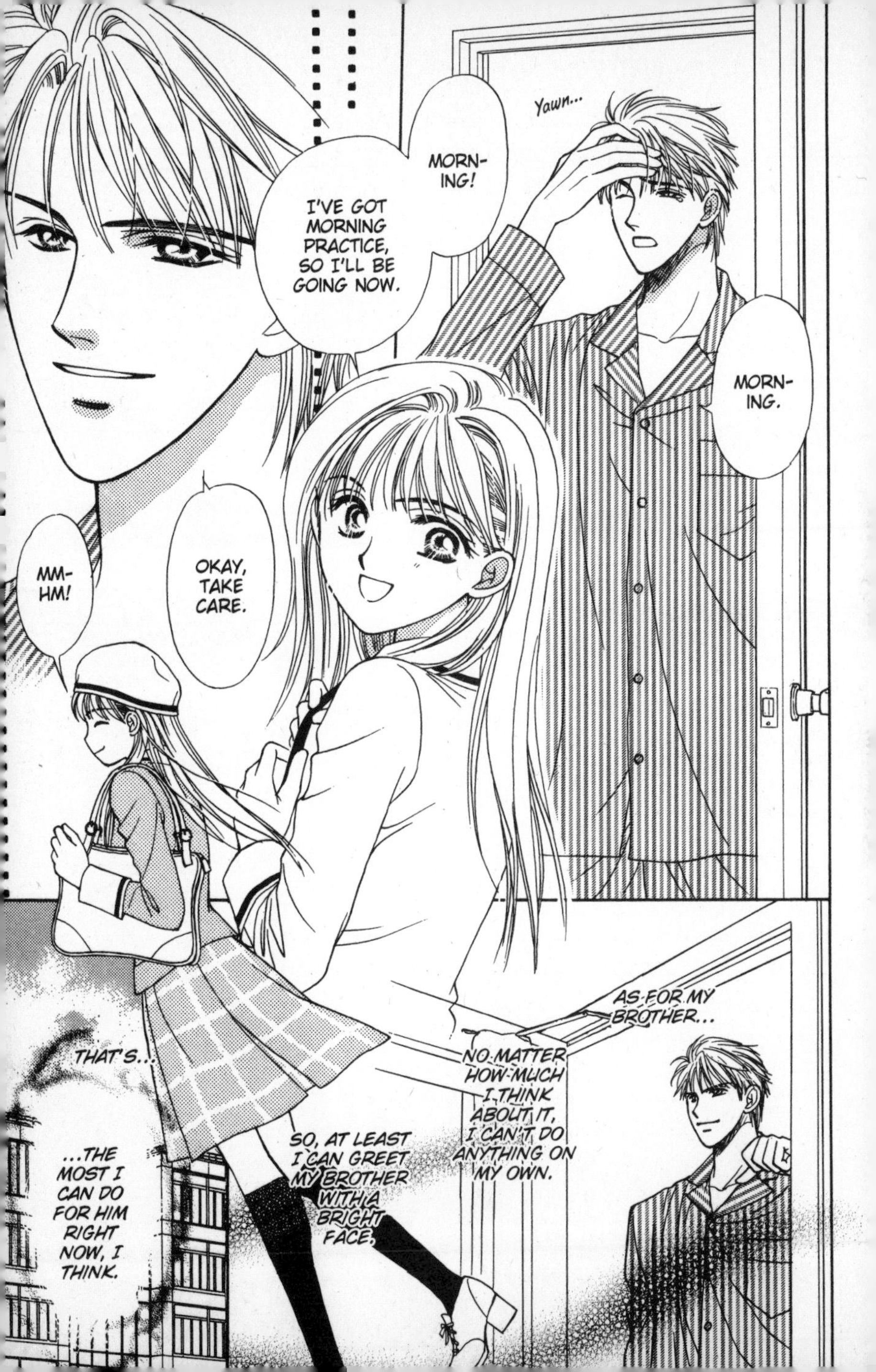
Yawn...
MORN-ING.
MORN-ING!
I'VE GOT MORNING PRACTICE, SO I'LL BE GOING NOW.
OKAY, TAKE CARE.
MM-HM!
AS FOR MY BROTHER...
NO MATTER HOW MUCH I THINK ABOUT IT, I CAN'T DO ANYTHING ON MY OWN.
SO, AT LEAST I CAN GREET MY BROTHER WITH A BRIGHT FACE.
THAT'S...
...THE MOST I CAN DO FOR HIM RIGHT NOW, I THINK.

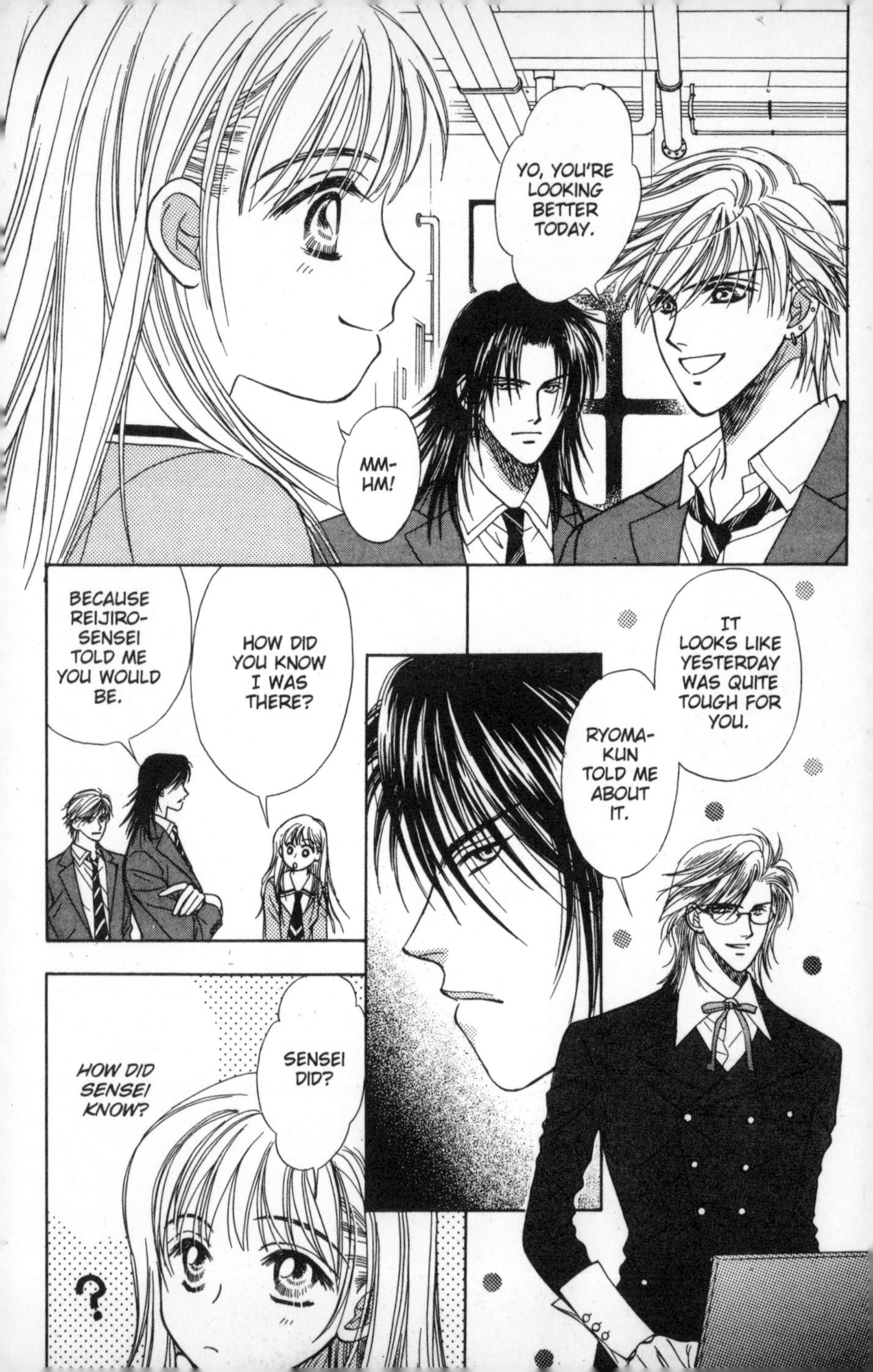
YO, YOU'RE LOOKING BETTER TODAY.
MM-HM!
IT LOOKS LIKE YESTERDAY WAS QUITE TOUGH FOR YOU.
RYOMA-KUN TOLD ME ABOUT IT.
HOW DID YOU KNOW I WAS THERE?
BECAUSE REIJIRO-SENSEI TOLD ME YOU WOULD BE.
SENSEI DID?
HOW DID SENSEI KNOW?

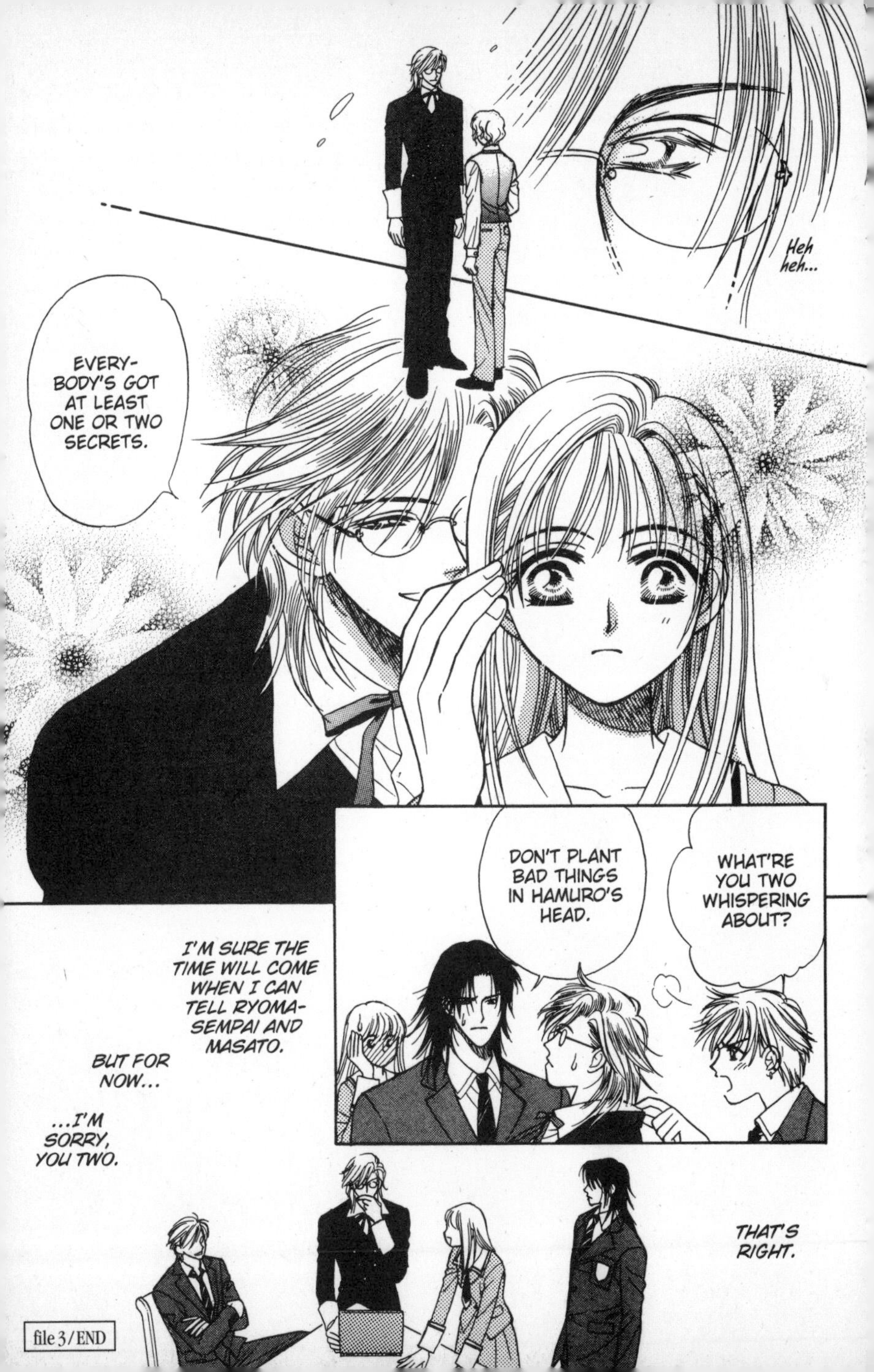
Heh heh...
EVERY-BODY'S GOT AT LEAST ONE OR TWO SECRETS.
WHAT'RE YOU TWO WHISPERING ABOUT?
DON'T PLANT BAD THINGS IN HAMURO'S HEAD.
I'M SURE THE TIME WILL COME WHEN I CAN TELL RYOMA-SEMPAI AND MASATO.
BUT FOR NOW...
...I'M SORRY, YOU TWO.
THAT'S RIGHT.
file 3/END

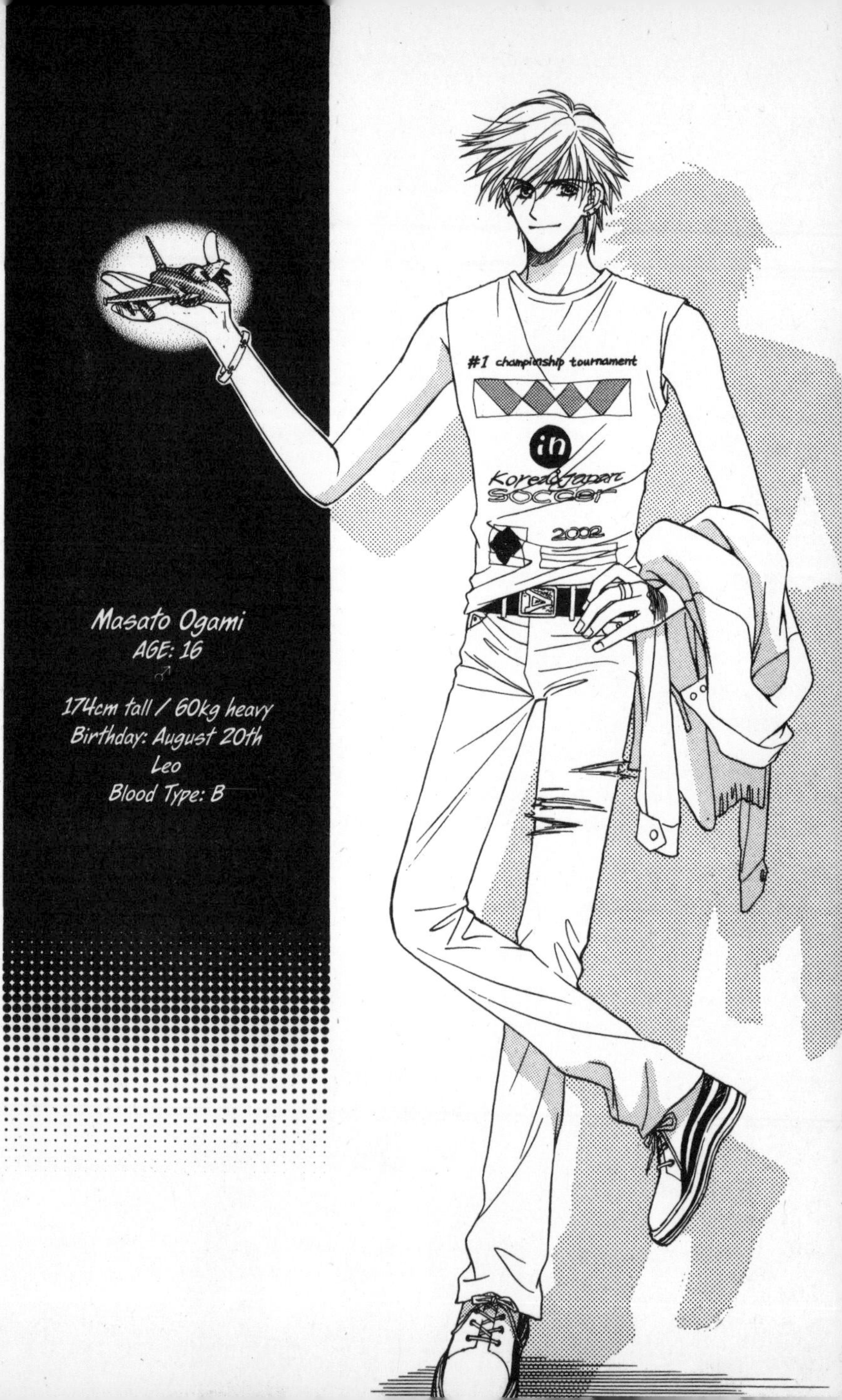
#1 championship tournament
in
Korea&Japan
soccer
2002
Masato Ogami
AGE: 16
♂
174cm tall / 60kg heavy
Birthday: August 20th
Leo
Blood Type: B

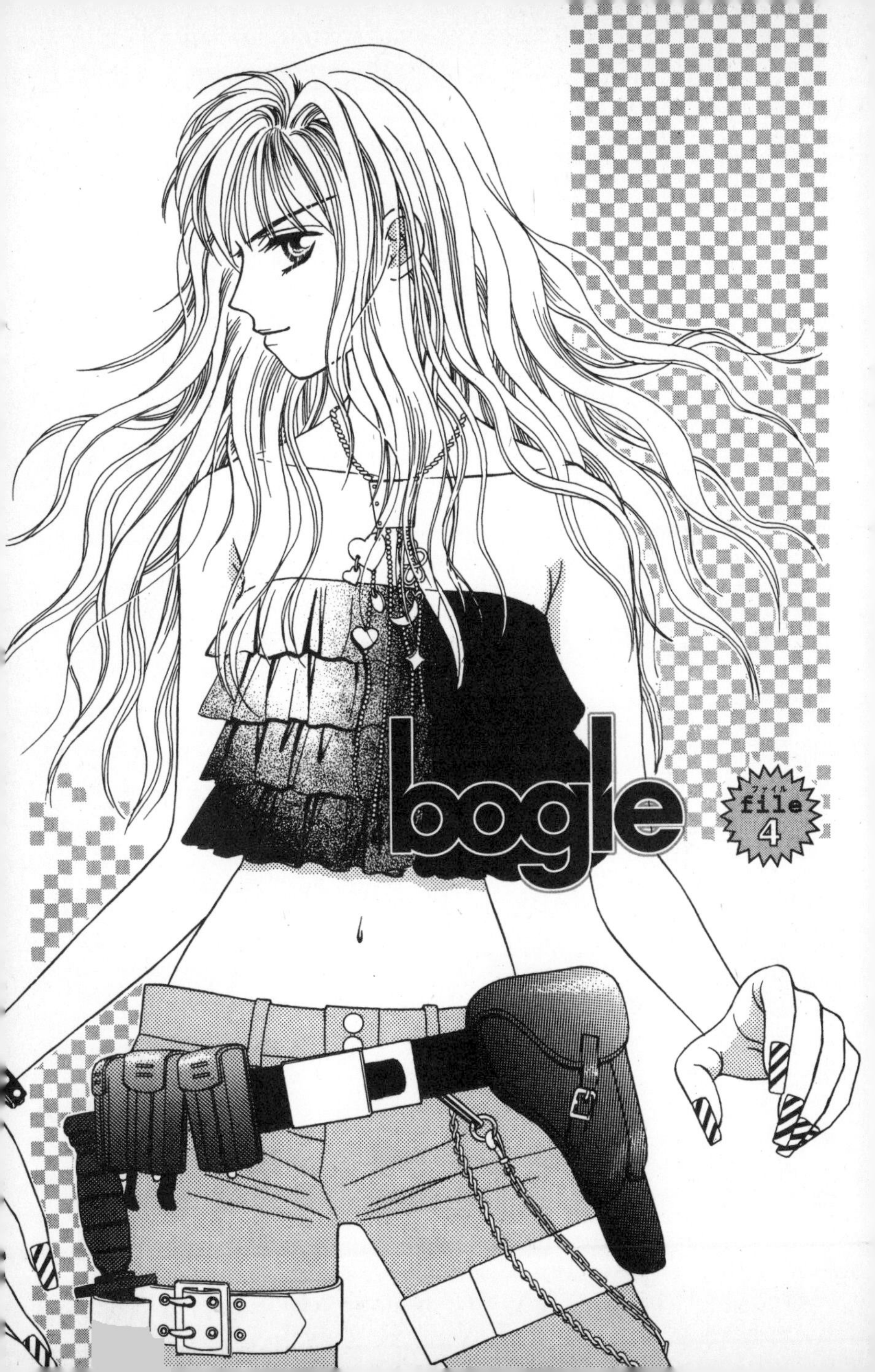
bogle
ファイル
file
4

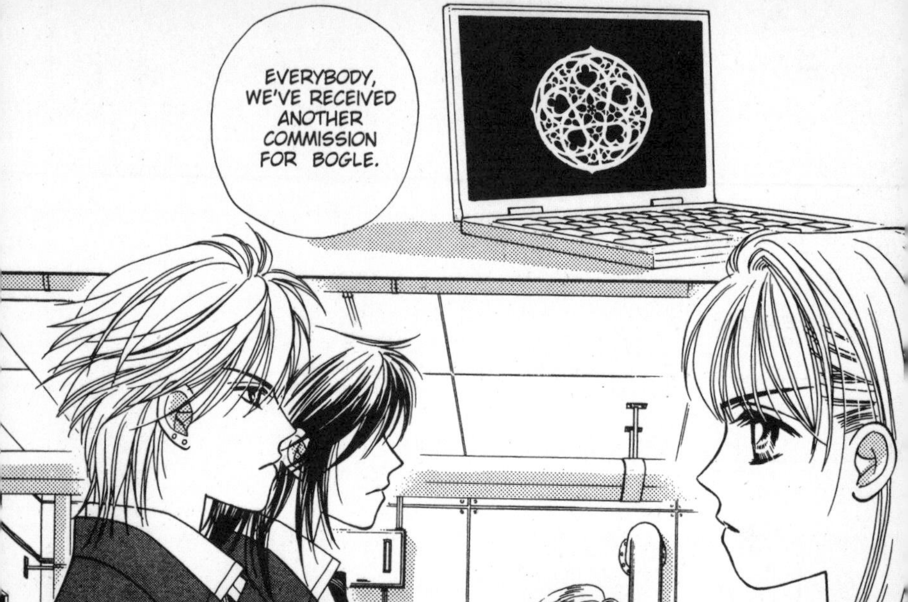
EVERYBODY, WE'VE RECEIVED ANOTHER COMMISSION FOR BOGLE.
IT'S FOR A RECENTLY DISCOVERED RENÉ MAGRITTE ILLUSION PIECE.
YOU ARE TO STEAL THE "WING OF THE SKY."

Actually, I've also got another book out from Akita Shoten. It's about a spiritually endowed clinic, called "Daughter of Pinocchio" (from Horror Comics Special). If you'd like, please read it.

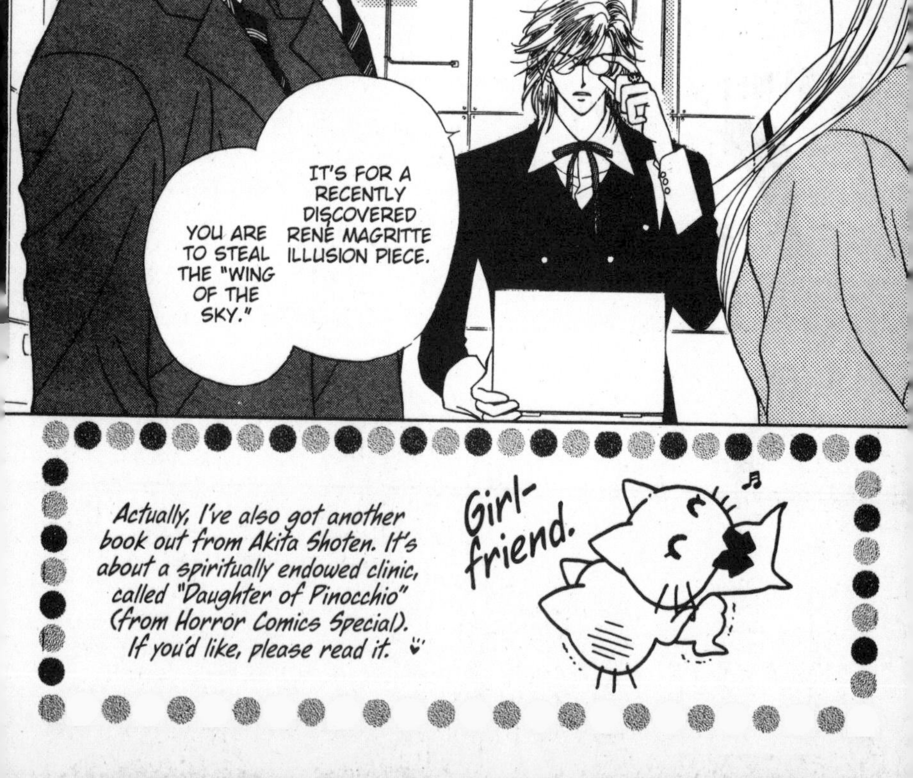
Girl-friend.

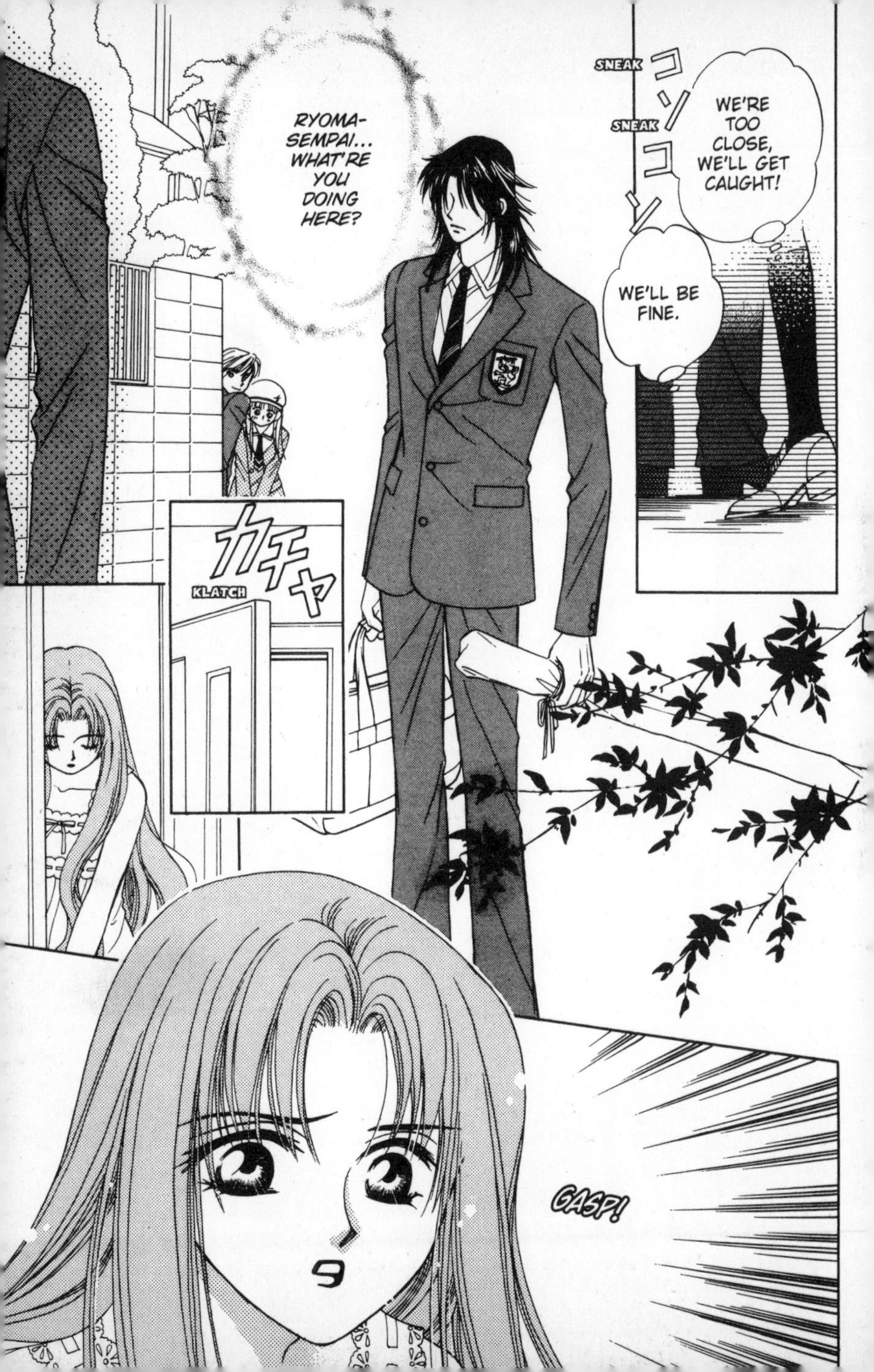
SNEAK
SNEAK
WE'RE TOO CLOSE, WE'LL GET CAUGHT!
WE'LL BE FINE.
RYOMA-SEMPAI... WHAT'RE YOU DOING HERE?
KLATCH
GASP!

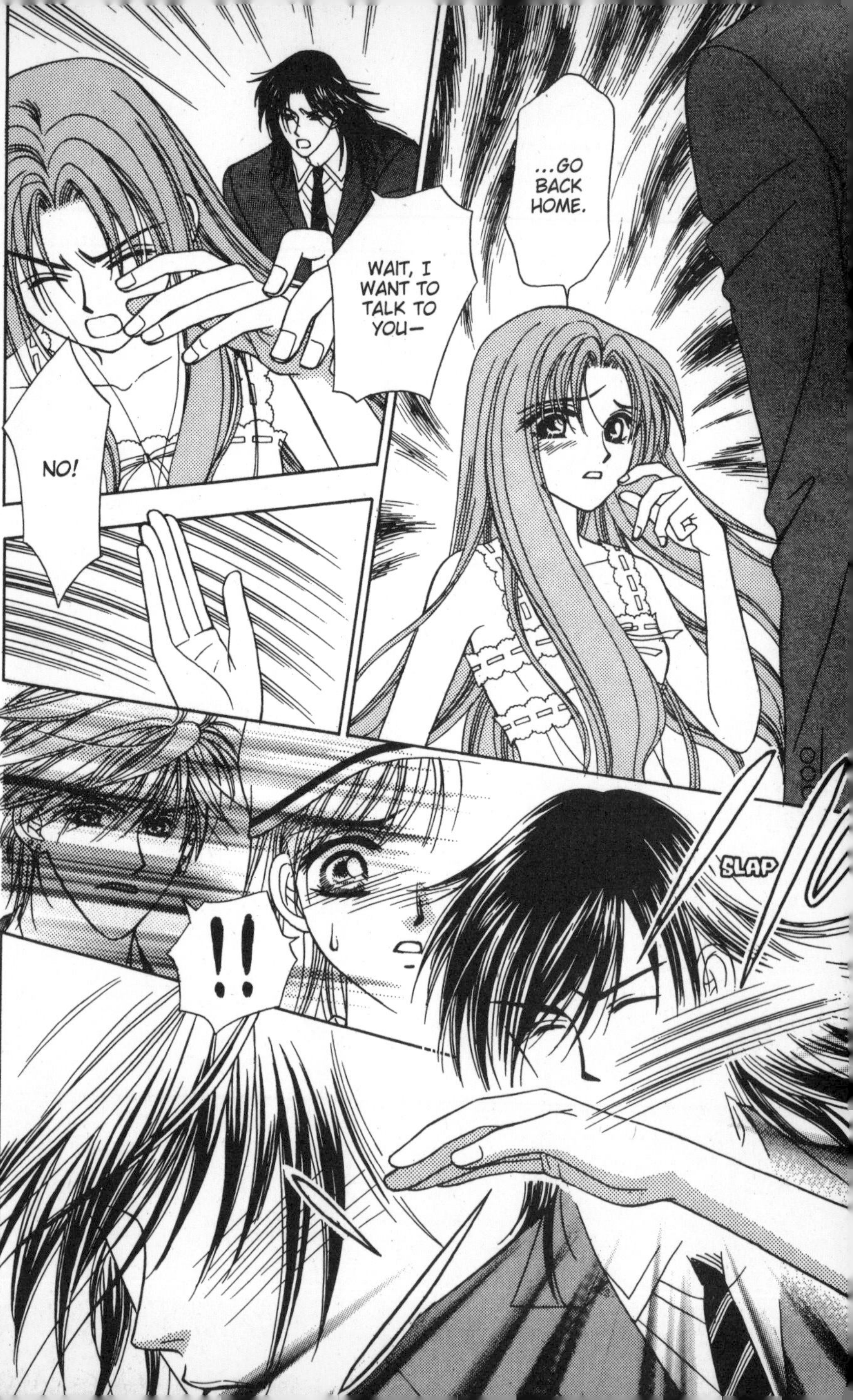
...GO BACK HOME.
WAIT, I WANT TO TALK TO YOU—
NO!
SLAP
!!

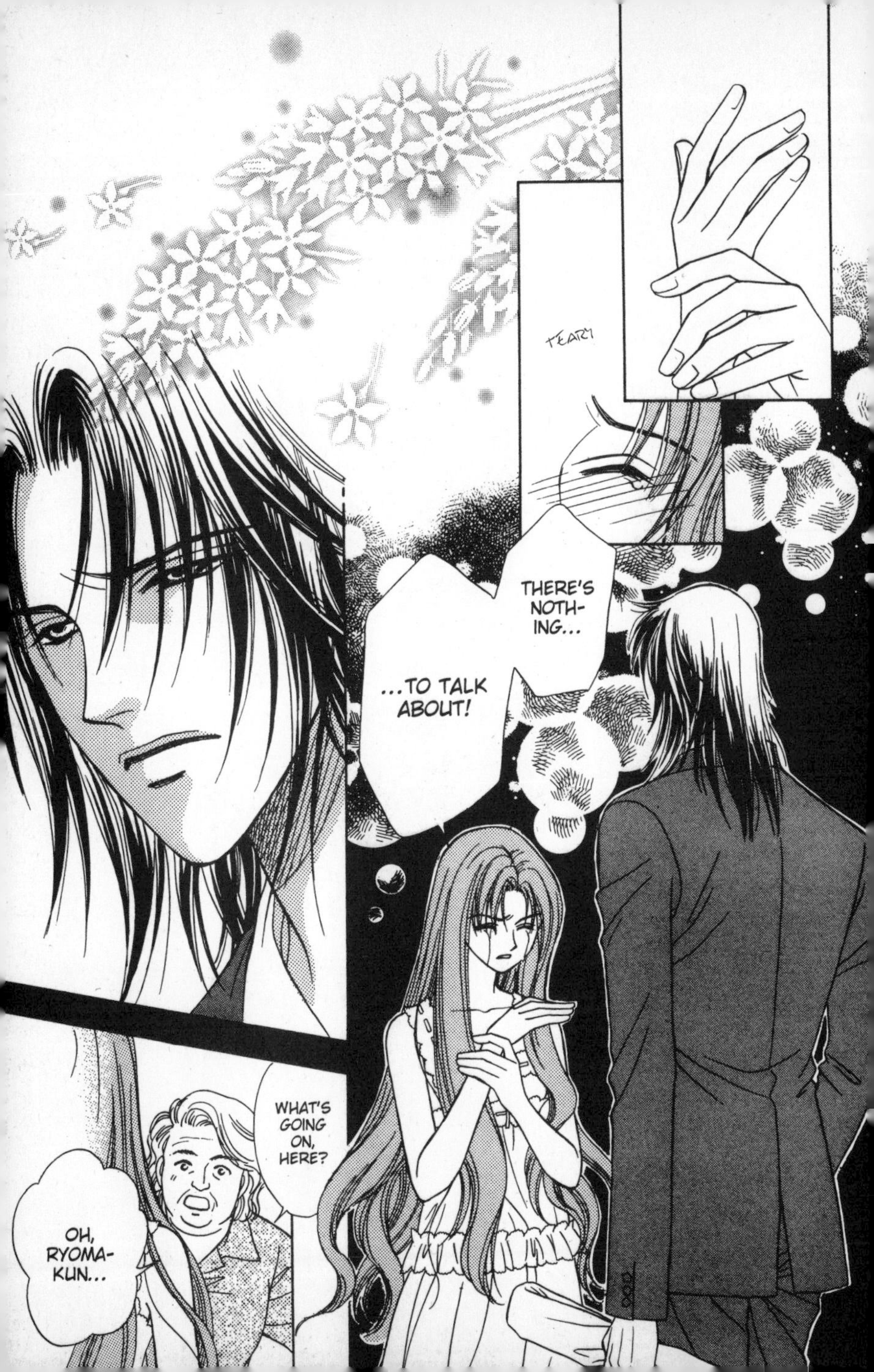
TEARY
THERE'S NOTH-ING...
...TO TALK ABOUT!
WHAT'S GOING ON, HERE?
OH, RYOMA-KUN...

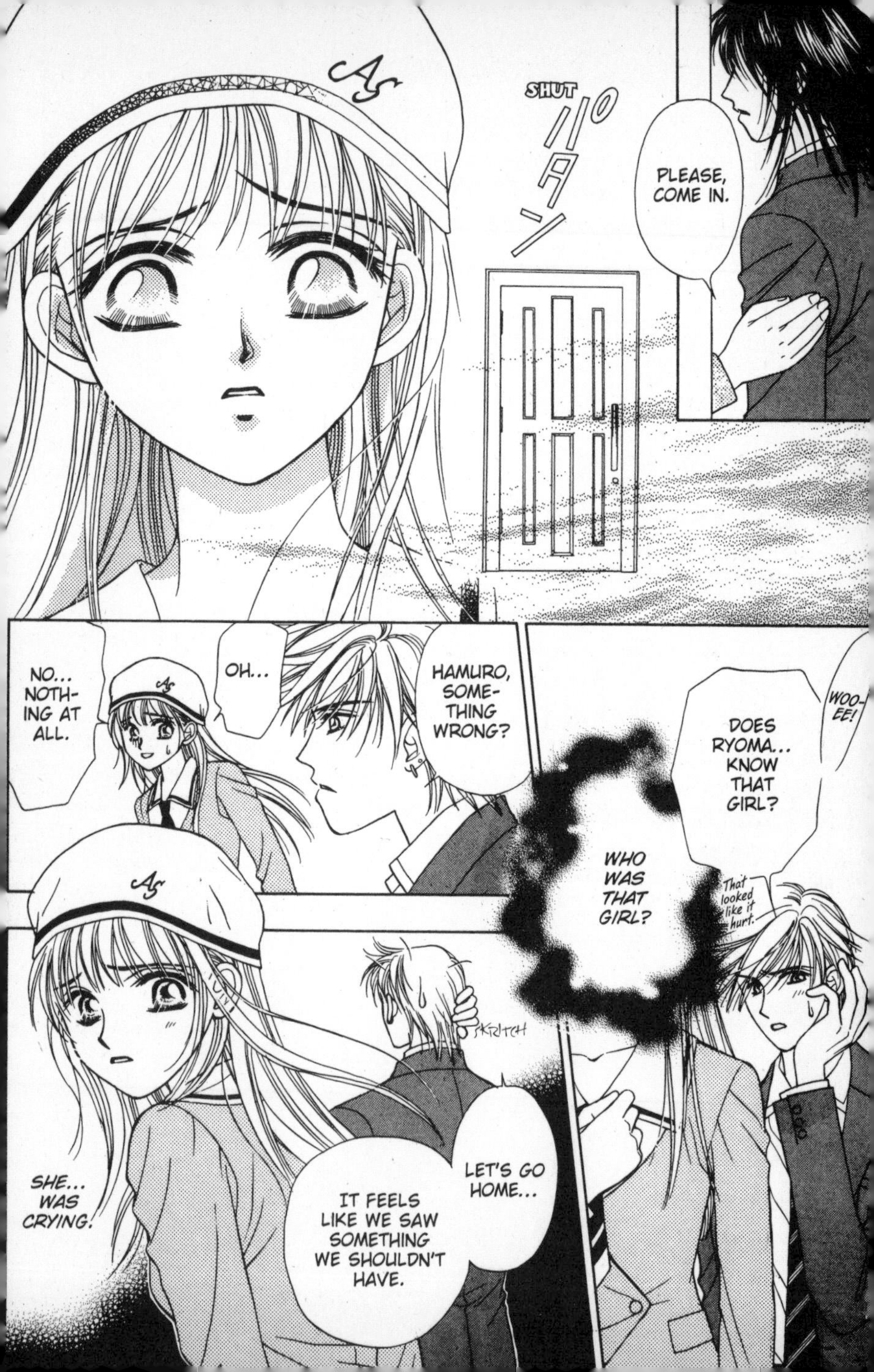
PLEASE, COME IN.
SHUT
パタン
WOO-EE!
DOES RYOMA... KNOW THAT GIRL?
That looked like it hurt.
HAMURO, SOMETHING WRONG?
OH...
NO... NOTHING AT ALL.
WHO WAS THAT GIRL?
SKRITCH
LET'S GO HOME...
IT FEELS LIKE WE SAW SOMETHING WE SHOULDN'T HAVE.
SHE... WAS CRYING.

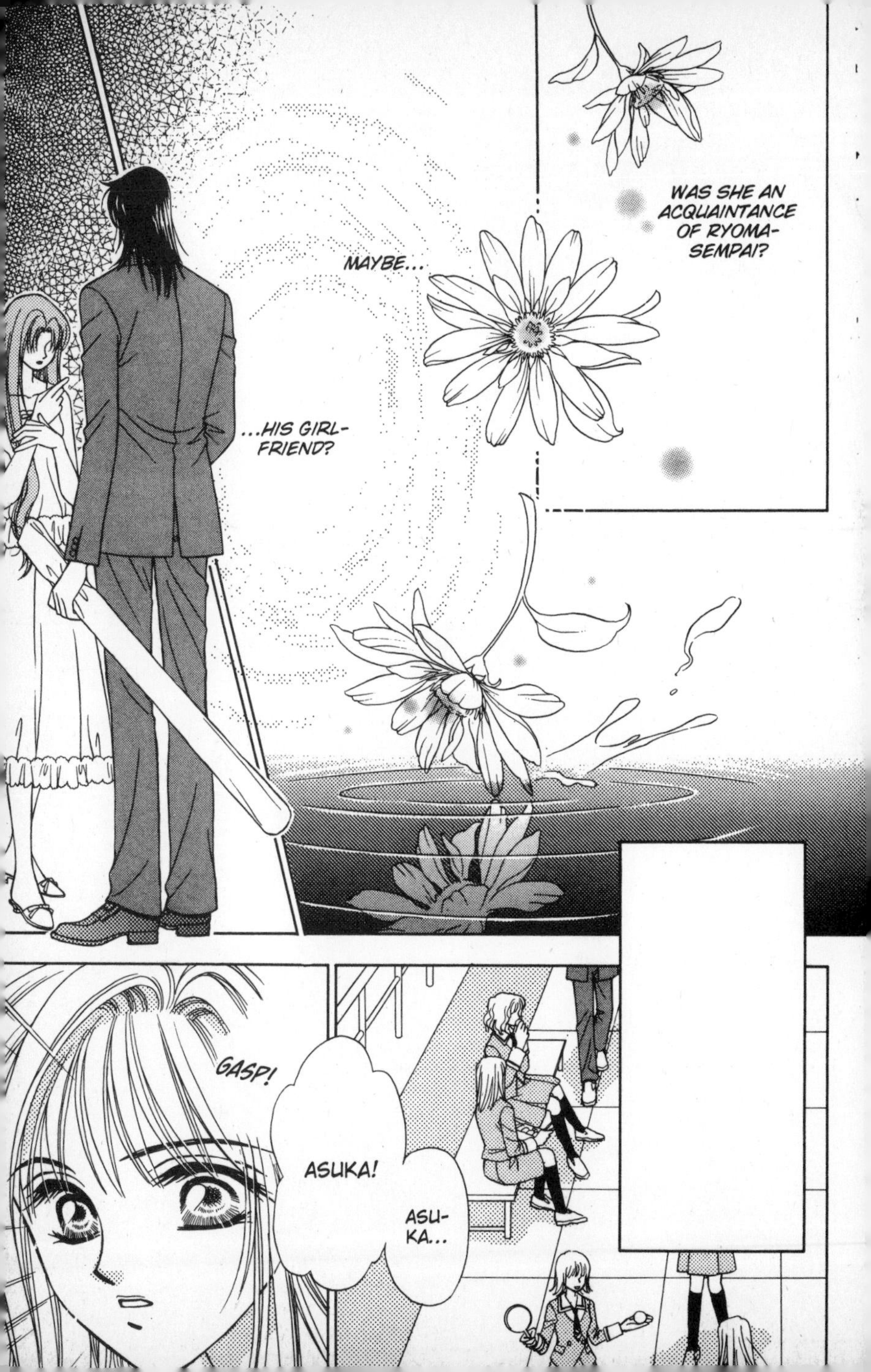

WAS SHE AN ACQUAINTANCE OF RYOMA-SEMPAI?
MAYBE...
...HIS GIRL-FRIEND?
ASU-KA...
ASUKA!
GASP!

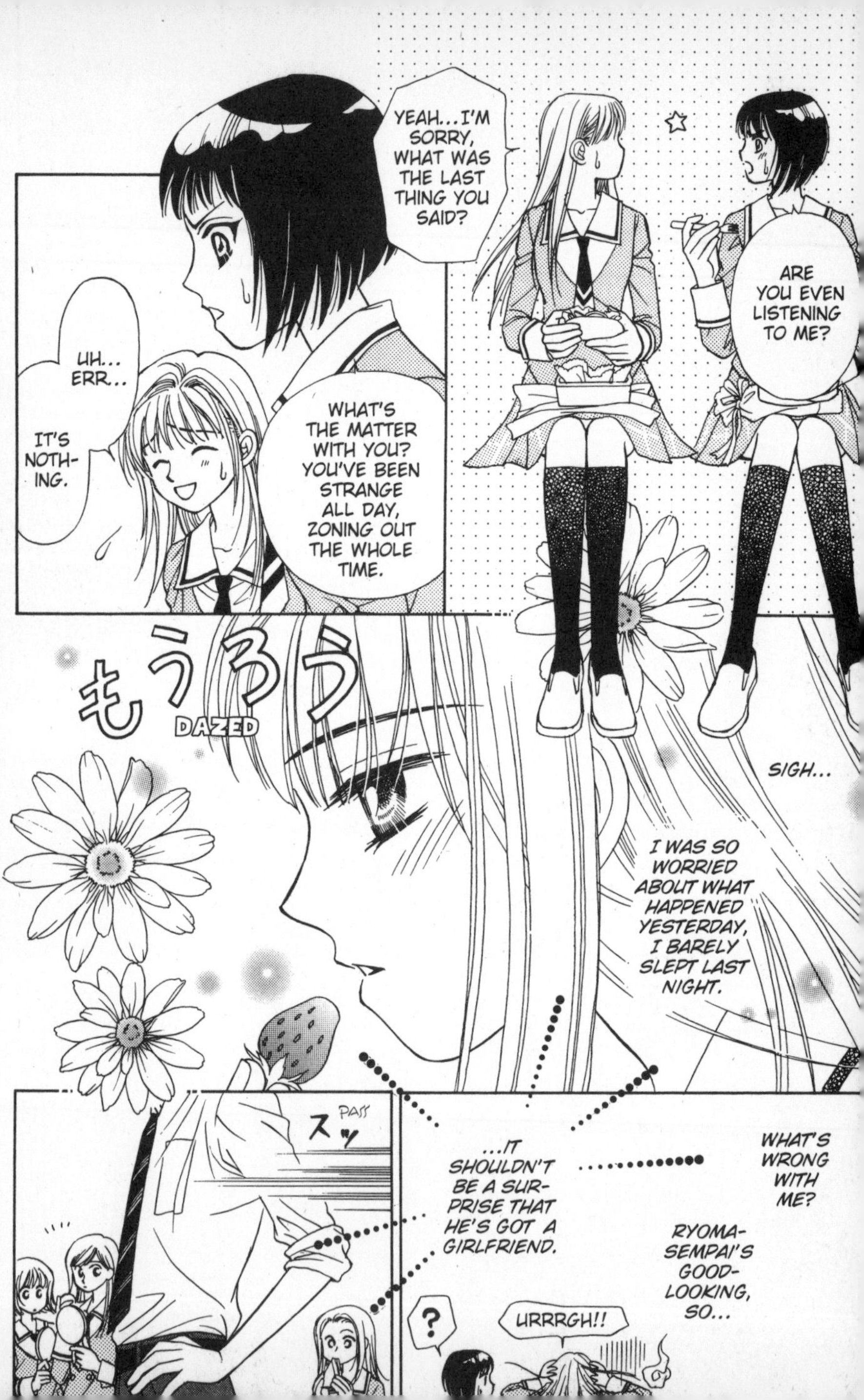

ARE YOU EVEN LISTENING TO ME?
YEAH...I'M SORRY, WHAT WAS THE LAST THING YOU SAID?
WHAT'S THE MATTER WITH YOU? YOU'VE BEEN STRANGE ALL DAY, ZONING OUT THE WHOLE TIME.
UH... ERR...
IT'S NOTHING.
SIGH...
もうろう
DAZED
I WAS SO WORRIED ABOUT WHAT HAPPENED YESTERDAY, I BARELY SLEPT LAST NIGHT.
WHAT'S WRONG WITH ME?
RYOMA-SEMPAI'S GOOD-LOOKING, SO...
...IT SHOULDN'T BE A SURPRISE THAT HE'S GOT A GIRLFRIEND.
URRRGH!!
?
スッ
PASS

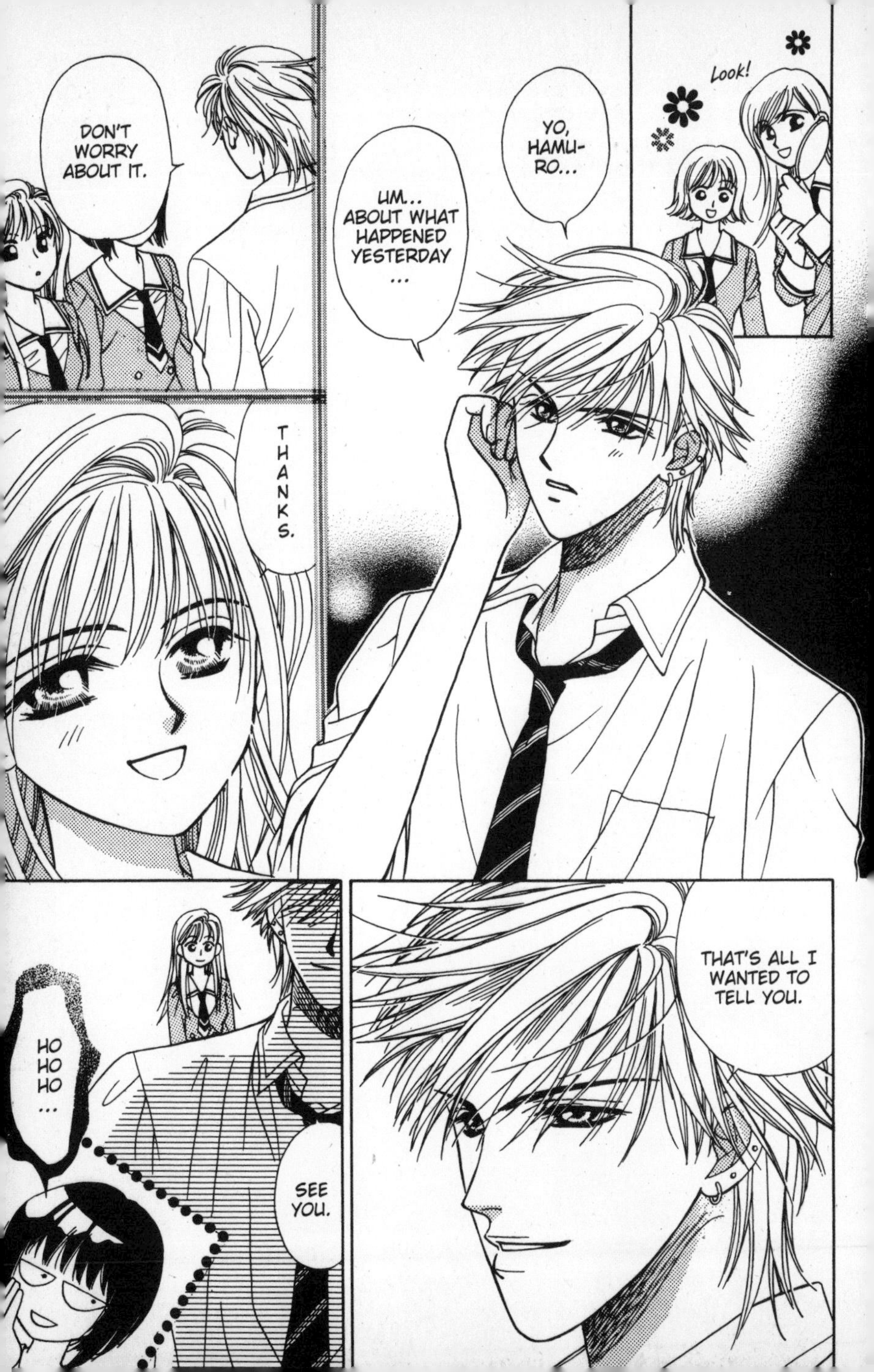
Look!
YO, HAMURO...
UM... ABOUT WHAT HAPPENED YESTERDAY...
DON'T WORRY ABOUT IT.
THANKS.
THAT'S ALL I WANTED TO TELL YOU.
SEE YOU.
HO HO HO...

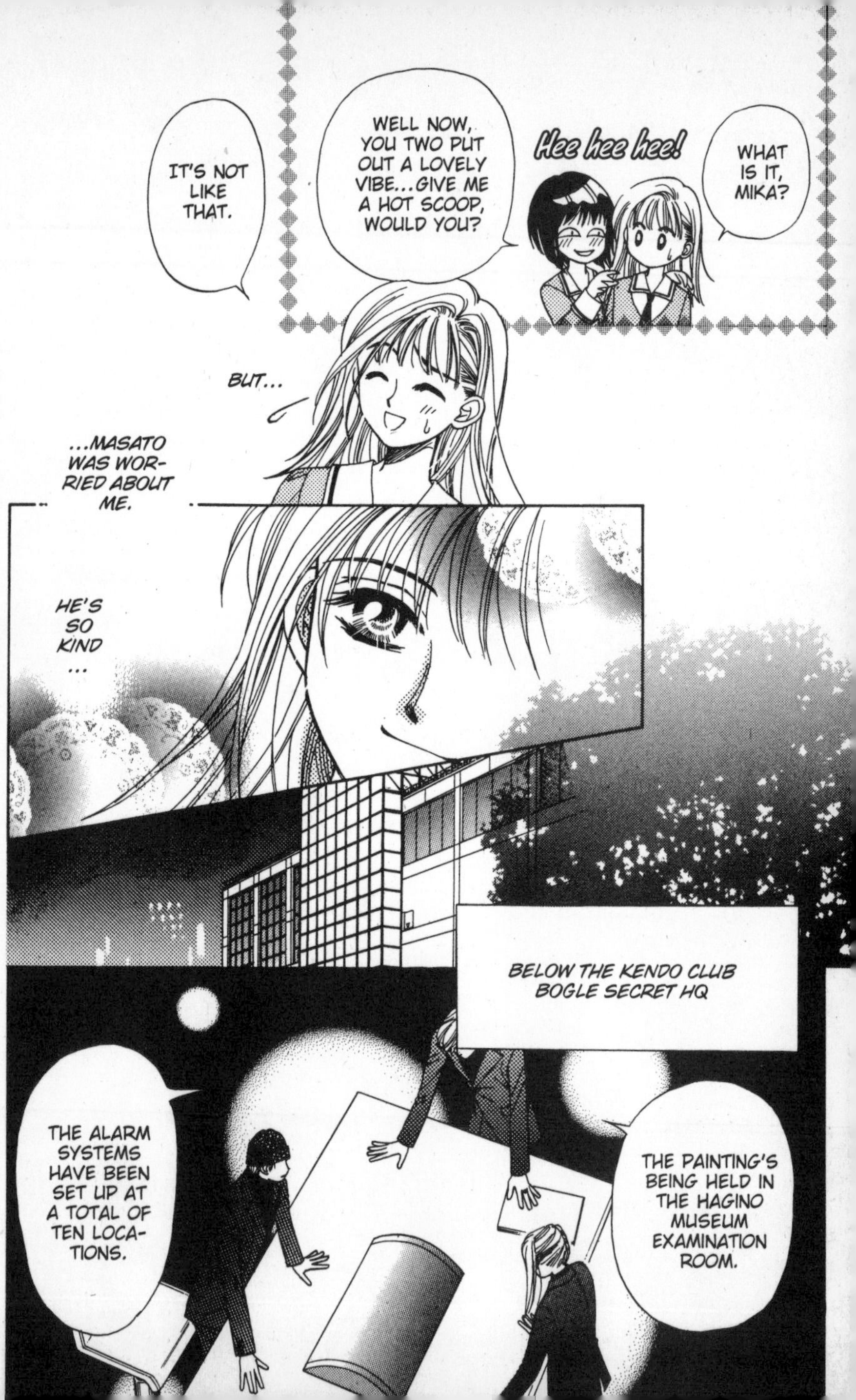

WHAT IS IT, MIKA?
Hee hee hee!
WELL NOW, YOU TWO PUT OUT A LOVELY VIBE...GIVE ME A HOT SCOOP, WOULD YOU?
IT'S NOT LIKE THAT.
BUT...
...MASATO WAS WOR-RIED ABOUT ME.
HE'S SO KIND ...
BELOW THE KENDO CLUB BOGLE SECRET HQ
THE PAINTING'S BEING HELD IN THE HAGINO MUSEUM EXAMINATION ROOM.
THE ALARM SYSTEMS HAVE BEEN SET UP AT A TOTAL OF TEN LOCA-TIONS.

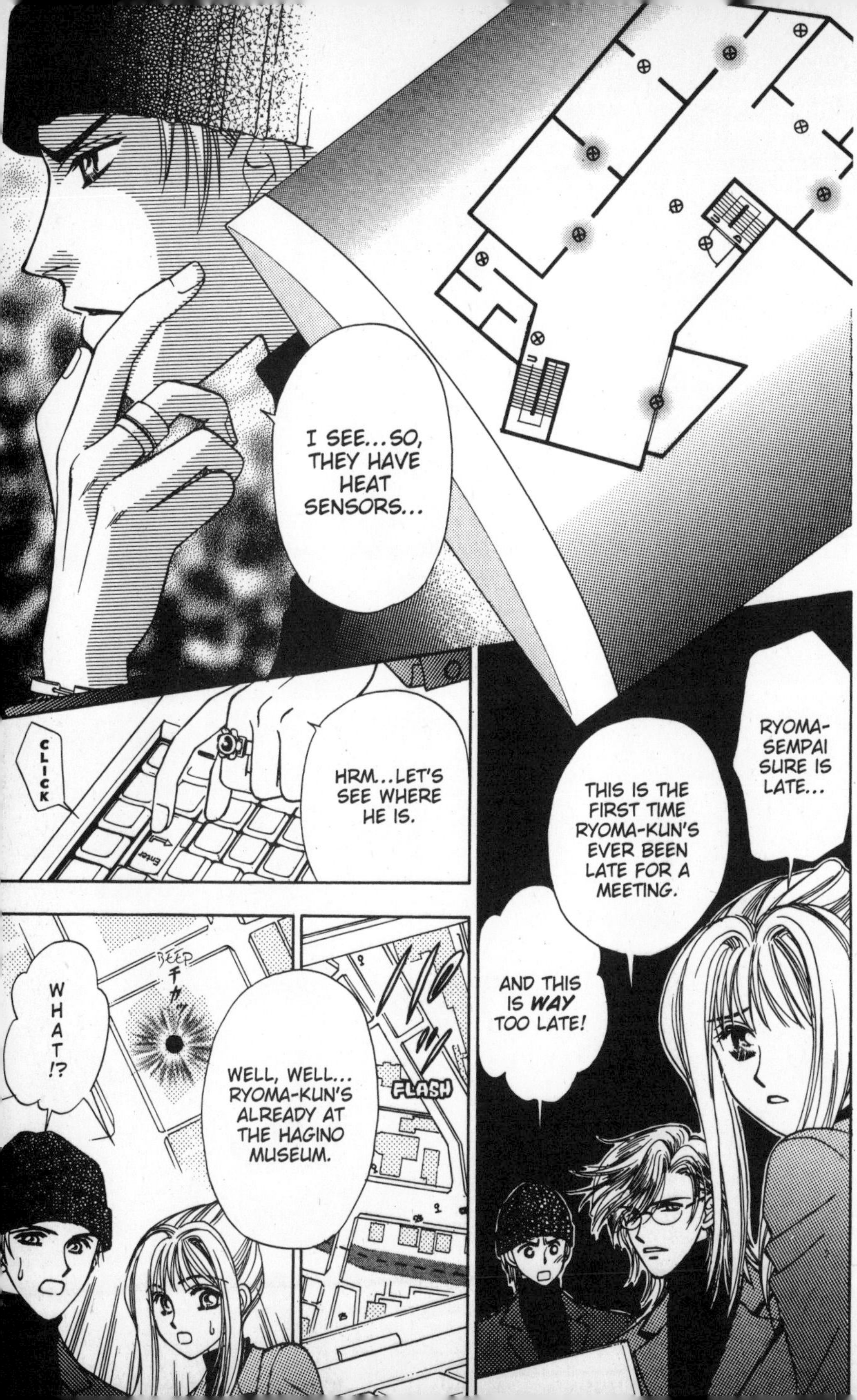
I SEE...SO, THEY HAVE HEAT SENSORS...
RYOMA-SEMPAI SURE IS LATE...
THIS IS THE FIRST TIME RYOMA-KUN'S EVER BEEN LATE FOR A MEETING.
AND THIS IS *WAY* TOO LATE!
HRM...LET'S SEE WHERE HE IS.
CLICK
Enter
FLASH
WELL, WELL... RYOMA-KUN'S ALREADY AT THE HAGINO MUSEUM.
BEEP
WHAT!?

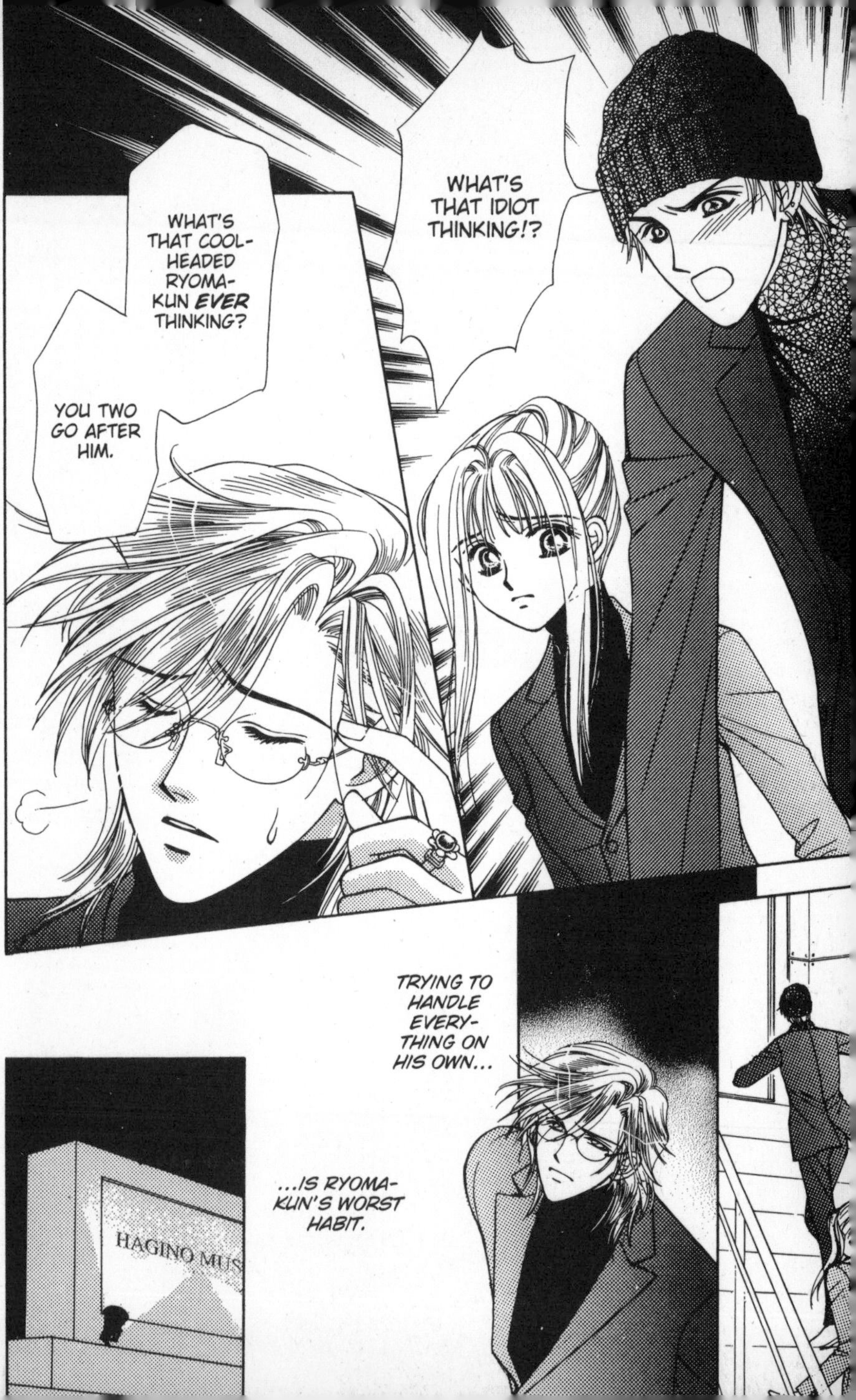
WHAT'S THAT IDIOT THINKING!?
WHAT'S THAT COOL-HEADED RYOMA-KUN *EVER* THINKING?
YOU TWO GO AFTER HIM.
TRYING TO HANDLE EVERY-THING ON HIS OWN...
...IS RYOMA-KUN'S WORST HABIT.
HAGINO MUS

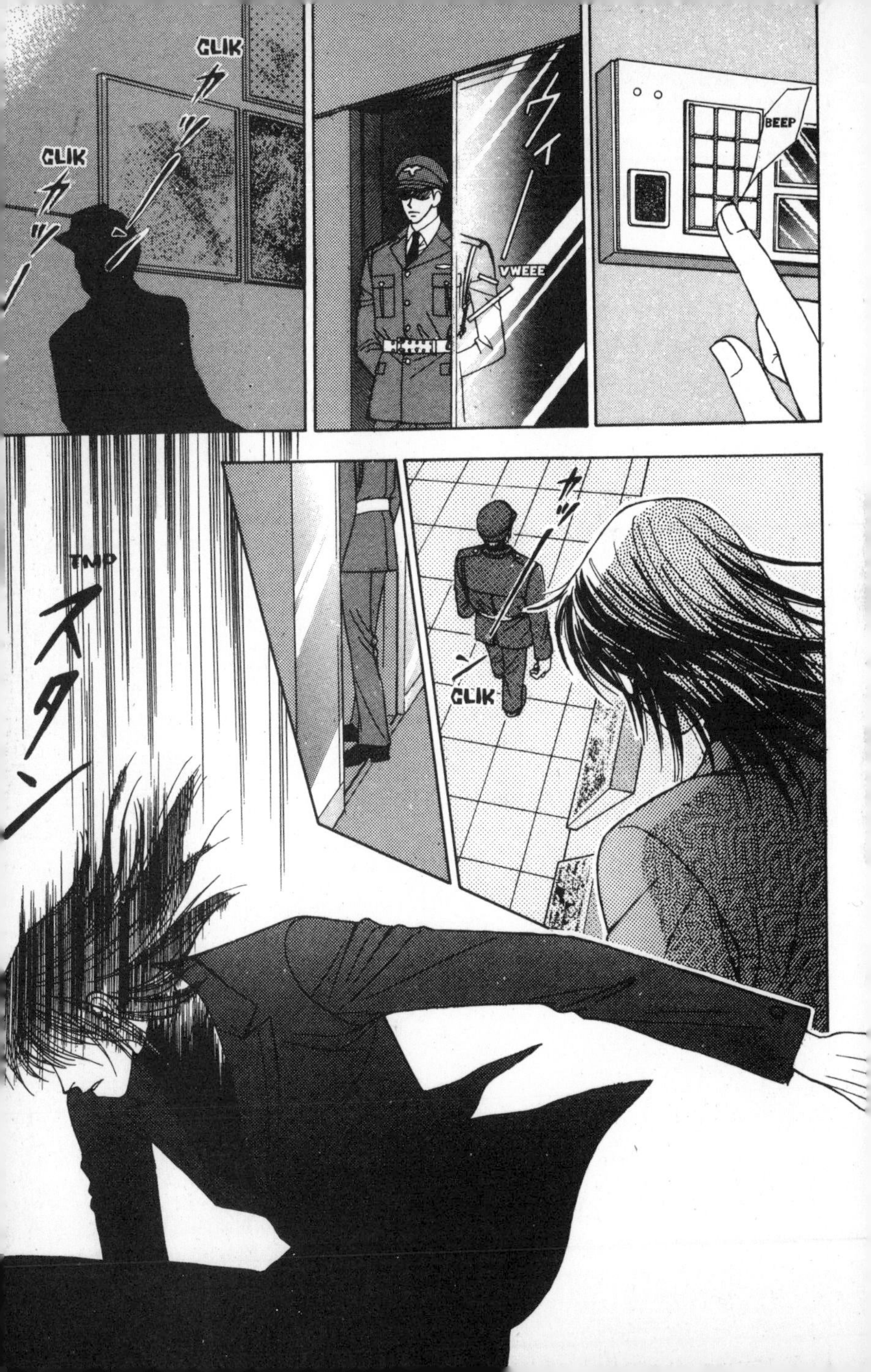
BEEP
VWEEE
GLIK
GLIK
GLIK
TMP

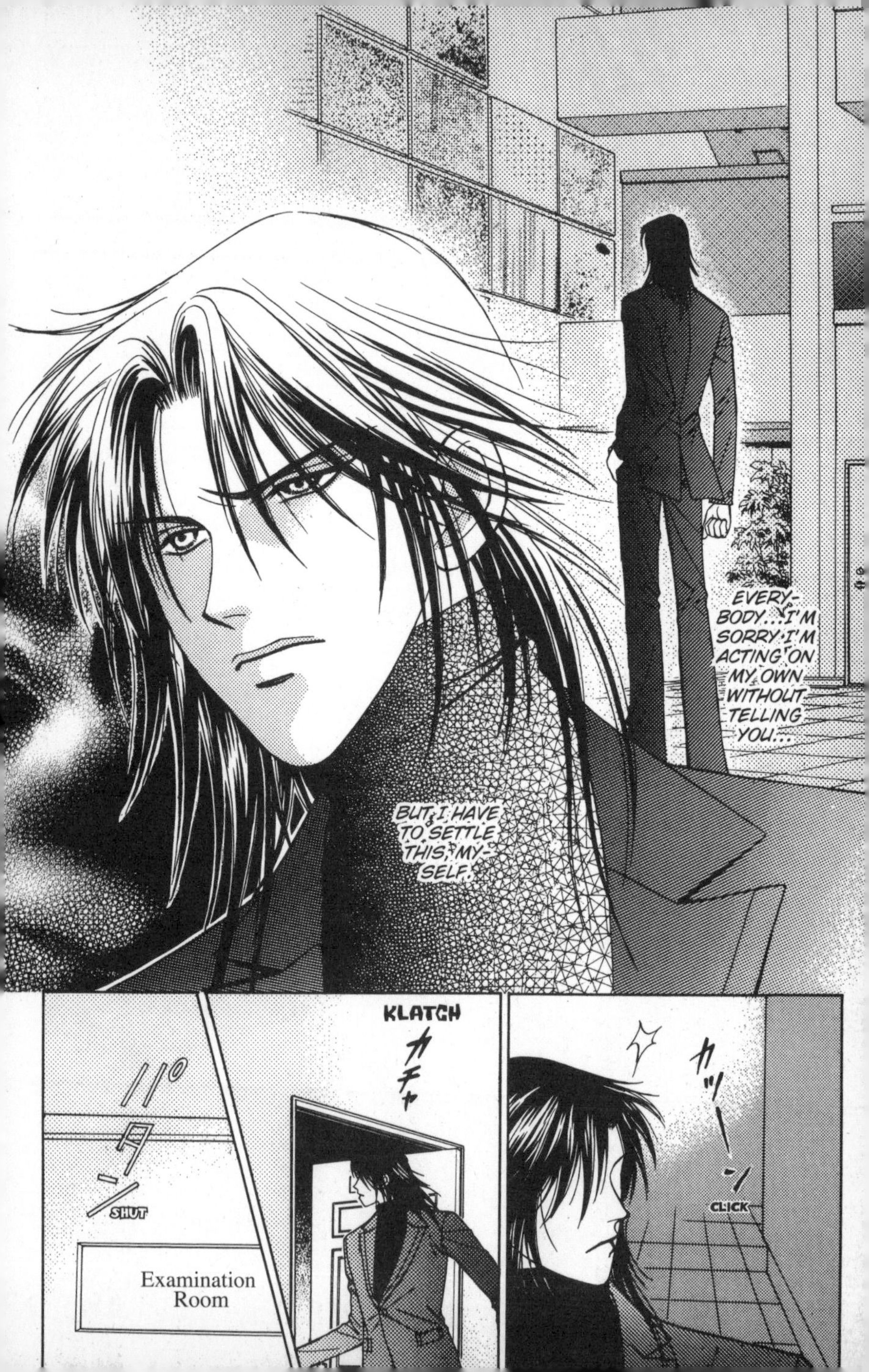
EVERY-BODY... I'M SORRY I'M ACTING ON MY OWN WITHOUT TELLING YOU...
BUT I HAVE TO SETTLE THIS, MY-SELF.
CLICK
カツーン
KLATCH
カチャ
パタン
SHUT
Examination Room

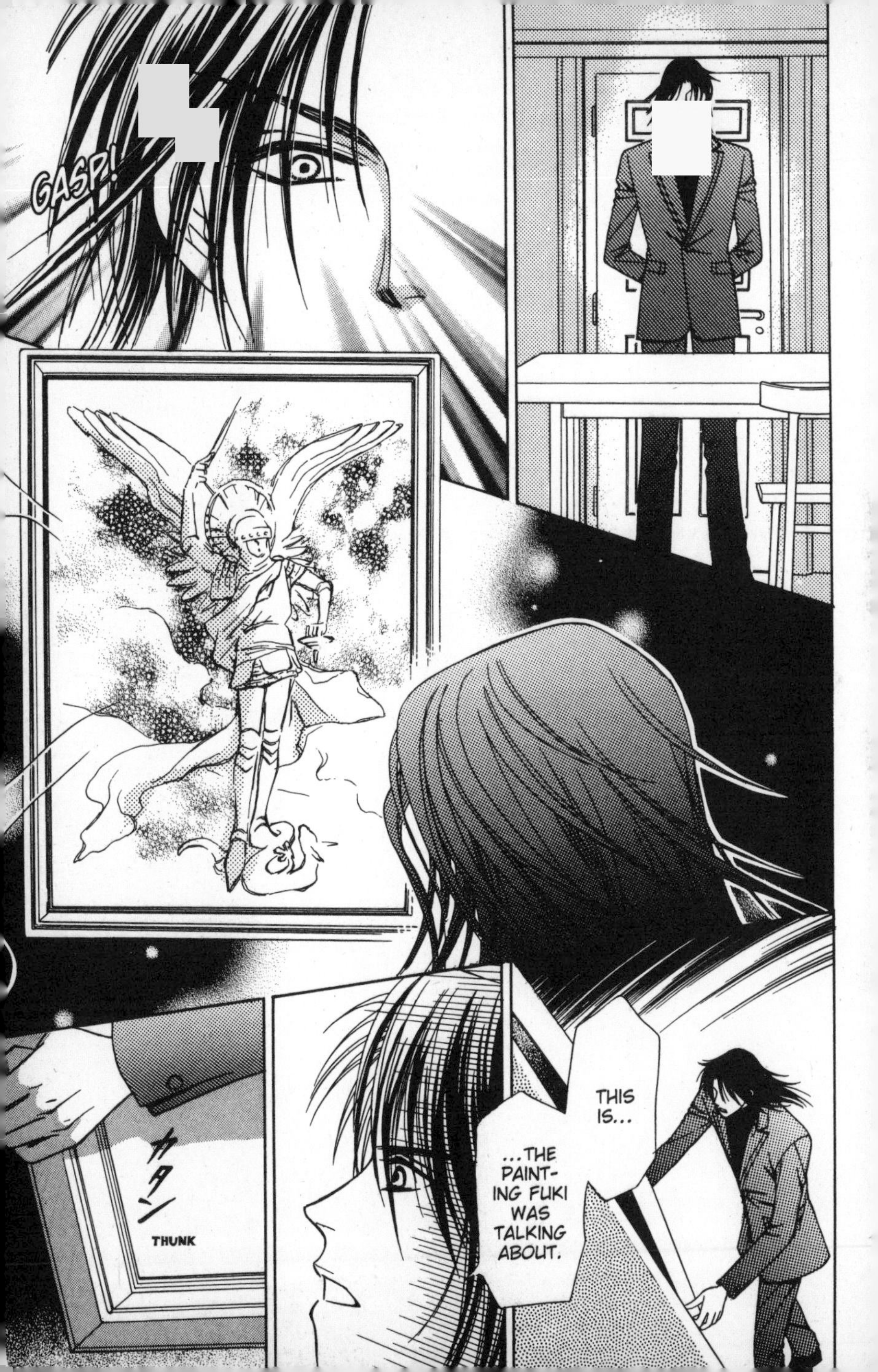
GASP!
カタン
THUNK
THIS IS...
...THE PAINTING FUKI WAS TALKING ABOUT.

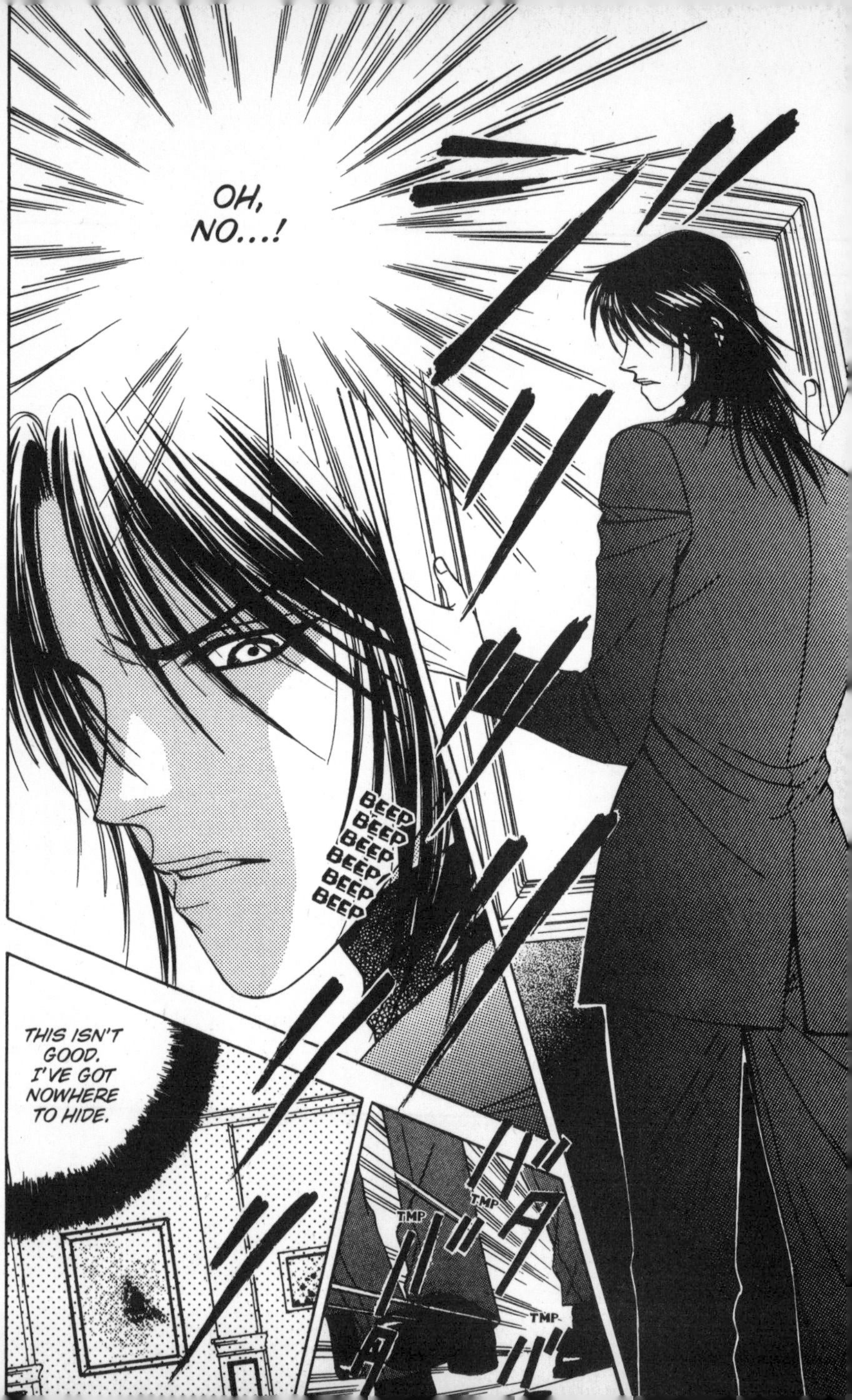
OH, NO...!
BEEP BEEP BEEP BEEP! BEEP BEEP
THIS ISN'T GOOD. I'VE GOT NOWHERE TO HIDE.
TMP
TMP
TMP

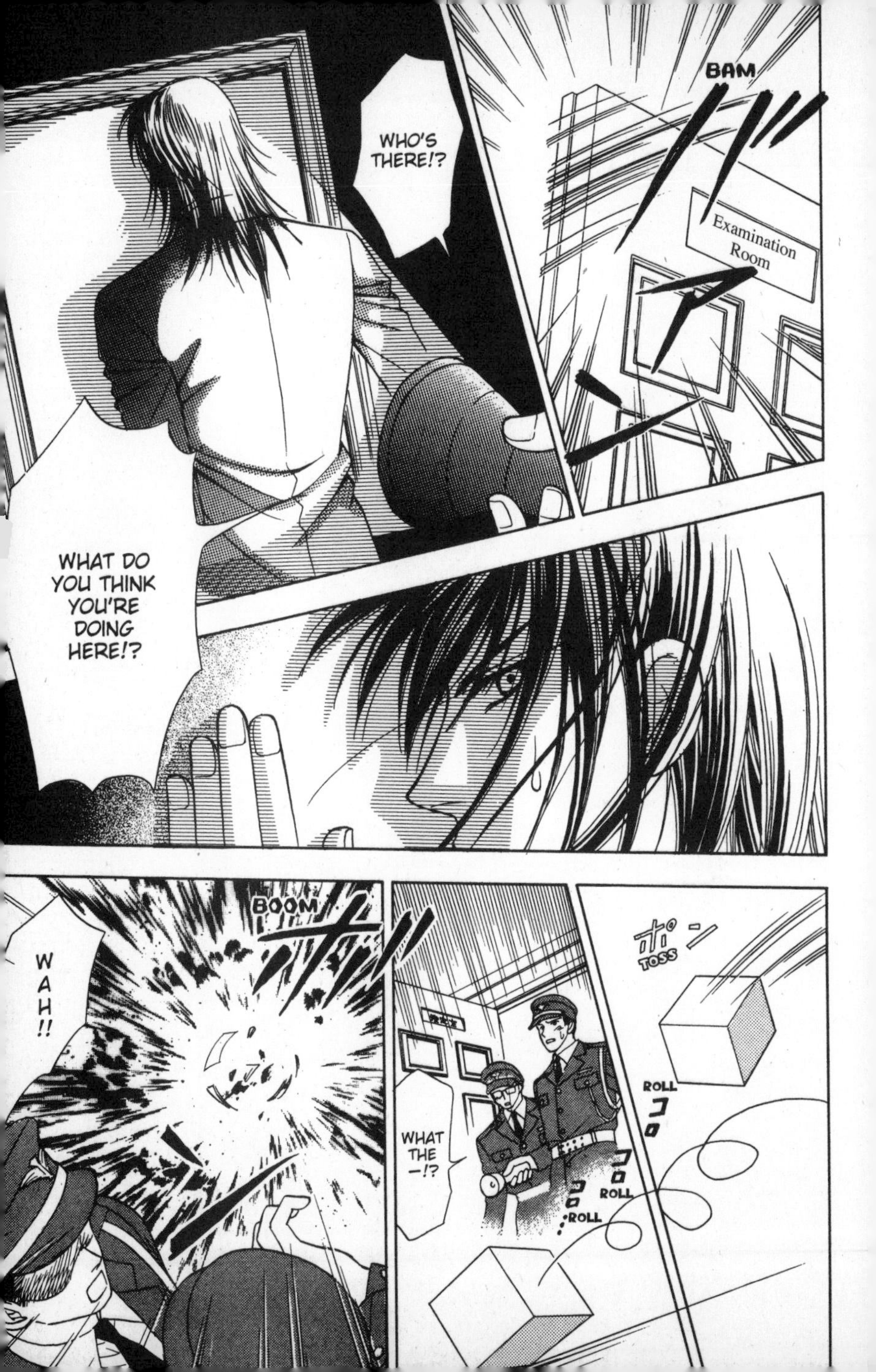
BAM
Examination Room
WHO'S THERE!?
WHAT DO YOU THINK YOU'RE DOING HERE!?
ポン
TOSS
ROLL
ROLL
ROLL
WHAT THE —!?
BOOM
WAH!!

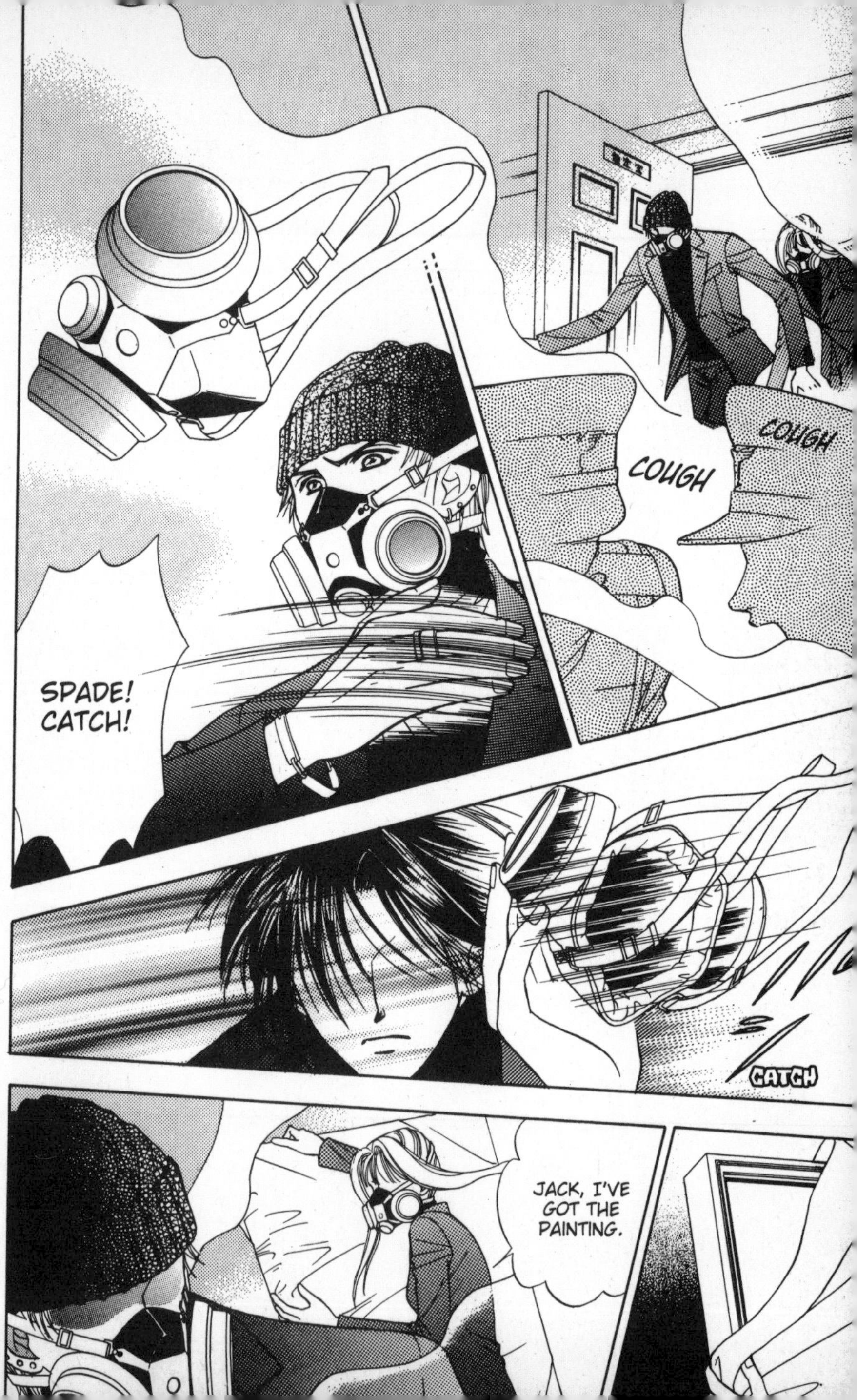
COUGH
COUGH
SPADE! CATCH!
CATCH
JACK, I'VE GOT THE PAINTING.

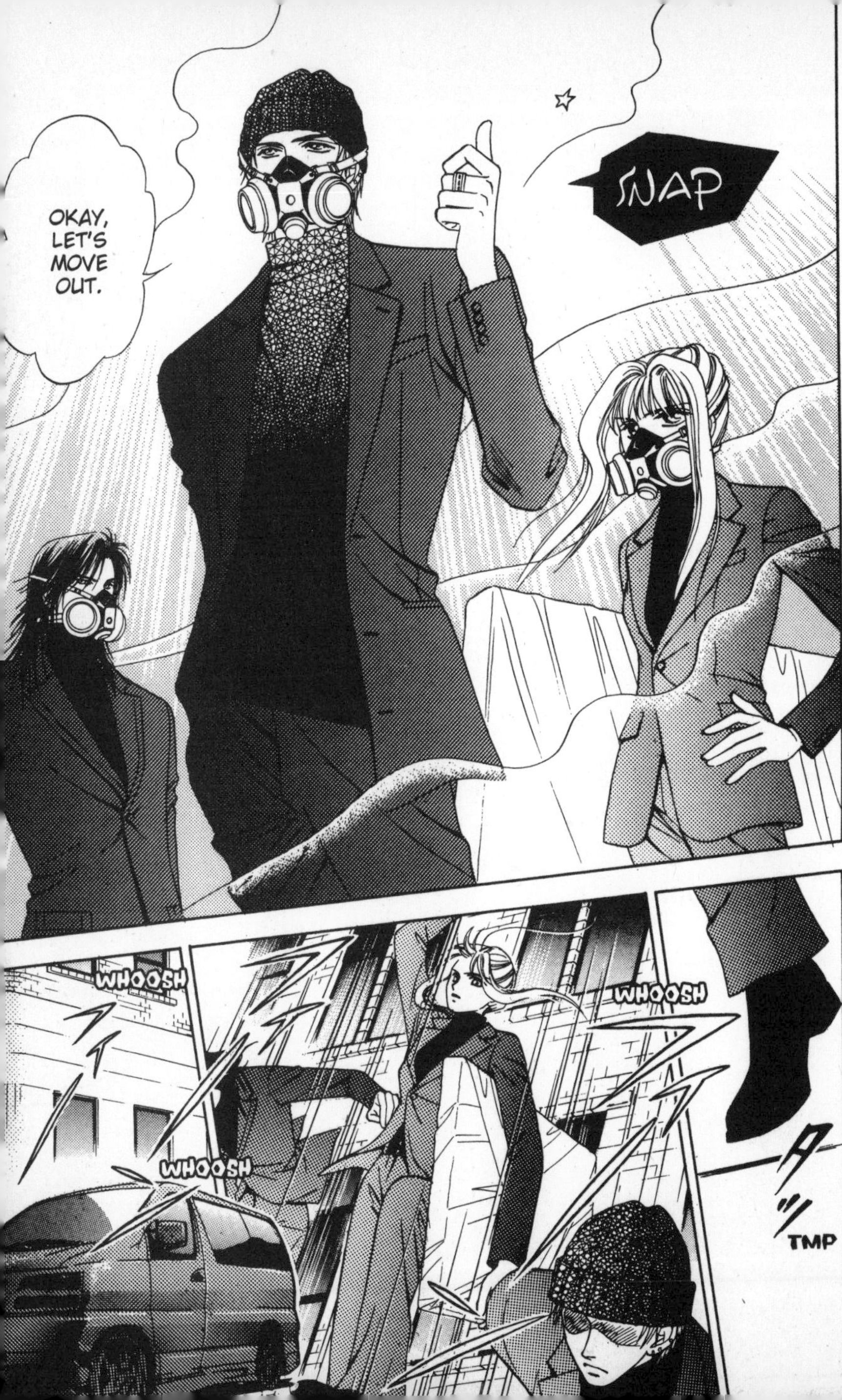
SNAP
OKAY, LET'S MOVE OUT.
WHOOSH
WHOOSH
WHOOSH
TMP

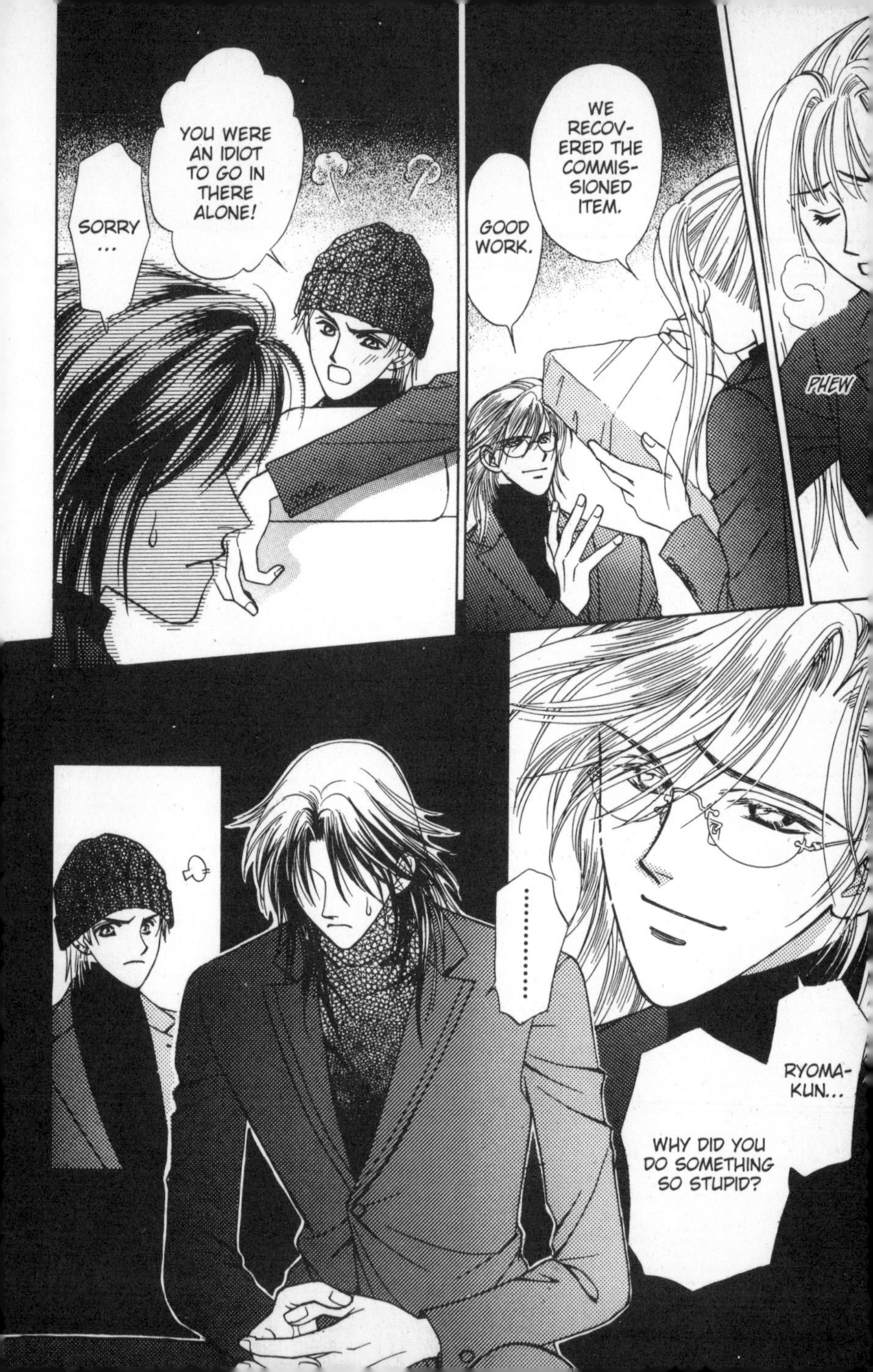
PHEW
WE RECOVERED THE COMMISSIONED ITEM.
GOOD WORK.
YOU WERE AN IDIOT TO GO IN THERE ALONE!
SORRY ...
RYOMA-KUN...
WHY DID YOU DO SOMETHING SO STUPID?
......

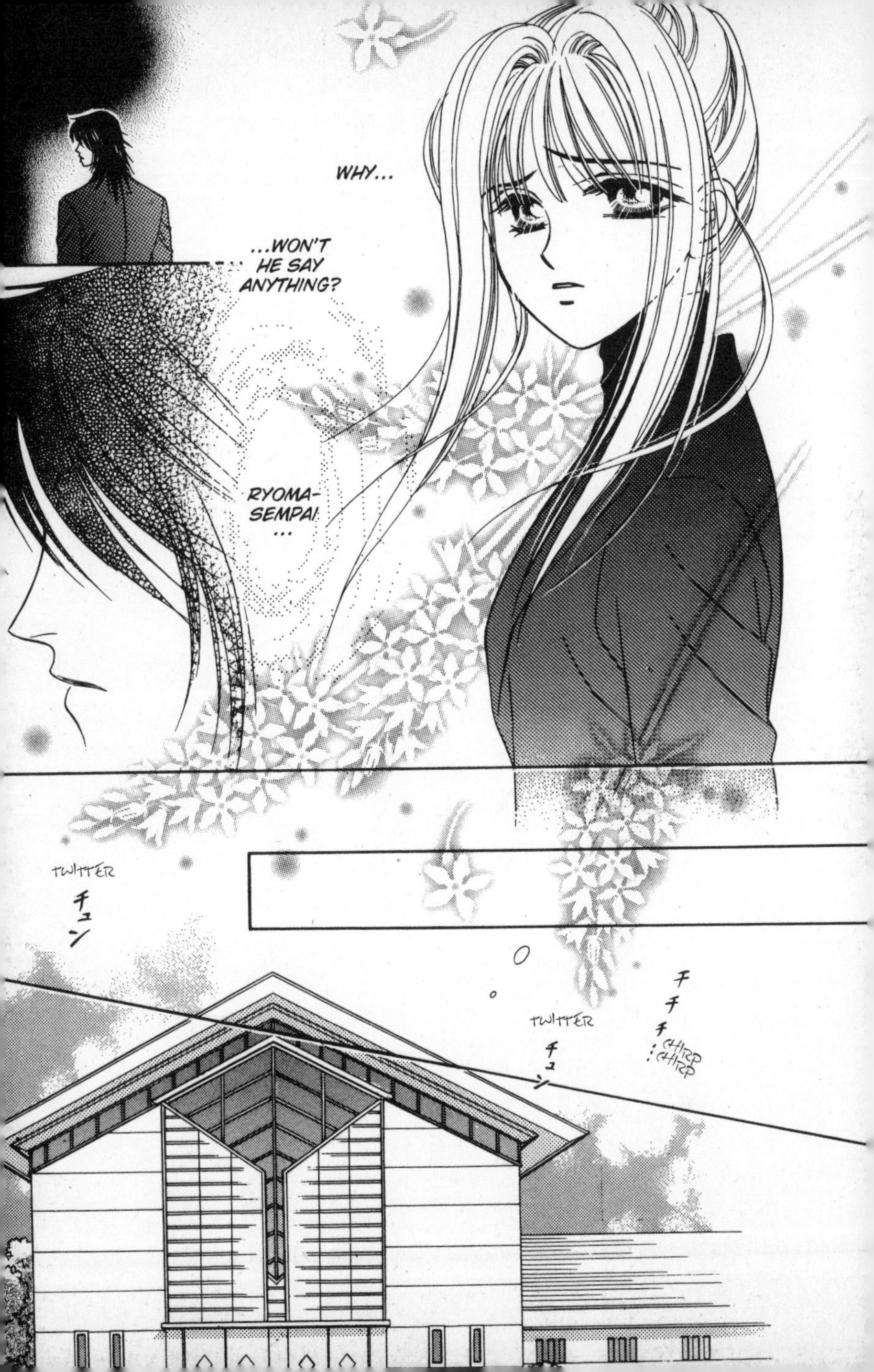
WHY...
...WON'T HE SAY ANYTHING?
RYOMA-SEMPAI ...
TWITTER
チュン
チチチ...
CHIRP CHIRP
TWITTER
チュン

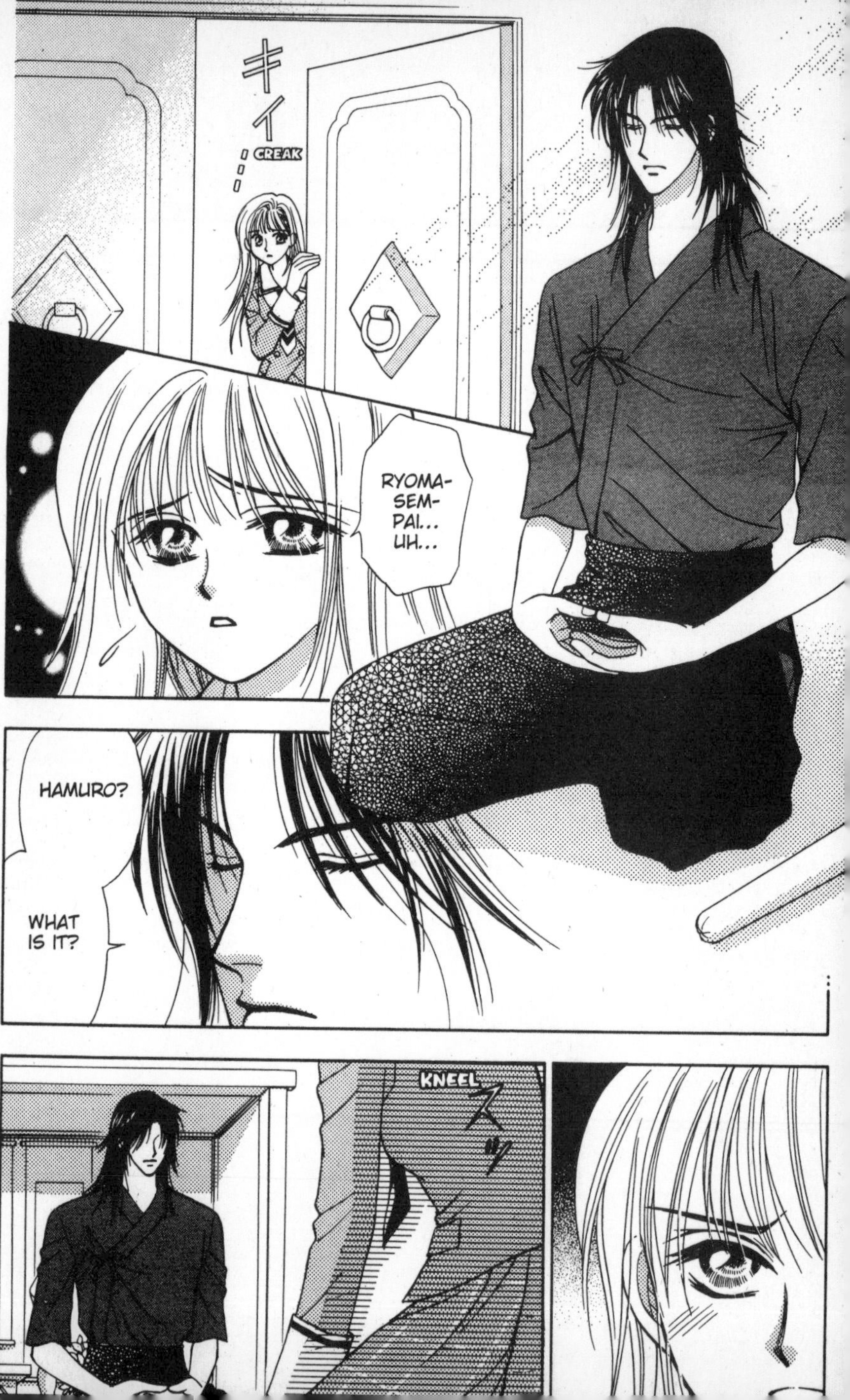
キイ
CREAK
RYOMA-SEMPAI... UH...
HAMURO?
WHAT IS IT?
KNEEL
スッ

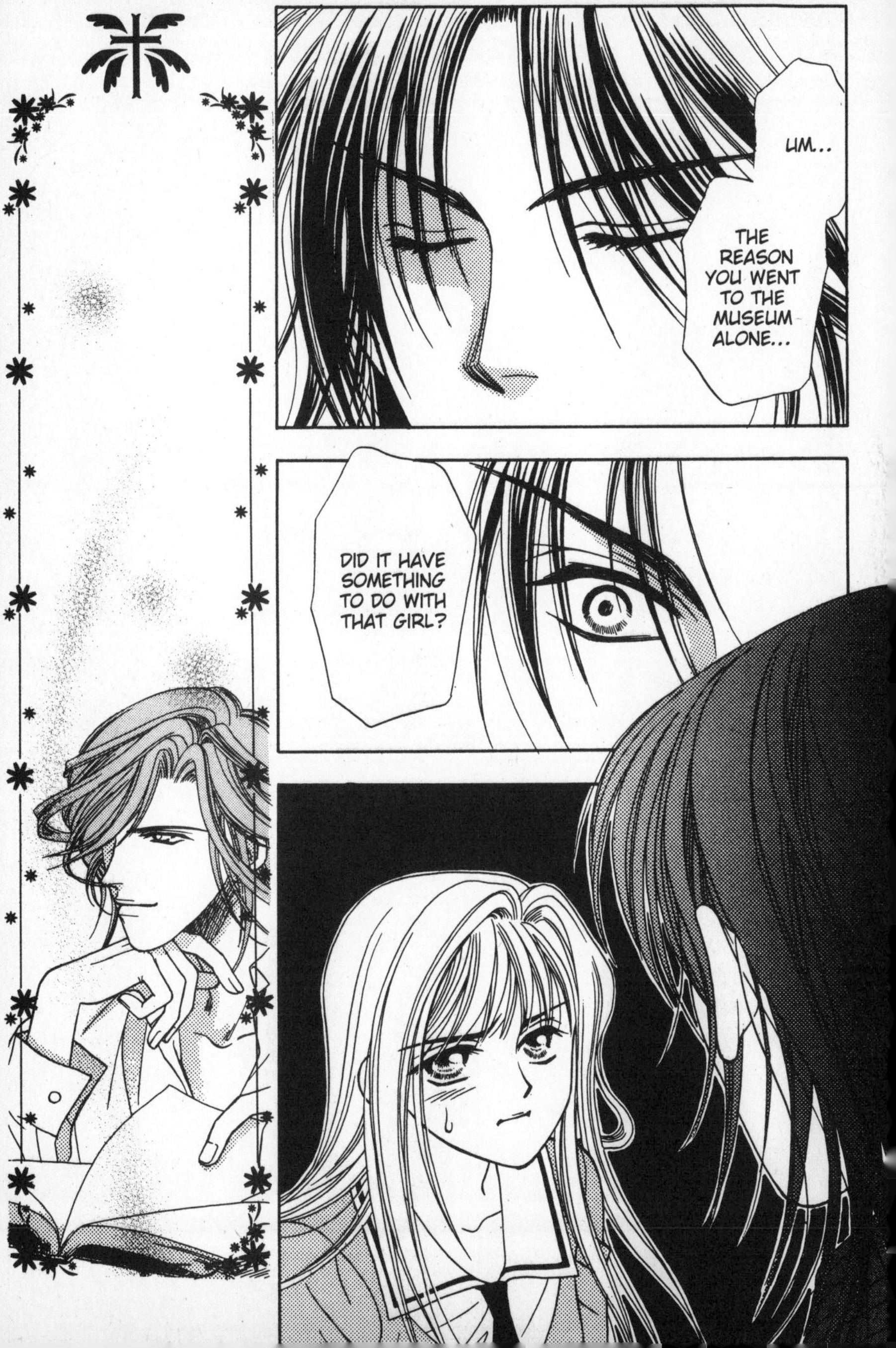
UM...
THE REASON YOU WENT TO THE MUSEUM ALONE...
DID IT HAVE SOMETHING TO DO WITH THAT GIRL?

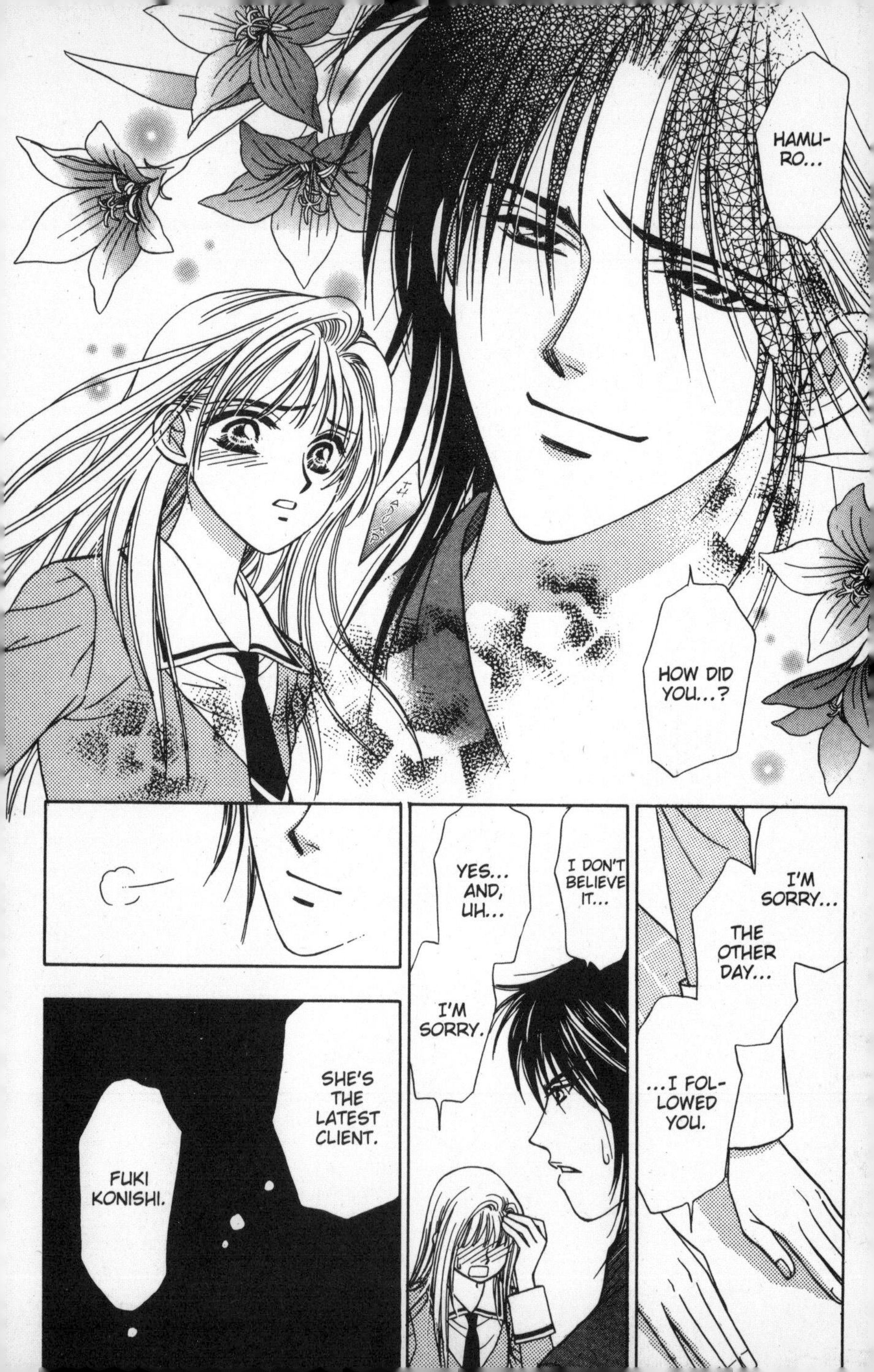
HAMU-RO...
HOW DID YOU...?
I'M SORRY...
THE OTHER DAY...
...I FOL-LOWED YOU.
I DON'T BELIEVE IT...
YES... AND, UH...
I'M SORRY.
SHE'S THE LATEST CLIENT.
FUKI KONISHI.

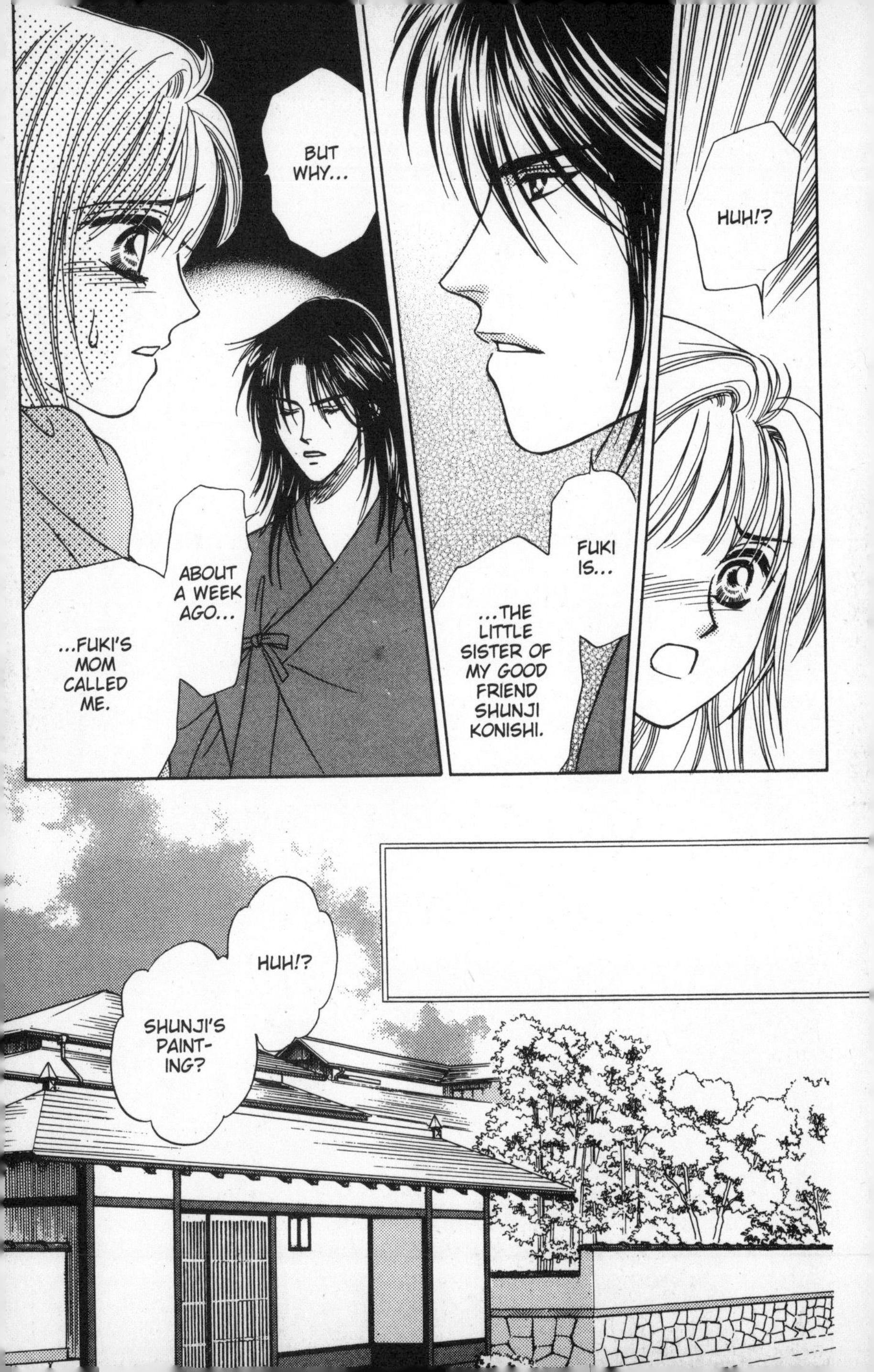
BUT WHY...
ABOUT A WEEK AGO...
...FUKI'S MOM CALLED ME.
FUKI IS...
...THE LITTLE SISTER OF MY GOOD FRIEND SHUNJI KONISHI.
HUH!?
HUH!?
SHUNJI'S PAINT-ING?

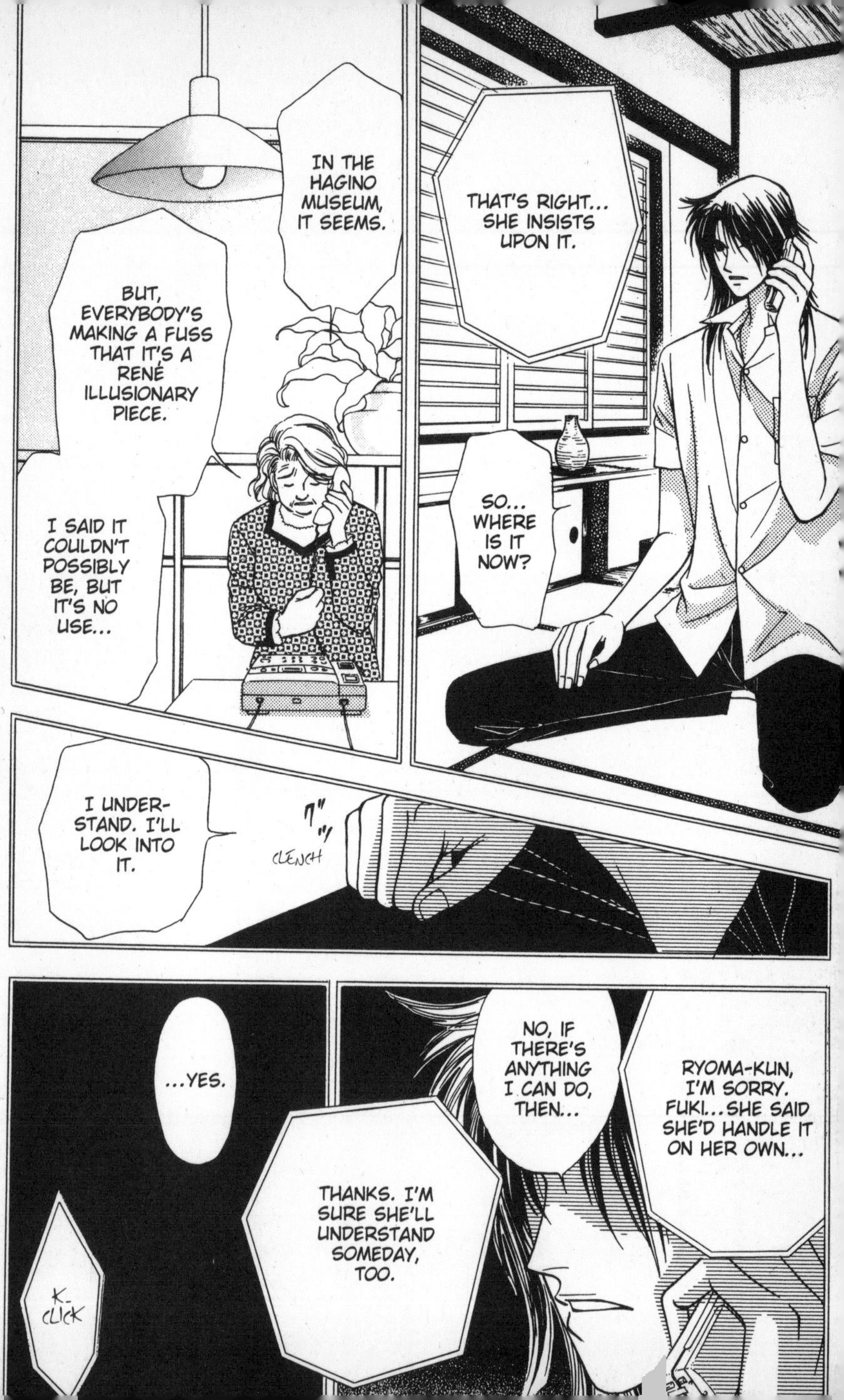
THAT'S RIGHT... SHE INSISTS UPON IT.
SO... WHERE IS IT NOW?
IN THE HAGINO MUSEUM, IT SEEMS.
BUT, EVERYBODY'S MAKING A FUSS THAT IT'S A RENÉ ILLUSIONARY PIECE.
I SAID IT COULDN'T POSSIBLY BE, BUT IT'S NO USE...
I UNDER-STAND. I'LL LOOK INTO IT.
CLENCH
RYOMA-KUN, I'M SORRY. FUKI...SHE SAID SHE'D HANDLE IT ON HER OWN...
NO, IF THERE'S ANYTHING I CAN DO, THEN...
THANKS. I'M SURE SHE'LL UNDERSTAND SOMEDAY, TOO.
...YES.
K-CLICK

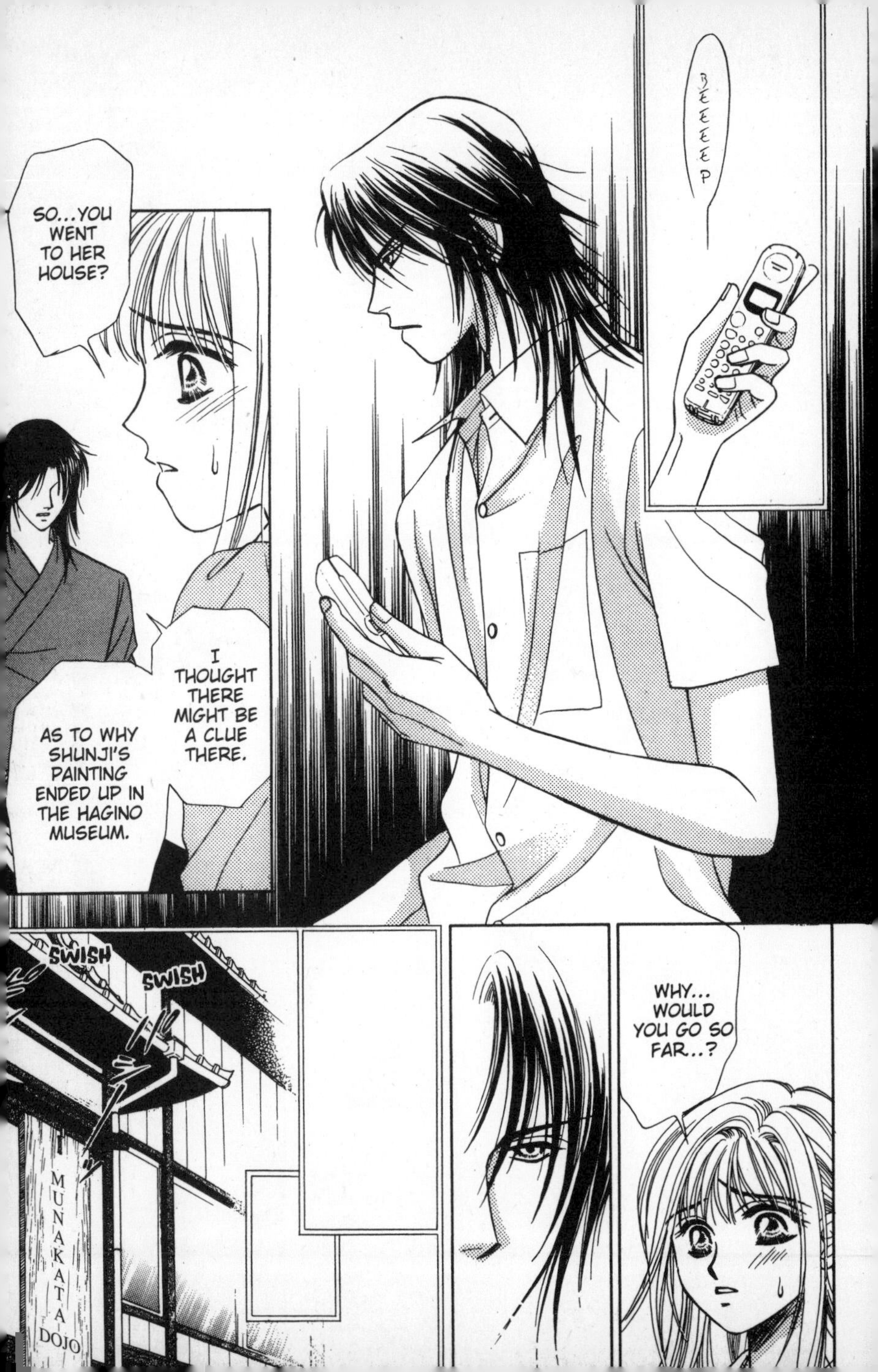
BEEEEEP
SO...YOU WENT TO HER HOUSE?
I THOUGHT THERE MIGHT BE A CLUE THERE.
AS TO WHY SHUNJI'S PAINTING ENDED UP IN THE HAGINO MUSEUM.
WHY... WOULD YOU GO SO FAR...?
SWISH
SWISH
MUNAKATA DOJO

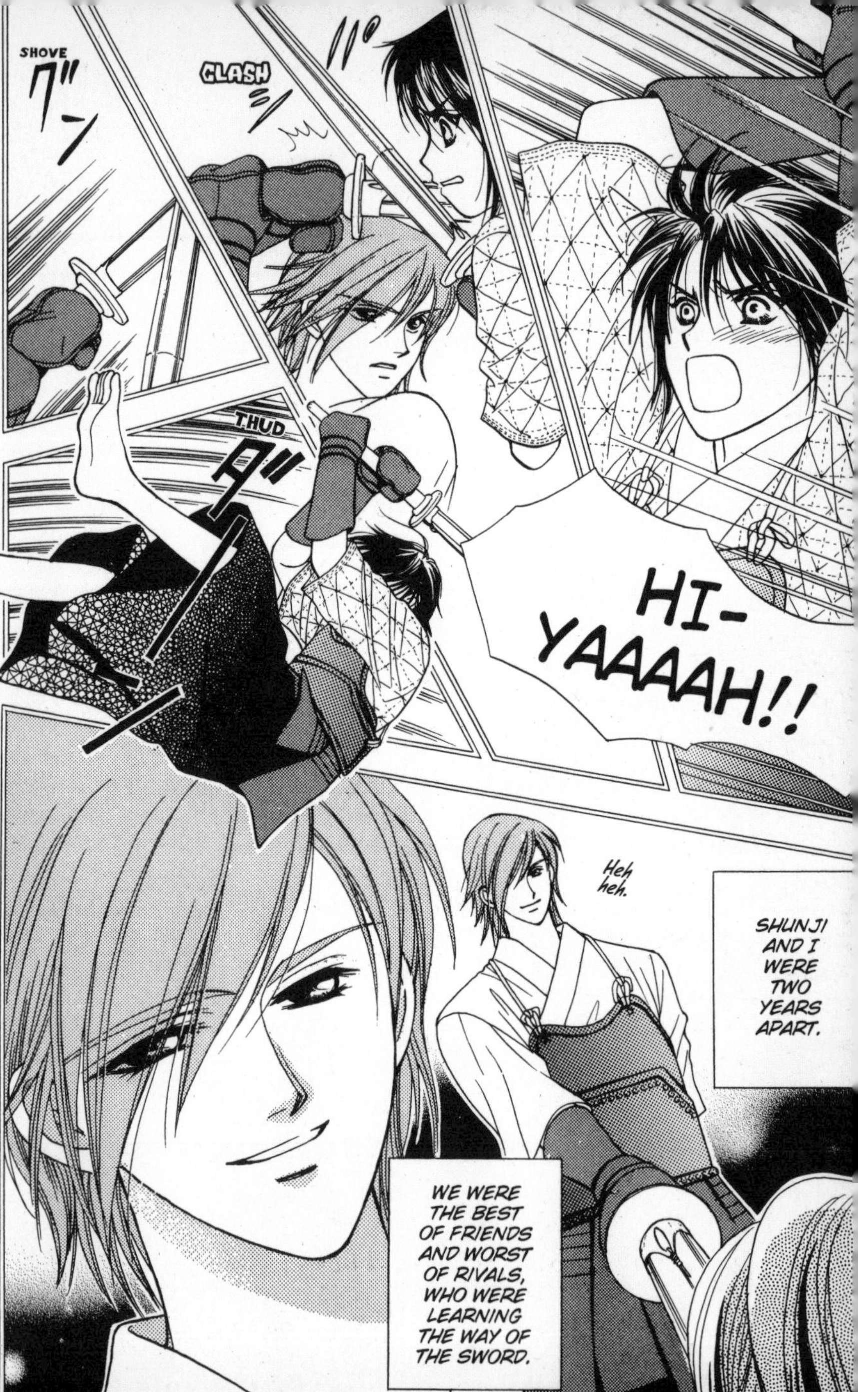
CLASH
SHOVE
THUD
HI-YAAAAAH!!
SHUNJI AND I WERE TWO YEARS APART.
Heh heh.
WE WERE THE BEST OF FRIENDS AND WORST OF RIVALS, WHO WERE LEARNING THE WAY OF THE SWORD.

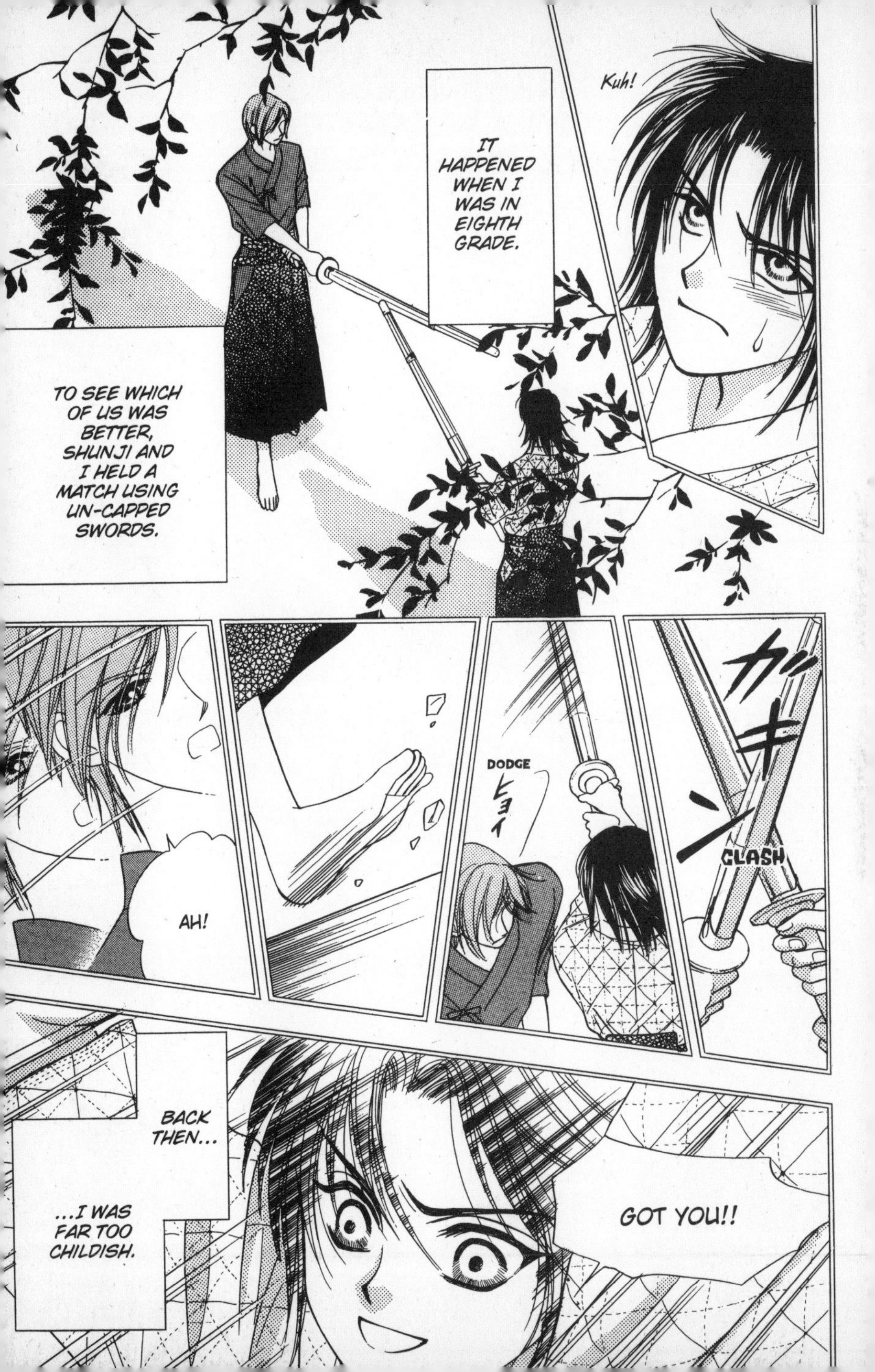

Kuh!
IT HAPPENED WHEN I WAS IN EIGHTH GRADE.
TO SEE WHICH OF US WAS BETTER, SHUNJI AND I HELD A MATCH USING UN-CAPPED SWORDS.
ガキ
GLASH
DODGE
ヒョイ
AH!
GOT YOU!!
BACK THEN...
...I WAS FAR TOO CHILDISH.

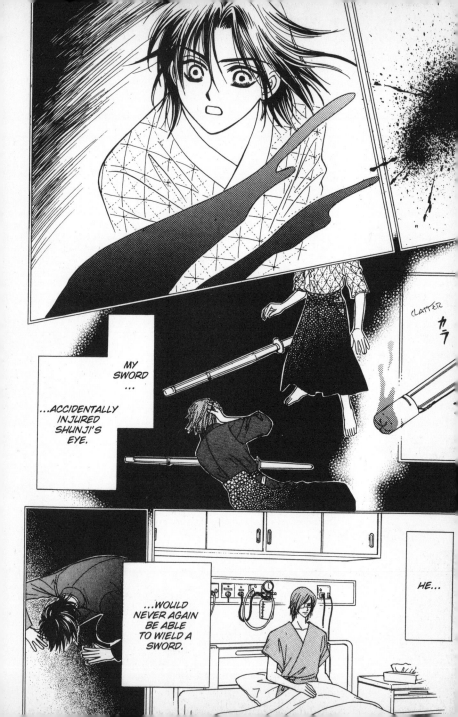

CLATTER

MY
SWORD
...

...ACCIDENTALLY
INJURED
SHUNJI'S
EYE.

...WOULD
NEVER AGAIN
BE ABLE
TO WIELD A
SWORD.

HE...

7

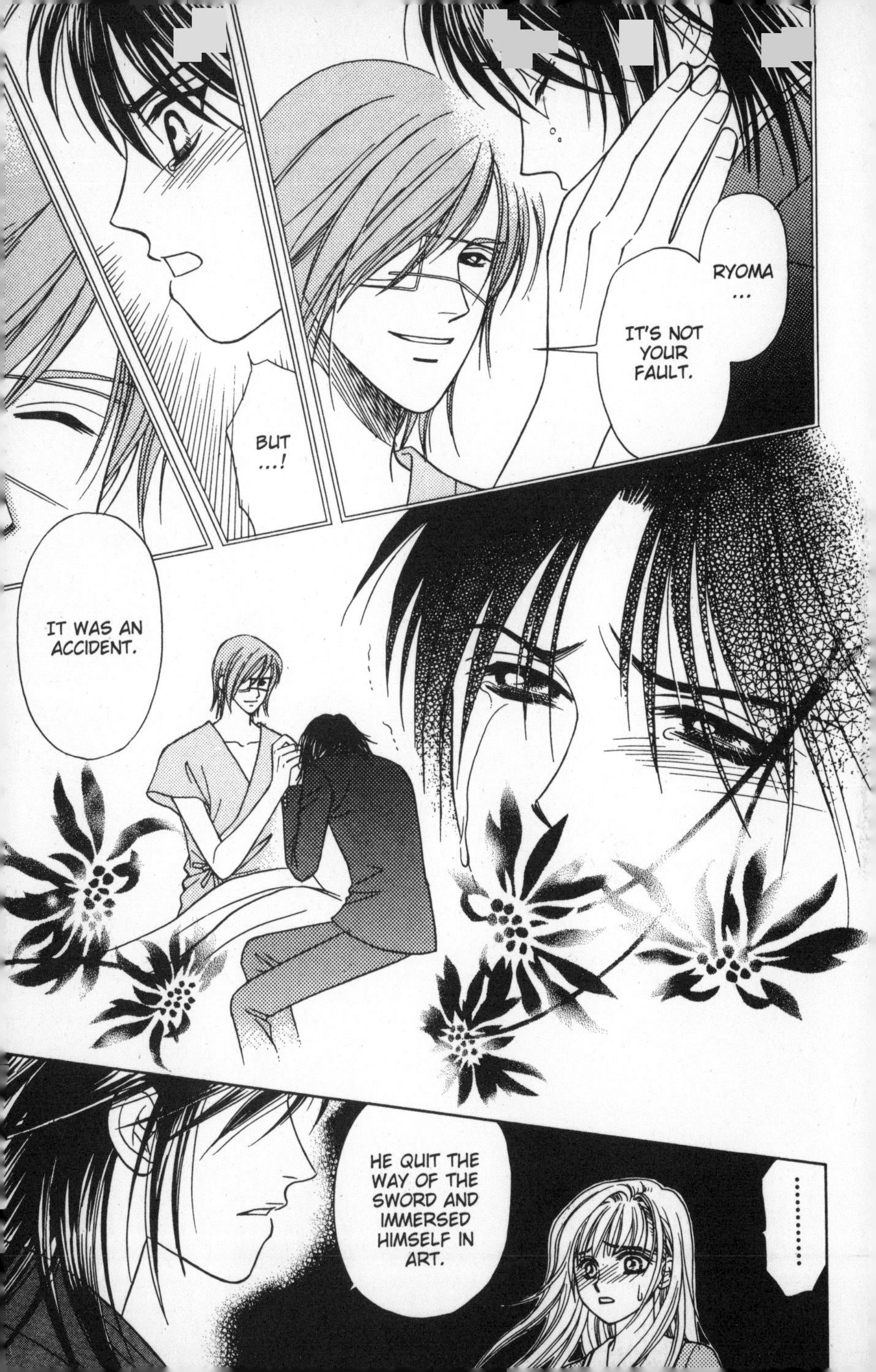
RYOMA ...
IT'S NOT YOUR FAULT.
BUT ...!
IT WAS AN ACCIDENT.
......
HE QUIT THE WAY OF THE SWORD AND IMMERSED HIMSELF IN ART.

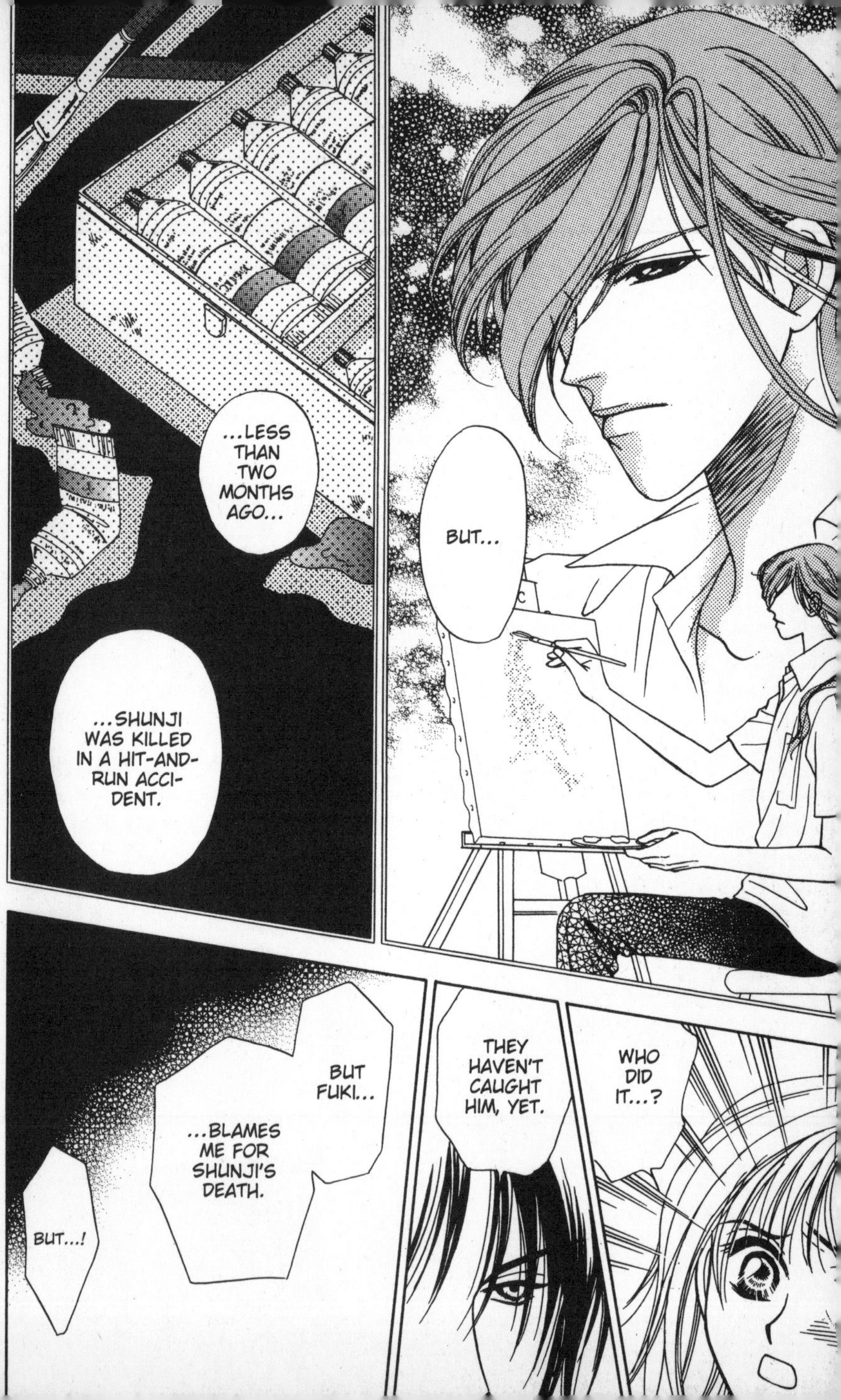
BUT...
...LESS THAN TWO MONTHS AGO...
...SHUNJI WAS KILLED IN A HIT-AND-RUN ACCI-DENT.
WHO DID IT...?
THEY HAVEN'T CAUGHT HIM, YET.
BUT FUKI...
...BLAMES ME FOR SHUNJI'S DEATH.
BUT...!

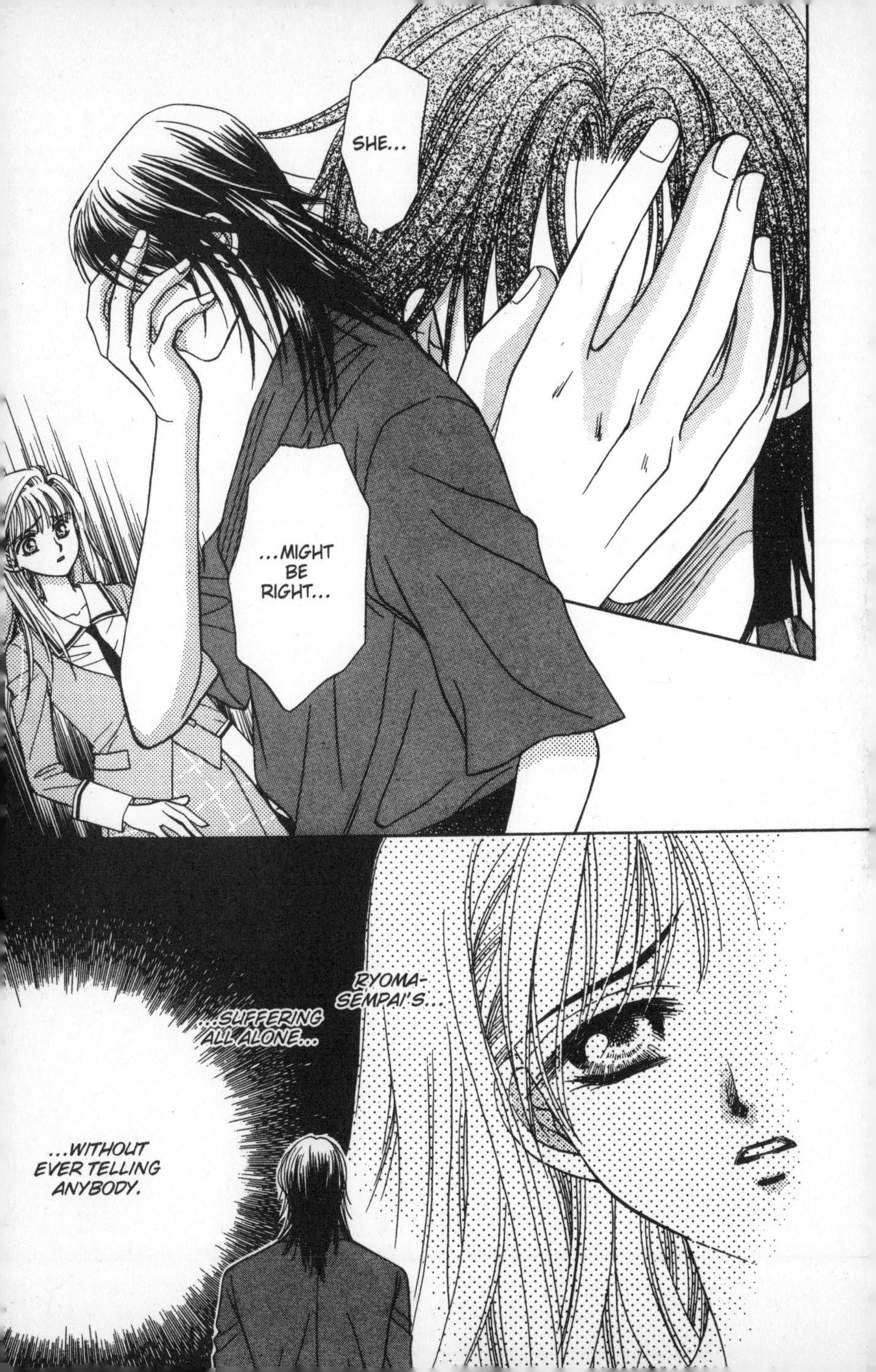
SHE...
...MIGHT BE RIGHT...
RYOMA-SEMPAI'S...
...SUFFERING ALL ALONE...
...WITHOUT EVER TELLING ANYBODY.

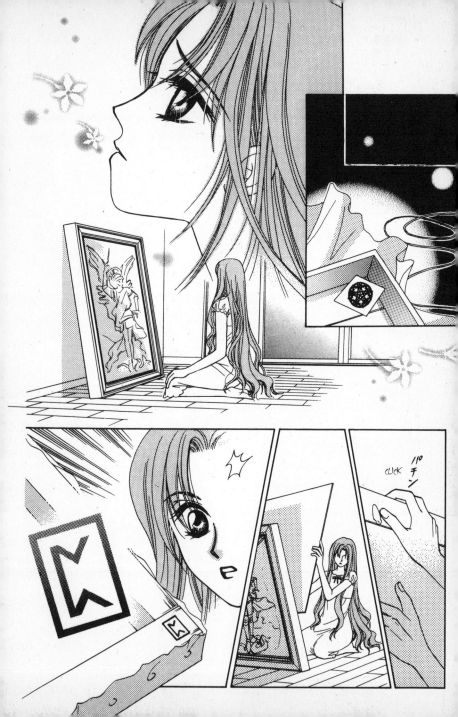

CLICK パチン

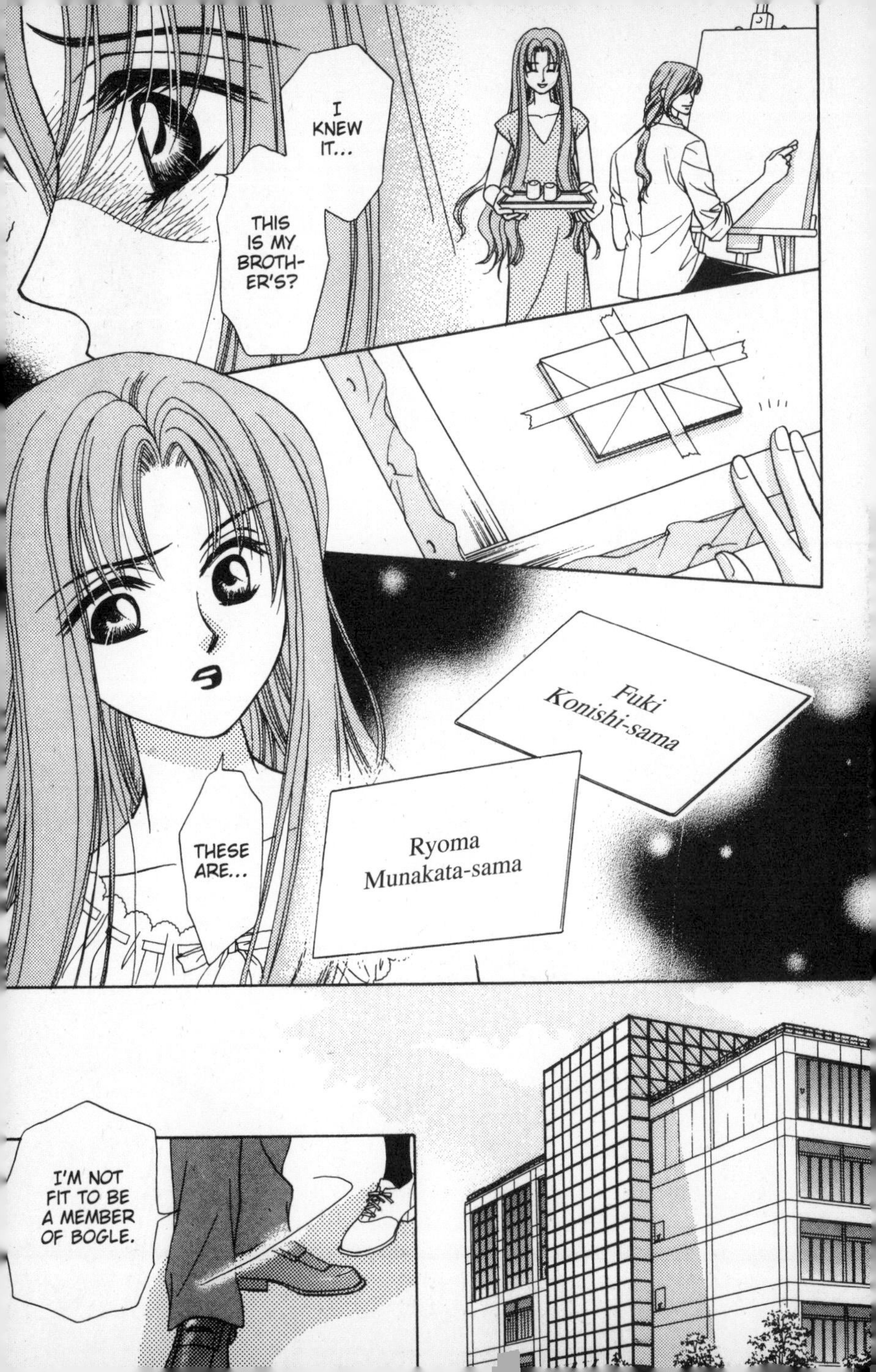
I KNEW IT...
THIS IS MY BROTHER'S?
Fuki Konishi-sama
Ryoma Munakata-sama
THESE ARE...
I'M NOT FIT TO BE A MEMBER OF BOGLE.

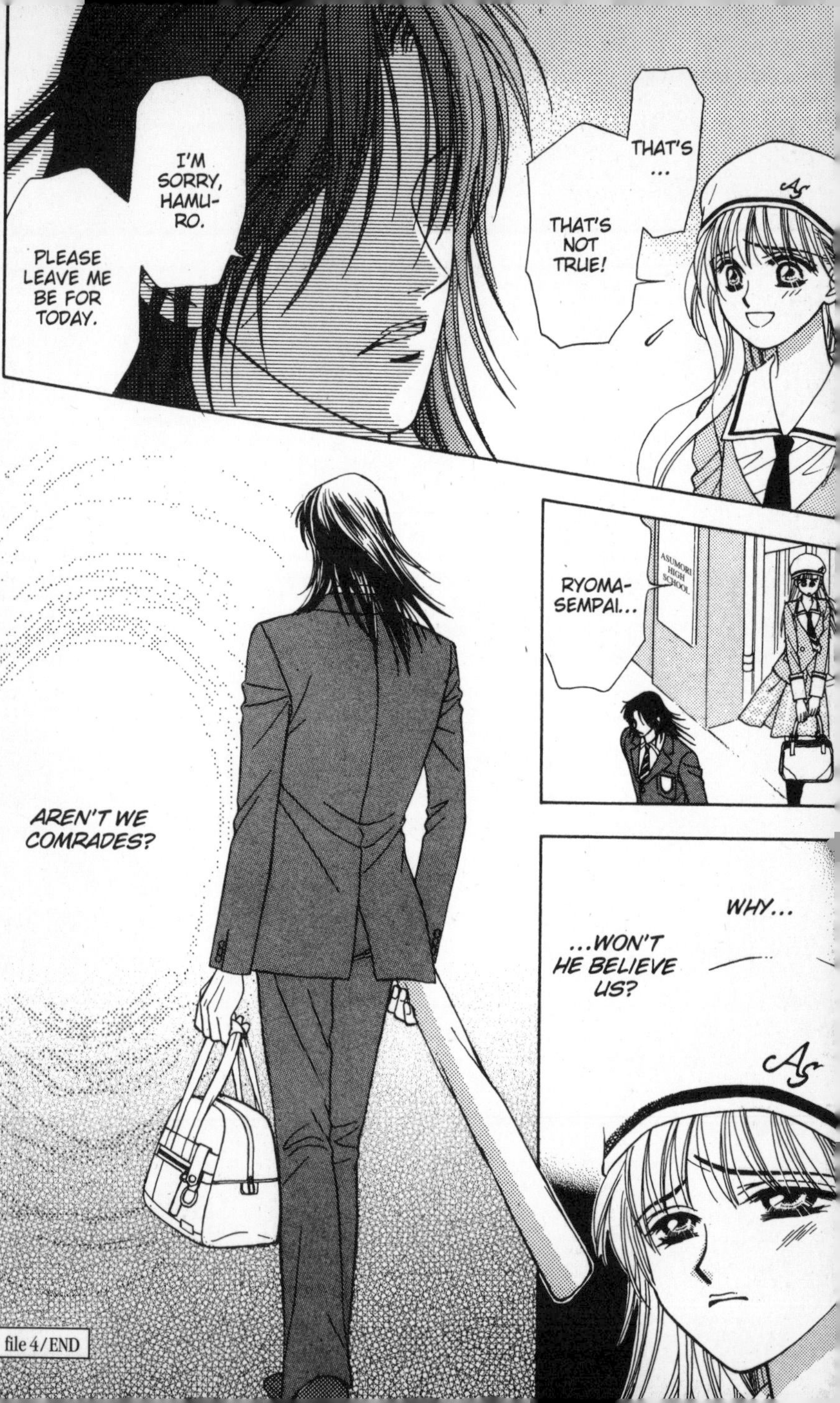
THAT'S ...
THAT'S NOT TRUE!
I'M SORRY, HAMURO.
PLEASE LEAVE ME BE FOR TODAY.
ASUMORI HIGH SCHOOL
RYOMA-SEMPAI...
WHY...
...WON'T HE BELIEVE US?
AREN'T WE COMRADES?
file 4/END

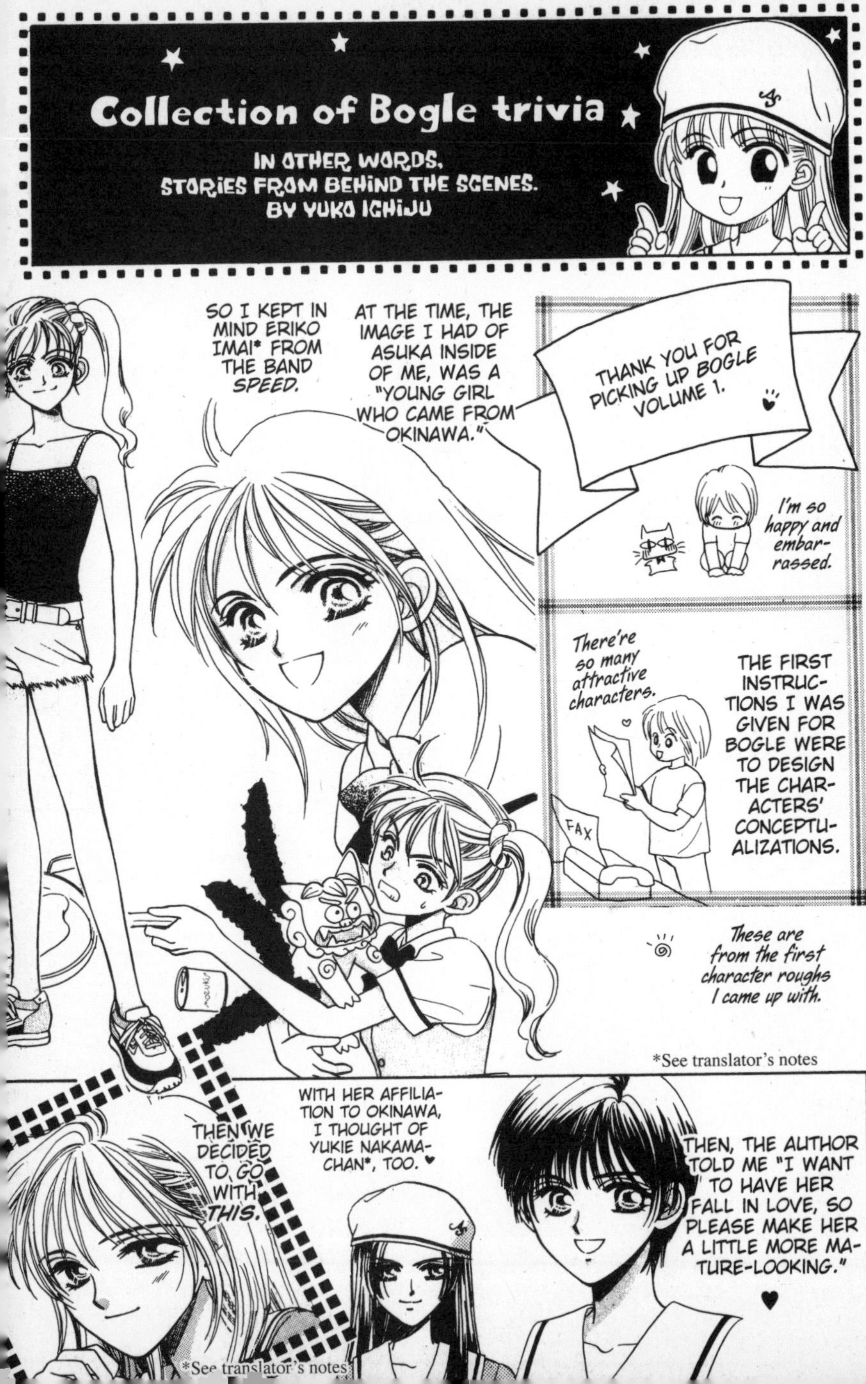
Collection of Bogle trivia
IN OTHER WORDS,
STORIES FROM BEHIND THE SCENES.
BY YUKO ICHIJU
THANK YOU FOR PICKING UP BOGLE VOLUME 1.
I'm so happy and embarrassed.
THE FIRST INSTRUCTIONS I WAS GIVEN FOR BOGLE WERE TO DESIGN THE CHARACTERS' CONCEPTUALIZATIONS.
There're so many attractive characters.
FAX
These are from the first character roughs I came up with.
AT THE TIME, THE IMAGE I HAD OF ASUKA INSIDE OF ME, WAS A "YOUNG GIRL WHO CAME FROM OKINAWA."
SO I KEPT IN MIND ERIKO IMAI* FROM THE BAND SPEED.
*See translator's notes
THEN, THE AUTHOR TOLD ME "I WANT TO HAVE HER FALL IN LOVE, SO PLEASE MAKE HER A LITTLE MORE MATURE-LOOKING."
WITH HER AFFILIATION TO OKINAWA, I THOUGHT OF YUKIE NAKAMA-CHAN*, TOO.
THEN WE DECIDED TO GO WITH THIS.
*See translator's notes

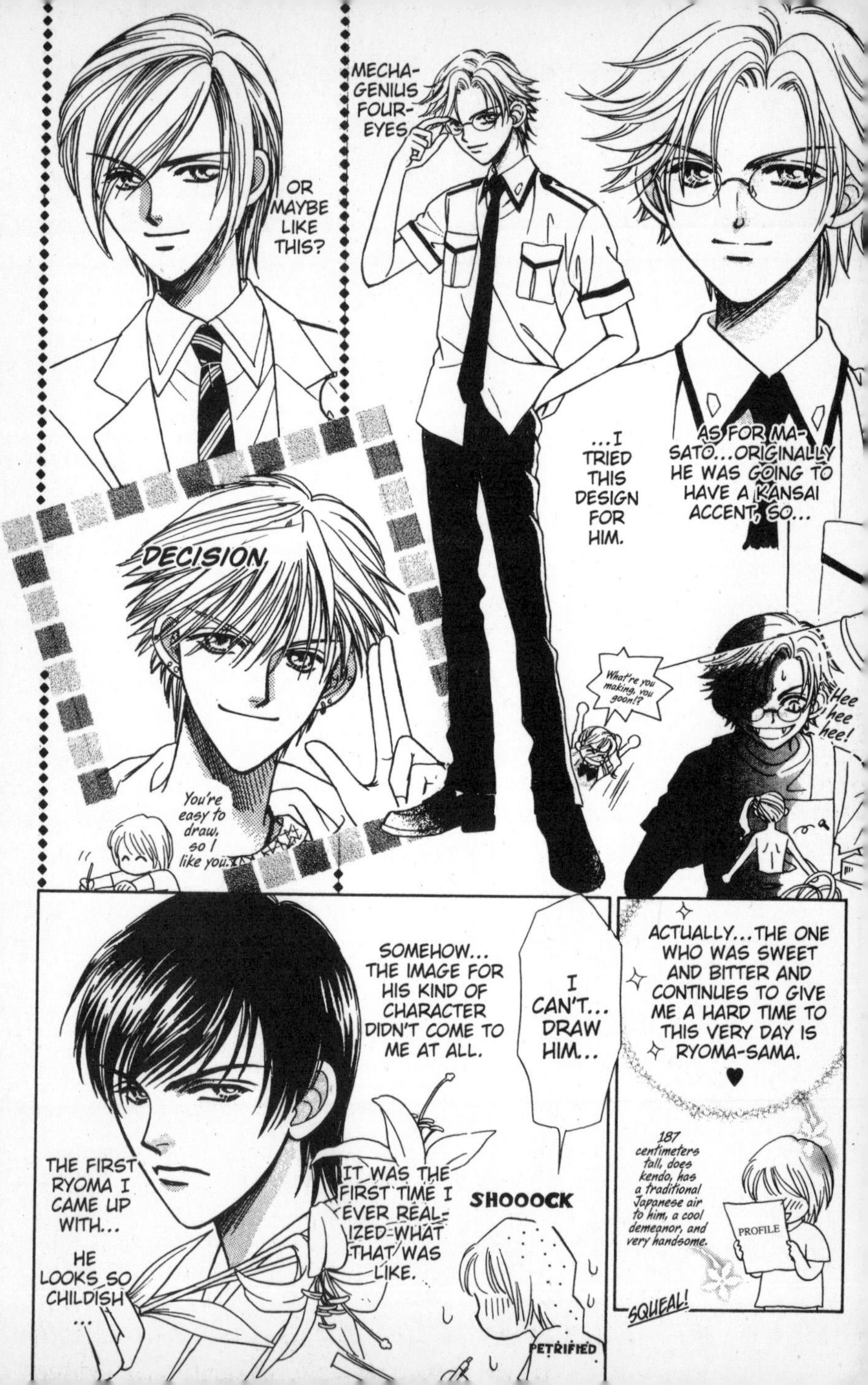
AS FOR MA-SATO...ORIGINALLY HE WAS GOING TO HAVE A KANSAI ACCENT, SO...
...I TRIED THIS DESIGN FOR HIM.
MECHA-GENIUS FOUR-EYES
What're you making, you goon!?
Hee hee hee!
OR MAYBE LIKE THIS?
DECISION
You're easy to draw, so I like you.
ACTUALLY...THE ONE WHO WAS SWEET AND BITTER AND CONTINUES TO GIVE ME A HARD TIME TO THIS VERY DAY IS RYOMA-SAMA. ♥
187 centimeters tall, does kendo, has a traditional Japanese air to him, a cool demeanor, and very handsome.
PROFILE
SQUEAL!
I CAN'T... DRAW HIM...
SHOOOCK
PETRIFIED
SOMEHOW... THE IMAGE FOR HIS KIND OF CHARACTER DIDN'T COME TO ME AT ALL.
IT WAS THE FIRST TIME I EVER REAL-IZED WHAT THAT WAS LIKE.
THE FIRST RYOMA I CAME UP WITH...
HE LOOKS SO CHILDISH...

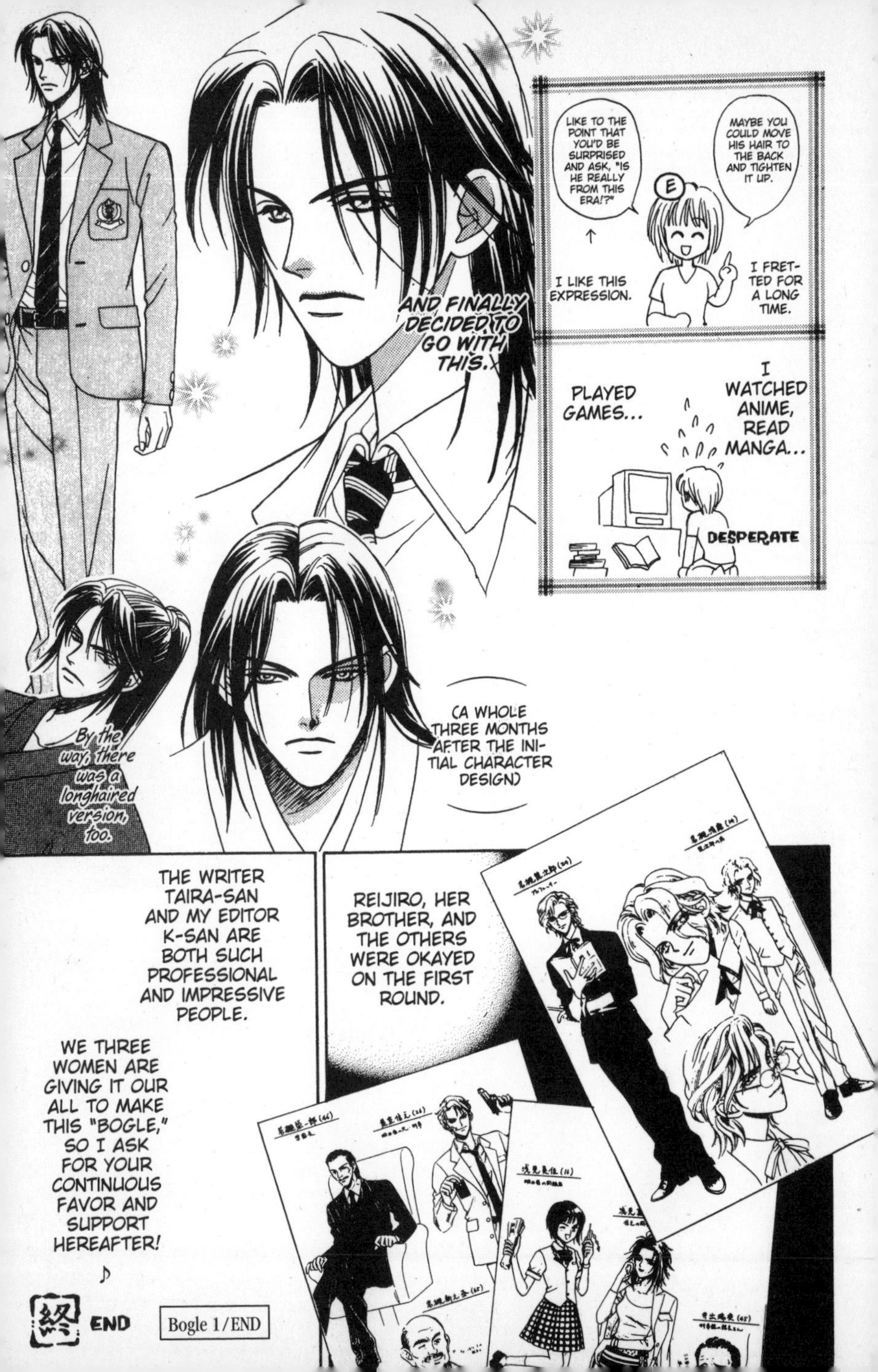
MAYBE YOU COULD MOVE HIS HAIR TO THE BACK AND TIGHTEN IT UP.
I FRETTED FOR A LONG TIME.
E
LIKE TO THE POINT THAT YOU'D BE SURPRISED AND ASK, "IS HE REALLY FROM THIS ERA!?"
I LIKE THIS EXPRESSION.
I WATCHED ANIME, READ MANGA...
PLAYED GAMES...
DESPERATE
AND FINALLY DECIDED TO GO WITH THIS.
(A WHOLE THREE MONTHS AFTER THE INITIAL CHARACTER DESIGN)
By the way, there was a longhaired version, too.
REIJIRO, HER BROTHER, AND THE OTHERS WERE OKAYED ON THE FIRST ROUND.
THE WRITER TAIRA-SAN AND MY EDITOR K-SAN ARE BOTH SUCH PROFESSIONAL AND IMPRESSIVE PEOPLE.
WE THREE WOMEN ARE GIVING IT OUR ALL TO MAKE THIS "BOGLE," SO I ASK FOR YOUR CONTINUOUS FAVOR AND SUPPORT HEREAFTER! ♪
終 END
Bogle 1/END

TRANSLATOR'S NOTES:

Pg. 7 – **"You can do it!"**
Okinawa is a southern island inhabited by Japanese, but with a distinct culture/dialect, the same way Louisiana is part of the United States but the Cajun dialect is almost a separate language. Standard Japanese for "you can do it!" is "Gabarou!" but here she used the dialect version which is "Chibaryou!" It's like the difference between most Americans saying "Hi!" and Southerners saying "Hey!" in greeting.

Pg. 16 – ***kendo***
Meaning the "way of the sword," this is the Japanese martial art of fencing. It is practiced wearing traditional armor and using bamboo swords.

Pg. 21 – ***onii-chan***
Though "*onii-chan*" means "big brother" Masato is not in fact Keita's older brother. It's similar to the way we'll call close, though not blood-related, older men in our lives "Uncle".
"*Onee-chan*" is used the same way, for women.

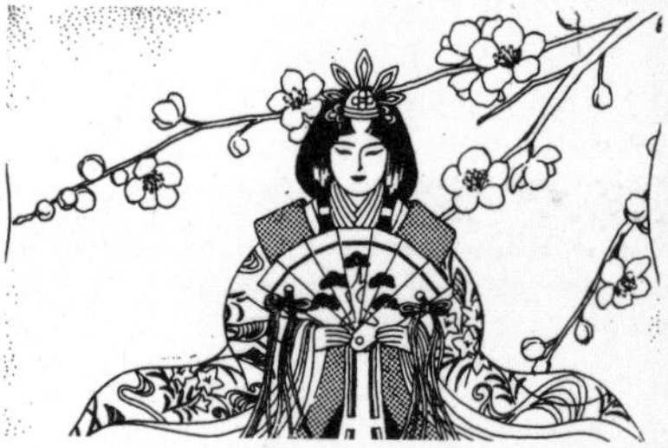

Pg. 34 – **hina doll**
This traditional Japanese doll is a key item in celebrating Girls' Day, March 3rd of every year. These ornamental dolls are set upon a red-clothed platform representing the Emperor, Empress, and rest of the court of the Heian period.

Pg. 102 – **bogle fairy**
This fairy from Scottish folklore is a trickster of a sprite who causes more mischievous harm to humans, than help.

Pg. 106 – ***bibimbap***
A popular Korean dish meaning "mixed rice" and consisting of a bowl of warm rice topped with seasoned vegetables, beef, a fried egg, and chili pepper sauce.

Pg. 110 – ***saataa andagii***
Reminiscent of the doughnut, this is a typical Okinawan snack flavored with pumpkin or purple sweet potato.

Pg. 189 – **Eriko Imai**
A Japanese pop idol who debuted in the 1990's as a part of the musical group SPEED. She's from Okinawa and was one of the main vocalists.

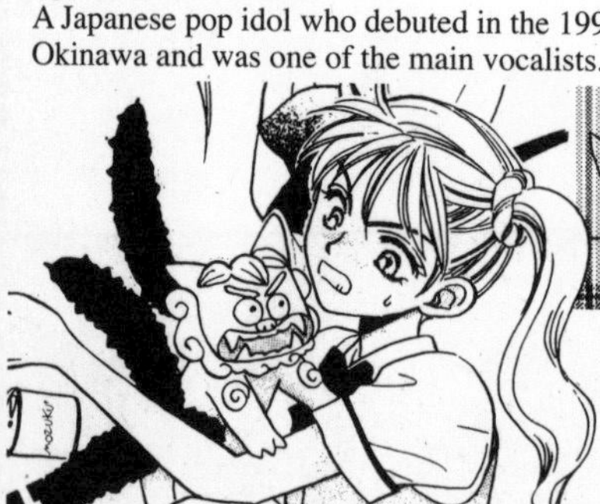

Pg. 189 – ***mozuku***
A stringy, crunchy type of edible seaweed, native to Okinawa.

Pg. 189 – **Yukie Nakama**
An Okinawan actress, singer, and former idol. She's starred in dozens of television dramas as well as movies and has even sung theme songs for *anime* shows.

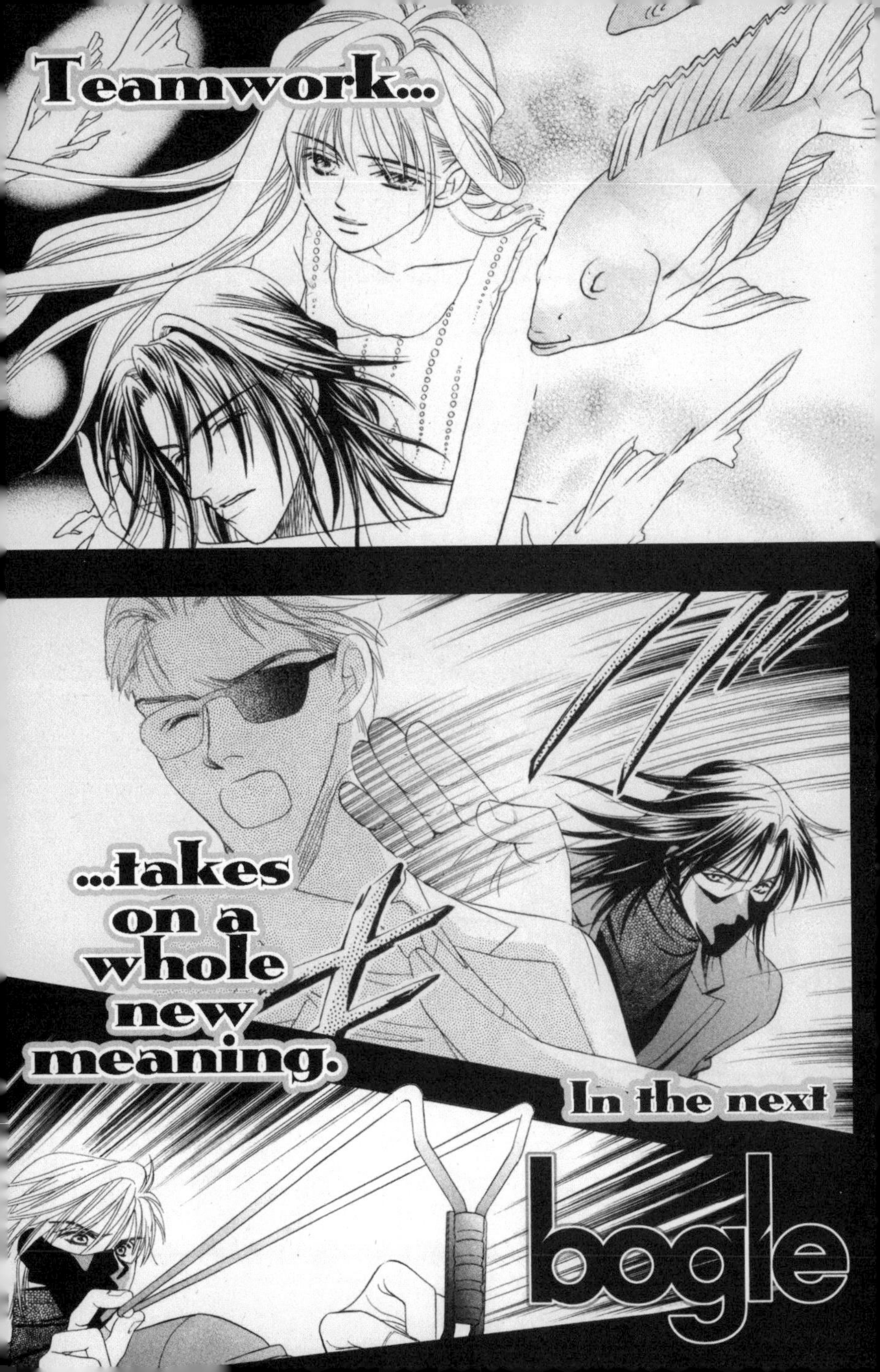
Teamwork...
...takes on a whole new meaning.
In the next
bogle

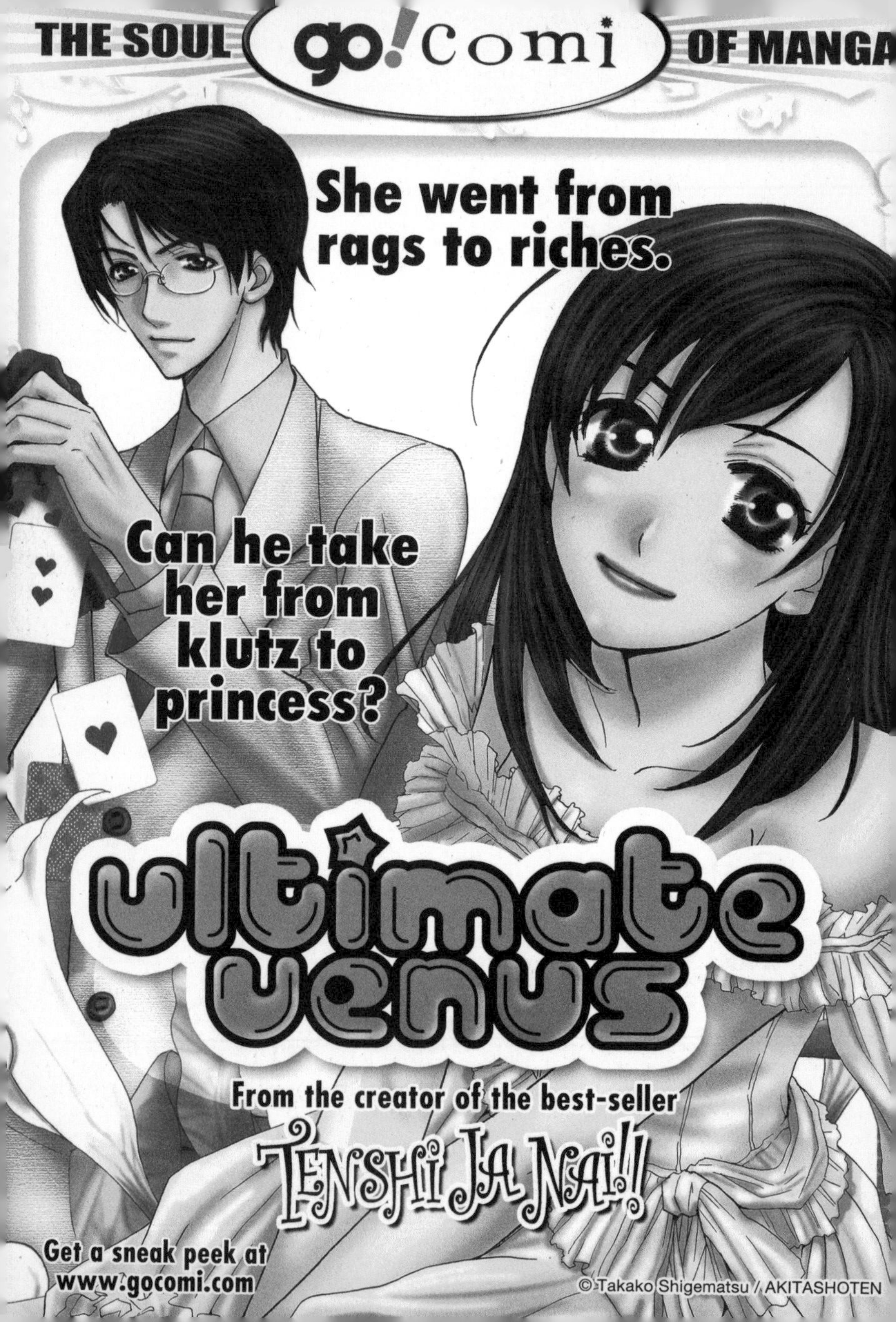
THE SOUL go!comi OF MANGA
She went from rags to riches.
Can he take her from klutz to princess?
ultimate venus
From the creator of the best-seller
TENSHI JA NAI!!
Get a sneak peek at www.gocomi.com
© Takako Shigematsu / AKITASHOTEN

They finally built a better boyfriend.
A.I. REVOLUTION
by Yuu Asami
go! comi
THE SOUL OF MANGA
© Yuu Asami / AKITA SHOTEN

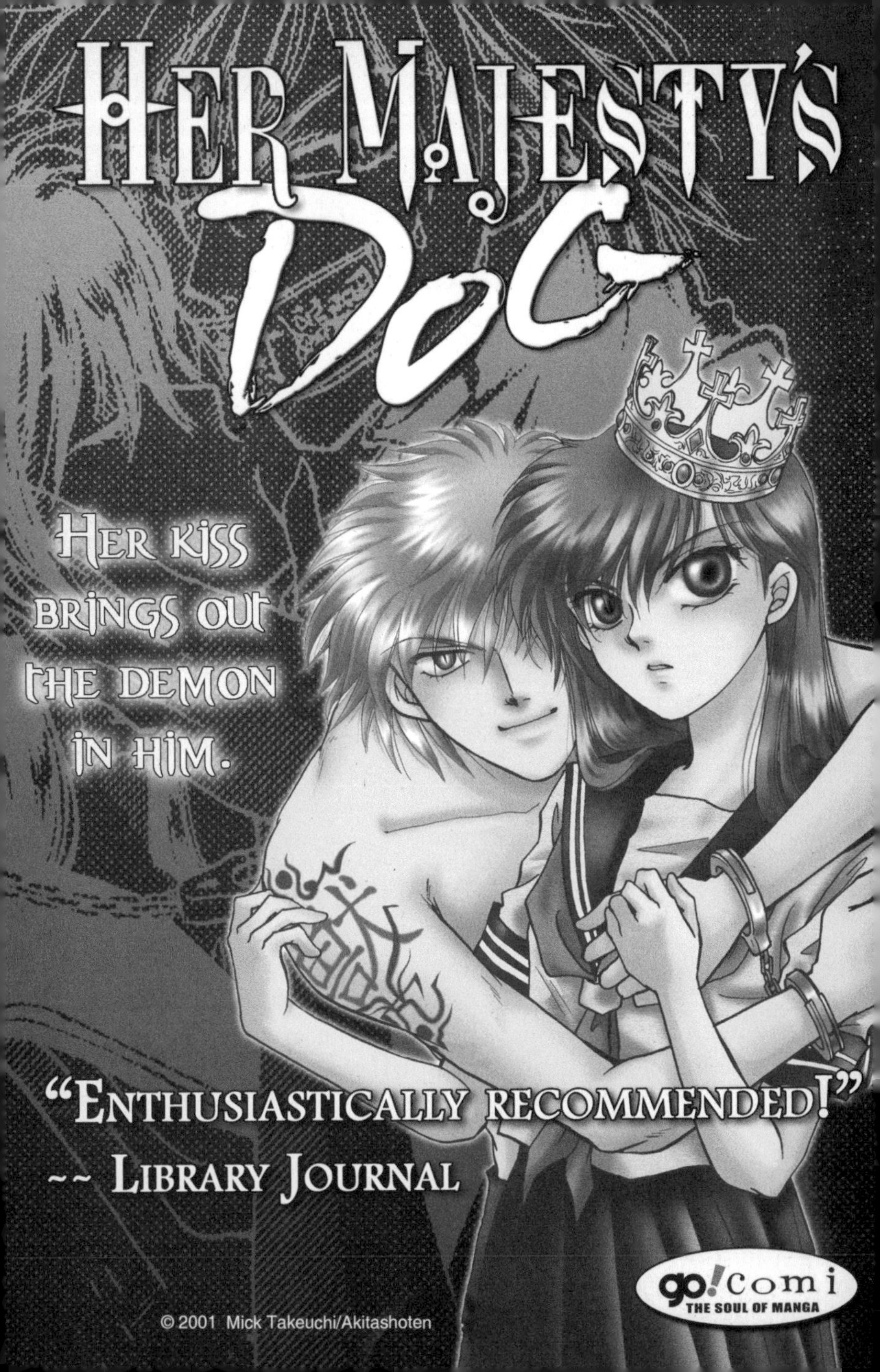

HER MAJESTY'S DOG
HER KISS BRINGS OUT THE DEMON IN HIM.
"ENTHUSIASTICALLY RECOMMENDED!"
~~ LIBRARY JOURNAL
go!comi
THE SOUL OF MANGA
© 2001 Mick Takeuchi/Akitashoten

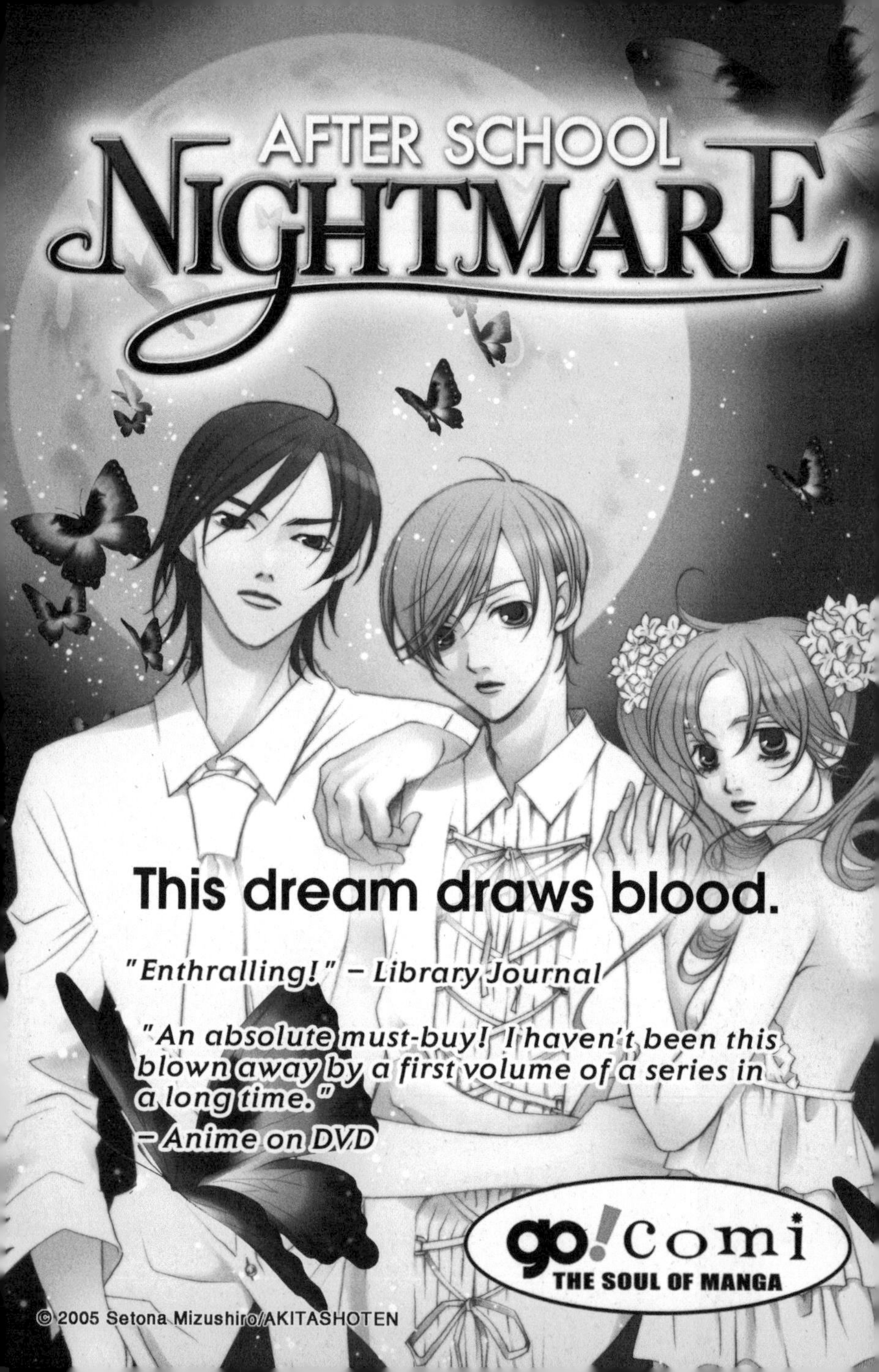
AFTER SCHOOL
NIGHTMARE
This dream draws blood.
"Enthralling!" – Library Journal
"An absolute must-buy! I haven't been this blown away by a first volume of a series in a long time."
– Anime on DVD
go!comi
THE SOUL OF MANGA
© 2005 Setona Mizushiro/AKITASHOTEN

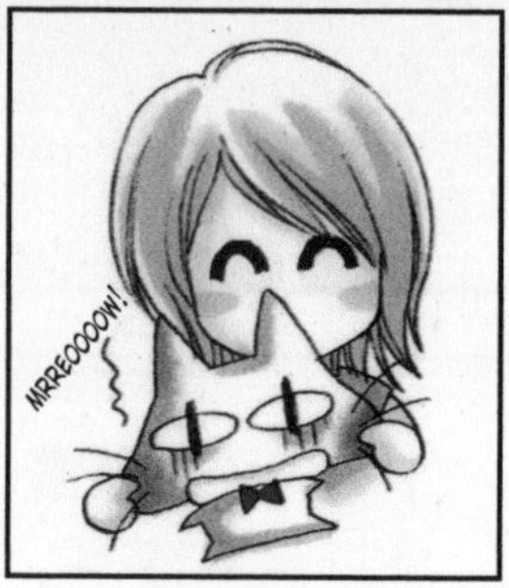
MRREOOOOW!

Yuko Ichiju

When I was a kid, I loved this certain action actress and so practiced how to do backflips by myself, and whatnot. There were times that I'd realize how lame and cowardly I was and would lament, "It's no use! I'll never be a spy!" (ha). But now I feel that my dream has come true to some degree through "Bogle."